D1558830

*Strategies for Deconstructing Racism in the Health and Human Services*

# Strategies for Deconstructing Racism in the Health and Human Services

*Editor*
Alma J. Carten

*Co-Editors*
Alan Siskind
Mary Pender Greene

OXFORD
UNIVERSITY PRESS

# OXFORD
UNIVERSITY PRESS

Oxford University Press is a department of the University of Oxford. It furthers
the University's objective of excellence in research, scholarship, and education
by publishing worldwide. Oxford is a registered trade mark of Oxford University
Press in the UK and certain other countries.

Published in the United States of America by Oxford University Press
198 Madison Avenue, New York, NY 10016, United States of America.

Library of Congress Cataloging-in-Publication Data
Names: Carten, Alma J., editor.
Title: Strategies for deconstructing racism in the health and human services / editor,
Alma J. Carten ; co-editors, Alan Siskind, Mary Pender Greene.
Description: Oxford ; New York : Oxford University Press, [2016] | Includes bibliographical
references and index.
Identifiers: LCCN 2016007594 | ISBN 9780199368907 (alk. paper)
Subjects: LCSH: Racism in social services—United States. | Racism in public
welfare—United States. | Discrimination in medical care—United States.
Classification: LCC HV91 .S7347 2016 | DDC 361.973089—dc23
LC record available at http://lccn.loc.gov/2016007594

9 8 7 6 5 4 3 2 1

Printed by WebCom, Inc., Canada

This book is dedicated to health and human services
professionals across the nation who work tirelessly
to achieve this level of humanity in practice.

*It's like everybody's sitting there and they have some kind of veil over their face, and they look at each other through this veil that makes them see each other through some stereotypical kind of viewpoint. If we're ever gonna collectively begin to grapple with the problems that we have collectively, we're gonna have to move back the veil and deal with each other on a more human level.*

Wilma Mankiller

# CONTENTS

# FOREWORD

## JOYCE M. JAMES

I am honored to write the foreword to *Strategies for Deconstructing Racism in the Health and Human Services*. The book makes an important contribution to the ever-expanding antiracist literature in bringing together the collective voices of an outstanding roster of contributing authors from academia and practice, who, in understanding that the time is now for systems change, have gone beyond the traditional literature, in an effort to introduce strategies that will illuminate new pathways for closing racial and ethnic gaps in the health and human services.

I have been a social worker for 35 years, starting my career as a front-line caseworker in Port Arthur, Texas. I have held the positions of Assistant Commissioner for the State of Texas' Child Protective Services Program, Deputy Commissioner of Department of Family and Protective Services, and my last position of Associate Deputy Executive Commissioner of the Center for Elimination of Disproportionality and Disparities and the Texas State Office of Minority Health. I am currently a racial equity consultant providing coaching, mentoring, leadership development, training, and technical assistance in multiple systems, institutions, and communities, with a specific focus on achieving racial equity through systems transformation. I knew early in my career that something was "just not right" in the way cases were handled, services provided, and decisions made, and it appeared to me that these traditional approaches were racially biased. But like most people without a language and an understanding of institutional and structural racism and of how it is manifested in systems, I hesitated to raise any issue that implied race as a factor—so I did like most people and I kept silent, struggling internally, which I later learned is a primary contributing factor in mental health disparities for African Americans.

One morning about 19 years ago, when I was a manager at the regional level, I made a decision to no longer be silent but to still be cautious in my approach. I asked for data about children in foster care for my region aggregated by race and ethnicity. The data were alarming! African American children represented 29% of the child population and almost 80% of the children in foster care in Jefferson County, Texas. The reality of what I had been feeling and the questions I had struggled with for so long created a burning desire within my innermost being to understand why. I had been silent for far too long, and like many other professionals I had not come to this work to pursue my own personal ambitions but because I wanted to make a difference. I had to own the painful fact that not only did my silence mean that I was not immune from the effects of the internalization of institutionalized racism but unknowingly contributing to its persistence. In fact, I learned that I was suffering from internalized racial oppression, a form of racism that manifests as internalized racial inferiority in some persons of color. The authors and many professionals in health and human services organizations struggle with the same issues that I struggled with more than 30 years ago. This book will do much to bring these issues to light, and in doing so reduce the stress and burden on these individuals, giving them strategies for elevating their voices and the language to describe and communicate on issues of race and racism that speak to systemic rather than individual factors—or speaking "truth to power," which is one of the integrating themes of the book as discussed by Carten in the introduction.

It has been a long journey from my early days as a caseworker and supervisor in the field. In my work and through my participation in numerous "Undoing Racism" workshops conducted by the People's Institute for Survival and Beyond, I came to understand institutionalized racism and to see its manifestations in systems, including those I worked in for so many years.

I don't know that we are ever immune from the long shadow cast by racism since the founding of our nation. But I do believe that we can counter its effects by commiting ourselves to work to expose it and its effects on the health and human services. It is racism that has shaped the attitudes and assumptions we hold about the poor, people of color, and other marginalized populations that are the primary consumers of the health and human services. These attitudes and assumptions facilitate "victim blaming" and make it easier to develop causal explanations that hold these populations complicit in their own suffering and unfortunate circumstances.

Institutional and systemic flaws are the root cause of the disproportionality and disparities that have produced poor outcomes for generations of vulnerable children, youth, and families. Despite changes in the laws, numerous new programs and services, and the good intentions of well-meaning professionals, racial inequities have persisted for the same populations over many generations.

Historically and today, health and human services agencies have internalized messages that have become deeply embedded in organizational and administrative structures, which have become accepted as "trusims" that place the full burden and responsibility for poor outcomes on individuals. This has led to a constant designing and redesigning in intervention and treatment strategies based in the same flawed assumptions and more and more programs designed to "fix broken people" that ultimately fail. The data indicate that this response has not been effective. In essence, we have become accustomed to using the same thinking that created the problem to resolve it, recycling the same old and inef-fective interventions, resulting in perpetuating and sustaining the problems.

The problem of institutional and structural racism that results in dispropor-tionality and disparities and the impact on the same population of people by multiple helping systems can be tracked to the community level. These out-comes have existed for so long that many practitioners in the helping systems have become immune to learning from the data. The time is long overdue for a new, bold, and courageous conversation that reframes the questions, to begin to examine systemic factors rather than assume individual pathology of the consumer. It is time for systems to "turn the mirror inward," to conduct critical examinations of their systems, and deeper analyses of the policies and prac-tices that have held disproportionality and disparities in place. Our helping systems must come to recognize that addressing disproportionality at the root cause is necessary and critical to racial equity, which we will achieve when race no longer is a predictor of individual outcomes. I have been privileged to lead one of the country's largest public child welfare systems that owned and sub-sequently courageously introduced institutionalized racism as the underlying cause of disproportionality and disparities in outcomes for families served by the system.

Under my leadership Texas passed three pieces of legislation related to sys-tems change in addressing racial inequities that were introduced and sponsored by Texas State Senator Royce West and Texas State Representative Dawnna Dukes: Senate Bill 6 in 2005 was the first groundbreaking piece of legislation in the country, requiring child protective services to address disproportionality in its enforcement actions, Senate Bill 758 in 2007 expanded the work to the entire state of Texas, and Senate Bill 501 in 2011 expanded the requirement beyond child protective services to examine and make recommendations to address dis-proportionality in all health and human services systems and in education and juvenile justice. I introduced the Texas Model for Addressing Disproportionality and Disparities, a model that proved effective in reducing disproportionality and disparities for African American and Native American children, and improving overall outcomes for all populations. The following provides a summary of the components of the model:

## DATA-DRIVEN STRATEGIES

All data are collected, researched, evaluated, and reported by race and eth-nicity and compared to the racial and ethnic composition of a defined geographic service area. These data are subsequently examined from a systemic and cross-systems perspective and in the in the interest of transparency shared with systems and the communities that will be affected by the data outcomes.

## LEADERSHIP DEVELOPMENT

Leaders must be grounded in antiracist principles and in their understanding of their own internalized racial oppression, seek to increase their knowledge about the documented causes of why people are poor, and must be equally accountable to their staff and their institutions and service consumers.

## CULTURALLY COMPETENT WORKFORCE

The importance of valuing the diversity of cultures within the service consumer community and the recognition that western cultural norms that shape the largest number of health and human service organizations cannot be imposed on all populations served by these agency.

## COMMUNITY ENGAGEMENT

Engaging the grassroots community through transparency in communication that is reflected in a receptiveness to hearing their ideas, and including them in dialogs, discussions, planning, and decision-making on efforts that will impact their lives and their communities.

## CROSS-SYSTEMS COLLABORATIONS

Understanding the relationship that systems have to one another and their collective impact on the same vulnerable populations and moving away from siloes to a more integrated and holistic approach.

As discussed by Billings in Chapter 6, the components of the model are reflected in the principles in which anti-racist training is anchored:

## TRAINING DEFINED BY ANTIRACIST PRINCIPLES

Learning from history
Developing leadership

Maintaining accountability to communities
Creating networks
Undoing internalized racial oppression
Understanding the role of organizational gate-keeping as a mechanism for
  perpetuating racism

My ability to lead large systems change efforts was grounded in these "Undoing Racism" principles. The training was a catalyst for the cultural and philosophical shift that resulted in a transformation of the Texas Child Welfare System and eventually in significant changes in other health and human services systems in the state. We learned that to be effective the work of health and human services systems must include staff and volunteers at all organizational levels and must be guided by antiracism principles with a goal of identifying and deconstructing the impact of oppressive systems on all marginalized populations served by the organization. Health and human services and other helping systems must be willing to become critical lovers of their systems and move toward greater accountability for achieving equity for all populations.

The importance of accountability at all levels of the system is lifted up in the chapters of this book and will no doubt inform practice in new and courageous ways that contribute to the development of a racial equity lens as the prism for health and human services professionals to view their work, and ultimately lead to the elimination of disproportionality and disparities. I am grateful to the authors for their contributions to the field of health and human services and for their boldness in raising an issue that I believe will elevate the consciousness of well-meaning professionals, causing them to reflect intently on race and racism and resulting in the necessary systemic changes that must occur to ensure equitable outcomes for the most vulnerable of populations.

This book will serve as that catalyst for the change we all want to see. It provides health and human services and other systems leaders with a sense of hope and optimism and new approaches and strategies based in the empirical evidence that makes change possible, and for the realization of our vision for the work we have chosen to do. For me that vision is "to be a witness to the transformation of systems so that the end result is equity for everyone."

# *PREFACE*

This book emerged from the experience of a New York City initiative undertaken in partnership with private and public social service agencies, the metropolitan schools of social work, the United Way of New York City, the Human Services Council of New York City, and the New York City Chapter of the National Association of Social Workers. The initiative brought the "Undoing Racism" workshop, the flagship project of the People's Institute for Survival and Beyond, to key players in the city's health and human service community.

The initiative was undertaken as one strategy for addressing the implications of race and racism in the administration and delivery of health and human services in New York City. Key participants included an interdisciplinary mix of policymakers, administrators, educators, students, and direct service practitioners. A smaller group subsequently emerged comprising individuals who took on the daunting task of providing the courageous leadership needed to address what they intuitively knew were the deeply rooted remnants of doctrines of white supremacy that contaminated social services systems in a city historically distinguished by its diversity and progressive social policy development.

Ann Hartman, in her classic editorial in the January 1990 edition of the *Journal of Social Work*, observed that "this edition takes the position that there are many truths and many ways of knowing. Each discovery contributes to our knowledge and each way of knowing deepens our understanding and adds another dimension or view of the world" (Hartman, 1990). This book endeavors to deepen our understanding of the influence of personal bias and structural and institutional racism in the health and human services. Unlike traditional projects that are anchored in a clear theoretical framework that integrates and builds on existing knowledge, the "Undoing Racism" initiative in New York City grew from a felt need that emerged from the seldom-acknowledged and underresearched realities of a system that reflected the values of a larger societal context that were incongruent with the social justice goals and humanistic values embraced by the helping professions.

New York City may well be viewed as a microcosm of the national landscape where service consumers are overwhelmingly people of color, a growing number of them new arrivals from countries with developing economies or undergoing violent political upheavals. Although highly diverse as to national origin, culture, race, and ethnicity, a common task of the largest share of this segment of consumers, whether they are representative of historically underserved populations or new arrivals, irrespective of the choice of the geographic location of resettlement, is that they must seek assistance from largely white-controlled health and human service organizations as they endeavor to solve problems of daily living or as they confront traumatic life-changing crises. Further, the worldviews of consumers of color that influence help-seeking and service-using behaviors are significantly different from the Eurocentric worldviews of helpers, and helping relationships are carried out in a systemic and organizational context of significant power imbalances. In light of these realities of the system, it is not surprising that despite high need, recent decades have seen extensive reports in the literature that clients of color have poor rates of service retention and are more likely to be noncompliant with service and treatment plans, which are often developed from misdiagnoses or flawed assessments of their presenting problems and service needs (UDHHS, 2001).

The New York City initiative set out to address these seldom-discussed realities of the influence of race and racism in the delivery of the health and human services. It emerged as a grassroots, bottom-up, formative approach to program development and knowledge building. The underlying assumptions of the initiative are anchored in the growing body of empirical evidence of the significance of race and culture as determinants of client outcomes, combined with "practice wisdoms" that are based in the extensive clinical observations gleaned from the many years of practice experiences of the human service professionals who participated in the initiative.

The initiative was launched in 2007 with funding support from the United Way of New York City. The Human Service Council, which is an umbrella membership organization for the city's human service providers, served as funding conduit, provided the pipeline for the recruitment of workshop participants, and identified sites where the workshops would be easily accessible. These recruitment and marketing efforts were supported by the New York City Chapter of the National Association of Social Workers, which is the nation's largest chapter, with a membership of approximately 10,000 social workers who practice in various settings in the city's five boroughs. The Jewish Board of Family and Children's Services, one of the city's oldest and most preeminent agencies in the nonprofit sector, played a major role by promoting the initiative to the city's social welfare leadership.

Over the first five years after startup, more than 2,000 members of the local human service provider community, including agency CEOs and senior executives and faculty members and deans of the schools of social work, attended the "Undoing Racism" workshop. In addition to the impressive and growing numbers of individuals who have completed the workshop, notable accomplishments to date include the following: (1) an issue of a local publication (*Mental Health News*, 2011) with a national circulation devoted exclusively to race and racism in the mental health system; (2) elective course offerings on "Undoing Racism" at a number of the city's metropolitan schools of social work; (3) the establishment of a field placement initiative under the auspices of the New York City Chapter of the National Association of Social Workers; and (4) an executive steering committee that meets monthly to continue to move the initiative forward.

The manuscript draws on these successful outcomes of the New York experience. Because some aspects of the initiative and its underlying principles may well be replicated or serve as anchoring principles for initiatives in other cities or social service jurisdictions, a primary goal of this volume is to disseminate information about lessons learned from the "Undoing Racism" approach to a national audience of health and human service providers. The experience taught us the value of deconstructing assumptions of what may be flawed attribution theories in designing interventions for consumers of color, and the benefits of drawing upon the growing body of relevant evidence-based research for shaping delivery strategies with service consumers of color. We also learned that cross-racial dialogs are essential for bringing to light the more subtle effects of interpersonal, institutional, and structural bias that are present in health and human service systems and professional educational programs. Lessons learned from the New York experience are increasingly reported in the literature as underlying themes of promising and best-practice approaches for eradicating the residual effects of doctrines of white supremacy that contribute to the persistence of ethnic and racial disparities in the health and human services despite our best efforts to close these gaps.

The chapters draw upon lessons learned from the New York experiences, as well as the original research conducted by national scholars who are among the roster of contributing authors. While some of the contributing authors draw a good deal on clinical observations gleaned from years of direct practice, they all recognize the need to bring science and practice in the human services closer together, and acknowledge the reciprocity of this undertaking: research must inform practice and practice must inform research. Their experiences also affirm, as Hartman posited, that there are "many ways of knowing." Moreover, the contributing authors recognize that the ambiguous and subtle forms of institutional and structural racism that are intertwined with personal bias are often difficult if not impossible to tease apart, isolate, and subject to the objective lens of the microscope, or attain the level of scientific rigor required by empirical inquiry. Combined with the underresearched area examining the implications of race and racism on service outcomes, these are longstanding realities of the helping professions that draw upon theories anchored in the behavioral sciences that too often confound the process of formulating bias-free research questions for hypothesis testing. In her editorial, Hartman makes reference to Walter Hudson's often-quoted axiom that "if you cannot measure the client's problem, it does not exist, and if you cannot measure the client's problem you cannot treat it." We do not concur entirely with this view when the subject of inquiry and knowledge building is concerned with matters of race. However, with the increasing emphasis on strengthening the scientific base of the health and human services, we hope that the clinical insights and impressionistic data gleaned from the five-year study period of New York's experience that are integrated in the content of some chapters will bring to light the difficult-to-measure, insidious effects of racism that have constrained the formulation of culturally relevant research questions for hypothesis testing essential for antiracist knowledge building in the health and human services.

Focusing on essential topics of service delivery, each chapter introduces the reader to some of the dimensions of race and racism that influence service outcomes and contribute to the ethnic and racial disparities that are present in virtually all fields in the health and human services. Some of the contributing authors offer alternative strategies for deconstructing the more subtle forms of racist practices that unintentionally contribute to the perpetuation and recycling of interventions of limited effectiveness in solving the problems of clients of color.

We envisioned that the book will have a high appeal to a broad and diverse audience, including social service provider agencies, policymakers, funders, and educational institutions that play a central role in the education and training of the health and human service workforce, advocacy groups, and professional membership organizations. It may also be of interest to service consumers and the general reading public who wish to gain new insights about their in-care experiences, and reasons for the persistence of problems among people of color despite their high visibility on health and human service caseloads.

## ORGANIZATION

The introduction defines ambiguous concepts for the purposes of this book, sets forth the conceptual framework and underlying assumptions, and introduces integrating themes that run throughout all chapters of the book.

### Part One: Building the Infrastructure: Supporting Sustainable Change and Renewal

Part One examines topics critical for establishing an organizational infrastructure essential for transforming agency culture and creating the context and climate conducive to the implementation and sustainability of antiracist practice approaches. In Chapter 1, drawing largely on the subjective experiences of one study agency, co-authors Pender Greene and Levine begin by analyzing the costs and benefits of transforming health and human services when weighed against traditional approaches that are blind to the proverbial "elephant in the room" that diminishes organizational effectiveness and efficiency. Siskind and Schenk in Chapter 2 advocate a top-down approach that begins with policymaking boards and executive leadership. Building on an eight year-effort of antiracist curriculum development in social work education, Tolliver and Burghardt in Chapter 3 set forth a model for the infusion of an antiracist approach into social work curriculum. In Chapter 4, Lee, Wang, Cao, Liu, and Zaharlick consider critical issues for establishing an antiracist research agenda that begins with the framing of culturally appropriate research questions and hypotheses that are anchored in a culturally relevant view of the norms and traditions of diverse consumer populations. In Chapter 5, using a race-specific lens for data collection and analysis to dispel the efficacy of colorblind approaches, Blitz and Abramovitz discuss the implications of the findings of a survey of respondents who had completed the "Undoing Racism" workshop for promoting racial equity in organizational development and change.

## Part Two: Reshaping Theoretical and Practice Paradigms

Part Two establishes the theoretical foundation for ethnically and racially inclusive practices that reject attribution theories anchored in Western ideologies in which assumptions of white supremacy are deeply embedded. Contributing authors examine the political dimensions of the health and human services that contribute to the persistence of racial and ethnic disparities in outcomes despite our best efforts to close gaps in consumer outcomes. In Chapter 6, Billings begins with an examination of the historical foundation and values underlying America's emerging social, economic, and political structures that shaped ideals of white supremacy and discusses the "Undoing Racism" workshop as a tool for bringing to light and deconstructing the flaws of these empirically untested assumptions. Subsequent chapters deconstruct assumptions of white supremacy in which structural and institutional racism is rooted. Finch, in Chapter 7, examines postmodern theories that are grounded in inclusive, equalitarian ideals and the concept of intersectionality. In Chapter 8, Hardy sets forth principles to reconceptualize and guide new antiracist and practice paradigms and tools for engaging in difficult racial dialogs.

## Part Three: Systemic Impacts and Special Populations

The contributing authors in this part examine the situation of underserved population groups and identify emerging programs and practice approaches that are enjoying considerable success in redressing the effects of practices that have given insufficient consideration to their special needs. In Chapter 9, McRoy and Mallon focus on the services to children and families and efforts to address disproportionality in the child welfare system. In Chapter 10, Huggins considers older adults, focusing on the elderly of color in urban areas, who are not well captured by the safety net programs. Lindsey and Watson, in Chapter 11, examine the circumstances of adolescents and emerging young adult males of color and offer effective approaches for engaging this underserved population.

## Part Four: The Helping Relationship

The contributing authors in this part examine varied topics that have implications for the establishment of trust in cross-racial and cross-cultural helping relationships, which is the vehicle within which all change occurs. Emphasizing the Hispanic experience and its within-group diversity, González in Chapter 12 considers the influence of ethnicity, race, and culture on consumer help-seeking and help-using behaviors. In Chapter 13, Klein examines the influence of transference and countertransference present in the helping relationship, and sets forth approaches for ensuring the establishment of effective cross-cultural alliances and communication with diverse consumer populations. In Chapter 14, Abramovitz and Mingus argue that the misdiagnosis of behaviors of school-aged children, which are symptomatic of untreated traumatic environmental conditions, combined with teacher bias creates a predictable pipeline that leads from school to the juvenile and criminal justice system.

## Part Five: Replicating Best Practices

Part Five integrates what has emerged as best-practice principles underlying high-performing programs serving ethnically and racially diverse populations in under-resourced urban communities, and those served by public agencies and characteristically jointly served by multiple agencies. Authors in this section describe two programs in the public and private sectors that are implementing strategies anchored in values of social justice and racial equity and new theoretical perspectives that are enjoying considerable success in closing the gap in racial and ethnic outcomes. In Chapter 15, Williams-Isom, drawing on powerful personal narratives, provides an insider's view of strategies that have launched the Harlem Children's Zone as a program model for national replication. In Chapter 16, Best-Giacomini, Howard, and Ilian describe a staff development "Undoing Racism" strategy for replication in public human services organizations serving a diversity of racial and ethnic groups.

Finally, closing thoughts are offered by the co-editors, Carten, Pender Greene, and Siskind, that synthesize major takeaways for the reader.

Alma J. Carten
May 2015

## REFERENCES

Hartman, Ann (1990) 'Editorial: Many Ways of Knowing', Social Work 35(1): 3–4.

Hartman, A. (1990). Many ways of knowing [editorial]. *Journal of Social Work*, 3–4.

U.S. Department of Health and Human Services. (2001). *Mental health: Culture, race, and ethnicity, a supplement to "Mental health: A report to the Surgeon General."* Rockville, MD: Author.

# ACKNOWLEDGMENTS

This book is the result of the experiences and work of many people, and we thank all of those who played a direct or indirect role in making it a reality. We would also like to acknowledge and thank the following individuals and organizations who played a direct role leading to the publication of the book:

Ronald Chisholm, co-founder of the People's Institute for Survival and Beyond, for bringing the "Undoing Racism" workshop to New York City, and to the Institute's master trainers who conducted the workshop during the early phase of implementation

The United Way of New York City, and Larry Mandell, former President and CEO, for providing the funding that made it possible to launch the program in New York City

The Human Services Council and former Director Michael Stoller for organizing the work, for serving as funding conduit for the grant, and for identifying sites for conducting the workshop

The New York City Chapter of the National Association of Social Workers and Executive Director Robert Schachter for providing an administrative home for the "Undoing Racism" initiative and the development of a field placement for a social work student to oversee the program

The deans, faculty, and students of the metropolitan schools of social work for bringing the "Undoing Racism" workshop to the academy

The Jewish Board of Family and Children's Services and former President and CEO Paul Levine for opening the agency up to serve as a laboratory for pioneering the implementation of the workshop in the city's not-for-profit sector

Ira Minot, Editor of the *Mental Health News*, for devoting a full issue of the publication to addressing issues of race and racism in the mental health system; this was the catalyst for the book

Members of the Executive Steering Committee of the "Undoing Racism" Alliance Monday Morning Collaborative for overseeing the work involved in the original publication and for assisting in the subsequent conceptualization of the book project

Our outstanding roster of contributing authors; we are especially grateful to each of them for lending their expertise to the project, and especially for their collegiality in responding to our editorial comments on their work To Joyce James for lending her name and prestige to the project in preparing the Forward, and for her transparency in sharing her personal journey of transformation in finding her race-conscious voice

Cassandra Coste, at NYU Silver School of Social Work, for providing administrative support to the project and for maintaining communication linkages with the contributing authors and publisher

We are grateful to Oxford University Press senior editor, Dana Bliss, and his special assistant, Andrew Dominello, and other Oxford staff for their expert consultation and guidance in bringing to publication a book on what is a highly controversial topic. We hope it will make a small contribution to diminishing the presence of the infamous "elephant in the room" when engaging in dialogs around race and racism relevant to the health and human services.

Finally, we offer a special thanks to all of those who attended the "Undoing Racism" workshop and took back what they had learned to their agencies and schools. In the end, it is they who will be the change agents who create and become a part of the critical mass that is essential for a true transformation of the health and human services.

# CONTRIBUTING AUTHORS

**Mimi Abramovitz**, DSW, is the Bertha Capen Reynolds Professor of Social Policy at the Silberman School of Social Work at Hunter College and The CUNY Graduate Center has written extensively about women, work, poverty, and social welfare policy. Her books include *Regulating the Lives of Women: Social Welfare Policy From Colonial Times to the Present, the award-winning Under Attack, Fighting Back: Women and Welfare in the US,* She is current writing *Gendered Obligations: The History of Activism Low Income Women in the US since 1900* as well as article on the importance of "place" and the impact of austerity policies on the human service workers. An activist and a scholar, Dr. Abramovitz has received numerous prestigious awards including membership in the American Academy of Social Work and Social Welfare and the Columbia University School of Social Work Hall of Fame and recognition as a "top leader" by the NYC Chapter of the NASW.

**Robert Abramovitz**, M.D., is a child psychiatrist and a Distinguished Lecturer at the Silberman School of Social Work (SSSW) at Hunter College. He prepares the next generation of trauma-informed social workers in his role as co director of the National Center for Social Work Trauma Education and Workforce Development and leader of the child trauma specialization program at SSSW. His work has always focused on the impact of adversity, violence, poverty, and racism on the lives of children and families and on resilience development in individuals, communities, and organizations. His medical degree is from Wayne State University and his adult psychiatry and child psychiatry training at the Yale University Department of Psychiatry and the Yale Child Study Center where he was an Associate Professor of Pediatrics and Psychiatry.

**Jeanne Bertrand Finch**, DSW, LCSW-R, is currently research associate professor, Department of Psychiatry, New York University and serves as secretary for the New York State Chapter of NASW. Previously Dr. Finch was associate dean for administration and MSW graduate program director within the School of Social Welfare, Stony Brook University, State University of New York. She has worked in the field of child welfare both in the U.S. and the U.K. and has presented at numerous national and international conferences on issues surrounding the challenges of teaching for social justice. She is co-author of *Learning to Teach, Teaching to Learn,* (2014, 2nd edition, CSWE Press).

**Christiana Best-Giacomini**, LMSW, Ph.D., is a social worker with 30 years of experience working in the New York City child welfare system. She is currently Senior Advisor for Child Welfare Policy, where she develops and revises child welfare policies. In addition to her work in child welfare, Dr. Best's body of work is focused on the immigrant experience and the myriad of issues related to transnational parenting and its impact on English-speaking Caribbean families, parents, and children. She is an adjunct lecturer at the Silberman School of Social Work.

**Rev. David Billings** has been an antiracist trainer and organizer with the People's Institute for Survival and Beyond since 1983. He is a part of the People's Institute's national staff and a member of its Community Organizing Strategy Team. In 1986 he co-founded European Dissent, a collective of white antiracist activists that continues its work today. Billings is a historian with an expertise in the history of race and racism. He expertly weaves history into the strategies of effective community organizing and institutional change work.

**Lisa V. Blitz**, Ph.D., LCSW-R, is a social worker with more than 20 years experience in mental health and social justice advocacy centering on efforts to incorporate racial equity and inclusion in organizations. She is currently an assistant professor in the Department of Social Work at Binghamton University, and assistant director of the BU Center for Family, School, and Community Partnerships.

**Steve Burghardt**, Ph.D., is Professor of Social Work at the Silberman School of Social Work at Hunter College. His areas of expertise include community organizing for the 21st century, transformative models of leadership, integrating the macro/micro spheres of social work practice, and cultural competency and humility. He was the co-recipient of the 2012 SAGE/CSWE National Award for Innovative Teaching. His most recent books include *Macro Practice in Social Work for the 21st Century* (2nd ed.) and (with Willie Tolliver) *Stories of Transformative Leadership in Human Services*.

**Yiwen Cao**, M.A., MSW, is a Doctoral Student and research associate at the College of Social Work, the Ohio State University. Her research interests focus on mental health disparities, neighborhoods, and organizational implementation of culturally responsive and evidence-based practices.

**Manny J. González**, Ph.D., LCSW-R, is an Associate Professor and Director of the MSW program at the Silberman School of Social Work at Hunter College where he teaches graduate courses in clinical practice, relational therapy, psychopathology, and evidence-based mental health practice. He has practiced as a clinician for 30 years, specializing in community mental health. Dr. González maintains a private practice in psychodynamic psychotherapy and clinical supervision and has published extensively in areas of clinical practice with Hispanic patients, mental health care of immigrants and refugees, evidence-based practice, and urban children and families.

**Kenneth V. Hardy**, Ph.D., is an internationally recognized clinician, author, and trainer. He is the Director of the Eikenberg Institute for Relationships in New York City, where he maintains a private practice specializing in working with traumatized and oppressed populations. Dr. Hardy is the former Director of the Center for Children, Families, and Trauma at the Ackerman Institute in New York City, and formerly served on the faculty at Syracuse University, where he held numerous positions, including Director of Clinical Training and Research, as well as Chairperson of the Department of Child and Family Studies.

**Alexis Howard**, LCSW-R, is a clinical social worker with experience in several practice settings: as a frontline practitioner, an administrator, and an educator. She currently serves as the New York City Coordinator for the New York Social Work Education Consortium at the University at Albany. In partnership with the New York City public child welfare agency her work focuses on strengthening the child welfare workforce. A key element of her work includes supporting the field education of MSW students within the context of child welfare practice. She is a Ph.D. student at the Silberman School of Social Work at Hunter College.

**Camille Huggins**, Ph.D., has over 10 years of experience working with older adults in long-term care and private practice. She has held administrative positions in rehabilitation and nursing facilities assisting multiracial seniors transitioning from living in the community into a nursing facility. Her dissertation research explored sociocultural predictors of mental health treatment utilization among African American and Caribbean black older adults experiencing depression, anxiety, and traumatic events.

**Henry Ilian**, Ph.D., Capsule is an evaluator at the New York City Administration for Children's Services (ACS), working primarily on an ongoing review of child protective casework effectiveness. For most of his career, he was involved in research and evaluation at the ACS James Satterwhite Academy for Child Welfare Training. He has researched child protective worker turnover, has conducted evaluations of training effectiveness and training needs assessments, and has developed tests for a variety of courses offered by the Satterwhite Academy.

**Eileen Klein**, Ph.D., LCSW, M.S., is an Assistant Professor and BSW Program Director at Ramapo College. Prior to teaching full time at Ramapo, Dr. Klein worked for over 30 years in public mental health and taught at several MSW programs in New York City. She has held an executive level position in a large urban inpatient health facility that focused on community reintegration for psychiatric inpatients, and the design and implementations of programs for reducing stigma for the mentally ill.

**Mo Yee Lee**, Ph.D., is Professor at the College of Social Work at the Ohio State University. She has a dual focus on intervention research regarding a solution-focused strengths-based systems perspective in social work treatment, as well as culturally competent research and cross-cultural integrative practice and research with individuals and families.

**Paul Levine**, LCSW, is the former CEO of the Jewish Board of Family and Children's Services. He played a key role in facilitating the "Undoing Racism" project in New York City and is currently a consultant with the Jewish Board of Family and Children's Services, examining a strong and continuing presence of child welfare services in the agency's service portfolio.

**Michael A. Lindsey**, Ph.D., is an associate professor at the New York University Silver School of Social Work. He is a child and adolescent mental health services researcher and is particularly interested in the prohibitive factors that lead to unmet mental health need among vulnerable youth with serious psychiatric illnesses, including depression. Dr. Lindsey has received research support from the National Institute of Mental Health (NIMH) to examine the social network influences on perceptual and actual barriers to mental health care among African American adolescent males with depression.

**Chang Liu**, MSW, is a doctoral student and research associate at the College of Social Work at the Ohio State University. Her research interests focus on mental health issues of Asian populations and integrative body-mind-spirit practice.

**Gerald P. Mallon**, DSW, is the Julia Lathrop Professor of Child Welfare and executive director of the National Center for Child Welfare Excellence at the Silberman Social Work at Hunter College in New York City. For more than 37 years, Dr. Mallon has been a child welfare practitioner, advocate, and researcher. He is the author or editor of 21 books and numerous peer-reviewed publications in professional journals. Dr. Mallon also serves as the Senior Editor of the peer-reviewed journal *Child Welfare*.

**Ruth G. McRoy**, Ph.D., holds the Donahue and DiFelice Endowed Professorship at Boston College Graduate School of Social Work. Prior to joining the Boston College faculty, McRoy was a member of the University of Texas at Austin School of Social Work faculty for 25 years and held the Ruby Lee Piester Centennial Professorship. She received her B.A. and MSW degrees from the University of Kansas and her Ph.D. degree in Social Work from the University of Texas at Austin. Her primary research and practice interests include such topics as barriers to adoption, racial and ethnic diversity issues, African American families, transracial adoptions, kinship care, family preservation, adoptive family dynamics, sibling placement issues, open adoptions, respite care, and other forms of postadoption services.

**Jessica Mingus**, LMSW, is a licensed social worker and trainer specializing in the impacts of trauma on learning and education access for students living in poverty. Her primary research and practice interests include trauma-sensitive program development, restorative practices for school inclusion and resilience-building embodiment practices for direct service workers. She currently works as the Interim Assistant Director for a City University of New York (CUNY) college transition program. She graduated with honors from the Silberman School of Social Work at Hunter College and has an AB in Cultural Anthropology from Princeton University.

**Todd Schenk** has been active in the human services field for 25 years, including the past 20 years at the Jewish Board of Family and Children's Services (JBFCS). Mr. Schenk has held roles ranging from oversight of program services to budget management and planning. As the Chief Operating Officer at JBFCS, Mr. Schenk oversaw the agency's program services for individuals and families with needs related to mental health, child welfare, domestic violence, developmental disabilities, and early childhood education.

**Willie Tolliver**, DSW, is on the faculty (1993–present) of the Silberman School of Social Work at Hunter College and the Social Welfare Doctoral Faculty at the Graduate Center of the City University of New York. Dr. Tolliver received his doctorate from the Graduate Center of the City University of New York. He has been a social worker since 1976 and has served on the faculties of Florida A&M University Social Welfare Department and the Boston University School of Social Work.

**Xiafei Wang**, MSW, is a doctoral student and research associate at the College of Social Work at the Ohio State University. She graduated from Peking University, China, with her bachelor and master degrees of social work. Her research interests focus on evidence-based practices in the systems of child welfare and juvenile justice.

**Amaris Watson**, MSW, LGSW, is a licensed therapist in Baltimore, Maryland. Her areas of clinical interest include depressive and anxiety disorders in ethnic minority youth. She plans to develop a nonprofit organization that specializes in the delivery of home-based mental health services to vulnerable youth in urban communities.

**Anne Williams-Isom**, Esq., is Deputy Director, Harlem Children's Zone, and former deputy commissioner for policy with the New York City Administration for Children's Services; she has published on the agency's reform efforts and program development for immigrant families.

**Amy Zaharlick**, Ph.D., is Emeritus Professor in the Department of Anthropology at the Ohio State University. Her areas of specialization are sociocultural, linguistic, and applied anthropology.

## CO-EDITORS

**Alma J. Carten**, Ph.D., ACSW, LCSW, is an Associate Professor, New York University Silver School of Social Work teaching in the Human Behavior and the Social Environment and Social Welfare Policies and Program curriculum areas. She has conducted research and published in child welfare, family preservation, maternal substance abuse, independent living services, child abuse in immigrant populations, and African Americans and mental health.

**Mary Pender Greene**, LCSW-R, is an Organizational Consultant, psychotherapist in private practice, career/executive coach, professional speaker, and Co-Founder of the Anti-Racist Alliance. She has a passion for assisting organizations in addressing structural racism and a commitment to the advancement of women and people of color in leadership roles. Her background also includes executive and management responsibility for the Jewish Board of Family and Children's Services, which is one of the nation's largest nonprofit, mental health and social service agency.

**Alan Siskind**, Ph.D., LCSW, is in private practice in New York City and Mount Kisco, New York, working with individuals, couples, and families. His practice is carried out through a race and ethnic critical lens. He is also a consultant on creating antiracist organizations, and formerly CEO of the New York City Jewish Board of Family and Children's Services. He has held adjunct faculty appointments with the Smith School for Social Work, the Columbia University School of Social Work, and the Silberman School of Social Work at Hunter College.

# INTRODUCTION

## The Overview

### ALMA J. CARTEN

... the ironic fact is that the students, research workers and professionals in the behavioral sciences—like members of the clergy and educators—are no more immune by virtue of their values and training to the disease and superstitions of American racism than is the average man.
Kenneth Clark (1972)

This volume is an outgrowth of a special issue of *Mental Health News* (Winter 2011) that brought together an interdisciplinary mix of mental health professionals to address the impact of race and racism on the mental health system. Contrary to the conventional wisdom that the subject of race was destined to be the constant "elephant in the room" that people would resist acknowledging, the responses to the publication revealed that practitioners and service consumers alike felt that the time was long past due for a coordinated effort to address the conundrum of issues resulting from past failures to forthrightly confront the implications of structural and personal bias that contributed to the persistence of ethnic and racial disparities in mental health outcomes. This encouraging response indicated that this topic was both timely and relevant and served as the motivation for preparing this book.

A central purpose of the book is to disseminate information about lessons learned from the New York City experience to a broader audience and to engage members of the helping professions practicing in the health and human services in difficult conversations around the controversial and ambiguous subject of race. There is an ample use of the words "racist" and "racism" in the volume. Not only are these terms equality ambiguous in their definition, but they are also potentially off-putting because they evoke strong emotional responses from Americans irrespective of their racial or ethnic identities.

Despite the ambiguities and lack of consensus about the significance of race in American society, the effects of race and ethnicity on producing unequal outcomes are well documented both quantitatively and qualitatively in the research and practice literature. The contributing authors draw on these data in an examination of the experiences of racial and ethnic groups who are segments of the population found to experience considerable disadvantage across virtually all societal domains, including the health and human services (Algeria et al., 2002; Hofrichter, 2003; McKernan et al., 2013; Smedley & Smedley, 2005; Smedley, Stith, & Nelson, 2003; Sue et al., 2007; U.S. Department of Health & Human Services, 2001). As reported in the first "Health Disparities and Inequalities" report (CHDIR, 2011), published by the Centers for Disease Control and Prevention, progress has been made in reducing these gaps. However, the work is far from done, since at the same time the report asserts that we need to move at a faster pace in closing what are modifiable gaps in health, longevity, and quality of life among certain segments of the population.

This book examines the combined and interrelated effects of various forms of racism for the health and human services. Over time these have evolved from blatant forms of legal segregation and discrimination to more subtle forms. There is no single or identifiable perpetrator for the latter, but they are no less harmful in their effects.

Racism is generally recognized as taking the form of institutionalized racism and individual personal bigotry. Institutional racism, also referred to as systemic or structural racism, is defined as the differential access and distribution of the resources, goods, services, and opportunities and power of society to the benefit of dominant racial groups. The pernicious and more subtle forms of individual bias and bigotry have more recently been described as "microaggressions" (Sue, 2010). Microaggressions are conceptualized as the invisible forms of racial bias that operate at an unconscious level of well-intentioned whites who see themselves as moral, fair-minded people and free of racial bias and prejudices (Sue, 2003). Whatever form it takes, none of these manifestations of racism can successfully operate alone or independently from one another. The supportive interactions of each of these have been essential for the persistence and sustainability of systemic and structural racism in the United States.

The terms "race work" and "race equity work," when used by contributing authors in describing the New York experience, may be understood as referring to a broad array of activities undertaken by practitioners at all organizational levels that are based in the core principles and philosophical approach of the People's Institute for Survival and Beyond as described by Billings in Chapter 6. These activities are purposefully undertaken as coordinated and planned approaches for bringing to light and eradicating all forms of racism that are a reflection of the residual influences of doctrines of white supremacy in an effort to reduce the persistent racial and ethnic disparities that are common in the health and human sector across the United States.

## THE CONTINUING DILEMMA OF RACE
## IN AMERICA

For some Americans the election of Barrack Hussein Obama as the country's first African American president was a much-welcomed signal that the United States had at last solved its troubled history of race. This optimistic belief that Americans were now living in a "postracial society" was soon shattered by carefully orchestrated challenges to the president's authenticity to serve in the office of the American presidency. For many Americans this opposition, coming largely but not exclusively from the conservative right of the Republican Party, was a more realistic measure of just how intricately the doctrine of white supremacy was interwoven into the fabric of American culture.

A close appraisal reveals that much of the questioning of President Obama's authenticity to serve in the American presidency focused on his personal attributes. The so-called birthers questioned his nationality and place of birth, calling into question his American citizenship; questions and doubts were raised about his religious beliefs and identification with the Christian faith; and accusations were made that he lacked an understanding of American values, as evidenced by what was claimed to be his leftist socialist leanings. Although unspoken, the nature of all of these doubts and questions about the president's personal attributes evoked the subliminal message that what was missing from his otherwise highly credible portfolio qualifying him for the presidency was that he was not white. The persistence of these efforts of nullification lends some credence to Harvard law professor Randall Kennedy's assertion in his analysis of the Obama presidency that everything about the nation's first African American president "almost unavoidably is interpreted through the lens of race" (Kennedy, 2011, p. 3).

Whatever one's point of view, responses that were unique to the Obama administration—the blatant racist portrayals of the president in the social media, the impulsive shouting out of "you lie" by a member of Congress, the singular focus on making his a one-term presidency, and the shutting down of the federal government by the Republican-controlled Congress—arguably are indicators that democracy has yet to triumph over racism as optimistically predicted by the Swedish sociologist Gunnar Myrdal (1944) in his classic study *An American Dilemma: The Negro Problem and Modern Democracy.*

## DEFINING THE AMBIGUOUS CONCEPT OF RACE

"Ethnicity" refers to a group of people who recognize a shared identity related to their ancestry, history, language, religion, national origins, and cultural attributes that distinguish them from other ethnic groups. Cultural norms and traditions that characterize various ethnic groups and are passed on across generations are learned and not biologically or genetically determined. Definitions of ethnicity are typically straightforward and there is little disagreement about them. However, despite considerable evidence that there is no scientific basis for classifying people based on their physical characteristics or skin color, there is far less consensus around the definition and meaning of race.

According to the statement of the American Anthropological Association (1998) on race, as scientific knowledge expanded in the 20th century beyond earlier classifications of people as Caucasoid, Mongoloid and Negroid, there was substantial scientific evidence that human populations are not clearly demarcated as biologically distinct groups. The Human Genome Project, undertaken as an international initiative to identify all the genes of the human body, concluded that humans share the same genetic code irrespective of their race or skin color. Moreover, the DNA analysis revealed that there is a far greater variation within what are currently classified as racial groupings than there are between them (American Anthropological Association, 1998; Collins, 1999).

The movement and intermingling of people across geographic areas throughout world history is added evidence that the notion of a "pure" white race is conventional wisdom that is not supported by science. Further, the "one drop of blood" rule historically used in the United States to determine who is black lends added insights into understanding the implications of the political dimensions of defining and classifying people into distinct racial groups. Given these political dimensions and the absence of scientific evidence to support the existence of the clearly demarcated classifications of racial groups as to biological traits, there is consensus among scholars in the fields of communication, cultural anthropology, and race relations that the concept of race is best defined and understood as a social and political construct.

## RACE AS A SOCIAL AND POLITICAL CONSTRUCT

Social constructionist theory posits that social phenomena and events and our perceptions of reality have meaning only because of the interpretative meaning assigned to them by a given culture or society within the context of time and place. Using race as an example, the social construction of whiteness and the definition of who is white have changed over the history of the United States. During different periods of American immigration history people of German, Italian, Irish, and Russian heritage were viewed as nonwhite, but today they self-identify and are generally considered to be white (Baum, 2006; Dee, 2003–2004). And as demographic and immigration trends saw an increasing diversity in the Hispanic population beyond traditional emigrants from Puerto Rico and the Dominican Republic, the racial classification system used by the U.S. Census Bureau currently gives Hispanics (the nation's largest ethnic group, with much within-group diversity) the option to self-identify as either white or black.

When applying social constructionist theory to racial politics in the United States, the practice of using skin color and physical features as criterion for assigning people to various racial groups has been historically used as a mechanism for the unequal distribution of power based on a socially determined definition of race. The process of racialization supported the doctrine of white supremacy and the advancement of empirically untested assumptions that spawned belief systems that whites are superior to all other racial groups (Carten, 2011, 2013). The racialization process, anchored in doctrines of white supremacy and scientific racism, provided justification for assigning unearned privilege and power to whites, the accepted dominant racial group in American society, and unearned disadvantage to people who have been viewed as "the other" at various times in the country's history. This process of disempowerment of people of color based on the social and political construction of race expanded to include what became associated with what was defined as aberrant cultural norms and behaviors, thus legitimating the growth and entrenchment of stigmatizing stereotypes purported to be an accurate representation of all members of marginalized racial groups.

Social constructions theory would also posit that the persistent racial stereotyping via blatant as well as subliminal messages and images contributes to internalized racism for both whites and racially marginalized groups. With societal validation, whites would naturally be conditioned to internalize a sense of superiority, privilege, and entitlement based exclusively on skin color. For members of racially stigmatized groups this may become reflected as the acceptance of negative perceptions about their own abilities and intrinsic worth. This "soiled sense of self" in turn engenders feelings of low self-esteem and self-worth for the individual that may be generalized toward others in their group of racial identification. Internalized racism and feelings of "less than" experienced by some people of color may be expressed in behaviors that embrace attributes of "whiteness" as being more desirable and a devaluing of attributes associated with their own racial group. For whites, this process results in an assumption of unwarranted and unearned sense of innate superiority that is based solely on skin color and the internalization of feelings of assumed privilege and entitlement that are taken for granted.

The implications of the social construction of race are elaborated by Finch in Chapter 7, and Billings' discussion in Chapter 6 examines how doctrines of white supremacy supported by scientific racism provided the socially constructed theoretical basis for the justification and legitimation of race-based discrimination that was sanctioned in both law and custom throughout the nation's history and are now deeply embedded in the country's institutional structures. Some examples are found in the years of the country, when policies of "manifest destiny" and beliefs about American exceptionalism led to the near-extinction of American Indians. During the early years of expansion in the West, the Chinese Exclusion Act exploited the labor of Chinese workers at the same that it placed restrictions on their immigration into the country and access to full citizenship. Jim Crow laws that were in place during the Reconstruction period following the Civil War effectively replaced the institution of slavery as the means for the disenfranchisement and oppression of freed blacks. The "separate but equal clause" of the Constitution was upheld by the U.S. Supreme Court until it was finally struck down by the Court in the landmark 1954 *Brown v. Board of Education* decision. And it was not until the enactment of the 1964 Civil Rights Act that segregation was banned in all public facilities.

Despite landmark legislation of the 20th century, the residual influence of doctrines of white supremacy justifying the unequal and discriminatory treatment of Americans based on race has had great staying power in the United States, with rippling and continuing effects into the present.

## RACE AS MYTH AND REALITY

Although it is viewed as a social and political construct, Smedley and Smedley (2005) argue that the effects of race are nonetheless very real in American society and for some population groups may extend over the entire life cycle, from the "cradle to the grave." According to data from the Office of Minority Health, African Americans are almost four times as likely to die as infants due to complications related to low birth weight compared to non-Hispanic white infants. Further, the rates for all major causes of death are higher for African Americans than for whites; this discrepancy accounts in part for the lower life expectancy for African American men and women (U.S. Department of Health & Human Services, 2013). The contributing authors present a more detailed statistical description of the disparate outcomes for various populations under discussion, and as they appear across various fields of practice in the health and human services.

## THE INTERSECTION OF RACE, CLASS, AND POVERTY

Racial and ethnic disparities are explained in part because of the disproportionate representation of people of color among the poor, which place them at greater risk for being impacted by the far-ranging consequences of poverty. African Americans and Hispanics are four times more likely to live in poverty than whites, are disproportionately impacted by social problems of concern to health and human service providers, and consequently have high visibility on the caseloads of practitioners in the helping professions. Children of color have historically been and continue to be the most disadvantaged age population of Americans. Findings from a recent report of the Citizens Committee on Children, an advocacy organization that tracks well-being outcomes for children in New York City, were not significantly different from the statistical picture of child well-being outcomes in urban communities across the country. According to this report's analysis of changing geographic patterns of poverty, more than 298,000 New Yorkers citywide are living in concentrated poverty. This number includes an estimated 124,000, or 1 in every 10 children, who are living in neighborhoods where the poverty rates exceed 40% and in which the majority of the population is black and Hispanic (Citizens Committee for Children, 2012).

While socioeconomic status plays an undisputable role in shaping the life course of individuals and provides an explanation of racial and ethnic disparities, it does not tell the full story. African Americans of all socioeconomic groups are found to be especially vulnerable to the adverse effects of race-based discrimination in health and human services systems that may be either real or perceived. They are also found to harbor feelings of mistrust of the health system based on ethical transgressions by the medical field in the interest of scientific discovery. The most blatant of these transgressions, which continues to fuel mistrust of the system among blacks, is the Tuskegee Study conducted by the U.S. Office of Public Health between 1932 and 1972. The study, which is common knowledge among blacks, involved 600 uneducated tenant farmers who were either infected or not infected with syphilis. The infected men were not told they had the disease, and during the study treatment was withheld from those infected, even though it became known that penicillin was an effective cure.

Unsurprisingly, cultural mistrust is identified as an important consideration for understanding service-using behaviors and in the diagnosis and treatment of African Americans (Snowden, 2001; U.S. Department of Health & Human Services, 2001). One of the social determinants accounting for the fact that African American women are more likely to die from breast cancer than all other women is their lack of trust in the health care system (Gerend & Pai, 2008). Increasing attention is being given to the adverse effects of perceived discrimination and racism on health and mental health outcomes for African Americans when controlling for socioeconomic status.

A meta-analytic review of the research conducted by Pieterse and colleagues (2012) on the mental health of African Americans found a relationship between perceived racism and adverse psychological outcomes, expressed as increased levels of anxiety, depression, and other psychiatric symptoms. Pascoe and Smart Richman(2009) made similar findings, concluding that the multiple forms of perceived discrimination have a significant negative effect on both physical and psychological health and also produce high levels of stress that are associated with unhealthy behaviors. Similarly, a study conducted by Franklin-Jackson and Carter (2007) found that race-related stress has implication for mental health and for the development of a positive racial identity for black Americans.

The negative impact of racism has been found to begin as early as the womb and to play a role in adverse outcomes for the infants of African American women. For example, African American infants are found to be at greater risk for low birth weight, which is a significant predictor of poor outcomes in early and later childhood. Giscombe and Lobel (2005) examined five explanations for the adverse birth outcomes among African American women that included the impact of racism acting either as a contributor to stress or as a factor that exacerbates stress effects; all were found to be contributing factors to adverse outcomes.

Focusing on children and youth growing up in poverty, Abramowitz and Mingus in Chapter 14 examine the detrimental impacts of race-based discrimination on schoolchildren that they argue contribute to a predictable school-to-prison pipeline. Research findings also indicate that schoolchildren, irrespective of their socioeconomic status, are equally impacted by the adverse effects of perceived racism or race-based discrimination. A study of ethnically and socioeconomically diverse elementary school–age children found that they developed an awareness of racial differences and stereotypes very early, and these perceptions impacted their responses to a variety of situations, including social relationships and test taking. Similar findings were noted in the comprehensive report of the Presidential Task Force of the American Psychological Association on Educational Disparities (2012). Beyond the reporting of well-documented gaps in the academic performance of African American, Hispanic, and some Asian populations in comparison to their white counterparts, the study identified the complex connection between racial identity and academic adjustment. Findings indicate that disparities in educational outcomes are associated with a variety of variables that included the awareness on the part of children and adolescents of discrimination and their stigmatized racial status. Other findings highlighted the complex connections between ethnic and racial identity and academic adjustment.

## SCOPE AND DEFINITION OF THE HEALTH AND HUMAN SERVICES

The health and human services, often used interchangeably with the terms "social services" or "social welfare services," have undergone considerable changes in scope, definition, and purpose since the federalization of these services with the enactment of the 1935 Social Security Act. The definition and scope of the health and human services are not always clear, and the boundaries of various fields of practices are overlapping. For our purposes the health and human services are defined as those services that operate under the U.S. Department of Health and Human Services and are concerned with providing services and benefits to meet unmet social needs. These services operate under the auspices of governmental, private, sectarian, nonsectarian, and faith-based organizations. With the emphasis on cultural competency and the increasing diversity among the nation's newest immigrants, recent decades have seen the emergence of minority-governed agencies and ethnic associations with strong roots in their communities of identification. The trend toward privatization occurring in the field during the 1980s and policies of "New Federalism" saw the field expanding to include agencies that operated for profit. However, health and human services have traditionally operated outside of the market because of the belief that all human life is of equal intrinsic value, and therefore access to these services should not depend on the individual's ability to pay.

## THE HELPING PROFESSIONS

The health and human service workforce comprises many professional disciplines and paraprofessional social service workers that are generically described as the helping professions. Each of the helping professions operates from a unique knowledge and skill base, but all share in common a valuing of human life, a service orientation, and a commitment to improving the quality of life of special populations as well as society as a whole.

This notwithstanding, health and human services in the United States since the federalization of these services under the Social Security Act emerged as part of larger institutional structures within which ideologies supporting racial discrimination and white supremacy prevailed. Therefore, these organizations and members of the helping professions who staff them have not been immune, by virtue of their mission statements, values, and training, to the effects of socialization experiences and cultural belief systems that reinforce and normalize racial bias at the personal, organizational, and societal levels. Reflecting the society's cultural norms, and in keeping with the legal mandate of the "separate but equal" clause of the Constitution, social welfare services in the United States developed along a two-track system of care—one for blacks and one for whites. This was the accepted pattern for public and private agencies and those operating under sectarian auspices. Even with the enactment of the Civil Rights Act that ended segregation in public facilities, these agencies continued to operate under misguided theories informed by notions of white supremacy.

## ONGOING REFORMS TO BRING RACE TO THE FOREFRONT

The health and human services field was challenged to rethink the policies and theories underlying its practices with historically underserved racial and ethnic groups with the push for social change and inclusion promoted by the many human rights movements that developed across the country during the 1960s (Carten, 2015). A number of professional associations were at the forefront in providing leadership in these reform efforts. Dr. Kenneth Clark was elected the first African American president of the American Psychological Association in 1969 and is credited with introducing the focus on social justice and the application of psychological principles in research as a tool for social change, These are continuing priorities as illustrated by the Association's guidelines for multicultural education, training and organizational change (on American Psychological Association, 2003).

The 1960s also saw the formation of professional associations that focused on the needs of ethnic and racial populations with which its membership shared a close identification. By 1967 African American, Hispanic, and Asian social workers peeled away from the National Association of Social Workers to form separate professional associations. The Black Psychiatrists of America was created in 1969 to advance causes related to the emotional and mental health development of African Americans who faced persistent racism. At the federal level, the National Institute of Mental Health established the Center for Minority Group Mental Health Programs. It also provided funding for the Council on Sial Work Education to establish the Minority Fellowship Programs, which has supported the doctoral education of underrepresented groups.

Concurrent with organizational and professional developments, the era saw the emergence of a new generation of scholars and researchers who were committed to deconstructing myths and stereotypes about people of color (Carten, 2015). This scholarship was instrumental in shifting theory building away from the use of a deficit model to a focus on the resilience, strengths, and adaptive and coping behaviors of African Americans (Billingsley, 1968; Chestang, 1972; Hill, 1972; Norton, 1978; Solomon, 1976). There was a cadre of clinicians during these years who were dispelling myths that people of color were not suitable candidates for the psychotherapies, adapting traditional approaches to clinical practice that were more appropriate for use with diverse client populations (King, 1967; Minuchin, 1967), and developing alternative practice models that achieved positive outcomes for clients of color.

The momentum established by these advances waned under the weight of a new conservatism that contributed to the increasing racialization of the political climate that was the context for the enactment of the 1996 Personal Responsibility and Work Reconciliation Act. While the new conservatism slowed progressive reforms in the health and human services, the new millennium saw the resurgence of these progressive efforts that gave greater attention to the combined effects of personal bias and institutional and structural racism.

Social work, psychology, and the allied health professions continued to be at the forefront as the professional disciplines that encouraged the use of culturally competent approaches, with recent years seeing new emphasis on the eradication of racism. All have modified their professional mission statements and objectives to include the eradication of racial and ethnic barriers to access to quality care as a major priority. For example, the National Association of Social Workers' (2008) Code of Ethics directs social workers to challenge social injustice as manifested in many forms and to engage in activities that promote sensitivity to and knowledge about oppression and cultural and ethnic diversity. Included among the imperatives adopted by the National Association of Social Workers 2005 Congress are those that address the impact of racism and other forms of oppression, social injustices, and human right violations through social work education and practice. A policy statement approved by the 2005 Delegate Assembly asserts that "racism is pervasive in the United States and remains a silent code that systematically closes the doors of opportunity to many individuals." The profession also subscribes to Culturally Competent Standards (2007) that promote respect for human diversity in many forms to eradicate the various "-isms" that contribute to disparities in outcomes between the dominant group and other social groups The Council on Social Work Education (CSWE), the accrediting body for baccalaureate and master degree social work programs, Educational Policy and Accredidation Standards require these programs to integrate content on human diversity across all curricula areas. An interdisciplinary mix of professional practitioners convened by the executive steering committee of the New York City Anti-Racist Collaborative indicated that social services practitioners across disciplines overwhelmingly favored approaches that looked at the issues through a prism of race that considers the combined and interrelated effects of personal bias and organizational and institutional barriers (Beitchman, 2011).

## ASSESSING AND PROMOTING SUSTAINABLE ORGANIZATIONAL AND STRUCTURAL CHANGE

As more attention is focused on the implications of race and racism for the health and human services, there has been a corresponding rise in the literature, resources, and tools for organizations to draw upon to support a systematic appraisal and study process required for understanding its position on the continuum of becoming a culturally competent and race-conscious system and for identifying potential barriers and obstacles to achieving desired diversity goals.

The National Association of Social Workers' statement on institutional racism provides guidelines and examples of what are not easily identified forms of structural and institutional racism. The document sets forth action steps and a framework agencies can use to conduct ongoing assessments of organizational structures and agency practices to identify manifestations of racism in their organizational culture, policies, and administrative practices. The literature review of assessment protocols published by the Annie Casey Foundation (2010) sets forth a range of models and frameworks for agencies to draw from and adapt for application that are tailored to the needs of individual organizations. It is also useful to review the strategy of the W.K. Kellogg Foundation that launched in 2010 a national grant-making program to address the interrelated issues of racial healing, structural racism, and racial equity.

The Office of Minority Health and the national Center on Minority Health and Health Disparities have developed "National Standards for Culturally and Linguistically Appropriate Services in Health Care" to increase the understanding of how an organization's cultural competence has been defined and measured. The National Association of Public Child Welfare Administrator has developed the Diagnostic Assessment Tool to address the inequities and disparate treatment of children of color in child welfare agencies nationally. The tool is designed for agencies to consider societal, systemic, and individual factors in an effort to identify the root causes contributing to disparate treatment of children of color and to assist them in developing more systemic and strategic approaches for tracking data trends and performance standards that allow them to examine strengths and weaknesses (Fabella et al., 2007). The Smith College School of Social Work is an exemplar of a graduate social work program that has undertaken a strategic antiracist approach for organizational change. This approach, which is designed to move the school along in the process of becoming an antiracist institution, is described in detail in the fall 2009 "School for Social Work Progress Report on Anti-Racism, Mission Statement."

The conceptual framework for the work undertaken under philanthropic, professional, governmental, and educational auspices in promoting organization change is anchored in the pioneering work of Cross and co-workers (1989), in which the following are considered essential elements: the system must (1) value diversity, (2) have the capacity for cultural self-assessment, (3) be conscious of the "dynamics" inherent when cultures interact, (4) institutionalize cultural knowledge, and (5) develop adaptations to service delivery reflecting an understanding of diversity between and within cultures. It is also widely accepted that to achieve long-term benefits and sustainable efforts, an essential first step is conducting an organizational assessment. This assessment can logically lead to the development of a strategic plan with clearly defined short-term and long-term goals and measurable objectives. Further, this comprehensive assessment, and can identify fiscal and personnel resources and required consumer and community partnerships (Cross et al., 1989; Lusthaus et al., 1999). Organizational assessment is an ongoing process rather than a one-time effort, which allows for opportunities to assess progress over time and identify and remove barriers to goal achievement in process.

Because organizational assessment may not be completely objective, a power/privilege analytical model may also be used as a companion when conducting an assessment of organizational policies and procedures that contribute to the perpetuation of white supremacy views (Roberts & Smith, 2002). A power/privilege analysis illuminates that the social policies and programs that serve as the context for the delivery of social services and practice theories that inform client interventions are neither value free nor neutral (McDonald & Colman, 1999; Pinderhughes, 1989). A good deal of emphasis is given to the experiences of African Americans in this volume, but many populations of color are negatively affected by the effects of discrimination based on skin color, which has been the dominant form of discrimination in the United States. Further, the racial discourse in the United States is no longer a black/white binary. There is a good deal of demographic, ethnic, linguistic, and cultural diversity within and among people of African, Hispanic, and Asian descent. In light of this significant diversity among and within service consumer groups, a power analytical model allows for a closer examination of practice theories based in a Eurocentric worldview of health and wellness and for the deconstruction of causal theories explaining the behaviors of racial and ethnic groups whose worldviews are fundamentally different.

## THE ANTIRACIST APPROACH

An antiracist model is emerging as one of the promising practices for uncovering the more subtle forms of institutional racism and personal bias that account for the persistence of racial disparities in well-being outcomes observed across virtually all fields of practice in the health and human services. The primary goal of this model is to raise awareness among practitioners at all levels of the organization about the effects of the insidious and often invisible forms of institutional racism that contribute to poor consumer outcomes.

Anchored in critical race, cognitive, and behavioral change theories, antiracist models encourage an examination of the implications of racism for society as a whole (Brunson Phillips & Derman-Sparks, 1997). As elaborated by Billings in Chapter 6, an underlying assumption of antiracist work is that racism has been consciously and systematically constructed in the United States since the country's founding. Therefore, it is the responsibility of every individual to engage in planned and sustained actions in an effort to dismantle the legacy of racism and white supremacy that pervades all institutional and organizational structures in American society and is deeply embedded in the American psyche.

Although African Americans and other populations of color are overburdened by the effects and consequences of racism, the antiracist approach encourages whites to weigh the benefits and gains accrued from "white privilege" against these larger human, economic, and societal costs and losses. These costs and losses are further exacerbated by the persistence of well-intention attitudes that we live in a color blind society that deny the significance of race (Nevielle, Worthington, Spanierman (2001)). Further, research findings suggest that a shared task for both people of color and whites in achieving a healthy racial identity in a society in which race continues to play a significant role is the recognition that on matters of race, "the personal is political." Concomitant to this is a willingness to "speak truth to power," or evidence the courage to take necessary risks involved with promoting dialogs around institutional and interpersonal racism in the face of resistance that can place one at risk of personal losses in prestige and status within their orgnizations. The psychological transformations necessary for achieving these tasks are manifested in the internalization of a feeling of comfort and authenticity with one's personal racial heritage and commitment to advancing a social justice, human rights agenda for many marginalized groups. This new awareness comes from the recognition of the intersection of racism and other forms of oppression and inequitable treatment based on socioeconomic class, gender, sexual orientation, citizenship or immigration status, or other personal attributes. Individuals who have evolved to this level of thinking also recognize that these inequalities contribute to high levels of social problems, including mental illness, and undermine the quality of life in the society. These assumptions are all captured in the following themes that are embedded in antiracist approaches.

## DECONSTRUCTING THE AMERICAN TRADITION OF "OTHERING"

Emerging against the backdrop of a capitalist economy and industrialization that favored values of self-reliance, individualism and influenced by Social Darwinism's "survival of the fittest," social welfare in the United States evolved with a predisposition toward understanding unmet human and social needs as resulting from shortcomings of the individual versus forces within the larger social order over which the individual had little or no control. This paradigm resulted in the entrenchment of biased assumptions about populations viewed as "the other" at various times in the country's history that continued to inform theory development in the behavioral sciences well into the 20th century. As cited in Thomas and Sillen (1972), the 1904 publication authored by E. Stanley Hall, the first president of the American Psychological Association, described African Americans, Indians, Chinese, and Mexicans as members of adolescent races that were on the lowest rung of the ladder of evolutionary development. Traditions of nativism of the colonial period favoring Anglo-Saxons continue to influence U.S. immigration policies and affect the experiences of new immigrants (Herndon, 2001). Despite this well-documented history of "othering" in the United States, we are reluctant to engage in an authentic dialog about the

inequitable treatment experienced by people of color; we would prefer to hold to
the belief that we live in a colorblind society.

## REJECTING THE CONSPIRACY OF SILENCE

Communication is a basic for effective practice in the health and human services.
Yet, cross-cultural dialogs dealing with race and racism are consistently found to
be the most challenging conversations in which to engage (Sue, 2005). According
to Hyde and Park (2002), faculty teaching in schools of social work consistently
report that content on race and racism is the most challenging and emotionally
charged content for them to teach. Classroom dialog among students is often
strained because of the fear of being "politically incorrect," and faculty and students alike often ascribe to a highly liberalized view that we live in a "colorblind
society" in which race is of little consequence. Consequently, they avoid or deny
the importance of this content because of its potential for divisiveness.

Commenting on the reluctance to engage in racial dialogs, David Brooks, in
his book *The Social Animal* (2011), suggests that for white executives a generation
of consciousness-raising has discouraged them from ever making racial comments or observations about minorities in public for fear of charges of racism,
discrimination suits, and career suicide. In a similar vein, Harvard law professor
and author Randall Kennedy's (2011) analysis of the Obama presidency centers
around the unspoken nuanced insinuations of racism that he suggest are conveyed between the lines or in subliminal messages, or sublimated racism, that
reflects the deep denial of the salience of race and the resistance to forthrightly
engage in a racial dialog.

## CHOOSING HEALTH AND WELLNESS

Professor John A. Powell, who heads the U.C. Berkeley Haas Institute for a Fair
and Inclusive society, and is an internationally recognized scholar on a range of
issues including race, structural racism, ethnicity, poverty, and democracy. He
frequently cautions in public talks that "out of sight" does not mean "out of mind."
He argues that suppressing prejudicial thoughts only increases them, while confronting them makes overcoming them more likely.

This view is supported in a number of publications that affirm the detrimental
effects on the mental health of individuals who are reluctant to engage in racial
dialogs. Williams (2008) makes an extensive use of case vignettes to support the
thesis that the unspoken emotional and psychological pain viewed as unique to
the African American experience is the root cause of the social problems and
mental health problems endemic to the black community. Similarly, DeGruy's

(2005) theory of "post-traumatic slave syndrome," developed from 12 years of quantitative and qualitative research, explains the etiology of many of the maladaptive survival behaviors observed in African Americans. Poussaint and Alexander (2000) apply DeGruy's theory in explaining the increase in male suicide rates in the African American community.

More recent research has been undertaken to examine more closely the consequences of racism for whites. For example, whites have reported experiencing anxiety, frustration, guilt, and shame when confronted with issues related to their own racism or to societal racism in general (Harvey & Oswald, 2000). These feelings are interwoven with anxiety, helplessness, and a sense of intense confusion around issues related to racism. Those who consider themselves to be egalitarian, while simultaneously holding that some forms of discrimination against blacks are justified, have been found to experience emotional and psychological discomfort and dissonance (Arminio, 2001; Iyer, Leach, & Crosby, 2003; Poteat & Spanierman, 2008).

## SPEAKING TRUTH TO POWER

Implicit in the expression of "speaking truth to power" is the concept of social justice, authenticity, and the need to bring to light injustices inflicted on disempowered and marginalized people in an effort to bring about change. This expression is most appropriate for advancing the purpose of this book because of its effort to reveal the benefits of moving beyond the conspiracy of silence that suppresses an authentic racial dialog, has a negative impact on mental health, and disempowers and diminishes the agency of people of color and whites alike. Further, the failure to forthrightly address these issues slows theory development essential for shaping effective practice interventions for people of color in need of the health and human services.

## SUMMARY

This introduction clarifies for the purposes of this book, the meaning of ambiguous terms that inform the race dialog. The disussion,elaborates the rationale and underlying assumptions of the antiracist approach as one strategy for addressing ethnic and racial disparities in health and human service outcomes. The authors in the following chapters draw upon their scholarship and on-the-ground experiences as clinicians, administrators, policymakers, researchers, advocates, and educators to examine more fully the implications of institutional racism for the persistence of these disparate outcomes in the health and human services. While each of the chapters is unique in addressing the area or practice of concern, all are interrelated and anchored in principles of the "Undoing Racism" approach and the core values of the helping professions that respect the multiple dimensions of human diversity and acknowledge the inherent worth of every individual and their right to opportunities and services that promote full self-actualization.

## REFERENCES

Algeria, M. Canino, G., Rios, J., Calderon, D. & Ortega, N.A. (2002). Inequalities in use of specialty mental health services among Latinos, African Americans, and non-Latino Whites. *Psychiatric Services, 53,* 1547–1555.

American Anthropological Association Statement on "Race." (May 17, 1998). Retrieved May 6, 2015, from. http://racialreality.blogspot.com/2005/12/aaa-statement-on-race.html

American Psychological Association. (2003). Guidelines on multicultural education, training, research, practice and organizational change for psychologist. *American Psychologist, 58,* 377–402.

American Psychological Association, Presidential Task Force on Educational Disparities. (2012). *Ethnic and racial disparities in education: Psychology's contributions to understanding and reducing disparities.* Retrieved from http://www.apa.org/ed/resources/r.

Annie Casey Foundation. (July, 2010). Leadership and race: how to develop and support racial leadership that contributes to racial justice. http://www.aecf.org/m/resourcedoc/aecf-LeadershipandRaceRacialJustice-2010.pdf

Arminio, J. (2001) Exploring the nature of race-related guilt. *Journal of Multicultural Counseling and Development, 29,* 239–252.

Baum, B. D. (2006). *The rise and fall of the Caucasian race: A political history of racial identity.* New York: NYU Press.

Beitchman, P. (2011, Winter). Noted panelists discussed the impact of race and racism on mental health professions, and on the therapeutic alliance. *Mental Health News.* The Impact of Race and Racism on Mental Health Clients, Practitioners, Organizations and Delivery Systems [special issue].

Billingsley, A. (1968). *Black families in white America.* Prentice-Hall Press: Englewood Cliffs New Jersey

Brooks, D. (2011). *The social animal: The hidden sources of love, character and achievement.* New York: Random House

Brunson Phillips, C., & Derman-Sparks, L. (1997). *Teaching/learning anti-racism: A developmental approach.* New York: Teachers College Press.

Capps, R. (1999). *Hardships among children of immigrants. Findings from the 1999 National Survey of American Families.* Number B-29 Series, New Federalism: National Survey of American Families.

Carten, A. J. (2006). African Americans and mental health. In J. Rosenfeld & S. Rosenfeld (Eds.), *Community mental health: Direction for the 21st century* (pp. Carten, A. J. (2013a). African Americans and mental health. In J. Rosenfeld & S. Rosenfeld (Eds.), *Community mental health: Direction for the 21st century* (2nd 125–138). New York, London: Routledge.

Carten, A. J. (2013b). African Americans and mental health. In M. Shally-Jensen (Ed.), *Mental health care issues in America: An encyclopedia.* pp. 9–15.

Carten, A. J. (2015). *Reflections on the American social welfare state: The collected papers of James R. Dumpson, PhD.* NASW Press: Washington, D.C.

Chestang, L. (1972). *Character development in a hostile environment.* Chicago: University of Chicago Press.

Citizens Committee for Children. (2012, April). *Concentrated poverty in New York City: An analysis of the changing geographic patterns of poverty.*New York: Author

Clark, K. B. (2004). The effects of prejudice and discrimination on personality development. In W. Klein (Ed.), *Toward humanity and justice: The writings of Kenneth B. Clark* (pp. 206–210). New York: Greenwood Press (the White House Conference report originally published in 1950).

Code of Ethics *of the National Association of Social Workers*Approved by the 1996 NASW Delegate Assembly and revised by the 2008 NASW Delegate Assembly. http://www.socialworkers.org/pubs/Code/code.asp

Collins, F. S. (1999). Shattuck Lecture—Medical and societal consequences of the Human Genome Project. *New England Journal of Medicine, 341,* 28–37.

Council on Social Work Education. (2008–). *Handbook of accreditation standards and procedures* (5th ed.). Alexandria, VA: Author. http://www.jsu.edu/socialwork/career/CSWE_EPAS.html

Cross, T. L., Bazron, B. J., Dennis, K. W., & Isaacs, M. R. (1989). *Towards a culturally competent system of care, volume 1.* Washington, DC: CASSP Technical Assistant Center, Georgetown University Child Development Center.

Dee, J. H. (2003–2004). Black Odysseus, White Caesar: When did "white people" become "white"? *Classical Journal, 99*(2), 162.

DeGruy Leary, J. (2005). Post-traumatic slave syndrome: America's legacy of enduring injury and healing. http://joydegruy.com/product/post-traumatic-slave-syndrome/ http://www.aphsa.org/content/dam/NAPCWA/PDF%20DOC/Resources/Disproportionality%20Diagnostic%20Tool/DisproportionalityArticle.pdf

Franklin-Jackson, D., & Carter, R. T. (2007). The relationship between race-related stress, racial identity and mental health for Black Americans. *Journal of Black Psychology, 33,* 5–26.

Gerendi, M. A., & Pai, M. (2008). Social determinants of black-white disparities in breast cancer mortality: A review. *Cancer Epidemiology Biomarkers, 17*(11), 2913–2923.

Giscombe, C., & Lobel, M. (2005). Explaining disproportionately high rates of adverse birth outcomes among African Americans: The impact of stress, racism, and related factors in pregnancy. *Psychological Bulletin, 131*(5), 662–683.

Harvey, R. D., & Oswald, D. L. (2000). Collective guilt and shame as motivation for White support of Black programs. *Journal of Applied Social Psychology, 30,* 1790–1811.

Herndon, R. W. (2001). *Unwelcome Americans: Living on the margins in early New England.* Philadelphia: University of Pennsylvania Press.

Hill, R. B. (1972). *The strengths of black families.* New York: Emerson Hall.

Hofrichter, R. (2003). *Health and social justice: Politics, ideology and inequity in the distribution of disease—A public health reader.* San Francisco: Jossey-Bass.

Hyde, C. A., & Ruth, B. J. (2002). Multicultural content and class participation: Do students self-censor? *Journal of Social Work Education, 389,* 241–256.

Iyer, A., Leach, C. W., & Crosby, F. J. (2003). White guilt and racial compensation: The benefits and limits of self-focus. *Personality and Social Psychology Bulletin, 29,* 117–129.

Kennedy, R. (2011). *The persistence of the color line: racial politics and the Obama presidency.* New York: Pantheon Books.

King, C. (1967). Family therapy with a deprived family. *Social Casework, 48,* 203–208.

Lusthaus, C., Adrien, M., Anderson, G., & Carden, F. (1999). *Enhancing organizational performance: A toolbox for self-assessment.* Ottawa: International Development Research Centre.

McKown, C. & Stambler, M. J. (2009). Developmental antecedents and social and academic consequences of stereotype-consciousness in middle childhood. *Child Development, 80*(6), 1643.

*Mental Health News.* (2011, Winter). The impact of race and racism on mental health clients, practitioners, organizations and delivery systems [special issue].

Minuchin, S. (1967). *Families of the slums.* New York: Basic Books.

Myrdal, G. (1944). *An American dilemma: The Negro problem and modern democracy.* New York: Harper & Brothers.

National Association of Social Workers Standards for Culturally Competency in Social Work Practice. http://www.socialworkers.org/practice/standards/NASWculturalstandards.pdf

National Association of Social Workers. Racism. http://www.naswdc.org/pressroom/events/911/racism.asp

Neville, H. A., Worthington, R. L., & Spanierman, L. B. (2001). Race, power, and multicultural counseling: Understanding White privilege and color-blind racial attitudes. In J. G. Ponterotto, J. M. Casas, L. A. Suzuki, & C. M. Alexander (Eds.), *Handbook of multicultural counseling* (2nd ed., pp. 257–288). Thousand Oaks, CA: Sage.

Norton, D. G. (1978). *The dual perspective: Inclusion of ethnic minority content in social work education.* New York: Council on Social Work Education.

Pascoe, A., & Smart Richman, L. (2009). Perceived discrimination and health: A meta-analytic review. *Psychological Bulletin, 135*(4), 531–554.

Pieterse, A. L., Todd, N. R., Neville, H. A., & Carter, R. T. (2012). Perceived racism and mental health among Black American adults: A meta-analytic review. *Journal of Counseling Psychology, 59*(1), 1–9.

Pinderhughes, E. (1989). *Understanding race, ethnicity and power: the key to efficacy in clinical practice.* New York: Free Press.

Poteat, V. P., & Spanierman, L. B. (2008). Further validation of the Psychosocial Costs of Racism to Whites scale among employed adults. *Counseling Psychologist, 36,* 871–894.

Poussaint, A. F., & Alexander, A. (2000). *Lay my burden down: Suicide and the mental health crisis among African-Americans.* Boston: Beacon.

Roberts, T. L., & Smith, L. A. (2002). The illusion of inclusion: An analysis of approaches to diversity with predominately white schools of social work. *Journal of Teaching in Social Work, 22,* 189–211.

Smedley, A., & Smedley, B. D. (2005). Race as biology is fiction, racism as a social problem is real. *American Psychologist, 60,* 16–26.

Smedley, B. D., Stith, A. Y., & Nelson, A. R. (2003). *Unequal treatment: Confronting racial and ethnic disparities in health care.* Washington, DC: National Academic Press.

Smith College School of SocialWork. (2011). *Anti racism commitment.* http://smith.edu/ssw/about_antiracism.php

Solomon, Barbara. (1976). *Black empowerment.* New York: Columbia University Press.

Snowden, L. R. (2001). Barriers to effective mental health for African Americans. *Mental Health Services Research, 3,* 181–187.

Spanierman, L. B., Armstrong, P. I., Poteat, V. P., & Beer, A. M. (2006). Psychosocial costs of racism to whites: Exploring patterns through cluster analysis. *Journal of Counseling Psychology, 53,* 434–441.

Sue, D. W. (2003). What is white privilege? In *Overcoming our racism: The journey to Liberation* (pp. 23–44). San Francisco: John Wiley.

Sue, D. W. (2005). Racism and the conspiracy of silence. *Counseling Psychologist, 33,* 100–114.

Sue, D. W. (2010). *Microaggressions in everyday life: Race, gender, and sexual orientation.* Hoboken, NJ: John Wiley & Sons.

Sue, D. W., Bucceri, J., Lin, A. I., Nadal, K. L., & Torino, G. C. (2007). Racial microaggressions and the Asian American experience. *Cultural Diversity and Ethnic Minority Psychology, 13,* 72–81.

Thomas, A., & Sillen, S. (1972). Racism and psychiatry. *Journal of the American Academy of Child Psychiatry, 11*(4), 737–739.

U.S. Department of Health and Human Services. (2001). *Mental health: Culture, race, and ethnicity, a supplement to "Mental health: A report to the surgeon general."* Rockville, MDL Author.

U.S. Department of Health and Human Services, Centers for Disease Control and Prevention. (November 22, 2013). *Health Disparities and Inequalities Report. CDC Health Disparities & Inequalities Report – United States, 2011,* Morbidity & Mortality Weekly Report (MMWR) Supplement, January 14, 2011, Vol.60, pg.1–116

Williams, T. (2008). *Black pain: It just looks like we're not hurting.* New York: Scribner.

W.K. Kellogg Foundation. *Truth, racial healing and transformation.* https://www.wkkf.org/what-we-do/racial-equity

*Strategies for Deconstructing Racism in
the Health and Human Services*

# PART ONE

# Building the Infrastructure

## Supporting Sustainable Change and Renewal

# CHAPTER 1

# Promoting Organizational and Systemic Change

MARY PENDER GREENE AND PAUL LEVINE

This book is about the implications of structural, institutional racism and personal bias in the quality of care provided to service consumers in the health and human services. Addressing structural racism is one of the toughest jobs that any leader can face. Although the reasons for this difficulty are myriad and complex, one major barrier is a lack of understanding about the meaning of structural and institutional racism. For many white staff, racism is viewed as "individual acts of meanness" (McIntosh, 2005). This may account for why any discussion of racism is often met with defensiveness and taken as an affront to personal integrity.

This chapter explains the need for organizations to create a culture that confronts racism, especially in its own policies and operation, and uses as a case study how a large sectarian agency based in New York City set out in 1991 to address racism. As a disclaimer, each organization has its own challenges when it comes to understanding and addressing race. Teasing out the common ground between the experience of the study agency and that of other agencies requires a close organizational analysis of the agency's mission, operating programs and policies, and organizational culture as well as a willingness to invest the necessary resources to support the planning and implementation process.

## COSTS AND BENEFITS OF TRANSFORMING THE ORGANIZATION

Antiracist policies and procedures benefit every staff member and client within an organization. According to an organizational behavior study conducted by King, Dawson, Kravitz, and Gulick (2012), antiracist approaches to organizational leadership not only reduced discrimination but also increased the loyalty of skilled employees, decreased rates of employee turnover, and improved overall job performance. According to the study, these benefits extended to all staff members, regardless of whether or not those particular staff members had previously been subjected to discrimination. (See also Buttner, Lowe, & Billings-Harrs, 2012; Hur & Strickland, 2012; McKay et al., 2007.)

Professional education programs for the health and human service staff members are carried out within the context of professional codes of ethics, which emphasize that all clients should be treated with dignity and respect and provided with the highest quality of care individualized to their service needs. Nonetheless, professional education programs often do not give sufficient attention to structural racism and its effect on engagement and collaboration with clients. Human service organizations are not immune to doctrines of white supremacy that are embedded in all American institutions (Sue, 2010).

The inequities in these systems contribute to disparate outcomes for people of color that are reported in virtually all domains of the health and human services, including education, housing, jobs, health care, and the criminal justice systems, to name a few. This is evident in the wage differences between whites and people of color. For example, in 2012, African American women earned 62 cents for every 77 cents white women earned and for every dollar white males earn (Cooper, Gable, & Austin, 2012). Moreover, institutional racism results in an "accumulation of discrimination," as Pager and Shepherd (2008, p. 200) clarify:

> Although traditional measures of discrimination focus on individual decision points (e.g., the decision to hire, to rent, to offer a loan), the effects of these decisions may extend into other relevant domains. Discrimination in credit markets, for example, contributes to higher rates of loan default, with negative implications for minority entrepreneurship, home ownership, and wealth accumulation (Oliver & Shapiro 1997). Discrimination in housing markets contributes to residential segregation, which is associated with concentrated disadvantage (Massey & Denton 1993), poor health outcomes (Williams 2004), and limited educational and employment opportunities (Massey & Fischer 2006, Fernandez & Su 2004). Single point estimates of discrimination within a particular domain may substantially underestimate the cumulative effects of discrimination over time and the ways in which discrimination in one domain can trigger disadvantage in many others.

When it comes to human service organizations, even the composition of the staff may reflect embedded racism. For example, according to a 2011 report by the National Association of Social Workers (NASW), people of color made up only 14% of the national human services workforce. Therefore, creating an organizational culture that factors in race is important because clients of color may not fully benefit from services/treatment if their racial/cultural identity, values,

communication style, and experience with oppression are not understood, surfaced, and addressed in the organization (NASW, 2011).

The key players in a human service organization include managers, direct
service practitioners, support staff, board members, and the recipients of service
themselves. They must avoid inadvertently applying societal oppressive concepts
to their service, including the assumption that clients are the sole cause of their
circumstance rather than the effect of various institutional, governmental, and
societal causes (Seipel & Way, 2006). Many service providers do not recognize,
for example, clients' wariness about receiving child welfare or mental health services because of power differences, concerns about stigma, or feeling misunderstood. Therefore, clients may stop using services without discussing concerns or
reservations with the providers (Seipel & Way, 2006).

## DEFINITION OF ORGANIZATIONAL AND INSTITUTIONAL RACISM

According to publications from the People's Institute for Survival and Beyond
(PISAB), the antiracist approach is based in the assumption that in a society organized around doctrines of white supremacy, the inherent social culture of that
society's institutions will naturally reflect bias unless there is deliberate action to
counteract that bias (Blitz & Pender Greene, 2006). Organizational racism as it
plays out in the workplace is succinctly described by Bobo and Fox (2003):

> Numerous studies show that contemporary workplace discrimination remains a
> significant concern. Employers often express stereotypical views of blacks, rate
> black workers as having weaker hard and soft skills than white workers, and openly
> acknowledge their own use of discriminatory recruiting and screening procedures
> during the hiring process. As a result, employers hire blacks at far lower rates than
> whites, even with controls for differences in levels of education.

Moreover, Dr. Shirley Better (2002), a prominent antiracist theorist and educator, proclaims that in institutions in which the mission of the organization, organizational culture, and operational programs and procedures indicate a limited
consciousness of racial bias, the social culture of unconscious racism will influence basic policies and practices. Unfortunately, even in institutions that have
a fairly high degree of awareness of racial bias, unconscious or unexamined aspects of the institution's social culture can unintentionally reinforce dynamics
that continue to privilege people with white skin (Blitz & Pender Greene, 2006).
It is in this manner that American institutions remain dominated by practices
that produce racial inequalities (Better, 2002). This is best measured by the
Continuum on Becoming an Anti-Racist, Multicultural Institution (Crossroads,

2007), in which an organization's full grasp of the effects of institutional racism, as well as the means to combat them, is represented in a spectrum from "exclusive" (i.e., a segregated institution) to "fully inclusive" (i.e., a transformed institution in a transformed society) (p. 72).

Structural racism requires institutional support and cultural nurturing to maintain the status quo (Pender Greene, 2007). At the study agency in the 1990s, various manifestations of organizational racism were revealed:

- In the early 1990s, analysis found that there was an increasing representation of people of color among the client population while the clinical managerial staff were almost all white. Of the 80 executives, department heads, and directors, five, or about 6%, were people of color. Among the hundreds of professional staff, MSWs, psychologists, and psychiatrists, the percentage was similar. Conversely, the direct care staff residential services were almost all of color.
- In 1990, almost 45% of the agency's 40,000 clients were of color. The change in service population was not a formal policy decision. The study agency had a long history of serving the Jewish population; in the 1980s it served the Jewish community and all New Yorkers. In 2008, following a strategic planning effort, the board changed the target population to simply "all New Yorkers." In reality, the change occurred as more third-party funding became available through Medicaid and Medicare. Children of color quickly became the majority of the agency's clients in its residential treatment programs.
- The agency was ignoring the client demographic shift. Empirically, clinicians observed a higher percentage of clients of color who left treatment prematurely. This dynamic is investigated in a study by McKay, Stoewe, McCadam, and Gonzalez (1998), who discovered that between 50% and 75% of urban, low-income children of color leave treatment prematurely. Several factors that influence client retention for clients of color include lack of insurance coverage, limited access to quality mental health services in poor neighborhoods, lower-quality care, staff making unilateral decisions about their clients' healthcare, stigma against mental health treatment, the disparate communication styles between staff and clients, and the small percentage of staff who are people of color.
- The clients of color at the study agency were "voting with their feet," but the demand for service was great and there were always new clients to replace those who had left. There were no financial consequences of client turnover, yet many senior executives and managers knew this trend did not bode well for the organization.
- At psychiatric residential services for adolescents, staff teams consisted of clinicians, who were mostly white, and direct care staff, who were mainly of color. When central office executives occasionally sat in on clinical team meetings, they observed that clinical staff related to each other as buddies;

the direct care staff were quiet. The direct care staff were sometimes called out of the meetings and would sometimes not return. The direct care staff also did not speak unless asked to and their reports were generally cursory. There was no meaningful interaction between milieu and clinical staff about observations of the adolescents. There was little discussion among the staff about how to redesign the roles of each of the staff to facilitate more progress for a resident. No one consciously was keeping staff of color "in their place," but the clinical team meetings reinforced the status hierarchy and the dominant culture norms of white privilege.

These indicators of organizational racism demonstrate cultural and sociological dynamics of power relationships. They do not reflect conscious personal efforts to demean others based on race, nor do the white clinicians, supervisors, or managers perceive themselves as behaving in a discriminatory way. According to Griffith, Childs, Eng, and Jeffries (2007, p. 292),

> People of Color represent a relatively high percentage of low-paid service workers and are underrepresented in health services management (Dreachslin, Weech-Maldonado, & Dansky, 2004). Also, People of Color who hold health care management positions tend to earn lower salaries and report less job satisfaction than their White counterparts (Dreachslin et al., 2004). Further, Dreachslin and colleagues (2004) found that job performance among People of Color was inversely related to exclusion from opportunities for power and integration into the organization. This suggests that increasing opportunities for advancement and to become more incorporated into the formal and informal structures within an organization may be a useful strategy for increasing productivity and job satisfaction. Although the authors note that the impact that placing more People of Color in leadership positions has on eliminating health care disparities is unclear, they conclude, "having an adequate representation of [People of Color] in all levels of the organization is considered pivotal to the provision of culturally appropriate care" (Dreachslin et al., 2004, p. 963).

The core of antiracist work seeks to identify and deconstruct institutional bias and to make structural changes that are supported by policies and procedures that are accountable with outcomes of equity (Chisolm & Washington, 2007). Antiracist work involves understanding how racism is a conscious and systemic effort constructed by the white privileged class throughout history, how it functions in society, and why it is perpetuated. The goals of antiracist work are to widen the circle of power and opportunity for people of color; share, respect, and nurture these cultures; develop intentional and systemic antiracist leadership within communities and organizations; be accountable to racially oppressed communities; and analyze and identify how institutional power affects communities of color (People's Institute for Survival & Beyond, 2015).

For an organization developing an antiracist practice, should the structural racist aspects of these various examples be surfaced for all to see? Yes. But then how does an organization focus on its own culture?

The business dictionary defines organizational culture as "the values and behaviors that contribute to the unique social and psychological environment of an organization." It develops over time and is based on shared attitudes, beliefs, customs, and written and unwritten rules that are considered valid. Every organization has its own type of culture; therefore, it is one of the hardest things to change. As a result, educating the organization and embedding antiracist policies and principles is the key to making lasting organizational culture change (Businessdictionary.com http://www.businessdictionary.com/definition/organizational-culture.html).

Where does individual responsibility start and end? And how does an organization face its own participation in the larger societal racism that infiltrates organizations and impacts even those individuals who consciously oppose racial discrimination?

Through a series of workshops that we described as "Difficult Race Dialogues," our managers were offered training on handling difficult race-based discussions. These workshops were led by outside consultants who shared common language and principles of antiracist work as developed by PISAB.

In choosing trainers, we used the guidelines developed by Gail Golden, MSW, Ed.D., an antiracist leader, educator, and consultant for over 25 years. According to Dr. Golden (2005),

- Training should be done by diverse, multicultural and multiracial teams, as one individual cannot possibly address all the issues.
- Trainers should have a power analysis, meaning that they need to go beyond prejudice based on skin color to a deeper understanding of racism.
- Trainers must teach that what we understand as racism is that those who hold prejudice based on skin color also have power, and control access to power based on skin color.
- Trainers must emphasize systemic, organizational, and institutional manifestations of racism rather than emphasizing racism as manifested as personal bias in interpersonal relationships.
- Trainers should focus on the phenomenon of the white culture's influence (i.e., dominant mainstream Western cultural norms) and its manifestations in organizations.
- Trainers need to be able to teach the link between racism and poverty.
- Trainers should have an understanding of racism that goes beyond its manifestation in the United States.

At the agency it became clear that managers needed specialized training to be able to fully integrate antiracist principles into the core of their administration. To realize this goal, the agency worked with the "Undoing Racism" program developed by PISAB and contracted with consultants who helped to develop a Leadership

Development Institute. This new institute was a cohort-based experiential leadership and management development program that provided mid- to senior-level managers with leadership development tools and formal training opportunities. Elements of the program were tailored to help produce antiracist leaders.

The entire group attended PISAB's two-and-a-half-day "Undoing Racism" workshops, which ultimately promoted authentic dialog among the racially and culturally mixed group members. The structure of the program allowed participants to incorporate and implement what they learned. It was a significant success and enhanced leadership skills and produced unexpected connections between managers who in the past had little or no relationship with each other.

## GOALS AND TRANSFORMATIONS

The process by which the agency transformed itself using antiracist principles was a long and complex one. Motivated by a variety of historical and contemporary ideas and events, the agency had five main goals it hoped to achieve through its antiracist work:

1. Improve outcomes by making clients, many of whom were of color, feel welcome in programs that had predominantly white and Jewish staffs. This required a second goal:
2. Recruit more professionals of color, specifically of the same race and ethnicity of people who lived in the community served by each program.
3. Formally announce to management and staff that leadership intended to racially diversify staff on all levels to reflect the clientele in the communities where programs were located. This was the new operational policy.
4. Begin an ongoing dialog about racial issues within the organization. To do so, create a diverse task force of well-regarded staff representing managers, clinicians, direct care staff, and preprofessionals who were known to be thoughtful and willing to speak at meetings.
5. All staff, both white and those of color, would be full stakeholders.

With clear goals outlined, the agency began by focusing on diversifying the professional staff to reflect the communities it served. Leadership questioned its earlier assumptions that very few people of color were getting MSW, Ph.D., and M.D. degrees and that the designation of the religion in the organization's name was discouraging applicants. The organization found out that the second notion was true, but the first was untrue—at least for MSWs. Once it was clear that there were many MSW candidates of color, a specific strategy was needed. It was decided that the agency had to come out and openly say that it wanted to be a place where professionals/MSWs of color were welcome and would have opportunities for advancement. Executive management acknowledged that it must do this dramatically.

Second-year MSW candidates of color began receiving stipends in exchange for a one-year commitment to become a social worker at the agency upon their receiving their degrees. This stipend program allowed the organization to be intensively involved with the graduate schools of social work in the assignment of second-year MSW interns to specific agency placements. The organization was able to not only interview candidates but also to persuade many of those who were not awarded a stipend to remain with the agency because of what they had learned during the application process. These candidates had no obligation to maintain their affiliation with the agency after receiving their degrees, but many did, along with the stipend recipients.

The most important change in the image of the organization came with the decision of the new chief executive to place a person of color in a top executive position. An African American female program director was appointed as chief of social work. Among her many responsibilities was the creation of more opportunities for social workers of color throughout the agency. It was also the responsibility of the chief of social work to manage the MSW and BSW internship programs and to look after the professional development of all social workers throughout their careers at the organization.

The chief executive carried great responsibility for the transformation. Since the start of the initiative, it was the CEO to whom all staff looked to see that race, antiracism, the role of white allies, and organizational racism remained high on the agenda. And while the chief of social work implemented significant changes in both diversifying the professional staff and supporting professionals of color, it remained a joint effort; the reliance on the top executive to sustain the initiative was always present. It was as if the agency was living in a tenuous world that could instantly disappear if the CEO stepped back too far. In part because racism is such a loaded issue from which we may all wish to flee, the CEO's leadership was needed to stay the course. The attitude of an agency's CEO and his or her willingness to move the initiative forward sets the tone for the rest of the organization. The role of the CEO and other top executives is to establish two fundamental aspects of multicultural antiracist practice: vision and accountability. An antiracist vision includes the following:

1. The ability to imagine and communicate the essential nature of multicultural practice. It is not enough to state that diversity is beneficial or preferred; it must be valued as necessary for the agency to move forward.
2. An analysis of power, privilege, and marginalization within the organization that highlights subtle inequities that discourage employees who are not part of the dominant cultural or racial group of the organization.
3. Modeling antiracism for senior leadership, including demonstrations of the learning and professional growth process on the path toward antiracist practice.

Accountability includes the following:

1. The willingness to take action to oppose acts of oppression, discrimination, or favoritism.
2. Readiness to allocate funds for professional development, specialized training, or access to needed resources to support multicultural antiracist practice.
3. Setting clear, well-articulated standards for multicultural antiracist practice that have been developed in collaboration with members of racial and cultural groups outside the dominant group of the organization.

Another action of the CEO was to create "affinity groups" both of staff of color and white staff who supported the agency's transformation. These groups met regularly and continue to do so in different geographic regions where the agency has programs. The groups discuss policy directions, obstacles to creating a racism-free work environment, advice to executive management, and mutual support on local issues that reflect personal incidents of racism as well as organizational racism. The CEO and COO made themselves available to meet with the affinity groups at their request. Leaders of each affinity group also meet together and discuss the concerns that have come out of their respective groups' meetings.

Managers and program directors have a vital role in the realization of the antiracist vision. Midlevel managers are typically the people responsible for hiring, developing, promoting, disciplining, and firing staff. They are often more closely connected to the community or populations served by their program than upper management and have a tremendous amount of power in the program or agency culture (Batts, 1998). Managers and directors, therefore, are responsible for the following:

- Defining cultural competency as including the ability to respond effectively to the dynamics of oppression and privilege and including this as a criterion for hiring, promotion, and professional development.
- Developing and maintaining a critical consciousness of all aspects of program functioning, including décor, policies and procedures, and relational practices, to ensure genuine multicultural inclusiveness.
- Creating flexible and responsive systems of accountability to the community or population served by the agency.

Supervisors often have the most direct contact with line staff and therefore maintain a central role in creating a program culture that is welcoming and responsive to the range of strengths and needs brought by the population served. Supervisors have the responsibility to do the following:

- Remain conscious of the differences and similarities between themselves and their supervisees, including an awareness of social distance, boundaries, how people interpret or experience authority, and relationships with people in authority.

- Promote and teach multiculturalism, cultural competency, and responsiveness to dynamics of difference, privilege, and oppression.
- Demonstrate mastery of the associated skills in annual evaluations and consideration for promotion.
- Actively recruit staff members who represent the range of clients or consumers served by the program and consistently respond to issues within the organizational culture that inhibit the growth and/or development of staff.

## TACTICS—HELPFUL AND OTHERWISE

The case study of the agency in the 1990s provides some tactical lessons that extend beyond that particular organization. Sustaining the commitment to address racial issues requires a combination of (1) leadership from the top; (2) a cadre of knowledgeable and articulate supporters on different levels of the agency; (3) structures such as committees and regularly scheduled events; and (4) written policies to make something important a sustainable component of a human service organization. All four elements are the responsibility of the CEO. At the study agency, the leadership, supporters, and structure were better developed than the written policies.

Over time, more than two dozen consultants who had expertise in areas related to racism were hired. Of great help were professionals who had substantial experience facilitating conversations among staff on racism. Each of them came to the agency for a series of scheduled small-group workshops primarily for the middle managers who directed programs and departments. Bringing the facilitators on board was in direct response to requests from the management group for training in how to help their respective staffs talk about race. Each year, sometimes more than once during the year, managers voluntarily attended a series (usually three sessions) with the experts and shared their efforts and challenges.

The agency made a commitment to finding the funds to support the training of management staff to implement the focus on race and racism. A decision was made to use the funds for the transformation. Once a month, a highly regarded academic clinician who had taught and consulted about racism spent a full day with the agency. In each case that person organized a group of 10 to 12 senior staff to study some aspect of racism from its appearance in clinical cases to the supervisory process. The lens was often a specific modality (family treatment, a women's group) or pathology, such as a child with behavior issues or post-traumatic stress disorder. The Cohen Chairs, as they were called, also led two half-day symposia each year for approximately 250 professionals and preprofessionals that reflected the work of the study group that they had formed.

The use of outside experts underscored that the work on race had broad interest and was the subject of examination by highly regarded academics and consultants. It was part of institutionalizing our initiative and communicating that the work was closer to the mainstream of fields of human and organizational be-havior than, perhaps, many staff realized. The outside experts were also free to confront the staff, and better at doing so, about their reluctance to face their own racism—whether its source was organizational or personal (i.e., prejudice). At these moments of confrontation, a great deal of emotion was expressed and the hesitance to address racism became sharply focused.

Policies and directives are also important tools that are used to institutional-ize changes in agency culture. Delaying the institution of written policies cre-ated a lack of clarity about directions and expectations. Understanding where the organization was headed relied too much on word-of-mouth messaging. If something is not published and disseminated, it lacks the power of the institu-tion's policies' importance.

One important example relates to a verbal "policy" that was stated strongly by the CEO but not codified as written policy for at least a year. All middle and senior managers were instructed that when hiring for any position for supervi-sor or higher, the manager was to seriously consider and interview at least one candidate who reflected the race or ethnicity of the local client population. Since the policy was not written and formally disseminated, many managers did not adhere to it. As a result, it became noticeable that there had been more racial di-versification of professional line staff than of supervisors.

Once the policy was written, it was also clear that the agency culture supported a manager valuing his or her individual program or division more than the needs and opportunities for staff promotion in the larger agency. Because programs operated with meaningful autonomy due to geographic decentralization, senior managers and executives believed they had to develop their own next generation of managers and supervisors who were very good at doing things in one specific way. What the agency learned was that supervisors needed to be developed for the entire orga-nization and not for just one location or service. The other lesson learned was the importance of tracking adherence to the hiring policy and other antiracist behavior by holding managers accountable for these things in their performance reviews.

Providing staff development and promotion opportunities also became more urgent. There is now an affinity group for administrators of color. Administrators in the group participate in peer support, management development training, and mentoring of other staff of color.

One effective policy that has continued is the mandate for all director-level staff to attend the two-and-a-half-day "Undoing Racism" workshop. The agency funds this training.

## COMPETING ADVOCACY PRESSURES

The agency took a firm position that racism was to have priority over other social injustice issues such as sexism/gender bias, homophobia, anti-Semitism, ageism, and so forth. The positive results were racial diversification of professional staff on all levels and the creation of ongoing affinity groups to monitor the agency's progress. Authentic conversations about race and racism occur now with more frequency in the clinical cases and in interpersonal staff relationships. Most indicative of the success is that in areas of sexual orientation/homophobia, staff developed a parallel initiative and found colleagues to invest energy to face these issues and to begin addressing the intersection of racism with other oppressions.

By focusing exclusively on the most difficult issue of racism and having success in a number of ways, managers and staff saw that other important issues related to improving clinical services to other stigmatized populations could be addressed. The agency has done some pioneering work with LGBTQ populations, both adults and adolescents. Most recently, the agency mounted an anti-stigma public information campaign to combat bias toward people with mental illness. It will become increasingly important to address the intersectionality of racism with other oppressions.

It is very important that the agency leaders continue their efforts to dialog with other people of color—Latinos, Asians, and others who do not share the white status—to hear and understand their experience with racial/cultural identity, structural racism, and immigration; share the history and present manifestations of structural racism toward various groups of color in the United States; and collaborate across cultural differences and similarities in confronting structural racism for clients and staff.

## UNANTICIPATED ISSUES AND THEIR IMPACT

Significant events had to be faced while the agency was incorporating a clinical and related management focus on race. Each issue absorbed a significant amount of energy, which, in turn, diverted some energy from the antiracism work. Each time the agency responded to other issues of consequence, it appeared to some staff that the racism work was being neglected. Many questioned whether management would resume the work on race. Was management just looking for a convenient excuse to let the matter of race alone for a while or maybe permanently? This was of greatest concern to staff of color and some white staff who were active with the affinity groups.

Executive leadership was aware of the anxieties of those who had the most invested in the transformation effort and had to balance the antiracism priorities along with the macro changes that were facing the entire human service world at that time. There is no doubt that there were periods when managers were increasingly preoccupied with adapting to economic and public policy changes. During those periods, it was necessary to reiterate that it was important that confronting racism remain a priority.

The ability to acknowledge and talk about race and structural racism is best practice in all human service organizations—including mental health, child welfare, juvenile justice, domestic violence, and others. We are clear that leaders, managers, and supervisors all need antiracist training to create an antiracist organization. The goal is to integrate antiracist policies, principles, and practices into the very core of the organization's culture. All of these changes require systemic and institutional change in order to truly impact an organization and its practice. It is important to remember that the pursuit of an antiracist organization is a journey and not a destination. For change to be lasting in an organization, these efforts must be sustained on all levels, beginning with the leadership, encouraged in management/supervision, and mandated in service to clients.

As leaders, we must be mindful that it is unrealistic to expect a comfortable and harmonious atmosphere as we seek to achieve an antiracist institution. We must expect a degree of discord and confusion. There is often a desire to let the antiracist conversation fade into the background. Therefore, it is necessary to develop a higher organizational pain threshold and tolerance for discomfort in order to stay the course. Growth begins where comfort ends.

## DISCUSSION QUESTIONS

1. Why is awareness of structural racism critical to realizing the mission goals of a human services organization?
2. How can an organization learn to face its participation in the larger society's racism that infiltrates organizations and impacts even those individual staff who consciously oppose racial discrimination?
3. What is the role of the top executive staff in creating a new culture that confronts organizational racism?

## REFERENCES

Anti-Racist Alliance (http://www.antiracistalliance.com).

Ayvazian, A. (2001). Interrupting the cycle of oppression: The role of allies as agents of change. In *Race, class, and gender in the United States: An integrated study* (pp. 809–815). New York: St. Martin's Press.

Batts, V. (1998). *Modern racism: New melody for the same old tunes.* EDS Occasional Papers, No. 2. Cambridge, MA.

Better, S. (2002). *Institutional racism: A primer on theory and strategies for social change.* Chicago: Burnham.

Blitz, L. V., & Pender Greene, M. (2007). *Racism and racial identity: Reflections on urban practice in mental health and social services.* Binghamton, NY: The Haworth Maltreatment and Trauma Press.

Bobo, L. D., & Fox, C. (2003, Dec.). Race, racism, and discrimination: Bridging problems, methods, and theory in social psychological research. *Social Psychology Quarterly* (Special Issue: Race, Racism, and Discrimination), *66*(4), 319–332.

Buttner, E., Lowe, K., & Billings-Harris, L. (2012). An empirical test of diversity climate dimensionality and relative effects on employee of color outcomes. *Journal of Business Ethics, 110*(3), 247–258.

Chetkow-Yanoov, B. (1999). *Celebrating diversity: Coexisting in a multicultural society.* New York: Haworth Press, Inc.

Chisom, R. (2005, Sept.). *Principles of anti-racist organizing.* Paper presented at meeting of Anti-Racist Alliance, New York, NY.

Chisolm, R., & Washington, M. (2007). *Undoing racism: A philosophy of international social change* (2nd ed.). New Orleans, LA: People's Institute Press.

Cooper, D., Gable, M., & Austin, A. (2012, May 12). Women and African Americans hit hardest by job losses in state and local governments. *Economic Policy Institute Report.* http://www.epi.org/publication/bp339-public-sector-jobs-crisis/.

Crossroads Anti-Racism Organizing & Training (2007). *Teaching and training methodology: Documentation and evaluation report.* Submitted to the Charles S. Mott Foundation.

DeRosa, P. (1996). Diversity training: In search of antiracism. *Bright Ideas, 5*:3.

Dudley, R. G. (1988). Blacks in policy-making positions. Reprinted from A. F. Coner-Edwards & J. Spurlock (Eds.), *Black families in crises: The middle class.* New York: Brunner/ Mazel.

Greiner, L. E. (1967, May). Patterns of organization change. *Harvard Business Review.* https://hbr.org/1967/05/patterns-of-organization-change.

Golden, G. (2005, Jan.). *Guidelines for choosing trainers to address racism, cultural diversity, issues of equity.* Paper presented at meeting of Anti-Racist Alliance, New York, NY.

Griffith, D. M., Childs, E. L., Eng, E., & Jeffries, V. (2007). Racism in organizations: The case of a county public health department. *Community Psychology, 35*(3), 287–302.

Hur, Y., & Strickland, R. A. (2012). Diversity management practices and understanding their adoption: Examining local governments in North Carolina. *Public Administration Quarterly, 36*(3), 380–412.

King, E. B., Dawson, J. F., Kravitz, D. A., & Gulick, L. M. V. (2012). A multilevel study of the relationships between diversity training, ethnic discrimination and satisfaction in organizations. *Journal of Organizational Behavior, 33,* 5–20. http://www.workplaceanswers.com/diversity-training-brings-unexpected-results/

Lorde, A. (1984). Age, race, class and sex: Women redefining difference. In *Sister outsider: Essays and speeches.* Freedom, CA: Crossing Press.

McIntosh, P. (2005). White privilege: Unpacking the invisible knapsack. In P. Rothenberg (Ed.), *White privilege: Essential readings on the other side of racism* (2nd ed.). New York: Worth. https://www.isr.umich.edu/home/diversity/resources/white-privilege.pdf

McKay, P. F., Avery, D. R., Tonidandel, S., Morris, M. A., Hernandez, M., & Hebl, M.R. (2007). Racial differences in employee retention: Are diversity climate perceptions the key? *Personnel Psychology, 60,* 35–62.

McKay, M. M., Stoewe, J., McCadam, K., & Gonzales, J. (1998, Feb.). Increasing access to child mental health services for urban children and their caregivers. *Health and Social Work, 23*(1), 9–15.

NASW Center for Workforce Studies and Social Work Practice. (2011). *Social work salaries by race & ethnicity occupational profile.* New York: NASW. http://workforce.socialworkers.org/studies/profiles/Race%20and%20Ethnicity.pdf

Pager, D., & Shepherd, H. (2008, Jan.) The sociology of discrimination: Racial discrimination in employment, housing, credit, and consumer markets. *Annual Review of Sociology, 34*, 181–209.

Pender Greene, M. (2007). Beyond diversity and multiculturalism: Towards the development of anti-racist institutions and leaders. *Journal for Non-profit Management, 11*(1), 9–17. http://www.socialworkgatherings.com/BeyondDiversityandMulticulturalism-TowardstheDevelopmentofAnti-RacistInstitutionsandLeaders.pdf.

People's Institute for Survival & Beyond. *Principles.* http://www.pisab.org/our-principles#undoing-internalized

Pierce, C. (1995). Stress analogs of racism and sexism: Terrorism, torture, and disaster. In C. Willie, P. Rieker, B. Kramer, & Brown, B. (Eds.), *Mental health, racism, and sexism.* Pittsburgh: University of Pittsburgh Press.

Pogue-White, K. (1998). *Continuing the work of developing cultural competence at JBFCS.* Paper presented at Meeting of Jewish Board of Family and Children's Services, New York, NY.

Seipel, A., & Way, I. (2006). Culturally competent social work: Practice with Latino clients. *New Social Worker, 13*(4). http://www.socialworker.com/feature-articles/ethics-articles/Culturally_Competent_Social_Work_Practice_With_Latino_Clients/

Sue, D. W. (2010). Microaggressions in employment, schools, and mental health practice. In *Microaggressions in everyday life: Race, gender, and sexual orientation* (pp. 207–231). New York: Wiley and Sons.

Thomas, D., & Ely, R. (1999, September/October). Making differences matter: A new paradigm for managing diversity. *Harvard Business Review 74*(5), 79–90.

Ware, B. L. & Bruce, F. (2000, April). Employee retention: What managers can do. *Harvard Management Update, 5*(4), 3–6.

*CHAPTER 2*

# Incorporating Antiracist Work
# at Staff and Board Levels

ALAN SISKIND AND TODD SCHENK

## INTRODUCTION

This chapter identifies some practical approaches to commence antiracist work in human service organizations, including how to build top-down support. The insidious effects of racism permeate all levels of organizations, transcending the worker–client relationship to include issues of staff relations, hiring and promotional practices, staff support networks, and the systemic effects of racism on communities and the disproportional representation of clients of color in many human service programs (e.g., child welfare, poverty, housing). We agree with the work of Griffith, Childs, Eng, and Jeffries (2007), who, in examining the effects of racism on institutions that deliver medical care, concluded, "in spite of professional standards and ethics, racism functions within organizations to adversely affect the quality of services, the organizational climate, and staff job satisfaction and morale" (p. 287). In a separate work, Griffith et al. (2007) contended, "a systems change approach is necessary to reduce and eventually eliminate healthcare disparities by illustrating how healthcare disparities are rooted in institutional racism" (p. 382). We agree with this approach, and with that article's further argument: "The theoretical framework for dismantling racism is an antiracist community organizing model that incorporates elements of power, sociopolitical development and empowerment theory" (p. 382). It is our contention that addressing this multitiered impact of racism in human service organizations requires that antiracist work incorporate executive leaders (staff and boards) who have a joint strategy and planning role and who formulate mission, set policy, create organizational structure, identify examples of disproportionality, advocate with public officials, and influence systems change.

*( 18 )*

## ESTABLISHING ANTIRACIST HUMAN SERVICE ORGANIZATIONS

Many challenges face those who endeavor to incorporate an antiracist perspective into the executive management of health and human service organizations, but the benefits of embarking upon this path are compelling. As Scott Page (2008) has pointed out, "What each of us has to offer, what we can contribute to the vibrancy of our world, depends on our being different in some way, in having combinations of perspectives, interpretations, heuristics, and predictive models that differ from those of others. These differences aggregate into a collective ability that exceeds what we possess individually" (p. 374). As the demographic shifts in the United States point toward a more and more diverse population, the need for culturally competent, race-sensitive practices in human service organizations grows (U.S. Census Bureau, 2012). The necessity of this work has been articulated by many organizations in many different forms. In an article for the *New Social Worker,* Barbara Trainin Blank (2006) noted, "The social workers and social work educators we interviewed indicated that while there has been some progress, the problem still exists—albeit in changed ways. They feel that reduced vigilance and a sense of satisfaction are premature."

While deliberation on such practices is helpful, organizations must go further to engage in action. Action plans may include the assessment of white privilege within the organization as well as intentional efforts to engage both staff and board members who mirror the populations of the communities being served. Trennerry and Paradies (2012, p. 22), drawing on the work of Ahmed (2006), have noted:

> In embarking on an organizational assessment, there is a need to ensure that findings from such assessments inform rather than replace action. Just because an organization is committed to being a diverse organization does not necessarily mean that they are one (Ahmed, 2006). Reflecting on developments in the U.K., where public bodies are required to have a race equality and action plan, Ahmed notes that the process of developing race-equality policies "quickly got translated into being good at race equality." Similarly, in undertaking an organizational assessment, what is essential then is not the process itself but the action that it generates. Accountability is therefore at the heart of this disjuncture between assessment, policy and practice.

Identifying manifestations of white privilege may require surveying staff at all different levels of the organization. Many scholars (DeAngelis, 2009; Hunter, 2011; Sue, 2010) have documented manifestations of white privilege in organizations, which frequently include instances related to the work culture. This may include the unspoken expectation of a white, European racial worldview in the workplace; microaggressions impacting professional identity, such as a majority white voice prevailing in case disposition discussions, even when the client is a person of color; agency systems that include disproportional white leadership in positions of power; professional opportunities such as promotions influenced by an "old boys" network; and client care where white staff may serve clients of color but the reverse may not often be true.

It would be unreasonable for two white male authors to embark upon a chapter about antiracist work in organizational leadership without first acknowledging the white privilege underlying this endeavor. The mere fact that we have held executive-level positions in large human service agencies already demonstrates the access to power and educational opportunities that have arisen from white privilege. Along the way, there have been numerous other manifestations of white privilege that valued our experience and background and paved the path for higher levels of responsibility. We acknowledge this privilege and the need to defer to the expertise of executives of color in our field; we share our perspective in the hopes that white people talking about and taking responsibility to integrate an antiracist approach into executive and board leadership will convey a useful perspective and, we hope, broaden the commitment of others to this important work.

As we know from the literature on change management (Gamson, 1992; Kotter, 2012; Lewin, 1945, 1951), effective change begins with a sense of urgency arising from dissatisfaction with the status quo. If an organization wants to maintain or grow "market share" and address emerging health and human service issues, then it is important to recognize the issues of the growing communities of color across the country.

In many cases, organizations that consider issues of becoming more culturally competent and race sensitive also need to reflect not only on the configuration of their staff but also the recruitment and retention efforts that allow staff to better mirror and articulate the racial and ethnic backgrounds of the communities being served. Bringing staff members into a work environment where they represent a small contingent of the overall workforce will present challenges. How does a staff member bring her or his authentic self into the workplace? Will that person's voice be heard in programmatic and clinical discussions if he or she brings a different perspective, or even a divergent view, from that of the dominant culture? Is there room at the decision-making table for people from diverse backgrounds, or are decisions still made by a homogenous (or at least not fully inclusive) subgroup of the organization's workforce? What are the implications for retention when someone is "the only" of his or her race in the room or part of too small a group to have a seat at the table? Creating a revolving door of entering/departing people of color is not an answer to the challenge of diversifying a workforce; in fact, it may be counterproductive to those goals.

Human service agencies are practiced in seeking broad input when it comes to decision making, albeit in arenas that are more clinical than administrative in nature. For example, while not analogous to the power dynamic and historical context of oppression, other recent shifts in human service organizations—such as multidisciplinary team conferencing, interdisciplinary clinical decision making, and the shift in mental health from the expert-to-patient relationship of clinicians toward a client-driven, recovery-based approach to service delivery—required a multipronged effort to educate staff, recognize and address the (perceived) loss of power of the privileged staff, and create feedback channels so that progress could be monitored. In human services, the concept and value of multidisciplinary or interdisciplinary teams—social workers, medical doctors, nurses, psychologists, counselors, direct care staff, family members, peers, and clients—is now widely accepted (Øvretveit, 1993; Schofield & Amodeo, 1999). But the understanding that these teams should also include cross-racial, cross-cultural, cross-class, and cross-gender representation is not yet as accepted.

Workplaces need to prepare to be more inclusive by rethinking how—and by whom—decisions are made. Embracing the views of an oppressed group may not be possible, however, until public consciousness is raised about the history of injustice and racism to which many clients and staff members have been and still are subjected. In his book *Erasing Racism*, Molefi Kete Asante (2003) described a "wall of racist ignorance" (p. 268); this wall continues to affect practices of disparate treatment in bank lending, insurance underwriting, ethnic and racial profiling, health care, educational opportunities, unemployment levels, and incarceration that disproportionately impact people of color in the United States. How, then, can we expect people of color to speak freely and inform the thinking about service delivery unless we acknowledge such disparities?

At the executive level, building the infrastructure for antiracist practice in an organization involves a long-term, multifaceted approach. The baseline conversation must directly address the case for redressing issues of racism for clients and the organization. However, it is uncommon for senior leaders of an organization to share a language to discuss issues of race and racism. Perspectives on racism are as varied as the people who make up the executive team, not to mention the program managers, supervisors, and front-line staff. In many cases, experience, history, shame, guilt, ignorance, and political "correctness" get in the way of an authentic workplace dialog about racism. The first task is to develop a common understanding and language through which to enter into a meaningful discussion. This early process must also include acknowledgment of differences around the table in definitions of racism.

Executive management must contemplate and create time, space, and structure for conversations and planning among the diverse racial and cultural groups represented in the staff. One structure for such conversations is the creation of "affinity groups," which is a proven strategy to help people with shared interests support one another and foster direct action (Gamson, 1992, pp. 62–64). Such affinity groups are already popular within not only within community organizations but also major corporations (General Motors, 2015; Skadden, Arps, Slate,

Meagher, & Flom, 2015). For example, one large mental health and social service agency in New York City developed affinity groups in each county to contemplate the impact of race and racism on the organization and its client base. Although it might seem counterintuitive, staff members specifically requested separate affinity groups for individuals who identified as white versus those who identified as persons of color. As one staff member astutely explained, without these distinctions, it would be like creating an art class in which advanced artists worked in the same studio as those only able to finger paint; the advanced students might become quickly uninterested if they needed to routinely discuss finger painting or the use of primary colors. This analogy helped to highlight the need to create space for beginner, intermediate, and advanced levels of discussion about race. Moreover, various strategies for ameliorating the impact of race on the organization and client service should be allowed to emerge.

Conversations about race and executive-level interest in antiracist work are important steps, but action needs to take place as well. Executive-level members of the staff need to shoulder ownership and accountability for addressing the manifestations of racism within the organization. When executives support the development of antiracist action plans, those plans are more likely to garner agency support and to acquire priority among the myriad challenges that the organization must address. Affinity groups may be asked to detail the various manifestations of white privilege within the organization, or task forces may gather to report these issues directly to executives. Such steps move the work beyond discussion to concrete steps that require and are met with action.

## CHALLENGES

Acknowledging the barriers as one begins a process is an important step, and it would be unproductive to write about antiracist work in organizations without contextualizing the potential pitfalls of the endeavor. These include the following:

- There may be competition with other *-isms.*
- Legal concerns that acknowledging structural racism may give rise to and lend credibility to discrimination claims in employment disputes may make some executive staff or board members wary about embarking on this work.
- Those who enjoy privilege and power may have interest in maintaining the status quo.
- There may be anxiety about and resistance to conversations about racism in the workplace.
- There may be reluctance to owning personal participation in racist systems.
- There may be a perceived lack of resources.

Experience has shown that focusing on one oppressed group can raise concerns that other oppressed people might be ignored. There are many other *-isms* that we face as organizations (classism, able-ism, sexism, anti-Semitism, heterosexism, and so on). A delicate balance is necessary to ensure that racism is not in competition with the organization's efforts to ameliorate negative consequences of other *-isms*. It is important to create space to fully and separately discuss racism and to make sure that the conversations about other forms of oppression do not become a way to avoid the difficult and often emotionally charged task of discussing issues of racism. Attempting to address all forms of oppression simultaneously might risk watering down all conversations so that no single issue is actually explored and addressed. It is also the authors' experience that exploring racism consistently allows other oppressions to be more effectively and authentically examined over time. It also encourages an organizational culture of openness and honesty.

Sometimes, antiracist work raises legal and/or human resource concerns about the increased likelihood for injurious conversations to occur in the workplace. Moreover, some feel that highlighting antiracist initiatives will call attention to previous and current problems in this arena, potentially lending credibility to claims of organizational racism. While these concerns have merit and particular caution needs to be paid to developing tools for managing emotionally charged discussions, there is also great value in demonstrating that an organization is publicly standing against racism and providing formal mechanisms to identify and redress the impact of racism in the workplace.

Many white people as well as many people of color respond to antiracist work within organizations with a refrain of "Why rock the boat?" Such a refrain presumes that the boat is not already rocking for many of the people on board. As mentioned previously, the demographics in the United States are shifting toward white people constituting the minority of the population; in this context, status quo thinking is not an option for an organization concerned with growing to meet the current needs of clients and staff as well as becoming a workforce of the future.

Organizations embarking upon this work may also have concerns of being met by expressions of intolerance or simply silence. Intolerance, while often feared by administrators, is actually the easier of these issues to address because people are talking and making their feelings known, which allows for productive dialog and sensitizing people to the needs of other staff and clients. If intolerance is then found to interfere with work performance and staff relations, it becomes a performance issue like others that we are already familiar addressing. Staff members who are wary of engaging in conversations about race and racism in the workplace often cite the issue of professional versus personal boundaries. In such cases, it is important to continue to link the antiracist work back to client service and staff relations to demonstrate the critical relevance of these issues to the workplace and the need to air those issues in a group conversation.

Concerns about lack of resources to incorporate antiracist work in an organization frequently focus on the unreimbursed staff time spent in meetings and trainings and developing policies/procedures or other structural cures to address the impact of race and racism. There may be foundation and philanthropic support available to support these unreimbursed efforts. Creating an affirming workplace where staff can bring their authentic selves into work, however, may lift morale, decrease the costly impact of staff turnover, and increase productivity, so that this work, in a number of ways, pays for itself. Similarly, when service delivery includes a focus on addressing the trauma of racism experienced by clients, then business may also improve as evidenced by higher client referrals and better client outcomes and satisfaction. Government and private philanthropic funders may also be encouraged that their investment in an organization dealing with these issues is a sound one.

## ISSUES OF BOARD INVOLVEMENT AND LEADERSHIP

The charge for executive leaders among all of these potential barriers is to set the stage for this work and explicitly endorse it. Antiracist work must permeate all levels of staff in the organization, and executives must build an organizational culture in which conversations about race, critiques of the organization, and constructive problem-solving proposals are welcomed.

Once those expectations for the organizational culture are established, then they must extend beyond the staff to include board members as well. Diversity on boards of directors of nonprofit organizations (as well as corporate entities) has a direct link to the effectiveness of the organization and, ultimately, to its perceived legitimacy by the community it serves. While we are focused here on racial diversity, the advantage of having inclusive boards in regard to gender, sexual orientation, and other areas is also critically important for many of the same reasons as those outlined above for staff.

An organization's board of directors can be a powerful resource in negotiating the turbulent environment nonprofits currently experience. There is intense competition for resources, increasing requirements for accountability, and increasing regulations from external government and foundation funders. We often think of the need for board members to bring wealth, work, and wisdom to their positions. It is not necessary that each member bring equal amounts of each, but it is essential that the organization's discussions about how to best achieve its mission are informed by a variety and a broad span of opinions and perspectives. Nonprofit boards are becoming more racially diverse or are facing pressures to do so. Board diversity has been increasingly seen as an important component of service outcomes and staff morale.

Analysis of board members' diversity, attitudes, and recruitment practices reveal that boards with a higher percentage of people of color had increased awareness of different experiences and opinions of clients and staff. This increased awareness, in turn, was positively associated with all aspects of board performance: analytical, educational, and strategic (Brown, 2002). Bantel and Jackson (1989) found, and Bradshaw and Fredette (2012) recently reaffirmed, that diversity encourages more creativity; a multiplicity of voices leads to more ideas, perspectives, and possible solutions. When boards initially diversify, they are more likely to exhibit conflict, but over time, as people are able to hear and learn from each other, they are most often able to accept the limits of their own perspectives and experience. Conflicts also create opportunities for creative problem solving for true learning to emerge.

There is broad consensus in both the literature and the reported experience of executives and organizations that racial diversity on boards goes beyond clear social value. The inclusion of more voices and more perspectives regarding the communities served promotes better program design and outcome, better community visibility and legitimacy, and better staff and board relationships. The U.S. Substance Abuse and Mental Health Administration (2006) affirms, "Having board members from diverse groups helps establish the program's credibility with members of those groups" (n.p.). LeRoux and Perry (2007) found that authentic diversity requires that people of color on boards represent and advocate for community needs and are not just on boards as tokens or to fulfill expectations about the organization's wish to meet a certain quota. Truly representative diversity is a positive asset not only in terms of the social responsibility of boards to communities served but also in providing a competitive edge to raise funds from both the public and private sectors. Although boards sometimes feel that their fundraising needs contradict their missions to be socially responsible and effective, these are not mutually exclusive aims. Both functions of a board of directors can exist in a dynamic and mutually advantageous relationship. Boards who are focused only on recruiting people of wealth to the exclusion of diversity are not always aware of lost opportunities in both spheres.

Boards typically recruit and attract people with whom they are familiar and comfortable. This results in board members who have similar experience, background, social class, race, and, therefore, perspective. Change, especially the prospect of interracial interaction, often creates fear of the unknown, anxiety about conflict, and the concerns of exposing underlying bias and racism.

Diversification often brings differences in perspective to historically white boards; in this way, it can be a precursor to change as it challenges status quo thinking at the board level. Difficulties need to be acknowledged and processed in order for the transition to be effective. There may very well be a sense embedded in the organizational history that the board already knows what communities of color need and want. Communities of color and others will often feel that those judgments are inaccurate and patronizing. Where there is a history of organizational success and long tenure, it is harder for boards to understand how true representative racial diversity enhances programs and legitimacy in the community. Boards project their own values and experiences as to what a successful service is, and what successful individuals, families, and communities look like.

A board that is considering diversifying racially must begin with an initial open conversation. The board may or may not have experience with gender diversity, sexual orientation diversity, age diversity, and so on. The process of including racial diversity, while it can benefit to some degree from past board experience in other areas of diversification, is quite different and, often, more complex. After asking the preliminary questions—Should we do this? Do we want to do this?—discussion needs to be structured, intentional, and deliberate. It is often useful to have a task force composed of board members and executive leaders that is tasked with carefully planning for the discussion by ensuring that all of the issues are presented in an organized way. The rationale, challenges, and ongoing nature of the process should be clearly laid out. Given the complexity of the issues and the anxiety that often attends discussions of race, it is frequently beneficial to include an outside facilitator who is an expert in the issues of board racial diversity and strategic planning.

It is important early on to establish that this process is never finished; it will need enduring attention, focus, and priority. Ongoing evaluations, status reports, discussions of barriers as they occur, and the use of consultation, as needed, are critical to the process. If diversity is approached solely to change numbers by bringing board members of color onto a predominately white board, then the project will most likely fail. Successfully establishing racially diverse boards will require representing the breadth of the communities that the organization serves. Smaller organizations with smaller boards will have a greater challenge here as there are fewer board positions available. Planning should take into account the changing demographics as well as the needs of the communities served.

Before the recruitment phase begins, clear goals for that process should be determined. There must be a plan for developing consensus among current board members on both the value of, and a process for, diversification. A planning work group should consist predominately of board members who are already convinced of the value of the effort and who have the leadership ability to bring others along. If the planning is weak, the outcome has less of a chance of being successful. Planning needs to be explicit about the challenges of diversification and the existing barriers the organization will need to address.

Board attitudes about racial diversity also need to be fully explored and discussed before a recruitment process begins. Board members of color might feel responsible for the success or failure of inclusion. White board members may consciously and/or unconsciously demonstrate a lack of commitment to an effective diversification effort and be concerned about what message that reveals about them and their organization. Moreover, board diversification efforts can only succeed with the full commitment and involvement of executive management. It may in fact be the executive leaders who provide the initial impetus for the board to address these issues. Executive leadership needs to be present in every step of discussion, planning, and recruitment. Executives, however, cannot be so far ahead of the board in "owning" the decision and moving ahead with the process that board members can never experience their own process and investment. Boards can and should expect full executive buy-in and support, but cannot diversify solely to please the executive or to meet his or her expectations. To be successful, board members need to commit to this effort and be prepared to support it of their own volition.

A database of potential candidates is a useful tool at this stage, and it should include names of people outside of the circles known by current board members. As presented in an article by Lisa Bertagnoli (2012):

> One factor hampering the search for minority and female board members is the current face of most nonprofit boards.
>
> "What happens on so many boards is that they recruit people who look like themselves—that's their circle of friends," says Edith Falk, chairman of Campbell & Co., a Chicago-based firm that consults for nonprofits. With such homogenous recruiting, "you're not getting the rich conversation that you would if you had" a more diverse group, she says.

Having constituents and/or their families on boards must be considered. Constituents bring their own unique perspective and set of experiences as well as accumulated wisdom (Lehman, 2005). They have clear ideas regarding what kinds of services are helpful and what strategies are (and are not) useful in service delivery. Nominations for potential board members can also be garnered by asking staff members of the organization, approaching elected officials about suggestions of active community members, and looking at board rosters of partner organizations. Consultants with experience in this area can also be helpful in suggesting additional ways to add to the database.

It is important to recruit potential board members who are committed to the organization's general mission, who have knowledge of the broad range of communities that the organization serves, and who have the ability to envision what an improved service system might look like. Furthermore, potential board members should have a sense of what questions to ask to bring the organization closer to achieving the maturity and tools necessary to better serve all of its constituents.

Whenever recruiting new members, boards must be clear about what skills are being sought and how those skills might be used. It is not enough to recruit a CPA or marketing professional, for example; board leadership must understand how each new board member's skillset will fit into the general mission and envision how that skillset will be put to work as soon as possible. In the process of diversification, it is especially important that the organization and older board members understand the "fit" and value of each person of color brought onto the board. Understanding what new board members will do (rather than just focusing on who they are) is important as part of the initial thought process so that integration and inclusion have already begun.

Similarly, the recruitment process must clearly define what is expected of board members. It is not useful, for example, to bring on members who are wealthy but who do not understand the expectations about giving and convincing others to give. In much the same way, it is unworkable, for example, to bring on a Latino board member who is not willing to use his or her connections with the Latino community or his or her perspectives of being Latino to enhance the services the organization provides or should provide to the Latino community.

It is helpful to bring on several board members of color at the same time to avoid tokenism or a sense that any one board member of color is responsible for representing all people of color. The initial plan needs to include quantifiable goals regarding the number of board members of color an organization intends to recruit. That way it is clear, from the beginning, that each new board member of color is just the beginning of the effort. Ideally, new board members of color will help in the recruitment of other board members of color. It is the full board's responsibility to diversify, however, and not a responsibility that should be given to only board members of color. This would reflect a lack of organizational commitment to the value of diversification. The goal, again, is not to make the board look more diverse. The goal is to make the board, in fact, more diverse.

The organization's plan for diversification should be intentional and specific; it should outline who will be responsible for what task and in what timeframe (the nominating committee, the whole board, a special taskforce), when reports will be due back to the board, who will evaluate the effectiveness of the plan's implementation, and when and how the plan will be evaluated and modified to ensure that it moves forward. Finally, the plan needs to include ideas of how to enhance board cohesion as new members join and are integrated.

Newer board members will need to be oriented to the organization and be ready to learn from the existing board about the history and issues involved in an organization's current functioning. This "onboarding" process is always important, but particularly so when attempting to orient new members who may bring different perspectives and experiences from the dominant culture. Older board members need to be ready to ask for, and really hear, the perspectives and experience of newer board members, and to encourage new members to share their ideas and perspectives even if they appear to be divergent from the dominant view. It is useful, where appropriate, to provide mentors and resource people (board and staff) for newer members. These resource people can also be an instrument for ongoing evaluation of how effectively newer board members are being integrated. Board leadership should conduct evaluations at different intervals to ensure that newer members are feeling included and valued, that they understand what is expected of them, and that they know what they can expect from others.

Diversification will ultimately fail if newer members are just dropped into current board activities and expected to simply adapt to preexisting ideas, policies, and processes. Such a situation defeats the value of diversification; soon enough, board members of color will feel as if they are on a board that does not really value their input or include them. New board members will depart or become inactive if there is not honest discussion of what went wrong and why inclusion did not work. One danger at this point is for boards to say, "Well, we tried," and revert back to business as usual, without ever really understanding or acknowledging how diversification was undermined.

While the benefits of diversification need to be subject to measurement, the benefits are nuanced and many will be less quantifiable at first. The quality and authenticity of organizational discussions at all levels, as well as the morale of constituents, staff, and board members, may be difficult to capture unless rigorously measured against past experience. Human service organizations have a paucity of reliable data on effectiveness of performance because while many measures of accomplishment are required by public and private funding sources, these may often be different from the actual effectiveness of services. Thus, retrospective research is not reported widely in the literature.

It is not clear what percentage of diversity a board needs to achieve to get improved service outcomes. Further research would contribute a good deal if it could provide answers to questions such as these: Is some diversity better than none? What are the minimum and maximum levels of diversity a board needs to achieve to have effective impact? Given the wide range of human service organizations and countless variables needed to evaluate organizational success, future research questions and methodology design will need to be carefully constructed.

Just as undoing structural or organizational racism itself is a continuous process, organizations cannot develop their boards and staff and be "finished." Organizations must remain vigilant to maintain their efforts by continuing to evaluate which goals have been reached and which have not. It is important to acknowledge that the work is challenging and ongoing; we must continually not only retool the work but also clarify the reasons for doing it. As Kathleen Fletcher (1999) explains, the effort to diversify "takes real commitment over time, constant flexibility and openness, and a true desire to succeed for the good of the organization rather than for the approval of outsiders." The knowledge that this continuing and demanding work will add immeasurably to the organization's relevance, legitimacy, and effectiveness will, ideally, be motivation enough for many to start and maintain the effort.

## DISCUSSION QUESTIONS

1. In considering my own (or one particular) organization, what challenges or barriers to antiracist work do I perceive? How might this answer be different if I asked a colleague of a race or background different than mine to respond to the same question?
2. What evidence of white privilege can I list in regard to this organization?
3. What benefits (emotional, structural, financial, or others) might come of a true commitment to diversification of this organization's staff and board?

## REFERENCES

Ahmed, S. (2006). The nonperformativity of antiracism. *Meridians: Feminism, Race, Transnationalism,* 7(1), 104–126.

Asante, M. (2003). *Erasing racism: The survival of the American nation.* Amherst, NY: Prometheus Books.

Bantel, K., & Jackson, S. (1989). Top management and innovations in banking: Does the composition of the top team make a difference? *Strategic Management Journal,* 10(S1), 107–124.

Bertagnoli, L. (2012, November 3). Why white men still dominate nonprofit boards. *Crain's Chicago Business.,* 1

Blank, B. (2006). Racism: The challenge for social workers. *New Social Worker.* http://www.socialworker.com/feature-articles/ethics-articles/Racism%3A_The_Challenge_for_Social_Workers/.

Bradshaw, P., & Fredette, C. (2012, December 29). The inclusive nonprofit board-room: Leveraging the transformative potential of diversity. *Nonprofit Quarterly (NPQ).* https://nonprofitquarterly.org/governancevoice/21570-the-inclusive-nonprofit-boardroomleveraging-the-transformative-potential-of-diversity.html.

Brown, W. A. (2002). Racial diversity and performance of nonprofit boards of directors. *Journal of Applied Management and Entrepreneurship,* 7(4), 43–57.

DeAngelis, T. (2009). Unmasking "racial micro aggressions." *American Psychological Association,* 40(2), 42. http://www.apa.org/monitor/2009/02/microaggression.aspx.

Fletcher, K. (1999). Building diverse boards: Lessons from a case study of Planned Parent hood affiliates. In *Perspectives on Nonprofit Board Diversity.* New York: BoardSource.

Gamson, W. (1992). The social psychology of collective action. In A. Morris & C. M. Mueller (Eds.), *Frontiers in social movement theory* (pp. 53–76). New Haven, CT: Yale University Press.

General Motors. (2015). Diversity at GM: Employee resource groups. Retrieved May 15, 2015, from http://www.gm.com/company/aboutGM/diversity/employee_resource_groups.html.

Griffith, D. M., Childs, E. L., Eng, E., & Jeffries, V. (2007). Racism in organizations: The case of a county public health department. *Journal of Community Psychology,* 35(3), 287–302.

Griffith, D. M., Mason, M., Yonas, M., Eng, E., Jeffries, V., Plihcik, S., & Parks, B. (2007). Dismantling institutional racism: Theory and action. *American Journal of Community Psychology,* 39(3/4), 381–392.

Hunter, R. L. (2011). *An examination of workplace racial microaggressions and their effect on employee performance*. Ph.D. diss., Gonzaga University.

Kotter, J. P. (2012). *Leading change*. Boston: Harvard Business Review Press.

Lehman, A. W. (2005). Racial diversity on your board of directors. Zimmerman Lehman. Retrieved May 15, 2015, from http://www.zimmerman-lehman.com/racialdiversity.htm.

LeRoux, K. M., & Perry, S. S. (2007, April 26). *The role of racial diversity in nonprofit governance: Does a "representation mismatch" influence stakeholder orientation?* Paper presented at a conference titled "Networks, Stakeholders, and Nonprofit Organization Governance: Whither (Wither?) Boards?" at the University of Missouri-Kansas City.

Lewin, K. (1945, May). The research center for group dynamics at Massachusetts Institute of Technology. *Sociometry, 8*(2), 126–136.

Lewin, K. (1951). *Field theory in social science: Selected theoretical papers*. New York: Harper and Row.

Øvretveit, J. (1993). *Coordinating community care: Multidisciplinary teams and care management*. Philadelphia: Open University Press.

Page, S. E. (2008). *The difference: How the power of diversity creates better groups, firms, schools, and societies* (new ed.). Princeton, NJ: Princeton University Press.

Schofield, R. F., & Amodeo, M. (1999). Interdisciplinary teams in health care and human services settings: Are they effective? *Health & Social Work, 24*(3), 210–219.

Skadden, Arps, Slate, Meagher & Flom LLP & Affiliates. (2015). Diversity and inclusion: Affinity groups. Retrieved May 15, 2015, from http://www.skadden.com/diversity/affinity.

Sue, D. W. (2010). Microaggressions in employment, schools, and mental health practice. In *Microaggressions in everyday life: Race, gender, and sexual orientation* (pp. 207–231). New York: Wiley and Sons.

Trennerry, B., & Paradies, Y. (2012, Spring). Organizational assessment: An overlooked approach to managing diversity and addressing racism in the workplace. *Journal of Diversity Management, 7*(1), 11–26. http://www.cluteinstitute.com/ojs/index.php/JDM/article/view/6932/7007.

U. S. Census Bureau. (2012, December 12). U.S. Census Bureau projections show a slower-growing, older, more diverse nation a half-century from now. http://www.census.gov/newsroom/releases/archives/population/cb12-243.html.

U. S. Substance Abuse and Mental Health Services Administration. (2006). *Substance abuse: Administrative issues in outpatient treatment*. Treatment Improvement Protocol (TIP) Series, 46. Rockville, MD: Center for Substance Abuse Treatment. http://www.ncbi.nlm.nih.gov/books/NBK64076/#A87857.

## FURTHER READING

Blitz, L. V., & Pender Greene, M. (2006). *Racism and racial identity: Reflections on urban practice in mental health and social services*. Binghamton, NY: Haworth Press.

Du Bois, W. E. B. (1988). *Against racism: Unpublished essays, papers, addresses, 1887–1961*. Amherst: University of Massachusetts Press.

Kivel, P. (2011). *Uprooting racism: How white people can work for racial justice* (3rd ed.). British Columbia: New Society Publishers.

Lavalette, M., & Penketh, L. (2014). *Race, racism and social work: Contemporary issues and debates*. Bristol, UK: Policy Press.

Lui, M., Robles, B., Leondar-Wright, B., Brewer, R., Adamson, R., with United for a Fair Economy. (2006). *The color of wealth: The story behind the U.S. racial wealth divide.* New York: The New Press.

McKissack, P., & McKissack, F. (1990). *Taking a stand against racism and racial discrimination.* Taking a Stand Series. New York: Franklin Watts.

Renz, D., et al. (Eds.) (2010). *The Jossey-Bass handbook of nonprofit leadership and management* (3rd ed.). New York: Wiley and Sons.

West, C. (1994). *Race matters.* New York: Vintage.

# CHAPTER 3

# Education and Training of a Race-Conscious Workforce

WILLIE TOLLIVER AND STEVE BURGHARDT

## INTRODUCTION

This chapter outlines the development of a year-long, foundational multimethod practice course offered to all 500 entering social work graduate students at the Silberman School of Social Work at Hunter College, which is the oldest and largest public social work program in New York City. The mission of the school focuses on preparing social work graduates for employment in the public and nonprofit health and human service agencies of the city. In carrying out its educational programs, the school places a preeminent emphasis on both anti-oppression content and mindful practice as central to students' skillsets and practice framework. Anchored in the school's mission, the course was initiated and enhanced over the past five years (2008–2013) and has emerged as an award-winning laboratory for faculty and students on how to deliver such content so that awareness of privilege, power, and oppression is understood to be integral to the social work practice that awaits them in the communities and agencies in which they live and work. This chapter offers lessons on curriculum development, staff preparation, and student response regarding the core issues and demands of preparing and sustaining an antiracist workforce capable of engaging in anti-oppressive work consistently in human services agencies.

## A BRIEF HISTORY

As is often the case in academic innovation, the push for curricular change regarding issues of race began with the students. They lobbied for a course on diversity in 1982, with a special emphasis on race and ethnic differences. Initially they were unsuccessful, as had the efforts of other student groups in 1989 and 1995. Interestingly enough, the requests of the students who lobbied in 1982 reflected the changing definitions and understanding of racial, gender, and sexual dynamics as they emerged within the larger society. For example, in 1989 the terminology was "cultural sensitivity"; in 1995, it was "cultural competency." The initiative that resulted from the activities of the 1995 student group was the establishment of a diversity taskforce on the Silberman campus with a designated faculty advisor. The students won faculty approval for a series of diversity workshops to be held over a two-year period during Common Days that allowed for the participation of the total student body. Ironically, students won this change during the year that Dr. Elaine Pinderhughes was the Moses Professor at the school. Dr. Pinderhughes is the preeminent and nationally recognized scholar on matters of diversity and is the author of the seminal text, *Understanding Race, Ethnicity and Power: The Key to Efficacy in Clinical Practice* (Pinderhughes, 1989). The book has had wide influence on both courses in clinical practice and in human behavior and the social environment curriculum areas.

At the end of the two years of student-run diversity workshops, the school launched a diversity orientation for all incoming students that was facilitated by members of the diversity taskforce with consultation from Dr. Pinderhughes. This was a significant change for the school because all incoming students participated in the orientation, which meant that the all students were introduced to the school's philosophical approach and model for understanding diversity at the beginning of their education experience. Previously, the students in the two-year full-time MSW program (mostly white traditional-aged students) attended an orientation during regular academic hours. In contrast, the evening students (mostly African American and other students of color, who were often employed) attended an orientation held outside of the traditional academic hours to accommodate their work schedules.

Over time the diversity orientation came to be viewed by incoming students as an opportunity for exposure to important privilege, power, and oppression content. However, the orientation did not provide them with the language and skills they needed to interrupt oppressive situations that occurred in classrooms or in their practice agencies. Further, feedback from the students revealed that there was unevenness in their classroom experiences in terms of course instruction that deepened their understanding of diversity content, and there were few faculty members with the skills to facilitate conversations dealing with issues of privilege, power, and oppression.

The school's inability to create a required course focused on oppression content over so many years was assessed as rooted in two distinct causes. First, although the students undertook these campaigns for a better integration of diversity content into the curriculum with great passion, they had not built broad enough bases of support among the student body for a continued momentum. Moreover, most of the core group were community-organizing students, who, while most often among the student leadership, made up only 10% of the total student body. In addition, there was definite agreement throughout the school on the more clinically focused courses and methods, but there was no established benchmark or widespread support that could serve as a schoolwide mandate for their community-organizing efforts. (Previous efforts were perceived as issues relevant only to macro practice or "community organizing.") The mandated diversity orientation created receptivity among all of the school's method majors of casework, group work, and community organization to the idea that diversity content was relevant for social work education and practice. However, students were reluctant to be at the forefront of student organizing for a required course on oppression.

The second distinct cause that was a major stumbling block was that the senior leadership of the faculty had begun their academic careers at a time when the emphasis on teaching and professional development was aligned with traditional psychodynamic and ecological theories. While these theories are not inherently hostile to structural approaches for understanding the dynamics of oppression, in application, content on oppression received marginal focus. Instead, traditional content consisting of Erikson (1968), Winnicott (1965, 1971), and other classical theorists and disciples remained central to the coursework taught by the senior faculty. Content on social oppression was viewed with skepticism—*how could it be of value in clinical treatment?*—or, in later years, was relegated to only one or two weeks of the overall course content.

Because it was perceived by curriculum chairs as being of interest to only a minority of students and an equally small number of faculty, the content on oppression was viewed as secondary to effective professional development. Thus, the anti-oppression material remained on the periphery of academic life until 2008.

## THE ENVIRONMENTAL CONTEXT
## AS CATALYST FOR CHANGE

The significant changes that occurred in 2008 were set in motion by three planned events that were under way in New York City as well as within the school itself. A fourth, unplanned stroke of luck played a part in the larger environmental context that led to the foundation-year curriculum evolving to include a central focus on anti-oppression.

The first trend was the growing influence of the "Undoing Racism: Unlocking the Structural and Historical Conditions of White Supremacy" workshops initiative. The initiative was spearheaded by the People's Institute for Survival, and the "Undoing Racism" workshop was offered to staff in the New York City public- and private-sector health and human service agencies, and to faculty and students in the metropolitan schools of social work. As described by Billings in Chapter 6 of this volume, the "Undoing Racism" workshop includes powerful content on the history of structural racism and white supremacy in the United States. Notably, the social work professionals who were instrumental in bringing the workshop to New York City first targeted academic and professional leaders who could be enlisted in supporting their community-organizing efforts and educating potential workshop participants about its value. With the local chapter of the National Association of Social Workers openly supporting the work, by 2008 there was increasing legitimacy within the profession of the value of making antiracist content and practice a core part of professional development in the curriculum of the schools of social work.

Second, a new group of school leaders was intent on developing a more innovative foundation course that exposed all students to the various methods of practice (administration, clinical, community organizing, and group). Led by a professor of policy and research at the school, the academic workgroup sought to develop a course that showed how each method would approach similar problems and client issues from the perspective of their major method. The course was designed as a class with a lab component. It brought together all of the students and faculty from three large sections (150 students each) with five or six faculty members in one large room. The faculty used role-plays, experiential activities, and their own case examples in the first laboratory hour with the large group. The second and third hours were spent in the individual classrooms that held each section led by the faculty members. The academic workgroup anticipated that this innovative and collaborative approach to the exposure of different perspectives on the same sets of social and individual issues would bring "from case to cause and back again" to life through the use of concrete role-plays, led by different faculty, across methods, generating conversations on race, gender, and sexuality.

Third, as this innovation was launched, a new group of students was entering the school. Some of them had attended the "Undoing Racism" workshop and were inspired to see this content brought more fully into the school through an oppression course that all students were required to take. Led by a community-organizing student, this time the group began with a more deliberative approach before making any demands for change. In addition, the students organized and formed the Anti-Racist Collective (ARCH) at the school; this student organization was an incubator for activism as well as a support for building camaraderie among students to sustain them in efforts to achieve systemic change. ARCH was the home base for student activists involved in organizing to win approval for a required course on oppression content.

Students first spoke with the faculty who had knowledge of previous efforts and why these had failed. Based on what the group learned from these conversations, their campaign began through classic planning techniques: They polled faculty members and sought support from the entire student body.

Interviewing faculty members and gathering student-body petitions took a considerable amount of time in the academic year, but the results paid off. Instead of only a handful of faculty members expressing support, the organizing group had over two-thirds of faculty members (many of whom by now also had gone to the "Undoing Racism" workshop) open to the development of an oppression course. Likewise, over three-quarters of the student body, including a majority of clinical students, signed a petition requesting the creation of such a course. In short, the two strategic problems that doomed previous efforts—lack of faculty support and modest student body interest—had been replaced with a level of support that gave their campaign legitimacy. Through relationships formed in ARCH the student leaders targeted the faculty-run Curriculum Committee that had slots for student representation. Student organizers filled all six student seats on the committee with people from across the student body, ensuring that the largely black people/people of color one-year residency students were involved.

By the time the students—a careful mix of clinical, administration, and community-organizing majors—attended a faculty meeting to give a 15-minute presentation on why such a required course should be offered, there was a new openness to their requests. As community-organizing historian Robert Fisher (2008) asserted soon after Barack Obama was elected as the nation's first African American president, "history moved."

And then there was that luck. At the time of the student presentation, the school was in the midst of the Council on Social Work Education's (CSWE) reaccreditation process. Reaccreditation requires an arduous and demanding audit of the school's curriculum, internship placements, and overall capacity to meet CSWE's accreditation standards, competencies, and outcomes as established by the Educational Policy and Reaccreditation Standards. While the students organized effectively to make certain the visiting CSWE member knew of the importance of this work and its widespread support (which was strongly acknowledged in the final CSWE report), it was also clear that creating an entirely new course while promoting the still-fledging practice lab throughout the first year would be unrealistic and might even foster destabilizing levels of change.

The dean of the school made this conundrum clear to the senior faculty supporting her. While actively supportive of the students' efforts, the dean, who had taken the "Undoing Racism" workshop, raised concerns about whether there was widespread support for the course at the school. Everyone wanted the content, including the dean, but creating a new course at the same time the practice lab was just getting under way raised concerns that the accreditation team might interpret this as unsound educational planning.

And here is where that luck struck. Could the material be integrated into the practice lab course itself? The dean did not hesitate: of course! There would have to be some significant work weaving this new material into the curriculum, but there was no longer any roadblock to focusing on anti-oppression content throughout a foundation course required of all students.

## NEW DILEMMAS ... AND OPPORTUNITIES

Freed to develop the content over an entire year, the full-time faculty developing the course were faced with two primary dilemmas. The first was one not unfamiliar to others who have been involved in team teaching: supporting a collaborative model across disciplines. Quite simply, full-time faculty are most often comfortable with the classroom as their single responsibility—and for which they have sole authority. Sharing the stage as well as ideas might sound wonderful in theory, but in practice developing and modeling a "win–win" approach to different ways of responding to the same case material would prove to be difficult. For example, as it turned out, even mild disagreement between how a community-organizing professor and a clinical faculty member would respond to a case caused nervousness in students and faculty alike.

Left unspoken, such differences could easily cause students to feel they had to choose sides—the very opposite of the collaborative intent of the course. It became clear that the six faculty members per section had to engage in careful planning where highlighted differences were acknowledged beforehand with students in each class as an example of how collaboration actually occurs: not by silent agreement, but by open differences in points of view. Faculty members learned to phrase their disagreements to minimize perceptions of hostility or antagonism. Over time, students overcame their nervousness at disagreement and become better able to handle their own disagreements in approaches to social work practice within their internship agencies as they tentatively approached supervisors and directors to engage in these issues.

The second dilemma-turned-opportunity was one that is essential to the anti-oppression work itself: Who would teach the course? With 18 sections to fill, finding full-time faculty members to teach this course always has been an uphill climb. Previous course commitments, the expectation for collaborative team teaching, and a quiet unease as to how to deliver/weave the anti-oppression material into foundational social work content meant that only a quarter of the teaching positions have been filled by full-time faculty members.

At the same time, those creating the practice lab course always wanted a consciously chosen mix of people teaching for reasons directly related to the anti-oppression material itself. Lab leaders sought to create each six-person section with a mix of senior, junior ,and adjunct faculty with an equal variety of social identities: African American men and women; Latinas and Latinos; open lesbians who were Jewish; older, straight, WASP males. Such a mix was crucial as a fundamental, experiential lesson that lab leaders knew would emerge over the year: How did students socially construct who was smarter and more knowledgeable? Was it the older, white, tenured professor with little clinical experience, or was it the much younger but far more clinically experienced Latina adjunct faculty member? Who was allowed to occasionally over- or understate a topic and be held permanently accountable for the mistake, and who got a pass?

These questions of power and privilege, all emerging as tacit, experiential knowledge, complete with discomfort for students and faculty alike throughout the year, are at the heart of the anti-oppression and mindful practice content of the course. It is through this content and how it is delivered that the Silberman faculty was one of the winners of the first annual CSWE-SAGE national award for curriculum innovation in 2012. We now turn to how this powerful, emotionally laden material has evolved from antiracist content to embrace both a broader anti-oppression focus and a mindful practice framework as central to transformative, sustained social work practice.

## ANTI-OPPRESSION SOCIAL WORK PRACTICE: TWO PROFESSORS' STORIES

The section tells how two faculty members came to articulate a place for anti-oppression content in social work education. It is also an example of the kind of discovery that we think illustrates how faculty members come to embrace this content as an essential component of social work education and practice.

### Full-Time Male Faculty Narrative

My social background underscores in triplicate what's meant by "white" in America. I'm an older, WASP, straight guy from New England. On my mother's side, my great-uncle sixteen generations back is the founder of the Pilgrims, John Robinson. (Yes, founder.) On my father's side, my Dutch grandfather nine generations back was the Massachusetts slave owner of a man who bought his freedom around the time of the Revolutionary War. That gentleman was the grandfather of another Burghardt, W. E. Burghardt Du Bois. (Yes, that W. E. B. Du Bois.) To say that my own life has benefitted from the myriad mix of power and privileges that such whiteness bestows is both self-evident and an understatement.

Therefore, for me, the larger community of my New England town was a fun laboratory of experiment, risk, and adventure. Schools were places to shine; the police were my family friends, even after I got picked up for hijacking cars ("just teenage pranks"); streets were to run free on, never to be stopped or frisked. It was an idyllic place for a young white boy like me to be.

Too bad it never felt as safe to go home. The combination of alcohol, a father's mental illness, and anger directed at a son's academic and social success served as sharp, psychic counterpoint to the world outside. While hardly politically or socially conscious, an inbred skepticism toward all forms of authority took root early. Early collegiate organizing efforts to examine possible discrimination in fraternities (against Jews; at the time, there weren't enough blacks on campus to count, let alone systematically discriminate against). Receiving my first death threat (after all, I was a WASP traitor, not a disaffected minority), I used my findings of bias to begin examining the college's admissions policies. Where they had been supportive of my initial efforts, suddenly there was a freeze. Warm back slaps of support were replaced with coldness and reproach. Parts of the outer world began to look a little like home.

While still unaware of systemic issues, this kind of tension between a desired belief in a just world and increasing exposure to systematic unfairness opened me to test more and more boundaries. Finding brilliance and soulful sustenance in jazz and the blues freed me in myriad ways: If jazz was "primitive," then Mozart was, too. Maybe they were both brilliant. If some people found the rhythm in James Baldwin's words too pulsating and angry, then I guess my pulse was angry also. That Malcolm X guy wasn't very nice with that "Chickens come home to roost" comment about Kennedy's assassination, but he sure wasn't stupid when I heard him speak. A young white's man journey to racial awareness was piecemeal and scattered, but it moved like Martin's arc, toward an understanding that what harmed another harmed us all. I couldn't get reelected class president any more, but little by little I could see where true freedom lay—and it wasn't in the fearful constrictions of white privilege and power being used to build edifices where one monochromatic color screened out the rich social mosaic I had come to feel was where my true home would be found.

Over the next many years, whether completing graduate school, organizing in the South Bronx, learning how to teach community organizing, or working with executives in child welfare, these beliefs were strengthened and expanded. Through the lens of Paulo Freire's work (Freire, 2000), I saw how easily it was to unconsciously replicate systems of racial and social dominance, even among progressive activists and educators. For me, the quest to shift dynamics of power and privilege in practitioners became a straightforward one in the classroom: The primary learning objective that I began to assert was that by the end of the academic year, students would have gained power while I would have lost none. That students were initially skeptical of such an objective was intensified as together we examined and worked on issues where race, class, gender, sexuality, and age were all at play in the classroom.

### Full-Time Male Faculty Narrative

Given the legally sanctioned construct of race, my social location is African American, middle class, able-bodied, Southern-born male. I acknowledge that I have always approached social work content from a particular standpoint that is informed by race. I have lived all of my life as a racialized minority in the United States of America as I was born during legally sanctioned segregation. From this location, race figures prominently into how I analyze all of my experiences. Therefore, it is important for me to state at the outset that race is front and center in my work to construct the place of oppression content in social work education. In addition, my work is grounded in my experience as a social worker engaged in the child welfare arena for almost 40 years.

My first job out of undergrad was in child welfare as a senior child care worker, and in two years my responsibilities increased to providing administrative/supervisory evening and weekend coverage for the residential care facility where I worked. There were about 200 children in residence, housed in cottages on a five-acre campus, and the agency was under the auspices of Catholic Charities. The executive director was a nun, and other key positions in the agency were held by both nuns and lay professionals.

The institution was mostly self-contained. There were chapels and a cafeteria that prepared all of the meals for the cottages. There was a school and an infirmary (health facility) staffed by a nurse 24 hours a day and on weekends. Notwithstanding the presence of a school on campus, children who had been removed from their caregivers because they did not attend school still remained absent from school. There were also a psychiatrist and psychologist as well as social workers.

I found my calling for social work while in this job. By 1976, I had earned the MSW and resigned from the supervisory position in institutional child welfare work. This decision was taken because of competing pulls: While the reuniting of some children with their families or placement of some children with new families was rewarding, the inability to find permanent homes for so many children engendered a desire to know more about the communities from which the children in the institution came.

My next job was with two professors from Columbia University School of Social Work in Central Harlem. In this setting, I learned that public schools were not working as well as they did when James Baldwin went to school in Harlem in the late 1930s. The civil rights movement resulted in integration of schools in the South. However, schools were already integrated in New York City, so the battle for equity was fought around community control of public schools. Community activists fought for and gained community control of public schools and the many employment opportunities schools afforded. This caused bitter divisions among teachers' unions (a Northern civil rights ally) and New York City black community activists. As community school boards worked to find their way in managing schools, academic programming suffered. By 1976, it was not uncommon to encounter in Central Harlem seventh graders who could not read.

The agency worked with children and families in Central Harlem, where people living at the lower socioeconomic level struggled to manage households on low-wage jobs and public assistance. People lived with housing problems, pest infestations, and challenges associated with drug sales, the criminalization of substance use, and the health problems caused by both alcohol and sustained drug use. There were also youth gangs, which resulted in police crackdowns on youth for gang involvement and drugs. Claude Brown's autobiography is a powerful portrayal of the challenges of coming of age in Harlem during these years (Brown, 1965).

By 1978, the Central Harlem program had a strong track record of success in using martial arts, sports, and the theater arts to engage youth. However, children and their families were still challenged by lack of affordable housing, health care, employment opportunities, and the additional resources required to meet their basic needs. Our work engaged young people and some parents at the micro level, and we did not have macro interventions to impact the resource structures that dispensed goods and services as well as social, civil, and political rights (Gil, 1996).

I returned to Florida and went to work for the Tallahassee-based Florida Center for Children and Youth as a research associate. In this policy think tank, we developed position papers that were used to provide information to statewide coalitions formed with the Junior Leagues of Florida as well as local community groups. The coalition building was facilitated in part by the board of directors for the organization. The board president was an activist and lobbyist with years of experience lobbying the Florida legislature. She found a way to use Federal Office of Juvenile Justice and Delinquency Prevention funds to establish the agency and drew on her extensive contacts to build coalitions to advocate for changes in Florida laws that would benefit children and families.

In this job, I learned that social work is political. Budd Bell (the board president), a seasoned social worker, was the volunteer lobbyist for the statewide National Association of Social Workers chapter. She worked out of the Petroleum Building a block from the state capitol in Tallahassee. The building was owned by the Pepper family, one of whom, Claude Pepper, was a congressman from Florida. Budd taught us (Center for Children and Youth employees and board members) how to lobby. David Gil from Brandeis University was keynote speaker at one of our child advocacy conferences, and after listening to the advocates' complaints about the legislators, David said to us, "Some of you must run for office." One of my colleagues, Bill Jones, an MSW graduate from Florida State University, had learned local politics in Columbus, Ohio. He became my tutor in political action, including learning the ropes in how to manage political campaigns.

By 1982, social workers were managing political campaigns for candidates running for school board, state prosecutor, and the state House of Representatives. In addition, social workers were involved in forming a coalition that won three of the five City Commission seats in Tallahassee. That same coalition gained control of the local Democratic Party in Leon County, Florida.

We use personal narratives to locate ourselves in the discourse on racial equity and social justice in the United States in general and in our approach to social work education specifically. Because anti-oppression practice finds its motivation at the personal level, we believe it is important for us to examine our personal narratives to learn how our personal stories influence our teaching and practice philosophies. Mapping our own lives to discern how power and privilege were bestowed on us by birth, gender, race, socioeconomic class, and sexual orientation is a significant part of the work of developing the self-awareness required for anti-oppressive social work practice.

People who do social work must understand how power dynamics manifest in our work. Pinderhughes (1988) notes, "A family's sense of power to control its destiny and to function effectively is affected by its fit with the environment" (p. 156). Richard Cloward taught social work students that many of the people using social services, who live at the bottom of the economic ladder, are viewed by their economic betters as the pariahs of society (Piven & Cloward, 1971). They are perceived by the powerful as powerless, and too often the people who work with them (social workers) come to think of themselves as powerless too. This is especially the case if the workers and the people they serve do not have the wherewithal to define their needs as deserving of resource expenditures. The narrative about working at the Florida Center for Children and Youth demonstrated that an organized and informed citizenry, working with social workers as gatherers and disseminators of critical information, could gain access to state and city budgets to make change.

The Tallahassee coalition won political campaigns by expanding their organizing to include the people at the margins. People living in public housing came to campaign headquarters on Election Day to watch the returns and cheered when their precincts' vote totals came in. Today, in the Bond section of southwest Tallahassee, there is a state-of-the-art public health facility delivered by the politicians who won their seats with the votes of the citizens of the Bond community. And one of the most successful advocates for people living in poverty in Tallahassee, and an integral part of this winning coalition, was Oliver Hill, a resident in public housing.

Among the many lessons learned by social workers and the community residents involved in these political experiences was the value of building coalitions, creating collaborative goals, and holding elected officials accountable.


## BUILDING THE PRACTICE LAB

We believe that this synopsis of a journey through arenas of social work practice illustrates the complex terrain social work practitioners find themselves in as they confront the myriad of social calamities befalling human beings in postindustrial societies across the world. Harrison Owen (1991) observed that human beings have long tried to control their environments. It is abundantly clear today that ordered social existence is desired yet rarely realized, particularly at the lower socioeconomic strata of society. Likewise, Patricia Hill Collins (2006) found that privacy is a privilege afforded the middle and upper classes in the United States. One hundred years of social work practice wisdom adds to our knowledge of who is denied privacy in the United States. Women, black people/people of color, people with disabilities, the elderly, children, religious minorities, trans people, and people whose sexual orientation is other than heterosexual are also marginalized in the United States. People living at the margins of society cannot prevent the agents of social control from intervening in their lives or the lives of their loved ones. After all, they often live in public housing, they attend public schools, and they receive publicly funded medical care that is dispensed in public health facilities.

These kinds of structural issues became more and more important as we continued developing and implementing this course. (Allen, 2001) When Silberman faculty took on developing the practice lab, what was initially envisioned was a course where social work students would develop a professional identity as a social worker. This was intentional, given that at Silberman students declare a social work method as their major method when they apply for admission. The faculty wanted Silberman graduates to know the roles of social workers across the methods and to understand how the whole of social work forms a network of skills and knowledge enabling social workers to intervene at micro, mezzo, and macro levels.

## Theoretical Underpinnings of the Anti-Oppression Practice Lab

In the first iteration of the lab, practice lab professors organized the course around stages of practice: pre-engagement, engagement, assessment, intervention, evaluation, and endings or termination. The syllabus was organized, distilling competencies, assignments, and requisite readings. Students and faculty members jumped in, and in time it was realized that the year-long course lacked an organizing frame. Why three hours instead of the two hours assigned for all other courses in the curriculum? Students and faculty members questioned the purpose of the large-group meeting for an hour where all six sections met: Did faculty members really expect students to speak in this huge forum?

Poole (2010) explores the question of what happens to social work graduates steeped in anti-oppressive practice tenets after graduation. We believe that the description of anti-oppressive practice found in this text closely aligns with our intentions for infusing oppression content into the social work practice lab at Silberman. Poole (2010) reviewed the anti-oppressive literature and offered the following description:

> Anti-oppressive practice (AOP) is a form of social work practice, which addresses
> social divisions and structural inequalities in the work that is done with people

whether they are users or workers. AOP aims to provide more appropriate and sensitive services by responding to people's needs regardless of their social status. AOP embodies a person-centered philosophy . . . a methodology focusing on both process and outcome; and a way of structuring relationships between individuals that aims to empower users by reducing the negative effects of social hierarchies. (Dominelli, 1994, as quoted in Poole, p. 2)

This description provides a framework for, first, supporting students to develop the capacity for a conscious and strategic use of themselves in the stages of social work practice. Through self-exploration informed by assigned readings, students reflect on their own backgrounds, social histories, and experiences as a way of mapping how these factors show up in their sense of who they are as people and how they think about the world. This reflective practice is introduced to the students and faculty members through readings on mindfulness (Epstein, 1999), where they learn to develop a skillset of a reflective practitioner. We believe that reflective practice and self-awareness help social workers to examine belief systems and values, deal with strong feelings, make difficult decisions, and resolve interpersonal and intrapersonal conflicts (Epstein, 1999).

The anti-oppressive practice framework also gives students the space and place to develop their understanding of the historical and structural conditions in the United States as they have impacted and continue to impact people, whether they are service users or workers. Students watch a documentary where indigenous people share their experience of historical and collective trauma and how it continues to impact them, their way of life, and their children. Students come to understand what Ventura (2008) observes as "[t]he issues enter the consulting room through individuals, but aren't able to be grasped by a psychology of individuals." For example, the hate crimes perpetrated against LGBTQ people in the United States can't be adequately understood by studying only the individuals responsible for the crimes. The context that sanctions such feelings and actions hold powerful lessons about what might be required to achieve a "good enough" fit between people and their environments (Ventura, 2008, p. 31).

Preparing social workers for effective practice in the private and public health and human services sectors, including child welfare, mental health, health care, and other fields of specialized practice where social workers are employed in the 21st century, is perhaps based on a premise that may no longer hold true. The challenges and difficulties experienced by the people who use these services cannot be separated into neat silos, unlike our best efforts to conceptualize specialties. There is spillover, and some of what manifest for individuals as issues for interventions planned and implemented by social workers and other disciplines in the health and human services are not the consequence of an individual's action or inaction alone. There are structural arrangements impacting the lives of people who seek these services, and the very same structural arrangements impact the lives of some of the social workers and other professionals who intervene. Both authors of this chapter listened as a Nigerian male student talked about being stopped by the New York City police over 30 times for no reason other than that he is a young black man who drives an expensive car. This is but one example that illustrates how social workers and their clients are subjected to overly aggressive policing.

Finally, the anti-oppressive practice framework description includes addressing social divisions and structural inequalities. The practice lab takes this directive up by exposing students to social work literature on power and privilege and exploring how these dynamics are manifest in our classrooms, social work agencies, and all the places where human beings interact. Before long, without any prompts from faculty, students begin to notice who speaks in the class, how often they speak, and how much "space" particular people take up in the conversations. This is simultaneously happening for all people, each with their own story and social background, in the classroom space. Faculty members are not excluded from these observations. Students begin to share their observations and ask that space be partitioned to privilege the voices of people who rarely speak in classroom forums. When this space is created, the students who speak up are invited to share what has contributed to the way they present themselves in the open forums, in terms of not speaking.

This awareness is but the tip of the iceberg in understanding power dynamics in social work practice. Pinderhughes' (1989) chapters on culture, understanding difference, and understanding power are used to ground our students in intercultural issues in the delivery of human services. We then layer onto this foundational content literature like Sellick's "Deconstruction of Professional Knowledge: Accountability Without Authority": "our accountability to the people we serve will come not from efforts to prove the authority of our knowledge, but from a more reflective and dialogic engagement with our knowledge and with the people served through it" (Sellick, 2002, p. 493).

Arriving at the mix of theory required to support foundational learning for social work practice is no easy feat. To begin with, it is important to highlight "Undoing Racism" content on the historical and structural conditions of racism when faculty and students are discussing, say, reasons for client resistance. Such content is crucial yet potentially discursive if not clear; it is hidden and ignored if not dealt with. Our work is unending. Practice lab professors recognized that the process of identifying the content for the course involves working with our students and alumni who continue to take an active interest in supporting the course. What we were not prepared for were the variety of issues that impact faculty members who commit to teach this course.

## CONCLUSION

How do social work educators prepare students for this level of complexity without overwhelming them with its sheer enormity? How can all social work method majors learn to assess and shape interventions to achieve desired outcomes in such intricately woven quagmires of suffering? How do we co-create with students a learning environment that challenges all of us to name our standpoints and critically examine what we know and believe about the world? How do we negotiate challenging the social work academy to, in the words of Wagner (2005), go beyond Eurocentric "objective," "apolitical," and (we add) ahistorical knowledge and "deconstruct domination couched in the language of detachment and universality"? Wagner (2005) notes that "broadening what is valued and foregrounding voices that had previously been silenced" is the work of antiracist/anti-oppression pedagogues (p. 261).

This is where our colleagues found themselves in 2008 as they welcomed the gift of developing a year-long practice lab that would provide students with foundational content for social work practice in a highly diverse world. Even in a year-long course, what would be the mix of theory, practice wisdom, skill development, and experiential learning required for social work practice in arenas like the ones described in this chapter?

## Implications for Social Work Faculty Recruitment and Development

First, schools committed to developing an antiracist and anti-oppressive workforce must openly recruit and support faculty members who are willing and able to take on the rigors and rewards of this kind of work. Making heartfelt statements of support for social justice and self-determination without a commitment to recruit faculty members who live and work at these issues each day is at best disingenuous and more likely openly hypocritical with relation to stated professional commitments. The practitioner adjuncts and full-time Silberman faculty members who commit to teach the practice lab are always excited by the idea of teaching a course that emphasizes anti-oppression, issues of human difference, and mindfulness to students entering the social work profession. Almost no one is prepared for the deep emotional and intellectual challenges that such material creates when working with a group of students whose social and personal stories vary widely, and whose awareness of their own power and privilege and their impact on their peers may be limited at best. Creating a classroom environment that creates a "safe enough space" can be extremely difficult when the content angers some students while others are liberated or feel guilty or confused.

Professors may become triggered by perhaps unintentional but nevertheless powerful examples of unconscious racism, homophobia, and social privilege. These issues are intensified for those of us who come from backgrounds rife with social oppression and historical trauma. Content and classroom reaction can re-activate one's own trauma that had perhaps been dormant and yet reappears in the classroom. This has especially been true for teachers who are women of color age 40 or younger. Wagner (2005) has documented that students challenge the knowledge, credentials, and skillsets of professors who are younger black women or women of color, in and out of the classroom. They also are given ratings significantly lower than their male and white colleagues. We have had to use significant debriefing time after each class so that oppressive comments and privileged challenges to competence are addressed, reworked, and reframed for the well-being of those who have been impacted.

Faculty members who are accustomed to the clarity of theory and the impersonal boundary often created between professors and students are challenged in new ways as well. Professors cannot expect students to reveal their stories of power and privilege, social oppression, or personal struggles without faculty doing the same in some form. Some faculty members have opted out of teaching this course because it requires effort well beyond what is needed for a course where the content is not so potentially unsettling.

In the early stages of this course (often most of the first term), students wrestling with internship demands often complain that they are not receiving enough skills to improve their practice. Experienced faculty members have to work with students and new faculty alike to hold the tension between "doing something" and understanding "the way something is done" so that the pragmatic need "to do" does not trump the deeper sets of issues at play in the development of a sustained anti-oppression model of practice.

### The Extraordinary Benefits of This Course

Given the above pressures and issues, why would anyone want to teach this course? In reality, almost everyone who has taught this course, both adjuncts and full-time faculty members, has returned again and again to the practice lab with an anti-oppression lens. Each faculty member has his or her own reasons, but they can be boiled down to just a few.

While students initially complain about the course, by the end of the year (and, equally important, later in their academic program), they report that it was one of the most valuable and helpful in their internships or their work (for students who work full time). Being able to weave in the content, becoming comfortable both with diversity and their own social identity, coming to terms with the dynamics of power and privilege, and understanding and becoming comfortable with others' stories (those of both clients and colleagues) combine to help them grapple with those skillsets needed for professional development. It is perhaps no accident that all the student graduation speakers of the past four years have highlighted the course—from the struggle to the inspiration—as one of the highlights of their career in our program.

Second, the faculty members, while often challenged in unexpected ways, find the course an equally unexpected arena for their own growth, heightened reflection, and deeper understanding of the human condition, often starting with themselves.

Finally, all of us have the opportunity to work with a group of colleagues whose beliefs, commitments, and individual stories allow us to live and work with anti-oppression material as a shared, collective experience. Instead of a lonely climb up a hill, we find comfort and even joy in approaching this work as a journey of opportunity and meaning for what the "United States of America" might be— and, sometimes, actually is.

## DISCUSSION QUESTIONS

1. How can anti-oppression/antiracist content be further developed throughout a school's curriculum so that the course content is not marginalized inside one course alone? How does this content become integral to all professional education?
2. In what ways can school administrators support faculty of color whose own lived experiences with oppression will inevitably be brought to the surface through teaching this content?
3. How can white faculty be encouraged to teach anti-oppression/antiracist courses?

## REFERENCES

Allen, J. A. V. (2001). Poverty as a form of violence: A structural perspective. *Journal of Human Behavior in the Social Environment, 4*(2/3), 45–59.

Brown, C. (1965). *Manchild in the Promised Land.* New York: Macmillan & Co.

Brown, C. (1976). *The Children of Ham.* New York: Bantam Books.

Collins, P. H. (2006). *From black power to hip hop.* Philadelphia: Temple University Press.

CSWE-SAGE. (2012, November). Award for Curriculum Innovation presented at CSWE Annual Program Meeting, Washington, DC.

Epstein, R. M. (1999). Mindful practice. *Journal of the American Medical Association, 282*(9), 833–839.

Erikson, E. H. (1968). *Identity: Youth and crisis.* New York: Norton.

Fisher, R. (2008, October 20). *Symposium on 21st-century activism.* Silberman School of Social Work, New York.

Gil, D. G. (1996). Preventing violence in a structurally violent society: Mission impossible. *American Journal of Orthopsychiatry, 66*(1), 77–84.

Owen, H. (1991). *Riding the tiger.* Potomac, MD: Abbott Publishing.

Pinderhughes, E. (1988). Significance of culture and power in the human behavior curriculum. In C. Jacobs & D. B. Bowles (Eds.), *Ethnicity & race: Critical curriculum concepts in social work* (pp. 152–166). Silver Springs, MD: National Association of Social Workers.

Pinderhughes, E. (1989). *Understanding race, ethnicity & power.* New York: The Free Press.

Piven, F. F., & Cloward, R. A. (1971). *Regulating the poor: The functions of public welfare.* New York: Vintage Books.

Poole, J. (2010). Progressive until graduation? Helping BSW students hold on to anti-oppressive and critical social work practice. *Critical Social Work, 11*(1), 2–11.

Sellick, M. M., Delaney, R., & Brownlee, K. (2002). The deconstruction of professional knowledge: Accountability without authority. *Families in Society The Journal of Contemporary Human Services, 83*(5/6), 493–498.

Ventra, M. (2008, May/June). The new social mind. *Psychotherapy Networker,* 26–33.

Winnicott, D. W. (1965). *The family and individual development.* London: Tavistock.

Winnicott, D. W. (1971). *Playing and reality.* London: Tavistock.

# CHAPTER 4

# Creating a Culturally Competent Research Agenda

MO YEE LEE, XIAFEI WANG, YIWEN CAO,
CHANG LIU, AND AMY ZAHARLICK

While American society has been blessed with and benefited from various forms of diversity, it has also been afflicted by racism, as illustrated in recent incidents such as the Ferguson shooting that involved the fatal shooting of an unarmed black teenage male by a white policeman, thus resurfacing claims of police brutality in the black community. While blatant forms of racism and discrimination have largely been outlawed by civil rights legislation enacted since the 1960s, systematic oppression and racism still exist and can be manifested in the less obvious forms such as microaggression, white privilege, denial, and claims of colorblindness (Bonilla-Silva, 2006; Rothenberg, 2004; Solorzano et al., 2000). Microaggression, a term originally developed in the 1970s by Chester Pierce to describe ways that black people were "put down" by their white counterparts (Pierce, 1974), has been expanded to describe both conscious and unconscious or even unintentional acts that reflect superiority, hostility, and racially inflicted insults and demeanors to marginalized groups of people (Sue, 2010). One negative consequence of racism, including the more subtle forms of microaggressions, is the well-documented social and health disparities experienced by many people of color (Children's Defense Fund, 2014; McLaughlin, 2010; Sanders-Phillips, 2009; Williams, 2007). For instance, children of color are disproportionately represented among the poor. One in 5 black children and 1 in 7 Hispanic children live in extreme poverty, compared to one in 18 for white, non-Hispanic children (Children's Defense Fund, 2014). The juvenile justice system is plagued with racial and ethnic disparities: children of color between the ages of 10 and 17 represent only 16% of the US population but account for 68% of this age cohort of children in restrictive residential placement (Children's

Defense Fund, 2014). There has been extensive research examining racial and ethnic disparities in health outcomes. Epidemiologic evidence indicates that compared with Caucasians, the African American population presented poorer outcomes on virtually all major health indicators, including coronary heart disease, type II diabetes, HIV, and infant mortality. Equitable access to quality health care is a major problem despite the high prevalence of these diseases in the African American population (Centers for Disease Control & Prevention, 2005, 2007; Forouhi and Sattar, 2006; Keppel et al., 2002; Myers, 2009; Smedley et al., 2003). Further, even when controlling for income, racial disparities in health (e.g., earlier onset and higher rates of cardiovascular disease; higher infant mortality; poor maternal health outcome) still exist for the African American population (Marsiglia, 2014).

While recognizing individual determinants, such as genetic predisposition, neuro-physio-biological characteristics that shape an individual's health behaviors, the concept of social determinants explicitly challenges previous explanatory paradigms that are primarily framed by individual risk behaviors. Pertaining to health disparities, the social determinants explanation concludes that "the conditions in which people are born, grow, live, work and age, including the health system, weigh more heavily in the cause and course of every leading category of illness than do any attitudinal, behavioral, or genetic determinant" (Robinson and Moodie-Mills, 2012, p. 2). The lived experiences of many people of color are shaped by societal racism, such as institutional discrimination, fixed social power, residential segregation, and perceived stress; those factors, and the limited access to or lack of essential resources, have negative impacts on their physical health, mental health, and social situations. Developing antiracism strategies that help narrow these disparities should be an imminent ethical responsibility for researchers and professionals in the health and human services.

## CULTURAL COMPETENCE AND ANTIRACIST RESEARCH AGENDAS

A classic definition of cultural competence was offered by Terry Cross and his associates. Their comprehensive definition refers to the ability of individuals and systems to respond effectively and respectfully to people of all cultures, races, socioeconomic status, ethnic backgrounds, sexual orientations, disabilities, and faiths or religions in a manner that recognizes, affirms, and values the worth of individuals, families, tribes, and communities. In doing so, it protects and preserves the dignity of each (Cross, Bazron, Dennis, & Isaacs, 1989). Sue and his associates developed a three-dimensional model in which cultural competence consists of cultural awareness, cultural knowledge, and cultural skills (Sue et al.,

2010). This model has informed the development of the American Psychological Association's guidelines (2002) and the National Association of Social Workers' (2007) standards pertaining to implementing cultural competence in practice across varied fields of professional practice. In the context of research, cultural competence is the capacity to respond to the unique needs of populations whose cultures are different from that which is considered the "dominant" or "mainstream" culture, or when the population being studied is different from that of the researcher. Cultural competence also implies the capacity to function within the context of culturally integrated patterns of human behavior defined by the group under investigation (Lee & Zaharlick, 2013).

Critics of cultural competence claim that by introducing multidimensional factors of oppression, it might lead to information diffusion. In other words, when the focus on race is "diffused" by so many other foci (e.g., gender, sexual orientation, disability, faith and religion), it might reduce or diffuse the focus on the negative effects of racism on racial minority groups (Schiele, 2007). However, we propose that cultural competence is integral to developing antiracist research strategies because this approach can address challenges of intersectionality, facilitate understanding of the biopsychosocial process, and promote the formation of multiracial minority alliances in the research process.

## Addressing Intersectionality

An individual's lived experience is often constructed by the interaction of multiple identities. For people of color, the intersectionality of their various statuses, such as gender, sexual orientation, ability status, age, race/ethnicity, socioeconomic status, immigration and acculturation status, and place of residence, may exacerbate the effects of the oppression of racism (Abrams & Moio, 2009; Marsiglia, 2014). For example, Wilson and colleagues (2004) studied the experiences and responses to social discrimination of Asian and Pacific Islander gay men. The study showed that the high-risk sexual behaviors among these men originated from discrimination by the gay community, rather than public homophobia. In an effort to combat the historically constructed stereotype of being submissive and weak, these men were more likely to undertake high-risk sexual behaviors, in particular forgoing the use of condoms, in an effort to please their non-Asian partners, and this contributed to the increased HIV risk. By applying the intersectionality analysis of race and sexual orientation, this study implied that the power differential between cross-race gay relationships should be the emphasis of HIV interventions. Understanding the experience of people of color with multiple identities (e.g., African American lesbians with disabilities) is far more complicated than when we only take the dimension of race into consideration.

Cultural competence is required when analyzing the multiple identities of people of color and helps avoid oversimplification of oppression from a single dimension.

## Understanding the Biopsychosocial Process of Disparity Formation

Myers' (2009) conceptual model of stresses due to ethnicity and socioeconomic status demonstrated that for people of color, the formation of ethnic and racial disparities is a complicated biopsychosocial process. Cultural competence, focusing on cultural awareness, cultural knowledge, and cultural skills, allows the researcher to understand the implications of social and economic inequalities on well-being outcomes that are rooted in institutional structures and race-based discrimination, as well as the adaptive and coping behaviors used to mitigate the effects of oppressive societal conditions. These coping behaviors include a person's tangible resources, social networks and support, personal agency, future orientation, racial/ethnic identity, and values (Myers, 2009). By identifying the unique risk or protective factors that constitute the cultural system of the studied population, researchers can create a research agenda that can contribute to knowledge building with diverse populations.

## Promoting Multiracial Minority Alliance

Dialogs dealing with antiracism tend to focus on ways and efforts to change the power differential between the dominant and subjugated groups; the misunderstanding and isolation among diverse racial groups are easily ignored. Racial groups often construct each other as a general and vague image—that is, the opposite of whiteness. Consequently, minority racial groups might have little interest in understanding each other's situation. Instead, they tend to focus on their own plights and suffering or, worse, construct other racial minority groups as competitors or enemies.

The conflicts and competitions among minority groups regarding economic resources, political power, and educational opportunities have been extensively demonstrated by historical facts and empirical studies (Cummings & Lambert, 1997; McClain, 1993; Weitzer, 1997). Korean merchants and African American community residents competed over limited economic resources in major cities (Weitzer, 1997). African American voters supported restrictive immigration measures that targeted Mexican immigrants (Cummings & Lambert, 1997). Recently, Asian Americans opposed legislation in California that proposed reinstating affirmative action measures to increase the admission rate of Hispanics and African Americans in the public education system.

Hostile interactions among these racial minority groups did not reduce their subordination and oppression. Instead, they had even less power to challenge the injustice imposed by the dominant group, thus becoming another way of promoting white supremacy. As Ikemoto (1992) commented on the tensions between African Americans and Korean merchants in Los Angeles, it seemed that both groups accepted their deprivation and assumed that competition must occur between the minority groups, but not between the minorities and the white population.

People of color are never a homogenous entity. By recognizing the vast diversity and heterogeneity among people of color, a focus on cultural competence has the potential to promote alliance among diverse racial groups. By highlighting the cultural aspects of the lived experience of different racial groups, cultural competence highlights the importance of mutual understanding, communication, and cooperation among and within diverse racial groups. For instance, a culturally competent Asian American researcher will be curious about the oppression and racism experienced by African Americans as a result of historical and institutional barriers, rather than holding them individually complicit in their own misfortune. Similarly, an African American researcher will recognize that Asian Americans are not insolent exploiters; instead, they experience discrimination by constantly being constructed as cultural others, foreigners, non-American, or "a model minority." Through mutual understanding and communication, different racial groups can transcend their particular race identities to form alliances, thereby making concerted efforts to ameliorate oppression and racism in the society.

## A CULTURALLY COMPETENT RESEARCH AGENDA

Culturally competent research is defined as research that is subjected to "a continuing, incessant, and open-ended series of substantive and methodological insertions and adaptations designed to mesh the process of inquiry with the cultural characteristics of the group being studied" (Rogler, 1989, p. 296). Culturally competent research is a dynamic system that highlights a researcher's commitment to critically examine his or her own values, to constantly engage with the study community, and to actively disseminate the culturally competent knowledge to the research community (Lee & Zaharlick, 2013). Researchers could use this system to guide their endeavors of conducting culturally competent research (Fig. 4.1; Lee & Zaharlick, 2013, p.13). This system builds on the work of Cross, Bazron, Dennis, and Isaacs (1989) that emphasizes five cultural competency components: valuing diversity, conducting cultural self-assessment, managing the dynamics of difference, acquiring and integrating cultural knowledge, and adapting to diversity and cultural context. These components do not

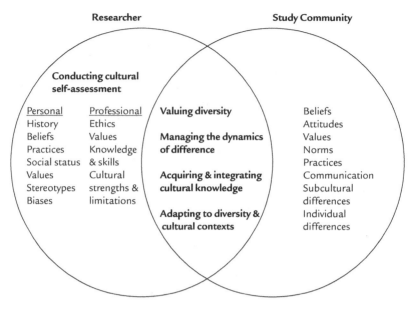

**Figure 4.1:** A Culturally Competent Research System.
Originally published in Lee, M. Y., & Zaharlick, A. (2013). *Culturally competent research: Using ethnography as a meta-framework.* New York: Oxford University Press, Figure 1.2, p. 13.

happen sequentially, but interact with each other in an iterative, dynamic, and ever-changing manner.

## The Study Community

The study community is defined as a fluid and evolving entity that includes the beliefs, attitudes, values, norms, and practices that are shared and learned by a group of people. The community is not viewed as an aggregate of attributes or characteristics. Core to this definition is that people interact socially and communicate symbolically with each other and themselves to give meaning to their lives. Yet, the shared nature of the community does not imply the elimination of subcultural (e.g., social class and occupation) or individual (e.g., age and gender) variations within cultures. Life for each member of every culture is meaningful in his or her idiosyncratic way. Fine (1979) developed the concept of "idioculture" to denote the webs of meaning produced in smaller groups within the broader culture. It is important for researchers to move beyond the acknowledgment of macro-level patterns for a given culture and to appreciate the diverse micro-level social process that individual members undergo to define their personal meaning.

## The Researcher: Conducting Cultural Self-Assessment

To conduct culturally competent research, researchers serve as the instrument to appreciate and acquire cultural knowledge that is achieved through their own personal journey of realizing, integrating, and adapting to diversity and cultural contexts. The extent to which researchers are able to value and appreciate diversity is largely mediated via their efforts to understand and assess their own cultures, including history, beliefs, values, stereotypes, and biases. It is not always easy to detect how our culture impacts our perceptions and thus our behavioral patterns. Because cultural influences usually occur outside of our consciousness, researchers must develop a practice of ongoing self-assessment, introspection, openness, curiosity, and self-observation. Researchers become aware of their own value systems and biases when actively engaged in a process of contrasting these with people or groups from another culture, as well as recognizing the individual differences that are present among people in their own culture or from a similar cultural background. One essential part of cultural self-assessment is to know "who you are" in relation to your own culture. Further, this process helps researchers to understand the ways in which their histories, cultural beliefs and practices, socioeconomic status, cultural values, stereotypes, and biases have shaped their personal identities. Self-awareness requires a critical examination of one's own prejudgments or biases on a daily basis. It also involves taking action to acquire and engage with multiple sources of cultural knowledge through advice seeking, consultation, or mentoring.

While it is important to be objective as a researcher, it is equally important to realize the influence of one's training, education, and professional experiences. This includes the professional values, knowledge and skills, and ethical standards researchers are obliged to abide by. We need to acknowledge the strengths and limitations resulting from our professional experiences. Does any part of our professional identify facilitate or hinder our understanding of a specific cultural group? Being reflective and reflexive as a researcher will help check our personal biases in the research process.

## Valuing Diversity: The Intermediate Zone

The capacity to manage, understand, and adapt to differences constitutes the intermediate zone between the researcher and the study community in a research context. The crucial step for researchers to undertake is to recognize and acknowledge the differences as well as similarities existing between themselves and the study community, people from various cultures, people within a given culture, or those within the same person. The appreciation of differences includes an understanding of differing beliefs, attitudes, values, practices, and policies as well as larger contexts and systems.

Becoming culturally competent means being aware of and understanding the dynamics stemming from the interaction between different cultures across multiple settings, whether these interactions are taking place in a professional or private setting or in formal or informal settings. Researchers constantly interact with the history and cultural meaning of the populations who are being studied. Culture is not perceived as a given; rather, it is ongoing and present in every single interaction. Researchers bring their own values, beliefs, and history and create a new meaning by learning and embracing the differences of the other group.

To manage the dynamics of differences, researchers must see and understand research participants in their context. While interpreting participants' cultural identity, researchers must hold back their own biases and allow participants to present their cultural meaning. Researchers allow this new knowledge of cultural differences in values and customs to sink in and be applied immediately in their interactions with participants. This new understanding may also lead to adjustments in the questions asked and the methods and interpretation that are culturally appropriate in the study community.

Cultural knowledge is produced by the experience and in the context of interaction with others. Thus, acquiring culturally competent knowledge requires continuous efforts to explore, define, and refine questions and adjust research designs that are well situated in the cultural context. The research approach is primarily inductive and involves spending time with people in their own settings. Researchers need to understand how patterns of communication, language, and speech play out in various sociocultural contexts. Researchers should assume the learner or apprentice role before interacting with people, as the purpose of the study is to acquire knowledge that researchers did not know before the study. In this way can researchers come to understand people's lives, sense of purpose, goals, and the meanings they assign to their interactions and can discover culturally based themes and relationships. The entire research process is a journey of discovery.

As part of the sociocultural scenes they research, researchers must keep track of their actions and reactions in the process. This means that they need to suspend judgment, preconceived stereotypes, and interpretation of behaviors based on their own cultural backgrounds while interacting with people. They should be prepared for any surprises from interpretations that are completely outside their experience, while being aware of the assumptions their own empirical questions are based on.

In conducting culturally competent research, researchers challenge themselves to go through the cognitive process of identifying confusion, modifying previously held beliefs, practicing new behaviors, and respecting other people's perspective. Adapting to diversity and cultural context involves taking actions.

Researchers need to learn how to communicate and understand the behaviors and underlying assumptions in intercultural interactions. Researchers must always bear in mind cross-cultural and intracultural differences. Each interaction is interpreted in light of the researcher's culture as well as other cultures and is also a chance to practice what the researcher has learned over time and simultaneously discover differences.

## ETHNOGRAPHY AS A META-FRAMEWORK

Because of the infinite possibilities of research and studies with diverse racial groups, conversations on efforts to create culturally competent research agendas will be more helpful if this dialog remains at the process level rather than the content level. Lee and Zaharlick (2013) proposed using ethnography as a meta-framework for conducting culturally competent research. Ethnography is a theoretically driven, systematic research approach to the study of the everyday life of a social group (Hammersley & Atkinson, 1983; Spradley, 1980; Zaharlick & Green, 1991). Ethnography employs both qualitative and quantitative research strategies in the research process as determined by the research questions. Ethnographic researchers engage in an intense investigation of people, places, and other phenomena to "discover" the culture of interest in their natural settings. Wolcott (1995) described ethnography as a way of seeing the sociocultural world as the social group sees it, in its totality, and for understanding their interpretations of that world. Because ethnography encourages developing contextual knowledge in which sociocultural interactions occur and focuses on understanding what the group's members need to know, do, predict, and interpret in constructing the ongoing events of their lives through which cultural knowledge is developed (Bogdewic, 1999; Spradley, 1980), this research method is especially helpful for conducting culturally competent research because of its respectful and collaborative approach with the study community, focus on a contextual understanding of the phenomenon, and an interactive-reactive process that allow ongoing intercultural learning and adaptation to happen in the research process.

While it is beyond the scope of this discussion to provide a detailed description of an ethnographic approach to conducting culturally competent research (for details please refer to Lee & Zaharlick, 2013), the core components of culturally competent research can be succinctly described as the following (Lee & Zaharlick, 2013, p. 65):

- A collaborative social relationship with the study group and community
- Researcher as learner and as research instrument
- Use of firsthand, long-term observation
- Participant observation and a contextual view of phenomena

- An interactive-reactive research process
- An eclectic approach
- Cross-cultural frame of reference
- A spirit of discovery

In sum, researchers taking an ethnographic perspective focus on establishing collaborative, intercultural relationships with the study community as a way to discover and learn from them. Through direct, long-term participant observation, using themselves as research instruments, and taking an eclectic approach to obtaining data and conducting analysis, researchers take a contextual and integrative view of events in their natural settings. More importantly, researchers adopt a dynamic, interactive-reactive process to frame, define, and refine research questions and continuously adjust the study design and research techniques in response to the idiosyncratic characteristics and needs of the study community. They search for explicit and implicit patterns, for their order, their purpose, and, ultimately, their meaning within the sociocultural and political context. As they learn something new about the culture under study, they try to understand how it connects with other aspects of the sociocultural system, and how it can be interpreted in light of what is known about all previously studied cultures and the broader culture (Lee & Zaharlick, 2013; Zaharlick, 1992).

## FRAMING THE STUDY QUESTIONS

Cultural competence is an integral part of each phase of a research study: deciding on the study topic, framing the study, designing research methods, collecting data, interpreting results, and disseminating findings. Culturally competent research processes adopting an ethnographic approach as a meta-framework provide helpful and explicit guidelines for the researcher. While it is beyond the scope of this discussion to provide a detailed description of the entire research process, we will provide an ethnographic perspective decision-making framework as a guideline for framing the study, which is a crucial and important first step in creating a culturally competent research agenda (Table 4.1, adapted from Lee & Zaharlick, 2013, pp. 69–70).

Designing culturally competent research using an ethnographic perspective emphasizes ongoing interaction, engagement, and consultation with the study community to frame the study, develop culturally appropriate research questions, and construct a relevant research design (Lee & Zaharlick, 2013). The researcher is likely to have an idea of the research area based on his or her expertise, previous research experience, and the existing literature. An ethnographic perspective emphasizes the importance of a collaborative relationship with the study community, researcher as a learner, and a contextual view of the studied phenomenon,

**Table 4.1.** CREATING A CULTURALLY COMPETENT RESEARCH
AGENDA: FRAMING OF THE STUDY

| | Questions to Be Considered | Culturally Competent Research Process |
|---|---|---|
| Purpose | What will be studied? | Ongoing interaction, engagement, and consultation with the study community to frame the study |
| Rationale | What is the rationale for engaging in the study at this time? What problems, concerns, issues, or interests will the study address? | The research should answer questions that are important for the community as determined by the community. The research should build knowledge that furthers localized and contextual understanding of the study community. |
| Significance | What significance does the study have for research, theory, policy, and practice? | The research should build knowledge that ultimately benefits the study community. The researcher should recognize the unique cultural characteristics and strengths of the community. |
| Locating the study | What information or literature exists regarding similar research (on the topic, the specific group[s], similar processes, etc.)? How do you conceptualize the phenomena to be examined, and how does it coincide with or vary from existing conceptualizations? What theory or theories and methodological approaches will you use to answer the question(s) you have posed, and why are they appropriate (cognitive, behavioral, developmental, etc.)? | The researcher is fully aware of the differences as well as similarities among the culture of the study population, the majority culture, and the researcher's culture. The researcher refrains from making assumptions and hypotheses about the studied phenomenon but actively collaborates with the study community to develop culturally relevant framing of the study based on informed and contextualized understanding of both the population and the phenomenon. |
| Research questions | What are the initial exploratory questions guiding your research project? | In an interactive-reactive research process, initial research questions could be adjusted and modified using new information and data obtained from the intercultural interaction between the researcher and the community. |

This table is adapted from Lee, M. Y., & Zaharlick, A. (2013). *Culturally competent research: Using ethnography as a meta-framework*. New York: Oxford University Press, Table 4.1, pp. 69–70.

which suggests the importance of an ongoing collaboration between the research team and the study community as well as firsthand and continuous observation of and participation with the study community in exploring relevant research topics and questions. This is the first step in creating a culturally competent research agenda. In other words, the framing of the study and the research questions should be developed in consultation with the study community because they are the "expert" of their lived experience and they are the "knowers." For instance, one of the authors of this chapter conducted a study exploring the perceptions of sexual violence against women in Asian American communities. She and her coauthor collaborated early on with the Asian American Community Services organization in central Ohio, with a team of community leaders, and with others interested in this issue to frame the research, develop the survey, and implement the study (Lee & Law, 2001). Likewise, Karina Walters and her research team at Washington University conducted studies with American Indian populations on issues of trauma, HIV, and mental health (Walters, Beltrán, Evans-Campbell, & Simoni, 2011; Walters, Mohammed, Evans-Campbell, Beltrán, Chae, & Duran, 2011). As a researcher, Karina Walters (2012) explicitly described how she made respectful and collaborative moves to connect with and gain trust from the elders and the community before initiating a conversation about research with the targeted community.

Rationales are usually needed to justify the implementation of any research. Regardless of the idiosyncratic rationales for different studies, culturally competent research agendas should be guided by the following meta-rationales:

1. The research should answer questions that are important for the community as determined by the community.
2. The research should build knowledge that furthers a localized and contextual understanding of the study community.
3. The research should build knowledge that ultimately benefits the study community.
4. The research should recognize the unique cultural characteristics and strengths of the community.

Useful questions could include why this research is important at this time and with this population. For example, a researcher who decides to study abused Asian American children should ask questions about the unique problems, concerns, issues, or interests for this community from their perspective. How is the experience of Asian American abused children being shaped by their historical, sociocultural, political, and economic context? How is it similar to or different from the experience of the majority culture? What is the significance of the proposed study for research, theory, policy, and practice with this community? The framing of the study is the most important initial step in creating a culturally competent research agenda.

In creating a culturally competent research agenda, researchers should be fully aware of the differences as well as similarities among the culture of the study population, the majority culture, and the researcher's culture. Researchers must be aware of their own possible biases and differences, must listen to the voice of the community, and must develop a contextualized understanding pertaining to the research area. For instance, the reason for and purpose of Asian parents' abusive behavior may be significantly different from those of Caucasian parents and African American parents. Asian parents may physically or verbally abuse their children because of their high expectations for their children, minority group pressures, and an authoritarian parenting style (Meston, Heiman, Trapnell, & Carlin, 1999). Those who have limited knowledge of this population might make assumptions based on the behaviors of the majority culture and overlook these possible differences.

Of course, not all differences among racial groups are a result of cultural differences. For example, not all Asian American parents have extremely high expectations for their children. Within-group variations and idiosyncratic individual and family characteristics and dynamics influence parenting behaviors and parent–child relationships in any particular dyad. A culturally competent researcher refrains from making assumptions and hypotheses about the studied phenomenon but actively collaborates with the study community to develop culturally relevant framing of the study based on informed and contextualized understanding of both the population and the phenomenon. Examples of research questions might be: What are the help-seeking practices of Latino family caregivers of elders with Alzheimer's disease? How do children who are deaf with hearing parents learn deaf culture? How do parents of murdered children deal with their grief? Other research questions may explore service or policy issues: What are the patterns of mental health service utilization of Native American, Asian American, White American, and African American populations? How can the differences be accounted for or explained? The initial framing of the study and research questions may be adjusted and modified with new information and data learned from the intercultural interaction between the researchers and the community, as a culturally competent research process is both interactive and reactive (Lee & Zaharlick, 2013). Regardless of the purpose of the study or the research questions, the importance lies in a process of inquiry that seek answers to questions through an examination of various sociocultural settings; the views, perspectives, and experiences of participants in those settings; and the structure and meanings people give to their lives and experiences. By doing so, culturally competent research provides a way of stepping beyond the known to enter the world of research participants to make discoveries that contribute to the development of empirical knowledge (Lee & Zaharlick, 2013).

## CONCLUSION

Integrating culture competence into the antiracism research agenda addresses the complexity of intersectionality among race and other cultural factors, facilitates better understanding of the biopsychosocial process of disparity and inequality formation, and promotes alliance among diverse racial groups. A culturally competent research agenda requires researchers to be culturally sensitive to the racial, ethnic, and cultural beliefs, attitudes, values, norms, behavioral patterns, and experiences of the people who are the focus of the research. Researchers must incorporate into the research process knowledge of relevant historical, environmental, and social forces that constitute the cultural background and cultural reality of the study community. Paying attention to these factors in the research process, from conception to final published report, promotes the development of cultural sensitivity, cultural awareness, and cultural knowledge that allows researchers to identify hypotheses to be developed, tested, modified, and refined to describe the experiences and perspectives of others and to suggest appropriate interventions. By doing so, culturally competent research studies generate knowledge that can lead to the transformation of beliefs, attitudes, and practices of those responsible for providing services to diverse communities, for identifying the unique needs of diverse populations, and for identifying and removing barriers that limit people's access to needed services (Lee & Zaharlick, 2013). Ultimately, culturally competent research agendas can help eliminate longstanding disparities in the incidence of illness, death, poverty, mental health issues, and other problems of people of diverse racial, ethnic, and cultural backgrounds as well as improve the access to, utilization of, and quality of health and other service outcomes (Goode & Dunne, 2003).

## DISCUSSION QUESTIONS

1. Why should culturally competent research be an integral part of an antiracist research agenda?
2. What should be included in a culturally competent research system, considering your own research agenda?
3. What are the important considerations in framing culturally appropriate research questions and hypotheses that are consistent with an antiracist research agenda?

## REFERENCES

Abrams, L. S., & Moio, J. A. (2009). Critical race theory and the cultural competence dilemma in social work education. *Journal of Social Work Education, 45*(2), 245–261.

American Psychological Association. (2002). Guidelines on multicultural education, training, research, practice, and organizational change for psychologists. *American Psychologist, 58*(5), 377–402.

Bogdewic, S. P. (1999). Participant observation. In B. F. Crabtree & W. L. Miller (Eds.), *Doing qualitative research* (2nd ed., pp. 33–45). Thousand Oaks, CA: Sage Publications.

Bonilla-Silva, E. (2006). *Racism without racists: Color-blind racism and the persistence of racial inequality in the United States.* Lanham, MD: Rowman & Littlefield Publishers.

Centers for Disease Control & Prevention. (2005). *National diabetes fact sheet: general information and national estimates on diabetes in the United States.* Atlanta, GA: U.S. Department of Health and Human Services, Centers for Disease Control and Prevention.

Centers for Disease Control & Prevention. (2007). *HIV/AIDS surveillance report, 2005* (Vol. 17, rev. ed.). Atlanta, GA: Department of Health and Human Services, Centers for Disease Control and Prevention.

Children's Defense Fund. (2014). *The state of America's children yearbook.* Washington DC: Children's Defense Fund.

Cross, T., Bazron, B., Dennis, K., & Isaacs, M. (1989). *Towards a culturally competent system of care. Volume I.* Washington, DC: CASSP Technical Assistance Center, Center for Child Health and Mental Health Policy, Georgetown University Child Development Center.

Cummings, S., & Lambert, T. (1997). Anti-Hispanic and anti-Asian sentiments among African Americans. *Social Science Quarterly, 78*(2), 338–353.

Fine, G. A. (1979). Small groups and culture creation: The idioculture of Little League baseball teams. *American Sociological Review, 44*(5), 733–745.

Forouhi, N. G., & Sattar, N. (2006). CVD risk factors and ethnicity—a homogeneous relationship? *Atherosclerosis Supplements, 7*(1),11–19.

Goode, T. D., & Dunne, C. (2003). *Policy brief, I.* Washington, DC: National Center for Cultural Competence.

Hammersley, M., & Atkinson, P. (1983). *Ethnography: Principles in practice.* New York: Tavistock Publications.

Ikemoto, L. C. (1992). Traces of the master narrative in the story of African American/Korean American conflict: How we constructed Los Angeles. *Southern California Law Review, 66,* 1581.

Keppel, K. G., Pearcy, J. N., & Wagener, D. K. (2002). *Trends in racial and ethnic-specific rates for the health status indicators: United States, 1990–1998. Healthy People Statistical Notes, No. 23.* Hyattsville, MD: National Center for Health Statistics.

Lee, M. Y., & Law, P. F. M. (2001). Perception of sexual violence against women in Asian American communities. *Journal of Ethnic and Cultural Diversity in Social Work, 10*(2), 3–25.

Lee, M. Y., & Zaharlick, A. (2013). *Culturally competent research: Using ethnography as a meta-framework.* New York: Oxford University Press.

Marsiglia, F. F., & Kulis, S. S. (2014). *Diversity, oppression, and change: Culturally grounded social work.* Chicago, IL: Lyceum Books.

Myers, H. F. (2009). Ethnicity-and socio-economic status-related stresses in context: an integrative review and conceptual model.Journal of behavioral medicine,32(1), 9–19.

McClain, P. D. (1993). The changing dynamics of urban politics: Black and Hispanic municipal employment—Is there competition? *Journal of Politics, 55*(2), 399–414.

McLaughlin, K. A., Hatzenuehler, M. L., & Keyes, K. M. (2010). Responses to discrimination and psychiatric disorders among Black, Hispanic, female, and lesbian, gay, and bisexual individuals. *American Journal of Public Health, 100*(8), 1477–1484.

Meston, C. M., Heiman, J. R., Trapnell, P. D., & Carlin, A. S. (1999). Ethnicity, desirable responding, and self-reports of abuse: A comparison of European- and Asian-ancestry undergraduates. *Journal of Consulting and Clinical Psychology, 67*(1), 139–144.

Myers, H. F. (2009). Ethnicity-and socio-economic status-related stresses in context: an integrative review and conceptual model. *Journal of behavioral medicine, 32*(1), 9–19.

National Association of Social Workers. (2007). *Indicators for the achievement of the NASW standards for cultural competence in social work practice*. Washington, DC: NASW.

Ramakrishnan, S. K. (2014). Asian Americans and the rainbow: the prospects and limits of coalitional politics. *Politics, Groups & Identities, 2*(3), 522.

Robinson, R., & Moodie-Mills, A. C. (2012). HIV/AIDS inequality: Structural barriers to prevention, treatment, and care in communities of color. Washington DC: Center for American Progress.

Rogler, L. H. (1989). The meaning of culturally sensitive research in mental health. *American Journal of Psychiatry, 146*(3), 296–303.

Rothenberg, P. S. (Ed.). (2004). *White privilege: Essential readings on the other side of racism*. New York: Worth.

Sanders-Phillips, K., Settles-Reaves, B., Walker, D., & Brownlow, J. (2009) Social inequality and racial discrimination: Risk factors for health disparities in children of color. Pediatrics, 124(Supplement 3), S176–S186.

Smedley, B. D., Stith, A. Y., & Nelson, A. R. (2003). *Unequal treatment: Confronting racial and ethnic disparities in health care*. Washington, DC: National Academies Press

Schiele, J. H. (2007). Implications of the equality-of-oppressions paradigm for curriculum content on people of color. Journal of Social Work Education, 43(1), 83–100.

Solorzano, D., Ceja, M., & Yosso, T. (2000). Critical race theory, racial microaggressions, and campus racial climate: The experiences of African American college students. *Journal of Negro Education, 69*(1/2), 60–73.

Spradley, J. P. (1980). *Participant observation*. New York: Holt, Rinehart and Winston.

Sue, D. W. (2010). *Microaggressions in everyday life: Race, gender, and sexual orientation*. Hoboken, NJ: Wiley.

Walters, K. L. (2012). *Indigenous voices in doctoral education: A model for the integration of pedagogy, scholarship, and service*. Plenary Speech, 2012 Annual Meeting of the Group for Advancement of Doctoral Education. Portland, Oregon, April 13–14.

Walters, K. L., Beltrán, R. E., Evans-Campbell, T., & Simoni, J. M. (2011). Keeping our hearts from touching the ground: HIV/AIDS in American Indian and Alaska Native Women. *Women's Health Issues, 21*(6S), S261–S265. DOI:10.1016/j.whi.2011.08.005

Walters, K. L., Mohammed, S. A., Evans-Campbell, T., Beltrán, R. E., Chae, D. H., & Duran, B. (2011). Bodies don't just tell stories, they tell histories: Embodiment of historical trauma among American Indians and Alaska Natives. *Dubois Review, 8*(1), 179–189. DOI:10.10170S1742058X1100018X

Weitzer, R. (1997). Racial prejudice among Korean merchants in African American neighborhoods. *Sociological Quarterly, 38*(4), 587–606.

Williams, D. R., & Mohammed, S. A. (2007). Discrimination and racial disparities in health: Evidence and needed research. *Journal of Behavioral Medicine, 32*(1), 20–47.

Wolcott, H. F. (1995). *The art of fieldwork*. Walnut Creek, CA: AltaMira Press.

Zaharlick, A. (1992). Ethnography in anthropology and its value for education. *Theory Into Practice, 31*(2), 116–125.

Zaharlick, A., & Green, J. L. (1991). Ethnographic research. In J. Flood, J. Jensen, D. Lapp, & J. Squire (Eds.), *Handbook of research on teaching the English language arts* (pp. 205–225). New York: MacMillan.

# CHAPTER 5

# When Does Race Matter?

## Examining Antiracist Organizational Change

### LISA V. BLITZ AND MIMI ABRAMOVITZ

Today, organizations of all types regularly address diversity. Reflecting corporate concerns, the organizational development literature provides ample guidance on how to "manage diversity" at the individual level with regard to staffing patterns and organizational functioning. Human service organizations have also begun to address racial disparities in child welfare, education, criminal justice, and other such areas, hoping to correct racially insensitive practices among individuals, be they overtly or unconsciously racist. However, a review of over 150 scholarly publications on this topic revealed very little information to inform antiracist work at the organizational level. Without empirical evidence, efforts to increase racial equity in the workplace become more difficult to initiate and more likely to falter.

Our research was designed to fill this knowledge gap by applying a race lens to data collected to examine organizational progress toward racial equity in the human services. This chapter (1) reviews the organizational development literature, (2) describes our research, and (3) examines efforts to achieve organizational racial equity by (a) the race of the respondents and (b) the racial composition of an organization's executive group. The use of the racial lens reveals that understanding the different experiences of white people and people of color is key to engaging all stakeholders in making progress toward racial equity in organizations.

## LITERATURE REVIEW

This review includes numerous empirical studies and a few important conceptual articles discussing the issue of race in organizational development efforts. The articles indicate that while institutions of higher education increasingly teach multicultural, anti-oppression paradigms, these ideas take longer to translate into practice. Rather, "colorblind" approaches that attempt to treat each individual without regard to race or ethnicity prevail (Plaut, Thomas, & Goren, 2009). Many organizations adopt the colorblind strategy in the fear that discussions of race will raise issues that elicit both differences and pain. Indeed, when people of color experience or perceive an organization as biased, they may initially regard efforts to promote racial equity as hypocritical—this, in turn, can stir up negative feelings (Triana, Fernanda Garcia, & Colella, 2010). On the other hand, white people may feel victimized by "reverse racism" (Norton & Sommers, 2011) and feel threatened or excluded if multicultural efforts do not specifically address their experience (Apfelbaum, Norton, & Sommers, 2012). Although colorblind approaches purport to transcend bias, critics see them as intentionally or unwittingly defending, if not justifying, the racial status quo by maintaining rather than eradicating institutional racism (Bonilla-Silva & Dietrich, 2011). They argue that colorblind strategies give insufficient attention to race-based structural bias and risk missing subtle, often unconscious, expressions of racial prejudice by the organization's staff. In turn, unchecked structural bias supports individual prejudice, resulting in racial microaggressions that can complicate supervisory relationships and harm both staff and clients of color (Constantine & Sue, 2007).

Unlike colorblind approaches, race-aware multicultural strategies have been shown to increase employee satisfaction (Price et al, 2005), improve client services, promote the value of difference, and otherwise effectively work to eliminate oppression (Hyde, 2004). They have also been shown to increase the retention of staff of color (Mckay, Avery, Tonidandel, Morris, Hernandez, & Hebl, 2007) and to lead all staff members to associate racial diversity with a stronger organizational performance (Choi & Rainey, 2010). However, these more difficult race-conscious approaches take more work to implement. Creating a positive diversity climate requires a major commitment of time and resources as well as a willingness to pursue a holistic transformation of the organization's culture (Martín Alcázar, Romero Fernández, & Sánchez Gardey, 2013). Embedding responsiveness to race into the organizational culture also requires continuous learning, knowledge sharing, skill development, and accountability for ongoing growth (Cocchiara, Connerley, & Bell, 2010). This systemic, multilevel, and nonlinear process requires a clear commitment to advance diversity goals, resources to support the creation of a positive diversity climate, and ongoing monitoring of all aspects of organizational functioning (Buttner, Lowe, & Billings-Harris, 2012).

The literature also highlights the importance of understanding how the race of organizational members and the racial composition of its leaders affect efforts to achieve racial equity. Racial identity (Helms, 1995), organization development (Thompson & Carter, 2012), and critical race theorists (Delgado & Stafancic, 2001) point out that achieving diversity goals often fall short because the dynamics of racism keep people divided along race lines. That is, social and historical race privilege benefits white people regardless of their economic situation or cultural background, while racism disadvantages people of color regardless of their ethnicity or economic status. Further, while many people of color are conscious of their racial identity development and the meaning of racism all of their lives, white people typically become race-aware only when challenged by circumstances or personal choice.

Research has also found that managers of color face several challenges not experienced by their white counterparts, including navigating both community perceptions and organizational dynamics (Melton, Walker, & Walker, 2010). Gender also affects perceptions of race. Women of color who face both race and gender stereotypes (Sanchez-Hucles & Davis, 2010) must develop race-based survival strategies to deal with both (Durr & Harvey Wingfield, 2011).

In multicultural settings, organizational performance is strengthened when work teams have the ability to (1) understand the experiences of people of color and address white privilege (Curry-Stevens & Nissen, 2011); (2) recognize troublesome race-driven organizational dynamics; (3) actively respond to members' unique backgrounds, talents, and personality styles; and (4) maintain a commitment to communication and relationship building (Hultman & Hultman, 2008). Tackling racial equity within an organization can be particularly challenging, however, as even people who are engaged in social justice work find it difficult to talk about inequality in diverse groups (Bell & Hartmann, 2007). Thus, it is also important to develop a mutual understanding about the need for racial equity, including developing a shared language to support communication and continued learning (Carter, Oyler, & Goulding, 2013).

Transformative organization change affects all members, and to succeed it requires the active support of the entire workforce. However, engagement in organizational change efforts is typically an additional responsibility assumed by members of an organization to support what they view as a valuable initiative. When such efforts are supported by effective outside advice and strong partnerships within the organization, they can lead to increased job satisfaction, career success, and organizational change (Aime, van Dyne, & Petrenko, 2011). When an organization's change efforts arise amidst a collective movement for change within the professional community, both organizations and their members stand to gain.

The role of race has received little attention in the ongoing efforts in the human services to create diverse teams to train the workforce to address racial disproportionality, to promote racial equity, and to overcome colorblind practices. While the literature on multicultural organizational development (see Hyde, 2004) offers valuable insights into the challenges posed by such change initiatives, few articles explore the role of the race of staff or the racial composition of an organization's leaders as related to organizational progress toward racial equity.

## DESCRIPTION OF THE RESEARCH PROJECT

This chapter seeks to fill this knowledge gap. To this end, we surveyed participants in the "Undoing Racism" workshop conducted by the People's Institute for Survival and Beyond and coordinated by the Anti-Racist Alliance. The Alliance was formed in New York City in 2002 to develop human services leaders to be equipped to pursue racial equity in their organizations. The Alliance placed the workshop at the center of its educational and organizing efforts to promote racial equity work. The two-and-a-half-day workshop explains the history of race discrimination in the United States, defines racism in the context of power and privilege, and teaches participants how to recognize institutional racism.

Our research was based on the premise that workshop alumni had developed knowledge about institutional racism and therefore could usefully describe their experiences and their organization's progress toward racial equity. Drawing on participatory action research methods, and in consultation with the Anti-Racist Alliance core team, we developed a survey that was distributed to 2,673 alumni between June 2010 and May 2012, using Survey Monkey, an online survey tool, with e-mail addresses supplied at registration. The survey was reviewed by multiple human service professionals for face and content validity, and the study was approved by the institutional review boards of the two collaborating universities.

Alumni were invited to participate in the survey a minimum of six months after they had attended the workshop. A total of 875 people responded; 258 e-mails bounced back, and 1,798 did not respond, yielding a response rate of 37.4%.

Using data from this study, Abramovitz and Blitz (2015) sought to understand alumni's perceptions of their organization's overall progress toward racial equity, the impact of the training on their knowledge and attitudes about structural racism, and their degree of engagement in organizational change efforts after attending the workshop. This chapter examines the respondents' experiences with antiracist work by focusing on both the race of the participants and the racial composition of their organizations.

This lens of race was applied to (1) understand who participated in the workshop, (2) examine ways in which the workshop experience and engagement in racial equity work varied by race, and (3) explore the relationship between the racial composition of an organization's executive group and its progress toward racial equity. While cultural and ethnic differences are important in many ways, the workshop focuses on the race privilege of white people as a general group and the oppression of all people of color to highlight the overarching dynamics of structural racism. Therefore, only two categories of racial identity were identified: white and person of color. In identifying the organization for which they worked, respondents were asked to identify general categories of "majority white," "majority people of color," or "racially diverse" (meaning no clear majority) for the executive group, staff, and people served by the organization. Data were treated as categorical, and analysis relied on frequency distribution, cross-tabulation, and chi-square tests. Similarities and differences among variables are discussed, including those that show statistical significance and those that have significance in practice and organization development. Statistical tables provide details of the findings.

## IMPACT OF THE RACE OF RESPONDENTS

The race lens reveals who participated in the survey and their post-workshop experience in the workplace. As shown in Table 5.1, of the 875 respondents (workshop alumni), over half (57.7%) were white and over a third (38.7%) were people of color, with a few choosing "other." Women predominated among both white respondents (75%) and respondents of color (80%). The predominance of women

*Table 5.1* DEMOGRAPHIC DESCRIPTION OF RESPONDENTS

| | White | Person of Color | | White | Person of Color |
|---|---|---|---|---|---|
| **Gender** | | | **Age** | | |
| Female | 81.4 | 75.4 | 18–35 | 30.5 | 33.3 |
| Male | 18.6 | 24.6 | 36–55 | 32.8 | 41.7 |
| **Education** | | | 56+ | 35.9 | 24.6 |
| Postgraduate degree | 18.6 | 10.5 | **Heritage** | | |
| Graduate degree | 65.0 | 65.5 | Born and raised in U.S. | 94.3 | 78.6 |
| Bachelor's degree | 15.0 | 13.1 | Born and raised | 2.7 | 11.8 |
| Less than bachelor's degree | 1.5 | 9.3 | elsewhere | | |
| **Professional role** | | | **Practice focus** | | |
| | | | Direct service | 44.2 | 53.5 |
| Administrator | 49.5 | 54.2 | Education | 39.2 | 24.8 |
| Educator | 21.5 | 15.0 | Advocacy | 9.0 | 11.9 |
| Direct practitioner | 14.0 | 21.5 | **Service focus** | | |
| **Length of employment** | | | Social work | 37.9 | 54.3 |
| 1–3 years | 31.2 | 29.6 | Education | 35.4 | 29.1 |
| 4+ years | 68.8 | 70.4 | **Number of "Undoing Racism" workshops attended** | | |
| **Organizational sector** | | | | | |
| Private nonprofit | 82.1 | 69.4 | One | 71.2 | 65.1 |
| Private for profit | 2.5 | 4.6 | Two or more | 28.8 | 34.8 |
| Public/government | 14.9 | 25.0 | **Attended other racial equity training** | | |
| **Attended cultural competency trainings** | | | Yes | 49.2 | 40.0 |
| Yes | 85.5 | 83.7 | No | 50.8 | 59.3 |
| No | 14.5 | 16.3 | | | |

White, $n = 505$; people of color, $n = 339$; other (not included), $n = 31$.

reflects the composition of the two major professional groups that participated in the workshop in New York City: social workers and educators. The age distribution also varied by race. White people predominated among those over age 56, while people of color predominated among those aged 18 to 35 and especially among those aged 36 to 55. Over three quarters of the respondents of color and almost all of the white respondents were born in the United States.

The group was well educated, with minimal differences by race. Over two thirds of both respondents of color and white respondents had a master's degree; 18.6% of white respondents and 10.5% of respondents of color had a doctoral degree; 15% of white respondents and 13% of respondents of color had a bachelor's degree; and a few more people of color than white people had less than a college degree. About 70% of each group had worked in their current organization for more than four years, indicating that they had a good deal of experience with the organization.

While most worked at both private nonprofit and public-sector agencies, more white alumni (82.1%) than alumni of color (69.4%) worked for a nonprofit organization. In contrast, a greater proportion of respondents of color (25.0%) than white respondents (14.9%) worked in the public sector. Many fewer—less than 5% of both respondents of color and white respondents—were employed by a for-profit organization. Alumni also worked in different fields. People of color were more heavily employed in social work (54.3%) than in education (29.1%), while white respondents were almost evenly divided between social work (37.9%) and education (35.4%). Among educators, approximately half worked in K–12 education; the rest worked in higher education. No differences emerged between respondents in higher education and those in primary or secondary education, so the categories were combined for analyses.

Respondents had experience with different types of racial disparity trainings (e.g., racial equity and cultural competency). About 85% of each group had participated in a cultural competency/diversity training; these are prevalent and often mandated in many organizations. These trainings tend to focus on individual and group differences rather than institutional structures. However, 49.2% of white respondents and 40% of respondents of color had participated in a racial equity training, such as the "Undoing Racism" workshop, which tend to highlight structural racism. More white alumni (71.2%) than alumni of color (65.1%) attended the "Undoing Racism" workshop just once, while a greater percentage of respondents of color (34.8%) than white respondents (28.8%) attended two or more times.

## ENGAGEMENT IN ORGANIZATIONAL CHANGE EFFORTS AMONG ALUMNI

The "Undoing Racism" workshop encouraged all alumni to become engaged in efforts to make their organization more racially equitable. However, only 531 respondents worked at organizations that pursued racial equity activities. Of these, nearly all participated in racial equity activities in their workplace. Some 119 respondents did not become engaged; the rest either skipped the question or did not work in such an organization. The following discussion explores the experiences of workshop alumni who did and did not become engaged in racial equity work on the job by race. Engagement was based on respondents' reports of whether they had "initiated," "participated," or "both initiated and participated" in various racial equity activities.

### Alumni Who Became Engaged

Of those who became engaged in racial equity work, more were white (87.8%) than people of color (81.1%) (Table 5.2), a difference that was statistically significant, but their experiences were often similar. About 70% of both respondents of color and white respondents reported positive attention from within their organization (see Table 5.2). More than 60% of each group reported sufficient peer interest. However, around 45% of each group also reported insufficient leadership support. Some 47% of the alumni of color and 45% of the white alumni reported resistance from organizational leaders, while about half of each group faced resistance from their coworkers.

Race made a greater difference in other areas of organizational life in ways that tended to reflect white privilege: the respondent's access to organizational decision makers and their feelings of safety and security. While two thirds of each group had access to outside advice (see Table 5.2), statistically more white respondents (84%) than respondents of color (74.7%) had access to organizational decision makers. Another statistically significant difference was the finding that a greater proportion of respondents of color (29.5%) than white respondents (18.9%) felt the need to keep a low profile when engaged in racial equity work. More white alumni (60.8%) than alumni of color (54%) stated that job security supported their ability to take action. Of those who limited their activities due to fear of getting into trouble, 24.9% were alumni of color and 15.1% were white. Finally, only 37.4% of the alumni of color and 41% of the white alumni stated that there was enough time on the job to do antiracist work.

### Alumni Who Did Not Become Engaged

Racial similarities and differences also arose among those who did not become engaged in racial equity work, but the differences were not statistically significant. About half of each group among the nonengaged explained that they did not have enough time on the job to become involved in racial equity work (see Table 5.2). Just over 50% of each group also said that they did not know how to

*Table 5.2* INFORMATION ON EXPERIENCES WITH RACIAL EQUITY WORK
BY RACE OF RESPONDENT

| Questions were "yes/no" responses, % of "yes" responses shown; *n* in parenthesis | People of Color | White | $X^2$ | *df* | Asymp signif |
|---|---|---|---|---|---|
| I engaged in racial equity activities at work | 81.1 (185) | 87.8 (295) | 4.75 | 1 | .029* |
| Positive attention received from organization | 72.7 (112) | 69.4 (170) | .51 | 1 | .476 |
| Sufficient peer interest for racial equity work | 66.1 (115) | 62.9 (171) | .48 | 1 | .489 |
| Sufficient leadership support | 44.7 (76) | 46.0 (125) | .07 | 1 | .797 |
| Engaged, but leaders resisted my efforts | 47.1 (64) | 44.9 (115) | .16 | 1 | .668 |
| Engaged, but colleagues resisted my efforts | 49.3 (75) | 50.6 (133) | .06 | 1 | .809 |
| Access to outside strategic advice | 65.9 (110) | 65.9 (170) | .00 | 1 | .996 |
| Access to organizational decision makers | 74.7 (130) | 84.0 (126) | 5.79 | 1 | .016* |
| I try to keep a low profile on my activities | 29.5 (46) | 18.9 (47) | 6.11 | 1 | .013* |
| I feel free to take action because I have job security | 54.0 (81) | 60.8 (138) | 1.71 | 1 | .191 |
| Limited activities, feared getting into trouble | 29.3 (46) | 15.1 (38) | 11.85 | 1 | .001** |
| Enough time at work to attend to related tasks | 37.4 (61) | 41.0 (98) | .52 | 1 | .471 |
| Not engaged, not enough time | 50.0 (22) | 47.4 (18) | .06 | 1 | .812 |
| Not engaged, did not know how to proceed | 53.3 (24) | 55.0 (22) | .02 | 1 | .878 |
| Not engaged, not enough peer support | 54.8 (23) | 42.5 (17) | 1.23 | 1 | .267 |
| Not engaged, do not know enough about issue | 13.3 (6) | 23.1 (9) | 1.35 | 1 | .245 |
| Not engaged, feared getting into trouble at work | 33.3 (15) | 23.7 (9) | .93 | 1 | .334 |
| Not engaged, only person here with an interest | 35.7 (15) | 27.0 (10) | .67 | 1 | .407 |
| Not engaged, not enough leadership support | 50.0 (21) | 40.0 (14) | .77 | 1 | .380 |
| Not engaged, racial equity at work is not a priority | 25.0 (10) | 15.4 (6) | 1.13 | 1 | .288 |
| Attended the workshop with coworkers | 71.7 (76) | 62.5 (125) | 2.60 | 1 | .107 |
| Coworkers had attended the workshop before me | 68.3 (69) | 71.8 (125) | .38 | 1 | .537 |
| The executive leader had attended the workshop | 66.7 (58) | 61.1 (102) | .76 | 1 | .381 |
| The workshop motivated me to support racial equity efforts outside of work | 79.0 (181) | 79.2 (266) | .001 | 1 | .971 |

* $p < .05$; ** $p < .01$.

proceed. However, 54.8% of the alumni of color and 42.5% of the white alumni said that a lack of peer support limited their engagement.

Other reasons for nonengagement varied by race. While more white alumni (23.1%) than alumni of color (13.3%) said they did not know enough about the racial equity issue (see Table 5.2), respondents of color reported other barriers. Thirty-three percent of respondents of color feared getting into trouble on the job compared to 23.7% of white respondents. Alumni of color (35.7%) were also more likely than white alumni (27%) to state that they were the only person at work with interest in addressing racial equity issues. They (25%) were more likely than white alumni (15.4%) to say that that racial equity work was not their top priority and more likely (50%) than white alumni (40%) to report insufficient leadership support.

## RACIAL COMPOSITION OF EXECUTIVES

Questions about the racial composition of an organization's leaders and staff are rarely included in research studies. In this study respondents were asked to indicate if the executives, staff, and people served by their organization were majority white, majority people of color, or racially diverse (meaning that there was no clear majority). The analysis of this data in Abramovitz and Blitz (2015) found that more than three quarters of the respondents worked in organizations where the majority of executives were white, while less than 10% worked in organizations where the majority of the executives were people of color or racially diverse (Table 5.3). Almost 50% of the respondents worked in organizations where the majority of the staff were white; 25% worked in organizations where the majority of staff were people of color and 21% where the staff was racially diverse. In contrast, less than a fifth were employed in organizations where the majority of people served were racially diverse, less than a third worked in organizations where the majority of people served were white, and almost half worked in organizations where the majority of people served were people of color.

The pattern of racial composition became more concentrated when analyzed by the race of the respondent (Table 5.4). While most respondents worked in organizations led by white executives, this applied to more white respondents (83.4%) than respondents of color (76.3%). In stark contrast, many fewer worked in an organization where the majority of the executives were people of color: only 7.3% of the white alumni and 13.7% of the alumni of color. More than twice the percentage of alumni of color (41.4%) than white alumni (16.5%) worked in

*Table 5.3* RACIAL COMPOSITION OF ORGANIZATION LEADERS, STAFF, AND PEOPLE SERVED

| Organizational Role | Primarily White | Primarily People of Color | Racially Diverse | Don't Know |
|---|---|---|---|---|
| Executive leaders | 78.1 (*n* = 439) | 9.8 (*n* = 55) | 9.6 (*n* = 54) | 2.5 (*n* = 14) |
| Staff | 49.6 (*n* = 274) | 25.0 (*n* = 138) | 20.7 (*n* = 114) | 4.7 (*n* = 6) |
| People served | 28.9 (*n* = 160) | 48.6 (*n* = 269) | 17.9 (*n* = 99) | 4.5 (*n* = 25) |

Table 5.4 RESPONDENTS' RACE IN CONTEXT OF THE RACIAL
COMPOSITION OF THE ORGANIZATION

| Respondent race | Primarily White | Primarily of Color | Diverse | $X^2$ | $df$ | Asymp signif |
|---|---|---|---|---|---|---|
| | *Race of the Majority of Executive Leaders* | | | | | |
| People of color | 76.3 (167) | 13.7 (30) | 10.0 (22) | 6.19 | 2 | .045* |
| White | 83.4 (262) | 7.3 (23) | 9.2 (29) | | | |
| | *Race of the Majority of Staff Members* | | | | | |
| People of color | 39.9 (81) | 41.4 (84) | 18.7 (38) | 39.42 | 2 | .000*** |
| White | 59.5 (184) | 16.5 (51) | 23.9 (74) | | | |
| | *Race of the Majority of People Served* | | | | | |
| People of color | 20.7 (44) | 63.4 (134) | 16.0 (34) | 23.52 | 2 | .000*** |
| White | 37.0 (112) | 42.2 (128) | 20.8 (63) | | | |

* $p < .05$; *** $p < .001$.

organizations where the majority of staff were people of color, while 59.5% of the white alumni and 39.9% of the alumni of color worked in organizations where most of the staff were white.

Finally, 9.2% of white respondents and 10% of respondents of color worked in an organization where the executive group was racially diverse, and 23.9% of the white respondents and 18.7% of the respondents of color worked in organizations where the staff group was racially diverse. Sharper differences arose in relation to the people served. More than 63% of the respondents of color but only 42.2% of the white respondents worked in an organization serving mostly people of color. In contrast, only 20.7% of respondents of color and 37% of white respondents worked in organizations where the majority of the people served were white. Sixteen percent of the respondents of color and 20.8% of the white respondents worked in organizations where the people served were racially diverse. In other words, both white respondents and respondents of color worked in organizations led by white executives. In contrast, white respondents tended to work in organizations where most of the staff were white, while more respondents of color worked in organizations where most of the staff were of color. The relationship to people served was less polarized, with both respondents of color and white respondents working in organizations where most of those served were people of color, but this was greater for respondents of color than white respondents.

## RACIAL COMPOSITION OF ORGANIZATION EXECUTIVES AND RACIAL EQUITY PROGRESS

"Undoing Racism" workshop goals included both individual and organizational development. The trainers encouraged participants to take their new knowledge back to their colleagues, organizations, and communities and to use it to promote institutional change (Anti-Racist Alliance, n.d.). The survey defined progress toward racial equity in terms of a set of 14 administrative activities that an organization seeking structural change in support of racial equity might take. For each activity, respondents indicated which of four steps toward racial equity their organization had reached: "already in place," "implemented," "under discussion," or "stalled." Respondents were asked to assess their organization's progress since the time that they had attended the workshop.

Table 5.5 shows the percentage of respondents reporting their organization's progress on the 14 activities. The four steps are grouped into four conceptual

*Table 5.5* ORGANIZATIONAL PROGRESS, CATEGORIZED BY RACIAL EQUITY DOMAIN

| Q # | RED* | My organization has . . . | Already in Place | Implemented | Under Discussion | Stalled | DK/ NA |
|---|---|---|---|---|---|---|---|
| 1 | AR EC | Policies that express a commitment to racial equity ($n = 406$) | 40.6 | 19.7 | 25.4 | 9.4 | 4.9 |
| 2 | AR EC | Procedures to implement policies that express a commitment to racial equity ($n = 405$) | 25.4 | 20.0 | 33.3 | 13.6 | 7.7 |
| 3 | ER | Deliberate strategy to hire, retain, and promote staff of color ($n = 401$) | 31.7 | 19.2 | 18.5 | 15.0 | 15.7 |
| 4 | ER | Involve community/ student representatives on organizational or advisory board ($n = 398$) | 30.4 | 10.8 | 17.1 | 15.8 | 26.9 |
| 5 | ER | Review composition of workforce to reflect racial diversity of community ($n = 397$) | 27.0 | 14.4 | 26.2 | 15.4 | 17.1 |
| 6 | ER | Review admissions policies so people served reflect racial diversity of community ($n = 399$) | 24.6 | 12.0 | 21.1 | 13.8 | 28.6 |
| 7 | ER | Review composition of leadership to reflect racial diversity of community ($n = 401$) | 20.9 | 11.0 | 24.2 | 21.4 | 22.4 |
| 8 | ER | Review composition of board to reflect racial diversity of community ($n = 399$) | 13.5 | 9.3 | 19.3 | 16.3 | 41.6 |

*(continued)*

*Table 5.5* CONTINUED

| Q # | RED* | My organization has . . . | Already in Place | Implemented | Under Discussion | Stalled | DK/ NA |
|---|---|---|---|---|---|---|---|
| 9 | DK | Committees or task forces to increase staff knowledge and skills about racial equity (*n* = 402) | 31.6 | 22.6 | 19.2 | 16.2 | 10.4 |
| 10 | DK | Orientation highlights racial equity (*n* = 405) | 27.4 | 13.1 | 23.5 | 21.7 | 14.3 |
| 11 | DK | Criteria for hiring and promoting includes assessing racial equity competency (*n* =394) | 19.3 | 11.2 | 20.1 | 22.6 | 26.9 |
| 12 | DK | Shared language or analysis about race and racism within the organization (*n* = 406) | 19.0 | 20.0 | 38.2 | 17.2 | 5.7 |
| 13 | MB | Internal strategy for dealing with possible backlash against racial equity efforts (*n* = 395) | 11.1 | 6.8 | 15.5 | 22.0 | 39.0 |
| 14 | MB | Specific mechanisms to follow up on racial bias complaints (*n* = 393) | 34.4 | 9.2 | 15.5 | 15.3 | 25.7 |

* Racial equity domain: AREC = addressing racial equity commitments; ER = ensuring representation; DK = deepening knowledge; MB = managing bias.

"racial equity domains:" (1) addressing racial equity commitment, (2) ensuring representation, (3) deepening knowledge, and (4) managing bias. The activities in each of these domains vary with regard to the degree of structural change involved, making some less challenging to address than others. In addition, the ensuring representation domain includes two levels of representation: (a) the bureaucratically more powerful organizational leadership (i.e., organizational executives and boards of directors) and (b) the bureaucratically less powerful groups (i.e., community members, students, and staff). The following discussion looks at these domains and the related activities in the context of the racial composition of the executive leaders.

For 8 of the 14 racial equity activities listed in Table 5.5, organizational progress reported by respondents for each of the four steps did not vary with the racial composition of the executive team. These activities were processes for reviewing the extent to which organizational policies and procedures expressed a commitment to racial equity (#1, 2) and for assessing the racial equity status of admissions policies (#6) and orientation programs (#10), use of shared language (#12), reviewing the racial composition of the workforce (#5), and dealing with backlash (#13) and racial bias complaints (#14). The eight activities were also evenly distributed among all four of the racial equity domains, with two falling into each one: an organizational "commitment to racial equity" (#1, 2), "ensuring representation" (#5, 6), seeking to "deepen knowledge" (#10, 12), and "managing bias" (#13, 14). That is, for some activities in each of the four racial equity domains, the racial composition of the executive team did not affect organizational progress.

The racial composition of the organization's executive leaders was related to organizational progress toward racial equity in relation to six racial equity activities: #3, 4, 7, 8, 9, and 11. These six activities differed from the eight activities where race did not play a role in two ways. First, they fell into just two racial equity domains ("ensuring representation" and "deepening knowledge"), while the activities without racial variation fell into all four domains. Second, these six activities tended to address more structural organizational issues, such as increasing the racial representativeness of more powerful members of the organizational hierarchies (i.e., top leadership groups and boards of directors), developing new strategies for hiring and retaining staff of color, and formulating criteria to assess the capacity of staff to address racial equity issues.

To deepen this analysis, the following discussion focuses on two of these four organizational progress steps: "under discussion" and "stalled." "Under discussion" includes the planning stage and indicates that an organization considered the activity important and planned to act on it. "Stalled" refers to activities where no action had been taken. "Already in place" was explored in depth in Abramovitz and Blitz (2015). The "implemented" step was excluded because only a few respondents reported progress at this step.

Table 5.6 compares the percentage of responses for "under discussion" across racial composition groups. Having activities "under discussion" is an important first step to any organizational change. Where the majority of executives were

*Table 5.6* RACIAL EQUITY ACTIVITIES "UNDER DISCUSSION" AND "STALLED" BY RACIAL COMPOSITION OF EXECUTIVES

| Q # | RED | White | | People of Color | | Racially Diverse | | $X^2$ | df | Asymp signif |
|---|---|---|---|---|---|---|---|---|---|---|
| | | Discussion | Stalled | Discussion | Stalled | Discussion | Stalled | | | |
| 3 | ER | 21.1 | 15.8 | 9.7 | 12.9 | 11.1 | 7.4 | 17.31 | 8 | .027* |
| 4 | ER | 14.5 | 13.3 | 22.6 | 32.3 | 14.8 | 18.5 | 14.82 | 8 | .063+ |
| 7 | ER | 23.8 | 23.0 | 22.6 | 25.8 | 33.3 | 7.4 | 15.91 | 8 | .044* |
| 8 | ER | 19.5 | 16.7 | 12.9 | 22.6 | 18.5 | 7.4 | 17.42 | 8 | .026* |
| 9 | DK | 18.2 | 15.8 | 41.9 | 25.8 | 14.8 | 14.8 | 17.62 | 8 | .024* |
| 11 | DK | 20.5 | 25.0 | 26.7 | 16.7 | 14.8 | 14.8 | 15.03 | 8 | .059+ |

Racial equity domain: ER = ensuring representation; DK = deepening knowledge.
+ $p < .10$; * $p < .05$.

people of color, "under discussion" received the greatest number of responses for three activities. Two of these (#9, 11) focused on "deepening knowledge" and skills of their staff, and one (#4) focused on "ensuring representation" of the community/student advisory board. Where the majority of executives were white, "under discussion" received the greatest number of responses for two activities "ensuring representation" (#3, 8). Activity #3 addressed hiring a racially diverse staff, and activity #8 focused on ensuring that the members of the board of directors reflected the racial composition of the people served by the agency. Finally, where the executive groups were racially diverse, "under discussion" received the greatest number of responses for only one activity (#7), ensuring the racial representativeness of their executive leaders.

A racial divide appeared within the activities "under discussion." The three activities most frequently reported as "under discussion" for organizations led by executives of color sought to increase staff skills and knowledge rather than change structure. They also sought to ensure the representation of people in less powerful organization roles (staff and people served), perhaps because many of the leaders were already people of color. In contrast, the three activities most frequently "under discussion" at organizations led by white or racially diverse executives targeted the structural issue of staff hiring and sought more equitable representation of higher-level personnel (boards of directors and executive leaders).

Where the majority of leaders were people of color, "stalled" received the greatest number of responses for four activities (Table 5.6). Three of these "stalled" activities (#4, 7, 8) focused on "ensuring representation" on the board of directors, among the organization's executives, and on community/student advisory boards. One of the "stalled" activities (#9) sought to "deepen the knowledge" and skills of the staff. Where the majority of executives were white, "stalled" received the greatest number of responses for two activities (#3, 11). Activity #3 was directed at ensuring the representativeness of the staff, activity #11 to deepening the staff's knowledge about racial diversity. Where the executive groups were racially diverse, "stalled" did not receive the greatest number of responses for any activities.

## OTHER FACTORS ASSOCIATED
## WITH ORGANIZATIONAL PROGRESS

To understand variances by racial composition of the executive leaders and other factors that might contribute to organizational progress, it is important to consider contextual factors.

White executives were more likely to lead large organizations, followed by racially diverse leaders and executives of color (Table 5.7). While smaller organizations may be more flexible, they may also have more financial or other resource constraints, limiting their ability to risk structural change. Large organizations,

*Table 5.7* FACTORS CONSIDERED BY THE RACE OF THE MAJORITY
OF EXECUTIVE LEADERS

| Variable considered; % of responses shown; *n* for each in parenthesis | Primarily White | Primarily of Color | Diverse | $X^2$ | *df* | Asymp signif |
|---|---|---|---|---|---|---|
| Work in a small organization (1–100 staff) | 29.1 (127) | 67.7 (36) | 42.3 (22) | 40.17 | 6 | .000*** |
| Work in a medium organization (101–750) | 27.8 (121) | 25.9 (14) | 28.8 (15) | | | |
| Work in a large organization (751+ staff) | 33.0 (144) | 5.6 (3) | 29.6 (14) | | | |
| I attended other racial equity training | 44.5 (191) | 49.1 (27) | 57.7 (30) | 3.43 | 2 | .180 |
| I attended cultural competency training | 85.6 (370) | 90.7 (49) | 75.5 (40) | 5.35 | 2 | .069+ |
| I have attended two or more "Undoing Racism" workshops | 30.0 (131) | 34.5 (19) | 46.3 (25) | 5.99 | 2 | .050+ |
| In-house racial equity training provided | 57.9 (143) | 40.0 (12) | 65.4 (17) | 4.35 | 2 | .114 |
| External racial equity training support provided | 62.2 (153) | 36.7 (11) | 57.7 (15) | 7.25 | 2 | .027* |
| Engaged, but leaders resisted my efforts | 47.3 (150) | 40.0 (16) | 32.4 (12) | 3.45 | 2 | .179 |
| Engaged, but colleagues resisted | 53.5 (176) | 28.3 (13) | 41.5 (17) | 11.46 | 2 | .003** |
| I attended the workshop with coworkers | 69.1 (170) | 54.8 (17) | 63.0 (17) | 2.77 | 2 | .250 |
| The executive leader attended the workshop | 61.2 (128) | 60.0 (15) | 71.4 (15) | 0.89 | 2 | .642 |
| Coworkers attended the workshop prior to me | 73.9 (164) | 48.1 (13) | 56.5 (13) | 9.69 | 2 | .008** |

+ $p < .10$; * $p < .05$; ** $p < .01$; *** $p < .001$.

which may be more bureaucratic, may also have more resources to devote to racial equity work. Larger organizations also may have more resources to provide financial support for staff to attend racial equity trainings. Additionally, the white leaders in our study are often supervising and serving diverse groups, which may add to the motivation to understand and address racial issues.

Respondents' exposure to racial disparity trainings varied by their race. The type of training in which they participated also varied by the racial composition of the executives of their organization. Respondents who had attended a cultural competency training were more likely to work where the majority of executives were people of color (90.7%), followed by organizations with a majority of white executives (85.6%) and a racially diverse team (75.5%) (see Table 5.7). Respondents were more likely to have attended two or more of the explicitly antiracist workshops when their organizational leaders were racially diverse (46.3%) than where the majority were people of color (34.5%) or white (30%). Organizational support for training also varied by the racial composition of the executives. Organizations led by racially diverse teams were more likely to support in-house trainings (65.4%), followed by white executives (57.9%) and then executives of color (40%). Support for external racial equity trainings targeted at structural racism was more likely where the majority of the executives were white (62.2%), followed by racially diverse leadership (57.7%) and then executives of color (36.7%).

The response received from leaders and colleagues is important to a worker's ability to engage in racial equity work on the job. Similar to the findings that a respondent's view of organizational progress varied by his or her race, views about the organization's responsiveness to his or her work also varied by the racial composition of the executive team. Workshop alumni described their leaders' response to their racial equity work as "very" positive at organizations led by executives of color (46.3%), followed by racially diverse (39.6%) and white-led (32.6%) organizations (Table 5.8). However, more alumni reported leaders' response as only "somewhat" positive. This includes 52.8% of respondents employed at organizations with racially diverse leaders, followed by 49.8% led by white executives and 33.3% led by executives of color. A similar rating was obtained for the response from colleagues. "Very" positive responses from colleagues were reported

### Table 5.8 PERCEPTIONS AND EXPERIENCES BY RACIAL COMPOSITION OF EXECUTIVES

| Frequency of responses are shown in text | Primarily White ($n$) | Primarily of Color ($n$) | Diverse ($n$) | $X^2$ | $df$ | Asymp signif |
|---|---|---|---|---|---|---|
| Leaders' response was very or somewhat positive (vs. negative) | 430 | 54 | 53 | 12.80 | 6 | .046* |
| Response of colleagues was very or somewhat positive (vs. negative) | 432 | 55 | 53 | 10.33 | 6 | .111 |
| Leader feedback was none, very, or somewhat negative (vs. positive) | 220 | 27 | 27 | 20.77 | 8 | .008** |
| Progress was very successful, successful, or limited (vs. not at all successful) | 427 | 54 | 51 | 12.35 | 6 | .055+ |
| Looking forward, I feel very or somewhat hopeful (vs. discouraged about future) | 428 | 54 | 51 | 18.70 | 6 | .005** |

+ $p < .10$; * $p < .05$; ** $p < .01$.

most often by respondents at organizations led by executives of color (46.3%), followed by organizations with racially diverse leaders (37.7%) and then white leaders (27.8%). More respondents at white-led organizations (59.5%) stated that their colleagues had a "somewhat" positive response, as did 58.5% of those led by executives of color and 47.3% of those led by racially diverse teams.

Alumni reported on feedback in addition to general responses. The feedback from leaders was "very" positive in organizations where the majority of executives were people of color (70.4%) compared to 51.9% for those led by racially diverse executives and 35.5% for white-led organizations. Leaders were reported as providing only "somewhat" positive feedback by 43.2% of the respondents at organizations with white leaders, 29.6% of those with racially diverse leaders, and 11.1% of those with leaders who were people of color.

In general, "very" positive responses and feedback were more likely to be received from both leaders and colleagues when the respondent worked for executives of color, followed by racially diverse and then white executives. "Somewhat" positive responses and feedback were more likely in white-led organizations. As noted earlier, many respondents who became engaged in racial equity work faced resistance on the job. However, this was more common in organizations led by white executives (47.3%), followed by organizations led by executives of color (40%) and then racially diverse executives (32.4%) (see Table 5.7). Resistance by colleagues was also reported by 53.5% of respondents in organizations led by white executives, followed by those with racially diverse leaders (41.5%), and executives of color (28.3%).

Sharing the "Undoing Racism" workshop experience with others from the workplace offers support for racial equity work on the job, and most respondents benefitted from this kind of support. More than 70% of the alumni of color and 62.5% of the white alumni had attended a workshop with colleagues (see Table 5.2). More than 70% of the white respondents and 68% of the respondents of color had attended the workshop after coworkers had done so. Respondents were more likely to have attended the workshop with coworkers in white-led organizations (69.1%) than those led by racially diverse teams (63%) and those where the majority of executives were of color (54.8%) (see Table 5.7). Coworkers were more likely to precede respondents to the workshop in organizations led by white executives (73.9%), followed by organizations with racially diverse leaders (56.5%) and leaders of color (48.1%). A slightly higher proportion of alumni of color (66.7%) than white alumni (61.1%) worked at an organization where the top executive had attended the workshop. However, this experience varied with the racial composition of the executive teams. The top executives in organizations with racially diverse leadership were more likely to have attended the workshop (71.4%) than where the majority of the leaders were white (61.2%) or people of color (60%). In sum, while the numbers were generally high, workshop attendance by the respondent's executive leader and coworkers was least common at organizations led by executives of color.

Alumni reported their views of the success of their organization's effort to achieve racial equity as "very successful," "successful," or of "limited or no success." This assessment varied somewhat by the racial composition of the executive leaders. "Limited or no success" was reported by 56.9% of the organizations led by racially diverse leaders, 56.2% of the organizations led by white executives, and 44.4% of those led by executives of color (see Table 5.8; see Abramovitz & Blitz, 2015). Reports of "successful" efforts were lower and were more common among respondents working at organizations led by executives of color (35.2%) and racially diverse leaders (33.3%) than by white executives (26.0%). Finally, regardless of the racial composition of the executive leaders, less than 10% assessed their organization's racial equity effort as "very successful."

Despite this view of organizational progress to date, many respondents remained upbeat about the possibility of achieving racial equity in their organization in the future. The majority of white respondents and respondents of color were hopeful about the future of racial equity in their organization. Regardless of the racial composition of the executives, all respondents reported a high degree of hope for the future. However, differences by race were also seen (see Table 5.8). Over 86% of the respondents employed by organizations with racially diverse leaders felt "somewhat" or "very" hopeful about the future. The percentages were lower for organizations led by white executives (71.8%) and those led by executives of color (70.3%). Yet, about 80% of each group stated that the workshop had motivated them to support racial equity work in venues other than their job, without any differences based on the racial composition of the executive leaders (see Table 5.2).

## LIMITATIONS AND AREAS FOR FUTURE STUDY

The study has some limitations that are important to consider. The first relates to the sample. Although the response rate was average for online surveys, we do not know whether the people who responded were representative of all those who received the survey and/or all those who participated in the workshop. There is the potential for selection bias, since only attendees who provided their e-mail address and only those who were most motivated to complete a long online questionnaire participated. Additionally, procedural bias is a concern, as the online survey eliminated potential respondents who lacked Internet access. Other concerns relate to the survey instrument, which was developed locally and has not been validated by previous research. The Organizational Progress Index contained a high rate of "don't know/not applicable" responses; the reasons for this are not known. Finally, while respondents were asked whether they had engaged in racial equity activities after attending the workshop, we did not assess whether they had also engaged in these activities prior to taking the workshop, so we cannot know for certain whether workshop participation was a primary catalyst for action. The cross-sectional research does not allow for causal interpretations, so further study is needed to explain the causal impact of workshop attendance and to identify mediating and moderating variables related to racial equity work.

## DISCUSSION AND IMPLICATIONS

The variances by race shown here support the benefit of race-aware multicultural approaches, and the rejection of colorblind approaches, to organizational development. The racial composition of the agencies represented in this study reflects disturbing racial disparities seen throughout the nation. Although there are many organizations led by people of color in New York City, agencies represented by the survey respondents in this study tended to be led by and staffed by white people rather than people of color or racially diverse teams. Meanwhile, the majority of people served were people of color. These structural disparities increase the need to pay attention to race. For example, Constantine and Sue (2007) found that people of color often report experiences of racial microaggressions. This was mirrored in this study, which uncovered clear differences showing that respondents of color were more likely to keep a low profile on antiracist activities, feared getting into trouble at work, and had less access to decision makers. That half of both respondents of color and white respondents experienced resistance from colleagues also points to the need for organizations to find ways to engage all members in racial equity work that serves the entire institution (Stevens, Plaut, & Sanchez-Burks, 2008).

The racial composition of the leadership team also mattered. For example, the racial equity activities "under discussion" fell into two distinct categories: eight that did not vary by the racial composition of leaders and six that did. More activities were "under discussion" in organizations led by people of color, but more racial equity activities were also "stalled" in these organizations. White-led organizations were more likely to tackle the structural issues. More research is needed to better understand these findings, especially since it is well known that leaders of color face unique challenges and potential scrutiny (Melton, Walker, & Walker, 2010). Respondents from white-led organizations were more likely to have attended the workshop after coworkers and to attend with coworkers. However, they were also more likely to experience resistance and least likely to receive "very" positive responses from executives and colleagues. Despite these workplace realities, regardless of the respondent's race or the racial composition of the executive team, most alumni felt hopeful about achieving racial equity in the future.

## DISCUSSION QUESTIONS

1. What does this chapter identify as some of the primary barriers to organizational development designed to address racial equity? Why do those barriers persist?
2. The study found that more white people became engaged in racial equity work at their organization than people of color. What are your thoughts on why this may be true? Could this be an anomaly of this study's respondents? What other differences struck you as important or surprising?
3. What actions can an organization's leaders take to promote the optimal involvement of all staff in racial equity efforts?
4. The study concluded that race-aware multicultural approaches are more effective than colorblind approaches to organizational development. What are your thoughts on this? How could an organization's leaders promote race-aware multicultural organizational development?

## REFERENCES

Abramovitz, M., & Blitz, L.V. (2015). Moving toward racial equity: The Undoing Racism workshop and organizational change. *Race and Social Problems, 4*, 97–110. DOI 10.1007/s12552-015-9147-4

Aime, F., van Dyne, L., & V. Petrenko, O.V. (2011). Role innovation through employee social networks: The embedded nature of roles and their effect on job satisfaction and career success. *Organizational Psychology Review, 1*, 339–361.

Anti-Racist Alliance. (n.d.). http://www.antiracistalliance.com/

Apfelbaum, E. P., Norton, M. I., & Sommers, S. R. (2012). Racial color blindness: Emergence, practice, and implications. *Current Directions in Psychological Science, 21*, 205–209.

Bell, J. M., & Hartmann, D. (2007). Diversity in everyday discourse: The cultural ambiguities and consequences of "happy talk." *American Sociological Review, 72*(6), 895–912.

Bonilla-Silva, E., & Dietrich, D. (2011). The sweet enchantment of color-blind racism in Obamerica. *Annals of the American Academy of Political & Social Science, 634*, 190–206.

Buttner, E., Lowe, K., & Billings-Harris, L. (2012). An empirical test of diversity climate dimensionality and relative effects on employee of color outcomes. *Journal of Business Ethics, 110*(3), 247–258.

Carter, R. T., Oyler, C., & Goulding, C. (2013). *Experiencing Diversity Project integrated report 2013: The research team's final observations and conclusions.* Retrieved from: http://blogs.tc.columbia.edu/experiencingdiversity/files/2013/05/Final-integrated_Experiencing-Diversity-report.pdf

Choi, S., & Rainey, H. G. (2010, January/February). Managing diversity in U.S. federal agencies: Effects of diversity and diversity management on employee perceptions of organizational performance. *Public Administration Review,* 109–121.

Cocchiara, F. K., Connerley, M. L., & Bell, M. P. (2010). "A GEM" for increasing the effectiveness of diversity training. *Human Resource Management, 49*(6), 1089–1106.

Constantine, W. G., & Sue, D. W. (2007). Perceptions of racial microaggressions among black supervisees in cross-racial dyads. *Journal of Counseling Psychology. 54*(2), 142–153.

Curry-Stevens, A., & Nissen, L. B. (2011). Reclaiming futures considers an anti-oppressive frame to decrease disparities. *Children and Youth Services Review, 33*(S1), S54–S59.

Delgado, R., & Stefancic, J. (2001). *Critical race theory: An introduction.* New York: University Press.

Durr, M., & Harvey Wingfield, A. M. (2011). Keep your "N" in check: African American women and the interactive effects of etiquette and emotional labor. *Critical Sociology, 37,* 557–571.

Helms, J. E. (1995). An update of Helms' white and people of color racial identity models. In J. G. Ponteroto, J. M. Casas, L. A. Suzuki, & C. M. Alexander (Eds.), *Handbook of multicultural counseling* (pp. 181–198). Thousand Oaks, CA: Sage Publications.

Hultman, K., & Hultman, J. (2008). Deep teams: Leveraging the implicit organization. *Organization Development Journal, 26*(3), 11–22.

Hyde, C. A. (2004). Multicultural development in human services agencies: Challenges and solutions. *Social Work, 49*(1), 7–16.

Martín Alcázar, F., Romero Fernández, P. M., & Sánchez Gardey, G. (2013). Workforce diversity in strategic human resource management models: A critical review of the literature and implications for future research. *Cross Cultural Management, 20*(1), 39–49.

Mckay, P. F., Avery, D. R., Tonidandel, S., Morris, M. A., Hernandez, M. & Hebl, M. R. (2007). Racial differences in employee retention: Are diversity climate perceptions the key? *Personnel Psychology, 60,* 35–62.

Melton, E. K., Walker, M. B. L., & Walker, S. A. (2010). Management strategies and performance: An examination of minority managers in public organizations. *Economics, Management, and Financial Markets, 5*(3), 131–159.

Norton, M. I, & Sommers, S. R. (2011). Whites see racism as a zero-sum game that they are now losing. *Perspectives on Psychological Science, 6,* 215–218.

Plaut, V.C., Thomas, K.M, & Goren, M.J. (2009). Is multiculturalism or color blindness better for minorities? *Psychological Science, 20*(4), 444–446. DOI: 10.1111/j.1467-9280.2009.02318.x

Price, E. G., Gozu, A., Kern, D. E., Powe, N. R., Wand, G. S., Golden, S., & Cooper, L. A. (2005). The role of cultural diversity climate in recruitment, promotion, and retention of faculty in academic medicine. *Journal of General Internal Medicine, 20,* 565–571.

Sanchez-Hucles, J. V., & Davis, D. D. (2010). Women and women of color in leadership: Complexity, identity, and intersectionality. *American Psychologist, 65*(3), 171–181.

Stevens, F. G., Plaut, V. C., & Sanchez-Burks, J. (2008). Unlocking the benefits of diversity all-inclusive multiculturalism and positive organizational change. *Journal of Applied Behavioral Science, 44*(1), 116–133.

Thompson, C. E., & Carter, R. T. (2012) *Racial identity theory: Applications to individual, group, and organizational interventions.* New York: Routledge.

Triana, M. D. C., Fernanda Garcia, M., & Colella, A. (2010). Managing diversity: How organizational efforts to support diversity moderate the effects of perceived racial discrimination on affective commitment. *Personnel Psychology, 63,* 817–843.

# PART TWO

# Reshaping Theoretical and Practice Paradigms

# CHAPTER 6

# Deconstructing White Supremacy

REV. DAVID BILLINGS

## INTRODUCTION

Most professional educators obtain degrees, publish, and teach with little under-standing of how white supremacy affects our lives and work. Those of us who are white, while understanding vague notions of "white privilege," rarely delve deeply into the impact of centuries of white supremacy on our current lives. We do not recognize how we have internalized messages of "better than" over cen-turies, right up to the present. Often people of color, while daily experiencing the impact of white supremacy, frequently attribute it to individual acts and atti-tudes, not to historical forces and contemporary psychological realities of racism. Without exploring how white supremacy has embedded itself in our culture, in-stitutions, and psyches, our good intentions and efforts serve only to keep the racial construct of this nation in place.

This chapter analyzes how white supremacy manifests itself in white individu-als and institutions as *internalized racial superiority.* The importance of under-standing this internalized superiority is a fundamental principle of the People's Institute for Survival and Beyond (PISAB). PISAB is a 35-year-old national, mul-tiracial, antiracist collective of organizers and educators who are dedicated to building a movement for social transformation. The goal of the collective is to end racism and other forms of oppression. PISAB's vision is captured in the fol-lowing statement:

> We envision a world where traditionally poor communities of color are healthy, vi-brant, whole, peaceful and self-sufficient; where the internal strength by which they have survived is free from oppressive forces such as racism. We envision these com-munities, girded with a clear sense of their own power, sustaining a quality of life that

is far beyond survival. We envision them nurturing their cultures, preserving their history, and cultivating their economies. We envision these communities being in harmony with one another and with other segments of the global community.

Nine principles inform PISAB's teaching and organizing. Through our "Undoing Racism™/Community Organizing" workshops, we analyze and give language to these principles:

- analyzing power,
- defining racism,
- exploring its manifestations,
- learning from history,
- sharing culture,
- accepting our roles as gatekeepers,
- committing ourselves to be accountable to those communities most oppressed by racism,
- developing leadership, and
- recognizing the internalized manifestations of racial oppression.

This chapter explores how this last principle can inform antiracist practice paradigms in human services.

## ABOUT PISAB

PISAB has trained more than 500,000 people, across the nation and internationally, through its "Undoing Racism™/Community Organizing" workshop. While organizing grassroots communities has always been fundamental to building effective social movements, PISAB believes that *antiracist organizing* requires a commitment to its nine principles. PISAB does not believe that racism can be educated away, although education about the history of race/racism is very important. Racism is not dismantled through studying about racism (Chisom and Washington, 1997), although scholars can also be effective organizers. PISAB also does not believe that racism can be legislated away; however, legislation is often a vital outcome of effective antiracist work. Rather, PISAB believes that racism was originally *created* by Europeans and Anglo-Americans as a social/political/economic ideology to establish and maintain their power. We also believe that since it was "done," it can be "undone"—eradicated—when communities come together with a common vision, whether the community is a neighborhood, an institution, or a profession. History teaches that racism will be undone when the nation builds a movement to undo it. Social transformations abound in our nation's history: the abolitionist movement was essential to ending slavery; labor movements of the early 20th century helped bring human rights for workers; the civil rights movement of the 1950s and 1960s forced an end to legal Jim Crow. These movements were organized, constituencies were built, and structural power was confronted. Because we are students of history, we have hope for the future: PISAB is committed to building an antiracist movement that will end white supremacy and allow this nation to fulfill its vision "That all [people] are created equal."

PISAB organizers are community workers, social workers, ministers, teachers, government workers, and human service practitioners. As antiracist organizers, they have learned to be directed by communities of color that have been long oppressed by racism. They take their marching orders from organized community leadership. Some of this leadership is educated, even highly educated; however, it is not vetted by academicians or racial critical theorists. While formal education is important, PISAB organizers recognize that most people's educational experiences do not deal with racism, much less with how to undo it; too often, in fact, their education reinforces it. PISAB's cofounders, Ron Chisom and the late Dr. Jim Dunn, were veterans of the civil rights movement, one a professor, the other a community worker. PISAB's vision of an antiracist movement, rooted in its nine time-hewn principles and informed by the experiences of struggling communities, binds together diverse groups in this work to transform institutions and society. Its effectiveness grows as organizers gain experience in undoing racism with families, with associates, in school, wherever they confront structural oppression.

Human service work is frequently with and in communities of color. Yet professionals rarely know anything about the history of race, how it was constructed, and how much structural power it embodies. One of PISAB's early influences was Dr. Frances Cress Welsing, who quoted lay scholar Neely Fuller in the dedication of *The Isis Papers: The Keys to the Colors* (1991): "If you do not understand White Supremacy (Racism)—what it is and how it works—everything *else* that you understand, will only confuse you." This was PISAB's mantra and still is.

PISAB asks, How did racism take such a foothold in the United States? What forms does it take today? PISAB studies white supremacy as a crucial factor in society today, especially in the nation's institutions and structures. How else can we explain the dramatic disparities between whites and black/brown people that exist in every institutional outcome in the United States? How else to understand why, by every measure of "quality of life," people of color fare less well and whites fare better? Are people of color less intelligent than whites? If the answer to this question is "No," then, asserts PISAB, we must look to the structural/institutional realities that continue to produce these startling disparate results.

## THE HISTORICAL ROOTS OF WHITE SUPREMACY

From the very outset of European efforts to control and exploit non-European parts of the world, dating from at least the last decades of the 15th century by

Portugal and Spain, policies and practices reflected assumptions about the superiority of European nations. An ideology was required to justify colonization, imperialism, the genocide of indigenous peoples of the "new world," and the enslavement of Africans. Color differentiation became a primary justification: whites being "naturally" superior to people of color became the norm and an entrenched belief system. Using such cultural manifestations as the Hebrew Bible and especially the Christian New Testament, Europe cloaked its imperial ambitions with dualisms of good versus evil, civilized versus savage, and believer versus heathen. In North America, Christian became synonymous with white people and heathen or savage with Indians and "Negroes." By the mid-18th century, such dichotomies were institutionalized and justified by a so-called scientific race theory of white supremacy. Racial polarization took on pseudoscientific trappings, with white people or "Caucasoids" said to be imbued with superior intelligence, morality, and beauty, and African people or "Negroids" designated as lesser beings devoid of traits of more civilized societies.

Today, the white supremacist ideology manifests itself in such dichotomies as Western civilization symbolizing human, technological, and cultural advancement. Because of a Western propensity to understand the world in terms of opposites, if Western civilization is best, all other peoples and nations are seen as less advanced, underdeveloped, and primitive. The scholar Winthrop Jordan, in his classic work *White Over Black* (1968), describes how white supremacy began in Northern European nations, took root in the "new world," and was codified by the United States. Indeed, as Higgenbotham (1978), Haney Lopez (1996), and Katznelson (2005) demonstrate, it was in the English colonies, later organized as the United States, that laws were passed to ensure that white supremacy would endure. This ideology, backed up by the hegemony of Western powers, led to a world order of haves and have-nots based on military force and economic exploitation. Just as important, the white supremacist ideology gave whites a sense of moral and cultural superiority. This twisted worldview has been internalized through white national hegemony so that white people understand themselves as representing all that is "normal" and "better than"—therefore, people of color represent inferiority and "less-than" minority status. (Thus today's curious "majority minority" phrase: people of color in the United States are always less than, even when they represent a numerical majority.) Thomas Gossett's great work *Race: The History of an Idea in America* (1963) and Ashley Montagu's *Man's Most Dangerous Myth: The Fallacy of Race* (1942, 1997) were among the earliest to describe how the myth of white supremacy wove its way into the entire U.S. culture: from popular magazines to literature, in science and theology, from the academy to the White House, white supremacy was preached and affirmed. *Everyone* "knew" white people were better. Only in the 1930s and 1940s, with Nazism demonstrating the logical outcome of "scientific" racism, did this nation's leaders begin to question white supremacy.

Centuries after legalized racism had seeped into the cultural DNA of the United States, Jim Crow laws were outlawed in the 1960s. Yet white supremacy remains: the institutions and structures of our nation, created by and for people who thought their ideas and worldviews were best, did not simply transform themselves after racial discrimination was outlawed. Rather, overt white supremacy became politically unacceptable, replaced by an even more pernicious ideology: colorblindness. Since the laws no longer sanction racism, it must be gone. Today, it is no longer culturally acceptable to espouse white supremacy, yet the institutions continue to function with the values and beliefs of their creators. People of color may enter, and sometimes flourish in, these institutions, but they remain virtually monocultural. Try as the nation might to remedy racial inequities, they stubbornly persist, sometimes more than before. According to Tim Wise (*Colorblind*, 2010), urgent institutional pressures oppress African Americans and other communities of color in virtually all domains of the health and human services as well as in housing, business, prisons, and schools. Despite the tremendous accomplishments and impressive strides blacks and other marginalized groups have made since the 1960s, the systems of the United States continue to produce outcomes drastically skewed against them. For example, recent findings from the Pew Research Center (August 2013) show that by 2011, black household wealth was 7% that of white households and Latino/Hispanic household wealth was 9% that of white households, a wealth gap that has *widened* since 1984. These outcomes for people of color are predictable: the institutions are doing what they were intended to do.

Despite these telling and persistent disparities, there continues to be a lack of consensus among Americans about the significance of race in the United States. Indeed, the notion of affirmative action for people of color is contested at every turn, despite the 350 years of "affirmative action for white people," as Ira Katznelson (2005) describes so well.

To colorblind theorists and practitioners, using race to explain outcomes is an excuse for personal deficiencies and personal lack of ambition and fortitude. The result of this new understanding of racism is that the words *race* and *racism* are no longer acceptable. Those who use them are "stuck in the past" or "using the race card." Yet, as Ian Haney Lopez demonstrates in his brilliant study of racism in the post–civil rights era (*Dog Whistle Politics*, 2014), policymakers, academicians, industry chief executive officers, politicians, courts, and nonprofit organizations all treat racial disparities as individual traits rather than structural deficiencies.

Whether in the educational system, where it is well documented that black and Latino children suffer in overly regimented and underfunded schools, or in the criminal justice system, with its profiling, police brutality, and sentencing disparities, the results are as predictable in Arkansas as in New York. Further, despite the Supreme Court's *Brown v. Topeka* decision enacted 60 years ago that outlawed segregation in public schools, America's public school systems are more segregated today than they were in 1960, largely due to housing segregation and entrenched poverty in communities densely populated by black and Latino families (Rothstein, 2013).

These institutional disparities have implications for the well-being of people of color and account in part for their high visibility in the health and human services population. These discrepancies are also reflected in the prison system, where according to a December 6, 2006, report by the U.S. Department of Justice, more than half of all prison and jail inmates were found to have a mental health problem (Glaze and James, 2006). Moreover, as Michelle Alexander demonstrates, systemic racial inequalities account for the overrepresentation of males of color in the prison system and for the United States having a higher mass incarceration rate than all other Western industrialized societies combined (Alexander, 2010).

If we are to challenge these structural inequities and transform health and human services, educators and practitioners must examine the roots of historical and structural racism in this country and analyze the persistence of ethnic and racial disparities across all domains.

## THE "UNDOING RACISM" WORKSHOP

The "Undoing Racism™/Community Organizing" workshop is the primary tool offered by PISAB for deconstructing racism in the health and human services system. The process of the workshop is crucial: it permits everyone in the room (all seated in one circle, when possible) to feel a sense of worth that their ideas and experiences matter. The goal of the workshop is for participants to glimpse the possibility that they are—or can be—part of a movement to transform unjust institutions. Trainers emphasize the urgency of the task of undoing racism. They explain that racism is part of our everyday experiences and that it affects every one of us. They explain that race is not just another issue; it is the major force throughout modern history that has divided movements for justice and equity. They invite participants to become part of an antiracist, multiracial movement to build a society in which all people "are healthy, vibrant, whole, peaceful and self-sufficient" (PISAB Vision Statement). PISAB believes such a movement is worthy and possible. It arises out of communities where people have gained a sense of their own power.

To the question of "why an 'Undoing Racism™/Community Organizing' workshop?" the trainers explain that people in this country are rarely educated to promote social change. Therefore, we need to reeducate ourselves, to think and act collectively, to have a common language for movement building. PISAB's workshops prepare people for mutual accountability, not to certify individuals to "do their own thing." Trainers promise that the workshop can be part of a lifelong journey. When we know that racism has been "done," we can organize to undo it.

PISAB trainers are all organizers, doing antiracist work within their own neighborhoods, professions, families, and faith communities. PISAB has 65 trainers (25 core trainers)—white, Native American, African American, Latino, Asian/Pacific Islander. It also has resource trainers who bring special experience and perspectives to workshops. The organization is headquartered in New Orleans, with offices in Seattle, Duluth, and New York and organizing committees in Houston, Atlanta, Springfield (MA), Greensboro (NC), Albuquerque, Portland (OR), Westchester County, NY, and Alaska. PISAB offers workshops wherever and whenever it is invited—in every state and all communities, rural or urban, indigenous nations, prisons, city halls, and boardrooms. PISAB trainers have worked in many countries, including South Africa, England, Japan, Central America, Ireland, and India. The majority of its revenue comes from fees for service.

A contract with participants guides the workshop and includes these expectations:

- Stay the whole time; don't come in and out.
- Listen to one another; respect one another's experiences and perspectives.
- Understand this is a liberated zone. Say what you have to say in the group; what's said here stays here. This is a safe space—even if it becomes uncomfortable at times.
- Struggle together; don't be afraid to ask questions.
- Don't blame the messengers (especially if you were mandated to attend).
- Expect to be enriched—accept that the workshop is for me.
- Participate; this is not a space to observe.
- Be flexible. Stand, sit, take breaks as needed.
- Stay with the process even when you are uncomfortable. This may be a place of resistance, and staying with the process, pushing through this growing edge, may result in new insights, understandings, "aha moments."
- There is no quick fix. Racism has been around for hundreds of years; it won't be "undone" in a couple of days.
- Disconnect from electronics.
- If you are confused about some language or an acronym being used, ask for a "literacy moment." You probably aren't the only confused one.

These guidelines shape the conversation in the workshop, enabling both white people and people of color to "get real" and share honestly with one another. Just as important, the contract offers effective strategies for building authentic relationships, whether at home, at work, or in a community. Workshop participants take a lot of time to introduce themselves, answering questions such as, "Who are you?" "What do you do?" "Why do you think it is important for you and for your organization to deal with racism?" PISAB believes that telling about ourselves is

important to effective organizing, since stories help us see one another's humanity and help us reflect on our own values and preconceptions.

The next workshop activity is the "Nine-Dot Exercise," in which participants
try to connect nine dots with four straight lines without lifting their pen or pencil
from the paper. This exercise dramatizes how we are all "boxed in" when it comes
to race—we are all socialized to see things certain ways. Our institutions are
boxed in by policies, structures, history, resources, time; individuals are boxed in
by fear, ignorance, denial, shame, worldviews.

"Why Are People Poor?" is an exercise that helps us understand how we are
socialized to think of "poor" as black/brown. Poverty has been racialized in the
United States. Although there are more poor white people than poor people of
color in this country, it is advantageous to the maintenance of inequitable systems
for white people not to identify with poverty. By using "single black mother" as the
face of poverty, white people feel distant from (black) poverty, and thus they are not
willing to build alliances across racial lines to combat poverty. In the United States,
mainstream media and schools teach us to distance ourselves from poor people
and to blame them for their poverty, even if we come from poor families ourselves.
PISAB believes that no one has the right to work with poor people or on their behalf
unless we understand the structural arrangements that keep them poor.

The "Undoing Racism™/Community Organizing" workshop focuses on
structural power: what it is, who has it, who doesn't have it, and why. Through
a series of questions and answers, workshop participants gain insight into
how institutions in this country are structured to disempower poor communities, particularly communities of color, and to benefit from their continued
existence. Participants confront their own role as gatekeepers—keepers of the
status quo—in this oppressive system. Then they explore strategies to become
accountable to those communities most oppressed by racism. PISAB's analysis
lets no one off the hook: all are part of the structural arrangement that keeps
racism in place.

PISAB's analysis of power is foundational to its understanding of racism,
which is defined as *race prejudice plus power*. Through an overview of the history
of racism, with its internalized messages of white supremacy, workshop participants learn how these racially constructed systems were built. They are challenged, finally, to become organizers in the movement to transform them.

## INTEGRATION OF "UNDOING RACISM™" PRINCIPLES IN PROFESSIONAL EDUCATION

A number of the New York City metropolitan schools of social work, as well as
the New York City chapter of the National Association of Social Workers, have
integrated PISAB principles into their course curricula and program initiatives.
Schools of social work that have adopted the "Undoing Racism™" principles

include Binghamton University School of Social Work, the State University of New York at Stony Brook, Fordham University Graduate School of Social Service, Hunter College's Silberman School of Social Work, and the New York University Silver School of Social Work. The goal of these schools is not only to prepare students to better understand the communities their constituencies often represent, but to influence other curricula being offered to prospective social workers at these same schools. In addition to schools of social work, the National Association of Social Work in Washington, DC, declared in 2013 that "Undoing Racism™" is a priority in all future strategic plans. As of January 2014 over 8,000 health and human service professionals, educators, and activists in the area have participated in the "Undoing Racism™" workshop.

## CONCLUSION

Deconstructing white supremacy is essential to transforming human services practice paradigms so that they are antiracist. A first step is to acknowledge that because our profession does not require knowledge of white supremacy, few professionals are so equipped. When we take that step, we become students— learners—who must listen to those most oppressed by racism. We must organize together. Yet collaborative work requires trusting relationships. In a race-constructed society, cross-racial relationships are fraught with centuries of inauthenticity.

PISAB offers a language so we can have honest conversations. We will make mistakes; how could we not? As we persist on this antiracist journey, our vision will become clearer, our words and acts more courageous. Our profession will be transformed.

## DISCUSSION QUESTIONS

1. How should this quote be understood in the helping professions: "If you do not understand White Supremacy (Racism)—what it is and how it works— everything else that you understand, will only confuse you"?
2. Is the role of history in human services merely to inform us of the past, or does it have influence as we look to the future?

## REFERENCES

Alexander, M. (2010). *The new Jim Crow: Mass incarceration in the age of colorblindness.* New York: The New Press.

Chisom, R., & Washington, M. (1997). *Undoing racism: A philosophy of international social change.* New Orleans: People's Institute Press.

Gossett, T. (1963, 1997). *Race: The history of an idea in America.* New York: Oxford University Press.

Haney Lopez, I. (1996, 2006). *White by law: The legal construction of race.* New York: New York University Press.

Haney Lopez, I. (2014). *Dog-whistle politics: How coded racial appeals have reinvented racism and wrecked the middle class.* New York: Oxford University Press.

Jordan, W. (1968). *White over black: American attitudes toward the Negro 1550–1812.* Chapel Hill: University of North Carolina Press.

Katznelson, I. (2005). *When affirmative action was white: An untold history of racial inequality in twentieth-century America.* New York: W.W. Norton & Co.

Montagu, A. (1942, 1997). *Man's most dangerous myth: The fallacy of race.* Lanham, MD: Rowman & Littlefield.

Pew Research Center. (2013, August). *Race in America: Tracking 50 years of demographic trends.* Washington, DC.

Rothstein, R. (2013, August 27). *For public schools, segregation then, segregation since: Education and the unfinished march.* Washington, DC: Economic Policy Institute.

Glaze, L., & James, D. (2006, July 6). *Mental health problems of prison and jail inmates.* Bureau of Justice Statistics, Washington, DC: U.S. Department of Justice, NCJ213600.

Welsing, F. C. (1991). *The Isis papers: The keys to the colors.* Chicago: Third World Press.

Wise, T. (2010). *Colorblind: The rise of post-racial politics and the retreat from racial equity.* San Francisco: City Lights Books.

Zinn, H. (1980, 2003). *A people's history of the United States.* New York: HarperCollins.

# CHAPTER 7

# Theoretical Perspectives for Transformation

## JEANNE BERTRAND FINCH

## INTRODUCTION

The work of justice requires ongoing consideration of existing barriers that impede achieving aspirations of individual and social well-being. This work is often made more difficult due to the complex and shifting terrain involved. In particular, the often emotionally laden issues associated with issues of social justice and racism require the help of theoretical frameworks to steer our responses and to act as a compass for a way forward. (Powers & Faden, 2006; Reisch, 2011). Theoretical frameworks guide our efforts to meet the challenge of achieving social justice; they aid our examination of the world and help make sense of our experience. They clarify how behavior evolves and change occurs. Moreover, these frameworks provide a rational approach for conducting an analysis of power imbalances. Within this context, theories help explain and predict behavior; they focus our responses and channel future enquiry. Theories also help elucidate principles regarding how and to whom resources are distributed; what obligations and entitlements exist regarding these resources; how practices surrounding implementation are conceived and realized; what role conflict plays; and under what conditions injustice is accepted and perpetuated (Payne, 2014; Robbins, Chatterjee, & Canda, 2012; Turner, 2011). With these concerns in mind, this chapter addresses theoretical perspectives that provide a targeted focus to aid our task for social transformation. This aim supports the purposes of this text in providing insights regarding service perspectives that guide the work of uncovering underlying barriers to achieve the change needed in undoing racism.

## USING CRITICAL SOCIAL THEORETICAL PERSPECTIVES TO PROMOTE ANTIRACIST PRACTICE: SETTING THE STAGE AND A CALL FOR ACTION

Postmodern critical social theory constructs a way of thinking about the world and questioning how knowledge evolves. It includes consideration of how knowledge is created; the role of language as a powerful expression of the dominant ideology; the roles of history and context; and the importance of social interactions to achieve change (Payne, 2014; Wulff, 2011). A fixed positivist stance is abandoned for an understanding that multiple views and truths are pertinent to lived experience. A humanistic approach to difference acts as a corrective to empiricism and a deficit approach that overly pathologizes divergence and perspectives of diversity. As such, within critical social theories all views are important and provide a valid perspective on the meaning of lived experience (Agger, 1998; Fook, 2008; Kohi, Huber, & Faul, 2010; Mullaly, 2007; Ortiz & Jani, 2010; Wulff, 2011). These perspectives set the stage for understanding social change and, just as importantly, incorporate a commitment and call for action. The act of attempting to understand the world is begun to promote action toward transformation (Agger, 1992, 1998).

## COMMON ELEMENTS OF ANTI-OPPRESSIVE THEORETICAL FRAMEWORKS

Agger (1998) presents shared assumptions of postmodern critical social theories as a means to identify common principles. Defining features include endorsing the following:

- Knowledge as socially constructed and not value-free; doubt whether objective truth can ever be captured; and opposition to positivism and reliance on testable, empirical truth (Fook, 2008; Love & Estanek, 2004; Robbins et al., 2012; Wulff, 2011)
- The possibility of progress as intricately linked and affected by both context and history; concepts of stability, predictability, and controllability yielding to an understanding that the world is at the same time complex, unpredictable, and interconnected; and change as a continuous feature of reality
- Hope for progress as an inherent product of change
- The path to social change exists through everyday occurrences, through increased awareness of the conditions that determine them, and through believing in people's individual agency and power to effect change. Yet, personal liberation is not adequate on its own, nor is it the sole aim of transformation. To be effective, evolution and change are required on both individual and societal levels; one is connected to the other (Agger, 1992).

Postmodern perspectives and critical social theories provide vital and practical frameworks that set the stage for the pursuit of change. Under this umbrella, a number of anti-oppressive theoretical and practice approaches emerge; their development and range have been described by several authors (cf. Allan, Pease & Briskman, 2009; Ashcroft, Griffiths & Tiffin, 2007; Baines, 2007; Dalrymple & Burke, 1995; Dominelli & McLeod, 1989; Fook, 2008; Leonard, 2001; Marchant & Wearing, 1986; Moreau, 1979; Mullaly, 2002, 2007; Payne, 2014; Robbins et al., 2012; Shera, 2003; Turner, 2011). However, these authors use different means for grouping the approaches; distinctions are often blurred by the many shared principles and the lack of explicated preferred applications. Interestingly, often missing within these anthologies, and of particular interest here, is critical race theory, which provides a clear focus for the work of undoing racism (Crenshaw, 2011; Delgado, 1995a, 1995b; Delgado & Stefancic, 2001).

Although anti-oppressive practice approaches take a somewhat different focus, they share common elements. Each places emphasis on understanding power and oppression and on divisions created by structural inequalities (Dominelli, 2002). Each proposes that change strategies are required at multiple levels. Becoming aware of how experiences of domination are individualized is stressed. This stance includes attempts to eliminate the potential negative impact of professional power that separates those who serve from users of service. Proponents of these approaches recognize the interconnections between the oppressor and the oppressed. They see domination as pervasive, accepted as normal, and often invisible. Uncovering underlying ideologies and operating assumptions is the key to understanding how social structures perpetuate social injustice. They propose that we create our own meanings and institutions, and therefore, that the possibility for a more just society is within our reach. Ways to create opportunities to develop increased awareness of these processes is achieved through a person-centered philosophy and egalitarian values. Mutuality, collaboration, and partnership characterize working relationships with those served. A call to action and a belief in the potential for transformation are endemic (Agger, 1998; Allan, 2009; Dominelli, 2008; Fook, 2008; Payne, 2014).

Certain concepts are embedded within these commonalities. These include social construction, notions of power, and how social identities are formed and maintained. A brief consideration of these concepts is provided below.

## SOCIAL CONSTRUCTION

Social construction is the process that accounts for individualized knowledge building; this is how we make sense of our lived experience and explains the meanings we attach to these events (cf. Berger and Luckmann, 1966; Gergen, 1985, 2009; Park, 2010). Knowledge, views, and beliefs are formed by our experiences and the way we interpret their meanings. Additionally, our views of reality are affected by history, culture, and economic context (Sahin, 2006). Contextual, interpretive, relational, and multiple views are the currency of importance; they shape our sense of ourselves and our worlds. Further, culture is shaped by our daily dealings and interactions with others (Gemignani & Pena, 2007). This process accounts for the multiple ways different individuals may respond to a similar experience and how certain groups of individuals may see the world differently from other groups. It is in these individualized frames of reference that historically underrepresented group voices and experiences become heard and given credence (Wulff, 2011).

## POWER AND SOCIALLY CONSTRUCTED REALITIES

Constructions are power-based (Foucault, 1988, 1999). This means that the way we form our realities is influenced by both social and political forces (Gemignani & Pena, 2007). This occurs both by accepting the cultural forces surrounding us and by questioning them. This interaction supports a sense of hope in our power to rewrite our stories and narratives—a direct means to affect antiracist thinking and redefine our social worlds. Power is not only lodged in large social structures and therefore outside of interpersonal relations, but it is also an integral part of our everyday interactions with others. Power is not just something possessed and something we are subjected to. It is present within each of us, is an available resource for our use, and is part of our relations with others (Foucault, 1988, 1999; Tew, 2006). This understanding is essential for work that aims to combat powerlessness within both large and more local systems of interaction and social operation.

## SOCIAL CONSTRUCTION AND SOCIAL IDENTITIES

As we construct our understanding of the world through lived experiences, these realities further shape what we expect to happen. These expectations are confirmed or challenged through our interactions with others and our experiences of the world. It is from these meaning making experiences that we establish our beliefs, goals, and subjective feelings (Park, 2010). How we construct our social worlds directly affects our social identities—that is, how and where we are socially located will influence how we are seen and how we see ourselves. The process is dynamic and entwined. Often we conform to the realities before us without questioning operating ideologies and their implicit underlying assumptions.

"Once a ruling idea (ideology) is normalized, it becomes common sense (as opposed to good sense), and is held, not only by the oppressors, but also by the mass of population (Gramsci, 1971). This is hegemony" (Armstrong & Ng, 2005, p. 43). Learned and internalized through socialization, this knowledge becomes part of how we interpret the world, our place within it, and what we expect to occur next.

If our expectations are not confirmed, the discrepancy between how we assess the event and our existing understanding creates a potentially stressful response to which resolution is sought (Agger, 1998; Blundo, 2001; Park, 2010; Robbins, et al., 2010). We normally seek explanations within the frames we have available to us; but the possibility for change may also occur at these junctures (Taylor, 2008). In Mezirow's (1997) terms, the possibility of a perspective transformation occurs.

This process creates possibilities and limitations for how we and our assumptions evolve. It accounts for the power of education to increase awareness and avert false consciousness, and it explains how critical consciousness is achieved through praxis—that is, connecting theory to practice, reflecting in and on action, and informing the ongoing development of theory (Friere, 1990; Freire & Macedo, 2000; Schön, 1983). The tenets described posit that we are not only products, but also creators and re-creators of the structures and conventions by which we live (Payne, 2014). Social interactions are potent determinants of the constructions we create, including those involving disadvantage or unearned privilege. "Human beings do not invent themselves in a vacuum, and society cannot be made unless people create it together" (Shor, 1992, p. 16). We are all capable of shaping our history (Freire, 1990) and, by implication, of shaping the future of antiracist thinking for ourselves and others. A call to action is central.

Challenges exist. For example, in applying our understanding of social constructions, we see that racial oppression involves endowing a group with characteristics or qualities that are shaped by cultural beliefs and assumptions "based on historical, contextual or other social considerations" (Ford & Airhihenbuwa, 2010, p. 31). Therefore, racism is not static; our ideas of race, racism, and antiracism change as our individual and social understanding evolve (Lee & Lutz, 2005). These new forms and contexts require evolving approaches.

A framework for analyzing structural issues of inequality and privilege—understanding social institutions and systems, and individual and group behaviors—requires supports at multiple levels. That is, if change strategies aimed at rupturing structural racism remain disproportionately designed for individual and interpersonal levels without attention to the larger social forces involved (or vice versa), efforts toward change remain limited. This is because efforts for change remain restricted by the lack of attention paid to the inherent forces exerting influence to maintain the status quo at one or another level of focus (Wildman & Davis, 1995). These elements are particularly crucial for work that attempts to untangle and confront existing dominant conceptions of race, racism, and power. Pervasive and persistent racist ideology requires change strategies targeted at individual thinking and behavior, and at the institutionalized social structures where these ideologies are embedded.

## CRITICAL RACE THEORY: HOW DOES A FOCUS ON RACE AID OUR EFFORTS?

Debates in the literature exist regarding the efficacy of focusing on one or another of the multiple ways oppression expresses itself in society. Critiques suggest that choosing one form of oppression over another creates a hierarchy of oppressions, splits the potential for coalition building, and ignores the vibrant interconnections between and among the various ways oppression is experienced (Constance-Huggins, 2012; Mullaly, 2010; Orelus, 2012). Likewise, equalizing all oppressions ignores the reality that domination differs in its effects and in the depth of the humiliation experienced (Schiele, 2007). Others suggest that bringing race to the foreground and underscoring its importance in debates about health and educational disparities, housing inequalities, and unemployment demographics gives appropriate attention to the realities of race as a factor in injustice (Ladson-Billings, 2011). The lack of such a specific focus is equated to taking a position of neutrality toward issues of race that, in turn, perpetuates inequality (Crenshaw, 1995; Delgado, 1995a; Ladson-Billings, 2011; Lavoie, 2012; Treviño, Harris & Wallace, 2008; Yosso, 2005). Critical race theory posits that critical theory without a focus on race and power is insufficient to undertake social transformation. Proponents challenge the presumed liberatory principle that "blindness" to race will eradicate racism. Instead, it is argued that the special focus on race spotlights blind spots connected to inequality and injustice linked to racism.

Critical race theory emerged as a powerful theoretical tool in the mid-1970s from the work of Derek Bell in response to the slow pace of racial social reforms (Crenshaw, 2002; Delgado, 1995a; Lipsitz, 2011). Based within the legal profession, it stood apart from critical legal studies, feminism, and other emerging critical theories by focusing on the complex ways that the social construction of race and the resulting racism affect our daily lives (Yosso, 2005). An emphasis was placed on understanding the institutionalization of oppression and on examining how the ideals of "the rule of law" and "equal protection" are affected by the racism embedded within our legal structures (Crenshaw, Gotanda, Peller, & Thomas, 1995).

The proponents of critical race theory were sparked by the stark reality that the social advances achieved by the civil rights movement were met with continuing (different but similar) challenges for equality. Even as "whites only" signs were disappearing, prejudice based on skin color persisted in more covert ways

(Lipsitz, 2011). The advances made were insufficient to stop patterns of power and continued privileges and burdens experienced across racial lines. "As the struggles over racial justice moved from buses and lunch counters to the gates of power and the logics that underwrote them, the 'sturdy structure' of racial hierarchy became increasingly evident" (Crenshaw, 2011, p. 1277). In the tradition of critical social theories, the examination and illumination of these conditions served as a start to breaking them apart.

## APPLICATIONS IN HEALTH
## AND HUMAN SERVICES

The core tenets of critical race theory posit that race is a social construction and that racism is widespread and embedded within the core structures of our culture. Racism permeates all aspects of social life (Ortiz & Jani, 2010). Therefore, it is often invisible and normalized. It results in a race-based ideology that determines who is considered in favor or out of favor at different times and in different contexts (Constance-Huggins, 2012). Further, critical race theory "asserts that human actions cannot be separated from the institutional arrangements of society" (Ortiz & Jani, 2010, p. 180). Although racism is rooted in a web of domination and subordination in which we all play a part, racism is not an individual matter (Valdes, Culp, & Harris, 2002). Allowing racism to rest on an individual level ignores the larger social system in which the individual is situated. It obscures the social support that perpetuates this ideology and behavior, and this obstruction thereby absolves the larger system from its role in shaping individual behavior (Wildman & Davis, 1995).

All forms of oppression or injustice, including sexism, ageism, homophobia, and economic exploitation, must be included in any attempt to address racism. Failing to account for these multidimensional and intersectional aspects of our identities potentially limits the discourse to a bifurcation of white versus black. This bifurcation constrains understanding of the varied configurations of discrimination and our responses to them. Therefore, the focus on race cannot ignore the reality that other social factors and oppressions are interrelated with race; instead, the issue is to place race in the foreground (Crenshaw, 1995; Ladson-Billings, 2011).

Critical race theory aims to transform the relationships among race, racism, and power (Delgado, 1995a; Delgado & Stefancic, 2001). It also seeks to expose "the mechanisms and structures that actually disadvantage people, even those ostensibly designed by social institutions to serve the needy" (Ortiz & Jani, 2010, p. 183). The complex nature of power and how it is implemented through encounters between users of service and welfare institutions is examined through this lens.

In summary, critical race theory seeks to expose principles that represent social exclusion and to identify tools for transformation by focusing on the experiences of those who are on the margins of society. It posits that because constructions of race and racism are normalized and accepted as "just the way things are," critical consciousness is required to bring race to the forefront of discourse and to uncover biases and develop understanding of the underlying assumptions embedded within the social order. The dominant ideology of a deficit perspective to race is disputed; instead, racial identities are seen as sources of strength for fulfillment and policymaking (Yosso, 2005).

Critical race theory provides theoretical support for transforming our understanding of the current context of racial injustice, and the resulting insight provides guidance for effecting change. Knowledge flows from a combination of ways of knowing, including theory, research, and personal experiences and practice; just as importantly, these various ways of knowing interact and inform each other (Delagdo & Stefancic, 2001; Ford & Airhihenbuwa, 2010; Ortiz & Jani, 2010). Emerging understanding is linked directly to change of the very social situations under examination. Understanding provides a means of shifting what is seen as an individual problem to one that is recognized as social and systemic. Critical race theory stipulates that a "call to context" provides a strategy and route to the achievement of civil rights by paying close attention to the details and realities that affect otherwise general principles (Delgado, 1995a). The purpose of this strategy is expressed as not merely for improved understanding, but also for change.

## COMPONENTS OF CRITICAL RACE THEORY TO FRAME OUR WORK: CRITICAL PERSPECTIVES, INTERSECTIONALITY, STORYTELLING, AND EGALITARIAN APPROACHES TO BUILDING RELATIONSHIPS

Establishing a critical perspective, intersectionality, storytelling, and egalitarian approaches to building relationships are embedded within critical race theory. Although not unique to this theory, they are directly connected to the tenets of critical race theory and highlighted within the literature (cf. Delgado, 1995a, 1995b; Delgado & Stefancic, 2001). Combined, they provide a powerful perspective for practice. For example, a stance of critical reflection on social and personal processes of power sets the foundation for the elimination of domination and the creation of emancipatory and egalitarian relationships in which dialog and collaboration may flourish. Recognizing the influences of storytelling and intersectionality within these relationships provides paths toward undoing racism on multiple levels. Each approach stands as a powerful construct for practice, and they combine to form potent means toward change. A summary of each follows.

## A Critical Stance to Understanding Race, Power, and Inequality

Fook and Gardner (2007) define critical reflection as "a process (and theory) for unearthing individually held social assumptions in order to make changes in the social world. It involves a deeper look at the premises on which thinking, actions and emotions are based. It is critical when connections are made between these assumptions and the social world as a basis for changed actions" (p. 14). This belief is broader than that of being self-aware or being open to others; it includes a social justice agenda. Just as importantly, a critical stance facilitates the ability to refute assumptions and to explore explanations that counter the dominant ideology of who benefits and who suffers. In this way, a critical stance informs our technique by helping us pose central questions to assess the conditions that produce inequality and oppression and to identify the barriers that exist for some to access resources. For instance, developing a critical lens provides a means to examine the complex interconnections among race, power, and inequality to maneuver clearer paths to structural change (Crenshaw, 2011; Delgado, 1995a; Dominelli, 2008). Our willingness to pursue increased understanding of our role and our professional power is an indispensable ingredient (Dominelli, 2004, 2008; Fook & Gardner, 2007; Ortiz & Jani, 2010; Reisch, 2011).

A critical stance seeks to uncover different conceptions of social justice and the seemingly invisible effects of structural racism that are ever present in our interactions and surrounding social systems; greater understanding of how social injustice manifests as unearned advantage and disadvantage; and how our own assumptions, personal and professional, are implicated. In this way insights about justice and the barriers preventing it are revealed. This notion embraces consideration of our, and our profession's, part in creating practices that divide us from those we serve—that is, barriers that enable inequality to persist and are created by our own efforts to serve (Foucault, 1994). It requires that we ask "What needs doing, who should do it and why? What allies/alliances are necessary? How will these alliances be formed and what targets need to be set? What blockages will be encountered? How can such barriers be overcome? Who will evaluate [and who will benefit from] the success (or its lack) of an action and how?" (Dominelli, 2008, p. 224).

For example, Ortiz and Jani (2010) propose that critical race theory aids our assessments and analysis by focusing our attention not only on an individual's or family's use of services, but also by considering the underlying assumptions embedded within the services proposed and whether the services address the needs of the community for whom they were designed. Taking this perspective enhances our understanding of the individual's or family's reaction to the services or interventions and shapes our understanding of the professional responses required on multiple levels of intervention to alleviate inherent injustice.

A critical lens, therefore, offers a way of looking at the situations presented for resolution through a structural analysis of power relationships and being prepared to reflect on our role in the equation for the purposes of change. These are different but similar processes and involve being able to ask discerning questions of ourselves and of the context we are in. Both accept the hidden influences of power and seek to uncover fundamental beliefs as a means of undoing the pernicious effects of oppression and racism. The growing understanding of these processes enhances notions of "professional use of self" (Fox, 2011; Urdang, 2010), from paying attention to our feelings, attitudes, and intersubjectivity to include examinations of how our own power, social location, and assumed statuses affect our work.

## Intersectionality

The concept of intersectionality contributes to our analysis of how multiple facets of oppression interact with people's identities and their worldviews. It is widely accepted that the concept of intersectionality surfaced from feminist women of color who called for a method of analysis that integrated the significant differences among women and their experiences of oppression (Hill-Collins, 1993, 2000, 2012b; Crenshaw, 1989, 1995; Gopaldas, 2013; hooks, 1984; Landry, 2006). A call for understanding our multiple dimensions of identity emerged. The premise within this construct is that focusing only on gender, for example, without paying attention to such factors as race, class, language, and religion fails to capture the full extent of felt oppression and will result in generalizations and essentialism (Bowleg, 2012; Crenshaw, 1995; Gopaldas, 2013).

Common themes within the concept of intersectionality include recognizing that markers of identity are contextual, and socially constructed. They are based on power relationships between and among groups, and experienced on both the individual and the social levels of our lives. Opposing forces may result as these identities concurrently exist within us (Hill-Collins, 2012a; Manuel, 2008; Weber, 1998). These themes suggest that the multiple dimensions of our identities do not function independently of one another. We are more than one facet of ourselves. Gender, class, and age intertwine and shape our sense of ourselves. They combine and interact. They locate us, and they produce dynamic effects and interchanges within our social worlds. The interchanges are also multidirectional. Different contexts and different situations place varying constraints or privileges on us and shape how we are socially located in time and place. This helps us move beyond a single or flat view of ourselves and others (Crenshaw, 1995; Hill-Collins, 1993; King, 1988; Sisneros, Stakeman, Joyner, & Schmitz, 2008; Zinn & Dill, 1996).

In this way, intersectionality offers a means to examine how individualized distinctions produce conditions for becoming subject to discrimination or benefiting from privilege. Both political and power relationships are embedded within these dimensions; making sense of these interrelationships requires attention to both structural and psychological factors. These dynamic interactions require a multifocal lens that considers all dimensions present at any one time, while also recognizing that one or another may predominate in influence or importance, depending on the context and situation. Potential conflict emerges when one dimension of our identity operates in opposite directions from other dimensions (Bowleg, 2012; Manuel, 2008). As our identities are located within two or more subordinated groups, our loyalties may be pulled in different directions that create competing allegiances. This has the potential to fragment and split potential connections among and between these different group identities (Brewer, 1993; Crenshaw, 1995; hooks, 1984). Yet, multiple identity locations may also provide a range of social advantages. Therefore, it is important to consider how these varying locations interact against or benefit each other (Manuel, 2008).

Thus, intersectionality is more than a way of viewing the multiple parts of our identities. It is also more than an accounting of the interconnections and entwined aspects of our identities and our social worlds. Understanding the import of intersectionality includes a focus on how our multiple social identities interact with larger structural factors and takes into account the ways multiple group identities and social positions impact our experiences of existing social barriers, including language, access to resources, poverty, citizenship status, and access to justice (Bowleg, 2012; Nelson & McPherson, 2003).

Crenshaw (1995) challenges us to question those parts of our identity we recognize as "home" and to expand our view of ourselves to include all aspects, even those where we might not feel as comfortable. She provides an example of how women may collaborate across boundaries of color and class, or how individuals might join across boundaries of gender and religion to form more effective coalitions on issues of common ground. This provides hope for coalition building, and for finding connections among us where we might not easily see they exist. A recent example is the links built across race, gender, and class among those concerned about the increasing gun violence in our schools and communities. Accordingly, intersectionality provides a means to understand experiences of oppression as well as a means to make use of our privileged statuses and social locations (Williams, 2004).

Contemporary meanings of intersectionality include considerations for various levels of intervention (Bowleg, 2012; Cho, Crenshaw, & McCall, 2013; Gopaldas, 2013; Manuel, 2008). On the micro level, intersectionality locates the multiple social locations of any one individual. It aids our assessments by providing a more rounded and inclusive view, and it creates the opportunity for a more nuanced dialog regarding the individual's lived experience. Bringing intersectionality to the surface offers a means of finding common ground within relationships while acknowledging the implications of differing or similar social locations. The aim is to avoid the dangers of stressing differences between us that lead to unintentional "othering" (Dominelli, 2008; Nelson & McPherson, 2003; Schiele, 2007; Yan & Wong, 2005).

On a broader social sphere, intersectionality provides an opportunity for an interdisciplinary examination of how social factors interact and interrelate with one another. Health disparities, domestic violence, and labor markets are examples of domains leading to the integration of previously "silo-ed" disciplines of study. This is a means for identifying potential coalitions of support. Channels result for posing questions about the process of policymaking and the nature of policy responses (Hankivsky, 2011; Manuel, 2008). Strategies emerge for social movements and collective change (Chun, Lipsitz & Shin, 2013). Finally, implications for how we conduct research and how we approach advocacy and policy formation are emerging (Bagilhole, 2010; Bowleg, 2012; Gopaldas, 2013; Manuel, 2008). An "intersectionality-informed stance" (Bowleg, 2012, p. 1270) commits research to understanding the interactions of multiple social identities and to framing research questions, analyses, and interpretations. The complexities of this task pose methodological challenges as well as opportunities (Bagilhole, 2010; Bowleg, 2012).

For example, Gopaldas (2013) provides a "comparison between traditional and intersectional research approaches on marketplace diversity" (p. 92). He points to the advantages of applying the construct of intersectionality to include research methods that reach historically silenced voices, to address interdependent social identities, to help explain consumer responses, and to help inform and formulate proposals for social change.

In summary, the concept of intersectionality takes our practice beyond that of understanding the fine distinctions within cultural differences that inadequately consider how one's culture is shaped, privileged, or constrained by context, time, and social forces (Abrams & Moio, 2009; Jani, Pierce, Ortiz, & Sowbel, 2011; Ortiz & Jani, 2010; Schiele, 2007). It also provides avenues to influence collective action, research and policy responses that lead to change.

## Storytelling

Language and discourse are vehicles for conveying dominant ideologies and shaping social structures. The stories built from this discourse help us make sense of our worlds and provide compelling normative and validating explanations (Delgado, 1995b; Montoya, 2002). Just as knowledge is open to interpretation and influenced by context, as well as influenced by those in power and by the existing master narrative/dominant ideology, discourse may sway reality in unbalanced ways (Lavoie, 2012).

Discovering that individual experience is part of a larger history bolsters the individual. It breaks down barriers of embedded preconceptions that keep people on the margins of social life (Devance, Casstevens, & Decuir, 2013;

Treviño, Harris, & Wallace, 2008; Yosso, 2005). The isolation of silence is broken and the individual finds support in being heard and is encouraged to act against continued isolation or misrepresentations of reality that have influence over him or her. An opportunity exists for the storyteller's own perceptions to change, for the narrative to evolve, and for new understanding to emerge (Fook, 2008). Narrative strategies and narrative therapy have evolved from these understandings as methods on the micro level of intervention (Kelley, 2011; Kerl, 2002; White & Epston, 1990).

These strategies yield benefits on the micro level but also produce effects on the macro level by impacting systemic misperceptions (Fook, 2008); they possess the power to challenge the dominant ideology and break down stereotypes (Delgado & Stefancic, 2001; Yosso, 2005). Recounting the experiences of historically oppressed groups from their own frame of reference, in particular, creates stories that counteract the dominant ideology and confront narratives that otherwise strengthen domination (Devance et al., 2013; Park, 2005; Roscoe, Carson, & Madoc-Jones, 2011; Schiele, 2007). Storytelling that confronts and destabilizes conventional wisdom and accepted normalized accounts challenges dominant regimes of discourse, power, and knowledge. By providing a glimpse that contradicts the dominant view, these "counter-stories" offer alternative explanations and enhance comprehension and appreciation of the complexities involved (Agger, 1998; Delgado & Stefancic, 2001; Fook, 2008). They enhance understanding while correcting misconceptions and challenging essentialism.

An important benefit of "counter-storytelling" lies in its power to break the silence of unheard and unrepresented voices of historically marginalized groups. Closely aligned with the concept of intersectionality, "counter-storytelling" emerges as a method to give credence to the lives of those who exist outside of the mainstream of social thought and who exhibit alternative patterns of behavior or ways of life. These storytellers benefit from an opportunity to have their experiences heard, affirmed, and normalized. They become empowered by hearing the echo of their own voices.

These individualized stories and perspectives provide explanations that offer insights and move us toward greater understanding (Crenshaw, 1995; Montoya, 2002). Further, well-written stories are a potent force to draw attention to otherwise ignored experiences and can kindle new connections among and between us (Delgado & Stefancic, 2001). Finally, listeners to these stories are in a position of bearing witness and calling attention to previously unheard stories, neglected points of view, or discounted realities.

Thus, storytelling serves as a way to normalize the dominant ideology and to destabilize this master narrative by reporting individualized accounts that provide insight into other realities and attack false consciousness (Freire, 1990). In this way, the powers of storytelling and "counter-storytelling" are witnessed on the individual level and in the larger social sphere.

## Egalitarian Empowerment Approaches

Egalitarian values are embedded within critical race theory, and empowerment approaches are embraced as a way for people to make their own decisions, gain access to resources, and become prime actors in their lives. Yet, inherent dangers exist because liberation cannot be given, nor can empowerment be achieved, unless those affected assume the power to lead themselves forward (Freire, 1990; Sakamoto & Pinter, 2005; Tew, 2006). Tew (2006) reminds us that "power together" may lead to oppressive forms of domination, and "power over" may not be oppressive when acting to protect those in vulnerable positions.

Egalitarian approaches argue against the misuse of professional power in our attempts to promote liberation. They are a means to achieve transformation by recognizing strengths within individuals, families, groups, and their communities; working jointly to overcome oppression; and sharing power in a mutually collaborative partnership that involves dialog and exchange. Freire (1990) elucidates the essential ingredients of mutuality, alliance building, partnership, and collaboration for this work. He argues for egalitarian relationships and blurring of the boundaries between helper and helped, and between teacher and learner, for the work of empowerment to be truly effective. This ingredient is required due to the inherent power differentials implicit in these roles; persistent attention is demanded to reduce their negative influences. The alliance built becomes its own model for sharing power (Tew, 2006).

In this frame, we are co-investigators and collaborators extending our expertise to fight alongside those we serve in the process of achieving transformation and freedom (Freire, 1990). If the work of empowerment does not include care for these intrinsic transformational aims, we perpetuate ourselves in a power position over those we serve, thereby diminishing their authority and expertise in finding their own route to liberation (Blundo, 2001; Payne, 2014; Reisch & Jani, 2012; Saleeby, 2002). This involves raising awareness through education in an inclusive, sharing process, communication, and dialog. Otherwise the danger is the perpetuation of oppression (Friere & Macedo, 2000).

Creating the conditions for dialog requires joining forces with those we serve and viewing our work as work together. Creating dialog ensures that differing points of view are not seen as better or worse but rather as additions and contributions to deepen understanding. Essential conditions are often expressed in terms of creating safety for these learning conversations to occur. Fook and Gardner (2007) point to the importance of tolerating confusion and uncertainty. Creating dialog requires establishing egalitarian relationships in which differing or "unsettling" opinions are respected and viewed as opportunities to improve comprehension (Fook & Gardner, 2007, p. 46). Embedded within the work of Freire (1990), a person with an egalitarian perspective engages with others as subjects, confronts "othering," and is determined to break down the negative effects of dealing with others as objects.

## REMAINING CHALLENGES: WHAT GAPS EXIST
## AND WHAT AVENUES PROVIDE HOPE?

A major area of concern is the marginalized position of critical social theoretical perspectives within American social work and other helping professions. In a sort of Catch-22, this reality produces doubt about the usefulness of these perspectives, thereby perpetuating their marginality (Payne, 2014; Reisch, 2011). More problematic is the cursory (or lack of) consideration given to anti-oppressive or antiracist theoretical approaches and, in particular, critical race theory.

This has particular implications for the education of new professionals. The challenge presented to students of applying theory to practice is directly affected by the absence of theories that take race and racism into consideration. Our efforts to undo racism is diminished and we are in danger of perpetuating a lack of attention to these issues. Related concerns are perceptions regarding the lack of guidance emerging from critical perspectives for intervention across multiple systemic levels (Reisch, 2011; Yosso, 2005). Critiques also suggest that there is too much emphasis on the power of ideas alone and in the belief that what is right and just will prevail if only people understood (Crenshaw, 1995).

The concerns regarding a lack of guidance for intervention appear connected to the bifurcation of micro- and macro-level interventions and a predilection toward focusing interventions on one or the other without considering how they could be applied at multiple levels. The diversity of views emerging from a social constructivist position when considering ideas of social justice often leads to confusion for practitioners in setting priorities and in deciphering meanings from the multiple perspectives presented (Reisch, 2002, 2011). The complex and confounding contradictions of multiple and opposing outlooks create confusion and barriers for practitioners searching for principles to guide their practice through a maze of competing priorities and through politically driven choices (Allan et al., 2009; Fook, 2008; Mullaly, 2007; Reisch, 2011).

A related area of concern is the attention given to teaching about the intricate processes of policy reformulation and large system change (Pimpare, 2011). A lack of appreciation for the complexity involved creates frustration and a lack of tolerance for the inherent tensions associated with conflict in ideological differences (Reisch & Jani, 2012). This creates additional tensions for practitioners as competing demands and as varying and opposing causes seek change or survival. The challenge is more complex than finding tools to grapple with the dichotomies involved (Mendez, 2009; Reisch, 2002, 2011; Reisch & Jani, 2012). Expertise regarding the process of how established patterns persevere is required. Paradoxically, it is within these complexities that opportunities and hope for effecting change exist. Fook (2008) suggests that the challenge of achieving solidarity in working toward change involves detailed analysis of existing differences to provide ways of discerning nuances of shared concerns from which common ground can be found. It is in this process that gains are also made in increasing local affiliations and individual awareness that contribute to larger-scale change efforts. The work of social change may be incremental and slow, but this is not the same as being static. Practitioners need to be educated about this process and given tools that assess gains to sustain their efforts while continuing to work for improvement. The slow and uneven incremental progress in addressing gaps in higher education graduation rates for black male students is a persisting illustration (Bowen, Chingos, & McPherson, 2009; Museus, Ledesma & Parker, 2015).

It is widely accepted that change requires more than a shift in perspective and increased understanding. Postmodern critical social theoretical perspectives, and critical race theory in particular, provide a compass to this work. Still, Lee and Lutz (2005) remind us that no simple answers emerge for the work ahead.

## CONCLUSIONS AND HOPE FOR THE WAY FORWARD

Paradigm shifts (Kuhn, 1962, 1984) occur when alternative perspectives emerge that challenge previously held theories or perspectives. Advances in knowledge are questioned as this information contradicts mainstream thought. The evidence may not be powerful enough to counter what is believed to be true and what has been—and might still be—taught. Old frames of understanding collide with new knowledge and new understanding. The shift challenges our worldview; differential acceptance occurs and creates periods of confusion until a new "truth" takes hold. It is proposed that in many ways practitioners must undergo a paradigm shift in thinking to undo racism. In addition to acknowledging race as a social construction, we must see problems as derived from the environment rather than the individual. Counter to predominant social mores, we must believe in the importance of breaking the silence about the impact of racism. We must be prepared to examine our own efforts at helping as potential repositories of racially oppressive practices. Likewise, we must be prepared to seek methods and approaches to tackle social, environmental, and economic injustice that include targets across multiple levels of concern (Abrams & Moio, 2009; Lavoie, 2012; Park, 2005; Reisch & Jani, 2012).

In the way that feminist scholars and activists focus on gender to achieve changes for women, and in the way that proponents of gay rights focus efforts for their community, it is legitimate to ask whether a focus on racial inequality may achieve change in the racial divisions in our culture and society. This does not mean that other dimensions of oppression are lost or ignored; it simply means that the conversation starts with racial inequality. It does, however, involve a shift in American ideology surrounding the political advantages of a colorblind position on race and power. Does critical race theory provide the needed focus as a direct means to our aims?

We are already using many of critical race theory's methods. The construct of intersectionality is slowly entering and informing professional practice, albeit on the individual level as an improved assessment technique. If more fully incorporated into our practice, intersectionality has the potential to improve all levels of intervention. It provides a mechanism to decipher existing social structures of oppression (Constance-Huggins, 2012; Jani et al., 2011; Jani and Reisch, 2011; Reisch & Jani, 2012), and it shifts our attention and target for change from an individual level to include a systemic structural level (Abrams & Gibson, 2007; Abrams & Moio, 2009). In this way it provides a remedy to reductionism, which inevitably leads to essentialism, stereotyping, and categorizing (Lavoie, 2012; Nelson & McPherson, 2003; Ortiz & Jani, 2010; Park, 2005; Schiele, 2007). However, if detached from its roots in critical social theory and a call for change, it becomes another instrument for individual assessment without turning to the larger issues it has the power to address.

Indeed, there appears a growing consensus, and implied within the precepts of intersectionality, that as we become more informed about the interactions of one form of oppression on another, the problems faced are recognized as interrelated and solutions are seen as requiring united interdisciplinary approaches "to create wider emancipatory networks that might confront these intersecting issues" (Trubek, 2011, p. 1503). This calls for a more integrated approach to intervention. In a similar manner, storytelling is a vehicle to achieve individual transformation; as exemplified in critical race theory, its uses for larger systemic change require equal attention. However, it is proposed here that we have further to go in applying a critical lens to our work.

Reisch (2011) proposes that we must connect theory with the experiences we encounter in our practice; that is, we must examine assumptions that lead to choices of interventions. We can identify the principles that inform responses to change and remain open to examining our own responses to difference by critical analysis of and critical reflection on our practice. These responses highlight the ways structural racism exists within our professional practices as well as in the larger social systems in which we operate. We cannot afford to neglect how we are educating for this work. We are obliged to consider how we address these issues in the curriculum and in the classroom--whose voices are silenced and ignored and whose are heard and valued (Patton, McEwen, Rendón & Howard-Hamilton, 2007).

Again, critical race theory provides a prime example. Proponents' analysis of how race and racial power are constructed began with an examination of their own professional education while considering the existing legal culture and the larger social structures within which their profession was based (Crenshaw et al., 1995). The tenets of critical race theory provoke thought and provide the means to achieve change. The work of Ladson-Billings and Tate (1995) presents another resource for examining how critical race theory may be applied to education (see also, Milner & Laughter, 2015 and Museus, Ledesma & Parker, 2015).

Crenshaw (2011, p. 1348) gives voice to the challenges ahead by asking, "Are the conceptual tools available to take on the ideological contours of today's racial apologia in the manner that critical race theorists took on liberal constitutionalism in the 1980s?" She answers her own question:

> [T]he task at hand is to interrogate (racial) power where we live, work, socialize and exist. For academics, that world is implicated in the ways that the disciplines were built to normalize and sustain the American racial project. A contemporary critical race theory would thus take up the dual tasks of uncovering the epistemic foundations of white as well as the habits of disciplinary thought that cabin competing paradigms through colorblind conventions. . . . What is needed is a crisp exchange of ideas, tools, histories and contemporary understandings from critical thinkers who are fully conversant with and able to deploy the conventions of their disciplines to explain how they contribute to racial hierarchy. . . . The critical call is for social constructionists to help contribute to a counter-narrative of how prevailing ideas about race have come to be, and how the post-racial agnosticism about their continuing imprint on social life contributes to rather than detracts from the continuing significance of race. Our attention should neither become trapped in the assertion that attentiveness to race only serves to reify it, nor by the moderate view that the best approach now that these historical missteps are exposed is to embrace a colorblind strategy to ignore it. . . . These are the poles of thinking out of which [critical race theory] emerged in law, and that may give way to the emergence of a similar kind of project across the disciplines today. (Crenshaw, 2011, pp. 1348–1349)

We must meet the uncomfortable challenge of bearing witness to discrimination by being prepared to confront privilege and oppression when and where we encounter it with theoretical frameworks to guide our journey. This task is before us.

## DISCUSSION QUESTIONS

1. What considerations are required to assess whether the services of your agency are relevant and responsive to the community's larger needs? How might you ensure that when acting as a gatekeeper to services, you also advocate for alternative designs and program adjustments to better respond to community demographics, strengths, and changing service needs of service consumers?

2. To what extent are your agency's services organized to help transform the social, political, and economic situations for those involved? Which critical

social theories and antiracist approaches are incorporated within your course outlines and/or staff development programs?

## REFERENCES

Abrams, L. S., & Gibson, P. (2007). Teaching Notes. Reframing multicultural education. Teaching white privilege in the social work curriculum. *Journal of Social Work Education, 43*(1), 147–160.

Abrams, L. S., & Moio, J. A. (2009). Critical race theory and the cultural competence dilemma in social work education. *Journal of Social Work Education, 45*(2), 245–61.

Agger, B. (1992). *The discourse of domination: From the Frankfurt School to post modernism.* Evanston, IL: Northwestern University Press.

Agger, B. (1998). *Critical social theories.* Boulder, CO: Westview Press.

Allan, J. (2009). Theorising new developments in critical social work. In J. Allan, L. Briskman, & B. Pease (Eds.), *Critical social work: An introduction to theories and practices* (2nd ed., Chapter 3, pp. 30–44). New York: Allen & Unwin.

Allan, J., Pease, B., & Briskman, L. (Eds.) (2009). *Critical social work: An introduction to theories and practices* (2nd ed.). New York: Allen & Unwin.

Armstrong, J., & Ng, R. (2005). Deconstructing race, deconstructing racism. In J. Lee & J. Lutz (Eds.),. *Situating "race" and racisms in space, time and theory: Critical essays for activists and scholars* (pp. 30–45). Montreal: McGill-Queens University Press.

Ashcroft, B., Griffiths, G., & Tiffin, H., (2007). *Post colonial studies: The key concepts.* New York: Routledge.

Bagilhole, B. (2010). Applying the lens of intersectionality to UK equal opportunities and diversity policies. *Canadian Journal of Administrative Sciences, 27,* 263–271.

Baines, D. (Ed.). (2007). *Doing anti-oppressive practice: Building transformation politicized social work.* Black Point, NS: Fernwood Publishing.

Berger, P. L., & Luckmann, T. (1966). *The social construction of reality.* New York: Anchor Books.

Blundo, R. (2001). Learning strengths-based practice: Challenging our personal and professional frames. *Families in Society, 82*(3), 296–305.

Bowen, W. G., Chingos, M. M., & McPherson, M. S. (2009). *Crossing the finish line.* Princeton, NJ: Princeton University Press.

Bowleg, L. (2012). Framing health matters: The problem with the phrase "women and minorities." Intersectionality—an important theoretical framework for public health. *American Journal of Public Health, 102*(7), 1267–1273.

Brewer, R. (1993). Theorizing race, class and gender: The new scholarship of black feminist intellectuals and black women's labor. In S. M. James & A. Busia (Eds.), *Theorizing black feminisms: The visionary pragmatism of black women* (pp. 13–30). New York: Routledge.

Cho, S., Crenshaw, K. W., & McCall, L. (2013). Toward a field of intersectionality studies: Theory, applications and praxis. *Signs: Journal of Women in Culture and Society, 38*(4), 785–810.

Chun, J. J., Lipsitz, G., Shin, Y. (2013). Intersectionality as a Social Movement Strategy: Asian Immigrant Women Advocates. *Signs: Journal of Women in Culture and Society, 38,* (4), 917–940.

Constance-Huggins, M. (2012). Critical race theory in social work education: A framework for addressing racial disparities. *Critical Social Work, 13*(2), 2– 6.

Crenshaw, K. W. (1989). Demarginalizing the intersection of race and sex. *University of Chicago Legal Forum, 140,* 139–167.

Crenshaw, K. W. (1995). Mapping the margins: Intersectionality, identity politics, and violence against women of color. In K. W. Crenshaw, N. Gotanda, G. Peller, & K. Thomas (Eds.), *Critical race theory: The key writings that formed the movement* (Part Six, pp. 357–383). New York: The New Press.

Crenshaw, K. W. (2002).The first decade: Critical reflections, or a "a foot in the closing door." In F. Valdes, J. McCristal Culp, & A. Harris (Eds.), *Crossroads, directions and a new critical race theory* (Chapter 1, pp. 9–31). Philadelphia: Temple University Press.

Crenshaw, K. W. (2011). Twenty years of critical race theory: Looking back to move forward. *Connecticut Law Review, 43*(5), 1253–1352.

Crenshaw, K. W., Gotanda, N., Peller, G., & Thomas, K. (1995). *Critical race theory: The key writings that formed the movement.* New York: The New Press.

Dalrymple, J., & Burke, B. (1995). *Anti-oppressive practice: Social care and the law.* Buckingham, UK: Open University Press.

Delgado, R. (Ed.). (1995a). *Critical race theory: The cutting edge.* Philadelphia: Temple University Press.

Delgado, R. (1995b). Storytelling for oppositionists and others: A plea for narrative. In R. Delgado (Ed.), *Critical race theory: The cutting edge* (Chapter 7, pp. 64–74). Philadelphia: Temple University Press.

Delgado, R., & Stefancic, J. (2001). *Critical race theory: An introduction.* New York: NYU Press.

Devance Taliaferro, J., Casstevens, W. J., & Decuir Gunby, J. (2013). Working with African American clients using narrative therapy: An operational citizenships and critical race theory framework. *International Journal of Narrative Therapy and Community Work, 1,* 34–45.

Dominelli, L. (2002). *Anti-oppressive social work theory and practice.* Basingstoke, UK: Palgrave Macmillan.

Dominelli, L. (2004). New directions for social work: Interdependence, reciprocity, citizenship, and social justice. In L. Dominelli (Ed.), *Social work: Theory and practice for a changing profession,* Malden, MA: Polity Press.

Dominelli, L. (2008). *Anti-racist social work* (3rd ed.). Basingstoke, UK: Palgrave Macmillan.

Dominelli, L., & McLeod, E. (1989). *Feminist social work.* Hampshire, UK: Macmillan Education.

Fook, J. (2008). *Social work: Critical theory and practice.* Los Angeles: Sage.

Fook, J., & Gardner, F. (2007). *Critical reflection: A resource handbook.* Berkshire, UK: Open University Press.

Ford, C. L., & Airhihenbuwa, C. O. (2010). Critical race theory, race equity, and public health: Toward antiracism praxis. Commentaries. *American Journal of Public Health, 100*(S1), 30–35.

Foucault, M. (1988). On power. In L. D. Kritzman (Ed.), *Michel Foucault: Politics, philosophy, culture, interviews and other writings, 1977–84* (pp. 96–109). New York: Routledge.

Foucault, M. (1994). The subject and power. In J. D. Faubion (Ed.), *Power.* New York: The New Press.

Foucault, M. (1999). Social work, social control and normalization: Roundtable discussion with Michel Foucault. In A. S. Chambon, A. Irving, & L. Epstein (Eds.), *Reading Foucault for social work* (pp. 83–97). New York: Columbia University Press.

Fox, R. (2011). *The use of self: The essence of professional education.* Chicago: Lyceum Books.

Freire, P. (1990). *Pedagogy of the oppressed* (32nd printing). New York: Continuum

Freire, A., & Macedo, D. (Eds.) (2000). *The Paulo Freire reader.* New York: Continuum.

Gemignani, M., & Pena, E. (2007). Postmodern conceptualization of culture in social constructionism and cultural studies. *Journal of Theoretical and Philosophical Psychology* (special issue, *Cultural Theorizing*), 27–28(1–2), 276–300.

Gergen, K. J. (1985). The social constructionist movement in modern psychology. *American Psychologist, 40*(3), 266–275.

Gergen, K. J. (2009). *An invitation to social construction* (2nd ed.). Los Angeles: Sage.

Gopaldas, A. (2013). Intersectionality 101. *Journal of Public Policy & Marketing* (special issue), *32*, 90–94.

Gramsci, A. (1971). *Selections from the prison notebooks.* Translated and edited by Q. Hoare & G. Nowell Smith. New York: International Pub.

Hankivsky, O. (2011). Intersectionality and public policy: Some lessons from existing models. *Political Research Quarterly, 64*(1), 217–229.

Hill-Collins, P. (1993). Toward a new vision: Race, class, and gender as categories of analysis and connection. *Race, Sex & Class, 1*(1), 25–45.

Hill-Collins, P. (2000). *Black feminist thought: Knowledge, consciousness, and the politics of empowerment* (2nd ed.). New York: Routledge.

Hill-Collins, P. (2012a). Social inequality, power, and politics: Intersectionality and American pragmatism in dialogue. *Journal of Speculative Philosophy, 26*(2), 442–457.

Hill-Collins, P. (2012b). Looking back, moving forward: Scholarship in service to social justice. *Gender & Society, 26*(1), 14–22.

hooks, b. (1984). *Feminist theory: From margin to center.* Boston: South End Press.

Jani, J. S., & Reisch, M. (2011). Common human needs, uncommon solutions: Applying a critical framework to perspectives on human behavior, *Families in Society, 92*(1), 13–20.

Jani, J. S., Pierce, D., Ortiz, L. O., & Sowbel, L. (2011). Access to intersectionality, content to competence: Deconstructing social work education diversity standards. *Journal of Social Work Education, 47*(2), 283–301.

Kelley, P. (2011). Narrative theory and social work treatment. In F. Turner (Ed.), *Social work treatment: Interlocking theoretical approaches* (Chapter 20, pp. 315–326). New York: Oxford University Press.

Kerl, S. B. (2002). Using narrative approaches to teach multicultural counseling. *Journal of Multicultural Counseling and Development, 30,* 135–143.

King, D. (1988). Multiple jeopardy, multiple consciousness: The context of a black feminist ideology. *Signs, 14*(1), 42–72.

Kohi, H. K., Huber, R., & Faul, A. C. (2010). Historical and theoretical development of culturally competent social work practice. *Journal of Teaching in Social Work, 30*(3), 252–271.

Kuhn, T. S. (1962). *The structure of scientific revolutions.* Chicago: Chicago University Press.

Kuhn, T. S. (1984). Revisiting Planck. *Historical Studies in the Physical Sciences, 14,* 246.

Ladson-Billings, G. (2011). Race . . . to the top, again: Comments on the genealogy of critical race theory. *Connecticut Law Review, 43*(5), 1439–1457.

Ladson-Billings, G., Tate, W.F. (1995). Toward a critical race theory of education. *Teachers College Record, 97,* 47–68.

Landry, B. (2006). *Race, gender, and class: Theory and methods of analysis.* Upper Saddle River, NJ: Prentice Hall.

Lavoie, C. (2012). Race, power and social action in neighborhood community organizing: Reproducing and resisting the social construction of the other. *Journal of Community Practice, 20*(3), 241–259.

Lee, J., & Lutz, J. (Eds.) (2005). *Situating "race" and racisms in space, time and theory: Critical essays for activists and scholars.* Montreal: McGill-Queens University Press.

Leonard, P. (2001). The future of critical social work in uncertain conditions. *Critical Social Work, 2*(1). Retrieved from/criticalsocialwork/the-future-of-critical-social-work-in-uncertain-conditions, June 24, 2014.

Lipsitz, G. (2011). "Constituted by a series of contestations": Critical race theory as a social movement. *Connecticut Law Review, 43*(5), 1459–1478.

Love, P., & Estanek, S. (2004). *Rethinking student affairs practice.* San Francisco: John Wiley & Sons, Inc.

Manuel, T. (2008). Envisioning the possibilities for a good life: Exploring the public policy implications of intersectionality theory. *Journal of Women, Politics & Policy, 28*(3/4), 173–203.

Marchant, H., & Wearing, B. (1986). *Gender reclaimed: Women in social work.* Sydney: Hale & Iremonger.

Mendez, P. (2009). Tracing the origins of critical social work practice. In J. Allan, L. Briskman, & B. Pease (Eds.), *Critical social work* (2nd ed., Chapter 2, pp. 17–29). New York: Allen & Unwin.

Mezirow, J. (1997). Transformative learning: Theory to practice. *New directions for adult and continuing education.74*(1997), 5–12.

Milner, R.H., Laughter, J.C. (2015). But good intentions are not enough: Preparing teachers to center race and poverty. *Urban Review, 47,* 341–363.

Montoya, M. E. (2002). Celebrating racialized legal narratives. In F. Valdes, J. McCristal Culp, & A. Harris (Eds.), *Crossroads, directions and a new critical race theory* (Chapter 8, pp. 241–250). Philadelphia: Temple University Press.

Moreau, M. (1979). A structural approach to social work practice. *Canadian Journal of Social Work Education, 5*(1), 78–94.

Mullaly, B. (2002). *Challenging oppression: A critical social work approach.* New York: Oxford University Press.

Mullaly, B. (2007). *The new structural social work.* Ontario: Oxford University Press.

Mullaly, B. (2010). *Challenging oppression and confronting privilege* (2nd ed.). Ontario: Oxford University Press.

Museus, S.D., Ledesma, M.C., Parker, T.l. (2015). Racism and racial equity in higher education. *ASHE Higher Education Report. Special Issue: Racism and racial equity in higher education, 42*(1), 1–112.

Nelson, C. H., & McPherson, D. H. (2003) Cultural diversity in social work practice: Where are we now and what are the challenges in addressing issues of justice and oppression? In W. Shera (Ed.), *Emerging perspectives on anti-oppressive practice* (Chapter 5, pp. 81–100). Toronto: Canadian Scholars' Press, Inc.

Orelus, P. W. (2012). Unveiling the web of race, class, language, and gender oppression: Challenges for social justice educators. *Race, Gender & Class, 19*(3–4), 35–51.

Ortiz, L., & Jani, J. (2010). Critical race theory: A transformational model for teaching diversity. *Journal of Social Work Education, 46*(2), 175–193.

Park, C. L. (2010). Making sense of the meaning literature: An integrative review of meaning making and its effects on adjustment to stressful life events. *Psychological Bulletin, 136*(2), 257–301.

Park, Y. (2005). Culture as deficit: A critical discourse analysis of the concept of culture in contemporary social work discourse, *Journal of Sociology and Social Welfare, 32*(3), 11–33.

Patton, L.D., McEwen, M., Rendón, L., Howard-Hamilton, M.F. (2007). Critical race perspectives on theory in student affairs. *New Directions for Student Services, 120,* Winter, 39–53.

Payne, M. (2014). *Modern social work theory* (4th ed.). Chicago: Lyceum Press.

Pimpare, S. (2011). Hopeful, active realism: A pedagogy of critical social policy, In J. Birkenmaier, A. Cruce, J. Wilson, J. Curley, E. Burkemper, & J. Stretch (Eds.),

*Educating for social justice: Transformative experiential learning* (Chapter 5, pp. 99–110). New York: Lyceum.

Powers, M., & Faden, R. (2006). *Social justice: The moral foundations of public health and health policy.* New York: Oxford University Press.

Reisch, M. (2002). Defining social justice in a socially unjust world. *Families in Society: The Journal of Contemporary Human Services, 83*(4), 343–354.

Reisch, M. (2011). Defining social justice in a socially unjust world. In J. Birkenmaier, A. Cruce, J. Wilson, J. Curley, E. Burkemper, & J. Stretch (Eds.), *Educating for social justice: Transformative experiential learning* (Chapter 1, pp. 11–28). New York: Lyceum.

Reisch, M., & Jani, J. S. (2012). The new politics of social work practice: Understanding context to promote change. *British Journal of Social Work, 42*, 1132–1150.

Robbins, S. P., Chatterjee, P., & Canda, E. R. (2012). *Contemporary human behavior theory: A critical perspective for social work.* New York: Allyn & Bacon.

Roscoe, K. D., Carson, A. M., & Madoc-Jones, L. (2011). Narrative social work: Conversations between theory and practice. *Journal of Social Work Practice, 25*(1), 47–61.

Sahin, F. (2006). Implications of social constructionism for social work. *Asia Pacific Journal of Social Work and Development, 16*(1), 57–65.

Sakamoto, I, & Pinter, R. O. (2005). Use of critical consciousness in anti-oppressive social work practice: Disentangling power dynamics at personal and structural levels. *British Journal of Social Work, 35*, 435–452.

Saleeby, D. (2002). *The strengths perspective in social work practice.* Boston: Allyn and Bacon.

Schiele, J. H. (2007). Implications of the equality-of-oppressions paradigm for curriculum content for curriculum content on people of color. *Journal of Social Work Education, 43*(1), 83–99.

Schön, D. (1983). *The reflective practitioner.* New York: Basic Books.

Shera, W. (Ed.). (2003). *Emerging perspectives on anti-oppressive practice.* Toronto: Canadian Scholars' Press, Inc.

Shor, I. (1992). *Empowering education: Critical teaching for social change.* Chicago: University of Chicago Press.

Sisneros, J., Stakeman, C., Joyner, M. C., & Schmitz, C. L. (2008). *Critical multicultural social work.* Chicago: Lyceum.

Taylor, E. W. (2008). Transformative learning theory. *New Directions for Adult and Continuing Education: Special Issue. Third Update on Adult Learning Theory, 2008*(119), 5–15.

Tew, J. (2006). Understanding power and powerlessness: Towards a framework for emancipatory practice in social work. *Journal of Social Work, 6*(1), 33–51.

Treviño, A. J., Harris, M. A., & Wallace, D. (2008). What's so critical about critical race theory? *Contemporary Justice Review, 11*(1), 7–10.

Trubek, D. M. (2011). Foundational events, foundational myths, and the creation of critical race theory, or how to get along with a little help from your friends. *Connecticut Law Review, 43*(5), 1505–1512.

Turner, F. (Ed.). (2011). *Social work treatment: Interlocking theoretical approaches* (5th ed.). New York: Oxford University Press.

Urdang, E. (2010). Awareness of self: A critical tool. *Social Work Education, 29*(5), 523–538.

Valdes, F., McCristal Culp, J., & Harris, A. (2002). Introduction: Battles waged, won and lost: Critical race theory at the turn of the millennium. In F. Valdes, J. McCristal Culp, & A. Harris (Eds.), *Crossroads, directions and a new critical race theory* (pp. 1–8). Philadelphia: Temple University Press.

Weber, L. (1998). A conceptual framework for understanding race, class, gender, and sexuality. *Psychology of Women Quarterly, 22*, 13–32.

White, M., & Epston, D. (1990). *Narrative means to therapeutic ends.* New York: Norton.

Wildman, S. M., & Davis, A. D. (1995). Language and silence: Making systems of privilege visible. In R. Delgado (Ed.), *Critical race theory: The cutting edge* (pp. 573–579). Philadelphia: Temple University Press.

Williams, C. (2004). Race (and gender and class) and child custody: Theorizing intersections in two Canadian court cases. *NWSA Journal, 16*(2), 46–69.

Wulff, D. (2011). Postmodern social work. In F. Turner (Ed.), *Social work treatment: Interlocking theoretical approaches* (Chapter 23, pp. 354–363). New York: Oxford University Press.

Yan, M. C., & Wong, Y. (2005). Rethinking self-awareness in cultural competence: Toward a dialogic self in cross-cultural social work. *Families in Society: The Journal of Contemporary Social Services, 86*, 181–188.

Yosso, T. J. (2005). Whose culture has capital? A critical race theory discussion of community cultural wealth. *Race Ethnicity and Education, 8*(1), 69–91.

Zinn, M. B., & Dill, B. T. (1996). Theorizing difference from multiracial feminism. *Feminist Studies, 22*(2), 321–331.

# CHAPTER 8

# Antiracist Approaches for Shaping Theoretical and Practice Paradigms

KENNETH V. HARDY

Regardless of the setting or circumstance, addressing intense interpersonal racial interactions remains a monumental endeavor. Whether these interactions are between colleagues, family members, or estranged racial groups hopelessly divided and unable to find common ground, progressive conversations involving race remain a major challenge. This chapter will provide a framework for conducting progressive conversations about race within the workplace and beyond. Establishing antiracist approaches for facilitating effective engagement around the difficult issues of race is one of the key elements in transforming health and human services systems. Demonstrating the willingness and skill to effectively navigate conversations about race that circumvent the usual paths of polarization and rapid escalation are central to the process of transforming health and human services systems.

## THE *PRIVILEGE AND SUBJUGATED TASK* (PAST) MODEL

The prevailing views regarding racial conversations are either that they should be avoided completely or they should just happen spontaneously. Unfortunately, neither of these perspectives appears to be very effective. The "not talk about it" strategy is ineffectual because it contributes to an undercurrent of racial tension that sabotages most racial encounters. It also promotes the flawed assumption that we live in a "colorblind society." The "let's just dive into it" approach seldom renders positive outcomes and usually quickly disintegrates into a type of interpersonal spontaneous combustion. Given the history of strained race relationships in the

United States, it is virtually impossible to have a spontaneous conversation about race that doesn't explode, implode, or spiral into a cauldron of suppressed anger, rage, and divisiveness. These typical and predictable reactions highlight the necessity for creating a more methodical and structured approach to talking about race.

The PAST Model is a power/privilege-sensitive framework designed to defuse contentious conversations and to facilitate constructive engagement across the divides of race and other dimensions of diversity. The model is predicated on the notion that power and privilege are two salient factors underpinning the creation, maintenance, and resolution of racially based conversations. These interlocking and overlapping principles undergird the PAST Model and serve as the basis for how it is constructed and implemented. The actual implementation of the model requires participants to do a racial self-analysis and to determine where their racial identities and broader cultural narratives regarding their identities locate them in the current conversation. Each participant must be clear whether his or her racial identity places him or her in a privileged or subjugated position (Berman Cushing et al., 2010). The outcome of this process should not be dictated or determined by whether the person in the privileged position "feels" or believes he or she is privileged or whether the person in the subjugated position personally feels privileged. It is common for many whites to denounce their racial privilege because they never felt privileged or because they simultaneously occupy other social identities that are undeniably subjugated positions (e.g., class, sexual orientation, religion, nationality). Similarly, it is also challenging for some people of color to embrace their racial subjugation, either because such an admission is tantamount to claiming inferiority or because they simultaneously occupy one or more social identities that are highly privileged in our society (e.g., class, education). It is essential that race is the critical determining factor and must be the singular focus of the interaction. Failure to do so refocuses the conversation from one that is skewed toward race to a free-flowing, splintered, ill-focused shouting match regarding whose pain and suffering is worse. This preparatory work is crucial because it helps to thwart many of the predictable and common pitfalls associated with having constructive and progressive conversations about race.

A central premise of the model is that each of us has multiple identities, one of which is a racial identity, which is the focal point of this chapter. Through a host of socially constructed messages and practices, race and more specifically racial identity is either associated with value and therefore privileged, or devalued and subsequently assigned to positions of inferiority and subjugation. In the United States, being white is a racially privileged position and being a person of color is a racially devalued position. The entire U.S. social structure has been and remains organized around a white supremacist ideology that unrelentingly reifies the reality that white is good, pure, better, and so forth, while black and other hues are inferior, animalistic, barbaric, and threatening. For this reason, within the framework of the PAST Model it is widely assumed that whites will be routinely assigned to the privileged position.

For the purposes of constructive conversations, the PAST Model recognizes two positions among those engaging to talk about race: (1) privileged and (2) sub-jugated. Each person or group occupying a given position is expected to perform certain tasks to facilitate a constructive conversation. The PAST Model posits that racial conversations can be constructive and progressive if one or more of the following conditions are adhered to:

1. Those in the privileged and subjugated positions rigidly adhere to performing their assigned tasks during an intense conversation about race.
2. Those in the privileged position rigidly adhere to performing their assigned task but those in the subjugated position fail to perform theirs.
3. Those in the subjugated position rigidly adhere to performing their tasks but those in the privileged position fail to perform theirs.

Obviously the first is the ideal option and holds the greatest promise for mean-ingful transformation. While the other options can be instrumental in promot-ing a positive shift in racial interactions, they can also be quite challenging and are not casualty-proof.

Whether in the workplace or other contexts, whites interested in having more progressive, less polarizing conversations with people of color can take a huge first step by exercising the tasks of the privileged. People of color also have a sig-nificant role in ensuring that conversations are constructive and progressive and can accomplish this feat by adhering to the tasks of the subjugated.

## THE TASKS OF THE PRIVILEGED

The tasks of the privileged are not specific to race, although this is the context in which they are presented in this chapter. These tasks, instead, are applicable to any situation, circumstance, or identity where one holds a position of power and privilege that is superior to that of those with whom one shares a relationship. The tasks are systemic and thus gain considerable potency and poignancy from their confluence. The tasks of the privileged are as follows:

### 1. Differentiate Between Intentions and Consequences and Always Start with an Acknowledgment of the Latter

It is common for whites, when discussing race and particularly after feeling at-tacked, misunderstood, or unappreciated by a person of color, to enter the con-versation by clarifying and at times restating (even overstating) their intentions. When a conversation focuses on the (pure) intentions of the white person who feels misunderstood, it obscures, possibly even "unintentionally" ignores, the original disclosure advanced by the person of color. Although "unintentional," a conversation that highlights the pure and good intentions of whites merely becomes another privileged conversation. The implication is that "having the good intentions" of the white person clarified takes precedence over whatever concern, hurt, or slight has been expressed by the person of color. This dynamic unfortunately and unwittingly reinforces a broader societal perception about who is valued and who isn't.

The hope is that the person in the privileged position would use his or her privilege responsibly and do so on behalf of (repairing) the relationship. When intentionality is introduced too quickly into the conversation, it primarily serves the person in the privileged position in lieu of the relationship. This is not to suggest that the intentions of the person in the privileged position are irrelevant, but it instead sounds a cautionary note regarding the significance of the timing of the disclosure. Once space (verbal and emotional) has been created (by the privileged position) and acknowledgment and validation have been extended, there may be a point where the clarification of intentions can be shared and received in a manner that appears less intrusive, evasive, and dismissive.

**Tactic #1:** Focus conversations on the consequences experienced by the subjugated person.

## 2. Avoid the Overt and Covert Negation of Subjugated Conversations and Disclosures

Conversations and disclosures that negate are never intended to do so, yet they do—and seldom inconsequentially. In conversations where whites and people of color have obvious differences in perceptions and experiences, it seems difficult for some whites to embrace, entertain, or authentically hold the position of the person of color without dismissing, correcting, reinterpreting, or attempting to expand their worldview by "teaching" them. All of these seemingly benign, innocent, and benevolent acts are tools of negation. The process of negation is a rather complex and sophisticated one. It is relatively easy to negate without knowing that it has happened. The most frequent acts of racially motivated negation are (a) challenges disguised as questions; (b) challenges disguised as advice; (c) silence; (d) "privempathy," and (e) undisguised challenge.

*Challenges disguised as questions* negate conversations/disclosure by appearing to seek information but really challenge the validity of a disclosure that has been made by a person of color.

> Mulani, an African American therapist, reported to her white supervisor, Helen, that she thought her white client, Rita, was racist as she continually made racially hostile comments throughout her sessions. Helen responded by asking, "Do you really

think she is racist, which is a very strong word, or do you think she just struggles with authority? ... Do you think it is possible that she may be triggering an emotional memory for you of someone in your family?"

The supervisor's questions were irrefutably clinically relevant, especially for clinical supervision. However, the timing of the questions and the invalidation of Mulani's perspective were problematic. The interaction would have been infinitely more effective and less racially charged had Helen validated Mulani's sentiment. She could have first invited Mulani to share more of her thoughts and feelings before posing "questions" that essentially called into question her version of the clinical experience. Mulani's response was to withdraw from the conversation and to conclude, as she later reported to her black colleagues, "white people always protect each other when it comes to race. Why should I have expected anything different from Helen just because she is a supervisor? At the end of the day she is still white!" Unfortunately, the conversation between Helen and Mulani was painfully reminiscent of most conversations about race that end prematurely and without resolution.

*Challenges disguised as advice* are also used to negate conversations about race.

> Lupa, a first-generation immigrant from Columbia and one of two Latinas working in a low-income multiracial community steeped in racial conflict, stated to her African American coworker Marva: "As a Latina I feel disrespected here. I feel like me and Selena get no respect because we are not African American. I feel like we don't fit in here and you don't want us here. It's a terrible feeling and it doesn't feel fair: it's not our fault that we aren't black!" Marva, listening attentively but shaking her head disapprovingly throughout Lupa's entire disclosure, responded, "I really think you and Selena would feel better about all of this if you learned more English. I think it would be helpful for you to enroll in one of the ESL classes at Community College—and they are free!"

It is conceivable that Marva's "advice" was relevant and could have been helpful to Lupa and Selena. However, what she did under the (dis)guise of disseminating helpful advice was to effectively dismiss and negate the heartfelt claims that Lupa made about race and their relationship. At no point did Marva acknowledge or validate any aspect of Lupa's claim.

*Silence* is another powerful tool of negation that is often used as an instrument of disconfirmation. When a person in the subjugated position makes a comment, particularly one that is laced with affect, and it engenders no comment or (expressed) reaction from the person in the privileged position, the original disclosure is de facto negated. The unintentional underlying message that gets communicated is "your message was not worthy of recognition or response."

*Privempathy* is the term I have coined to refer to the empathy of the privilege. It often negates the disclosures of persons in the subjugated position by offering parallels or similarities to the shared disclosure while simultaneously negating it by advocating false notions of equality.

> In a graduate-level cultural diversity course, Jaipaul nervously stated: "As the only brown person in the class I often feel racially marginalized. I feel like when we talk about race it is always about black people. I have no objections about talking about blacks, but I just wonder why there isn't space for people like me. I feel totally invisible, like I really don't matter." Both the tension and the silence in the classroom were deafening. Richard, the only white male in the class, nervously scanned the room and then stated: "Jaipaul, I know what you mean and I feel your pain. As a white male I have that same thought every class. It's like I'm either invisible or demonized. When do I get to talk about all of the reverse racism that I experience from people of color, especially blacks? I always have to hear shit like 'you're white, YOU DID THIS, YOU DID THAT.' You talk about being invisible—I am totally invisible in here!"

What commenced as Richard's "empathy" for Jaipaul quickly shifted to a disclosure about his suffering as a white male. In the process there was very little, if any, overt acknowledgment of or attention devoted to Jaipaul's painful disclosure. Richard made a number of painful disclosures in his own right that certainly warrant close and acute attention, but not at the moment he shared them and not at the expense of his classmate. Richard's *equalization* of his and Jaipaul's "suffering" essentially overshadowed and negated the latter's experience as "a brown person" who felt uniquely marginalized within the class culture. The subtext of Jaipaul's message was "this is how I am marginalized in this class based on my unique identity " and Richard countered by (indirectly and unintentionally) implying that the experience that Jaipaul considered unique was anything but, because it applied to him as well.

> The tension in the classroom intensified as Monique, an African American student, passionately shared her perspective. She appeared to be oblivious to Richard's comments and directed her comments to Jaipaul. Without seemingly taking a moment to breathe, she turned to Jaipaul and stated tersely: "In THIS country it IS about black and white. As black people we have had to deal with shit that no other group has ever had to deal with. Before some cultures ever came to this country, we were slaves, we were denied the right to vote, beaten up, hosed down, and raped. THIS is why we talk about black and THIS is why we SHOULD keep talking about black issues!"

Unlike her classmate Richard, Monique did not engage in privempathy; instead, her negation of Jaipaul's disclosure was a direct rejection of his point of view. It was an *undisguised negation*. Jaipaul's perspective was completely and categorically rejected. As in the case with Richard's disclosure, what reasonable-thinking human being could deny the cogency of her remarks? Yet her disclosure and subsequent negation of Jaipaul's comments were just as problematic as Richard's. Both responses demonstrate some of the inherent complexities in discussing race and avoiding conversations that negate.

**Tactic #2:** Practice the art and skill of validation.

### 3. Avoid Reactive Reflexes: Acts of Relational Retrenchment, Rebuttal, and Retribution

Conversations about race, especially cross-racially, can be very emotionally taxing for all parties involved, and in some ways can be even more so for many whites. These conversations are often emotionally destabilizing for many whites and provoke a bevy of intense feelings ranging from sadness and guilt to anger and fury. Accordingly, it is also relatively easy for many whites to quickly feel personally attacked and/or hurt by the unbridled and expressed rage of many people of color. Under these emotionally evocative circumstances it becomes almost instinctual for many whites to reactively retreat toward self-soothing and/or self-protective strategies for coping. Unfortunately, these tactics do very little to facilitate the effective engagement of a progressive conversation about race.

In light of these dynamics, it is imperative for whites to avoid reactions that will either facilitate their withdrawal from the conversation (and ultimately the relationship) or contribute to the escalation of conflict. Comments such as "I have nothing else to say . . . I'm done with the matter . . . I can't convince you, so why bother" are all statements of *relational retrenchment*. These are statements of surrender. They become expressions of exasperation, frustration, and futility that justify retrenchment from both the conversation and the relationship. Relational retrenchment ultimately eradicates the *will* to stay in the conversation.

While staying in the conversation is critical to having a progressive conversation about race, its benefits can be quickly undermined if *rebuttal* is used as the primary tool for accomplishing the task. When those in the privileged position, in this case whites, rely heavily on *acts of rebuttal* to remain in the conversation/relationship, a dynamic analogous to a sparring match typically ensues. These types of interaction are often characterized by incessant talking, perhaps even yelling, blame-affixing, little listening, and a principal focus on who is "right." Other than offering an opportunity for the immediate release of underlying, deeply felt affect, these types of encounters seldom offer anything constructive.

*Acts of retribution* is another reactive reflex commonly used by those in the privileged position. These acts can range from thinly veiled threats directed toward those in the subjugated position to verbal disclosures deliberately designed to provoke strong affect or to emotionally injure in the spirit of revenge.

Although each of these acts has been presented here discretely, they are intricately intertwined, which makes their dynamics hard to identify and deconstruct in the midst of conversation. Becoming more mindful of these "reflexes" and consciously avoiding reliance on them can be one of the most challenging and beneficial tasks executed by the privileged.

**Tactic #3:** Develop thick skin.

## 4. Avoid the Issuance of Prescriptions

*The issuance of prescriptions* refers to a seemingly benign but often explosive dynamic that involves those in the privileged position offering what is believed to be value-free, "objective," and benevolent advice to those in the subjugated group regarding their well-being. The underlying implication of the prescription issuance is that those in the privileged position know the needs of those in the subjugated position better than they do themselves. This dynamic reinforces extant broader societal messages regarding superiority/inferiority and who is intelligent and who isn't. Although it clearly may not be the "intention" of the privileged to reify such polarizing and devaluing messages, the "consequence" is almost always to the contrary.

> Awinita, a Cherokee social worker, stated to Stephanie, her white coworker, that she was frustrated with the lack of respect that the agency they worked for demonstrated toward Native people and their healing methods. "I'm sorry, but it's the same old way it's always been. It's as if the ONLY way and the RIGHT way is always the white way," Awinita stated with a sense of anguish. Stephanie, appearing slightly irritated, responded firmly: "Well, Awinita, I don't know what to say. Maybe you and the other Native people here should just focus on learning how to be the best social workers you can be and stop worrying about whether it's 'Native' or not . . . healing is healing. I think all of you will be less frustrated if you stop obsessing over whether it's Native or not."

Stephanie's response to Awinita was to issue her a prescription for how she could be less troubled about their agency's failure to expand its intervention practices to take into consideration the cultural needs of some of its clients. Implicit in Stephanie's response was the notion that it was she, not Awinita, who knew what was in the best interest of the Native Americans in the agency.

**Task #4:** Supplant prescriptions with vulnerable disclosures about one's self.

## 5. Avoid Speaking from the KNOE (Knowledgeable, Neutral, Objective, Expert) Position

One of the major impediments to conversations between the privileged and the subjugated is the presumption that the former speak from a position of neutrality, objectivity, and, in some cases, expertise. Thus, in conversations about race, the phenomenon and influences of whiteness are rarely if ever overtly acknowledged (Hardy, 2008). Positions taken by whites and the opinions they express are often considered knowledgeable, neutral, objective, and free of the influence of race. There is a persistent and predictable disconnect between the whiteness of whites and what they say. It is common to assume that the disclosures of many whites are free of racial contamination and bias. For example, a person of color makes a reference to race, and a white person responds, "Why are you playing the race card?" It is rarely commented on or considered that the mere asking of the question could also be construed as playing a race card. This rarely happens because exploring how race informs the attitudes and behaviors of whites in their execution of everyday life is a foreign concept. The unacknowledged, unexplored, hidden dimensions of whiteness (racial privilege) on whites are a major impediment to having effective conversations about race. It is this dynamic that provides the fuel for every task discussed in this section.

**Tactic #5:** Always locate one's racial self in the conversation.

Several other tasks of the privileged cannot be discussed here due to space limitations, but the five that have been presented can have a powerful positive impact on otherwise difficult racial conversations.

## THE TASKS OF THE SUBJUGATED

It is equally important for people of color to use the tasks of the subjugated as a guide to their participation. The following is a description of these tasks and the tactics for implementation.

### 1. Challenge Silencing and Voicelessness

Silence is the hallmark of oppression. Regardless of the type or origins of oppression, "voicelessness" is a common denominator. Voicelessness is a hidden trauma wound that is a response to the process of "silencing," a principal tool used by those who oppress. Silencing is a powerful tool of oppression that teaches the oppressed that "speaking" and "self-advocacy" can have severe consequences. Thus, voicelessness, the counterpart to silencing, refers to an "inability" to speak on one's behalf, specifically in regard to self-advocacy. Voicelessness can be manifested as remaining silent when one *wants* to speak but *can't* or by assuming positions of subservience or hypercompliance, or adopting a sense of selflessness. The reticence or "inability" to speak or act on one's behalf is usually rooted in a fear of reprisal by whites or is a byproduct of a racial socialization process that teaches people of color that silence is not only golden but is integral to one's survival. "I don't want to come across as an angry black male," "I don't want to be perceived as the minority who is always complaining about race," and "I didn't say anything when that racist comment was made; I just tried to ignore it and let it go" are all expressions of voicelessness. No matter how much these claims are rationalized or euphemized, they mask a deeply seated underlying pain for many people of color that contributes to the birth of other conditions that make healthy race relationships and conversations virtually impossible. One of the major detrimental and unintended consequences of voicelessness is that it is a prelude to rage, which is a strong emotion inextricably tied to experiences of degradation, devaluation, and/or domination. Once rage invades a relationship, it either overshadows or destroys the potential for trust, goodwill, and respectful engagement.

People of color cannot initiate or participate in constructive conversations about race if their voices remain muted. Attempts at conversations are often quickly short-circuited by trepidation and highly constrained disclosures on the one hand or emotional explosiveness and rage on the other. Either way the result is always the same: misunderstanding, polarization, and continued strained racial relationships.

Overcoming voicelessness and reclaiming and exercising one's voice require risk taking. The process involves making a concerted effort to make just one comment more than one is comfortable making and not worrying about whether anyone is listening, whether anything will change, or how one might be perceived. After all, the principal purpose in speaking is to reclaim one's voice and overcome voicelessness.

**Tactic #1:** Use "I" messages and embed all statements within the framework of "I think, I feel, and I wish." Practice and take risks in making just one comment more than you are comfortable making.

## 2.  Regulate and Rechannel Rage

Rage is a common and predictable byproduct of silencing and voicelessness (Cose, 2011). In fact, the two phenomena are very closely intertwined. The more one has been silenced, the greater the degree of voicelessness, which inevitably intensifies rage. As rage increases in intensity, the more difficult it is to manage effectively. Rage is a normal reaction to experiences of injustice and can be a powerful resource when it is appropriately managed and rechanneled (Hardy & Laszloffy, 1995). On the other hand, it also can be quite destructive when it is improperly managed and free-floating. In conversations about race, particularly cross-racially, it is often the intense semifiltered, free-floating, unmanaged rage expressed by some people of color that compromises attempts to engage in constructive dialog. Thus, it is the failure of people of color to appropriately manage and rechannel their rage, coupled with the failure of whites to exhibit "thick skin" (see "Tasks of the Privileged" #5) during these moments, that significantly hampers attempts to have productive conversations about race.

The goal for those who are "enraged" is to mobilize their energy to become "outraged" (Hardy, 2013). The latter requires overcoming voicelessness and establishing the ability to express rage proactively and constructively. The goal is never to eradicate rage, but to use rage appropriately, people of color must *identify, embrace*, and ultimately *rechannel* rage. Since rage is often entangled with a host of other feelings and experiences, people of color need to sharpen their rage-detection abilities to develop a more comprehensive understanding of how rage infiltrates their lives. Rage can be manifested in a number of expressions and experiences, ranging from sadness and depression to self-destructiveness and violence. Identifying rage is an essential and fundamental step to moving toward effective management of it.

Once rage has been identified, the next crucial step is to embrace it. When people of color begin to embrace rage, they inevitably begin to develop a clearer understanding of the distinctions between rage and anger. They become willing to relinquish their preoccupation about whether they are reinforcing the stereotype of "being angry." Instead, embracing rage enables people of color to own these complex feelings without shame or disavowal. This is an important developmental step because repudiating one's anger is often an attempt to counteract a description of people of color that has been predominantly promulgated by whites (see "Tasks of the Subjugated" #3). Finally, embracing rage allows people of color to be more fully integrated. No longer will it be necessary to be enraged by assaults on one's dignity, and then have to deny them to avoid "appearing angry," and then being left to live with the "anger" of being angry but not being "allowed" to express it. This is the perfect recipe for the buildup of destructive rage.

**Tactic #2:** Use rage as an energy source to foster and reinforce your voice and self-advocacy. Resolve to stay engaged in difficult conversations. Attack ideas, not people.

### 3. Engage in a Process of Exhaling

The process of embracing rage is directly related to the task of exhaling. Part of the privilege of privilege is that those who possess it are empowered to define others' experiences, behaviors, and realities. As a result, it is more common for those in the subjugated position to "be defined" than it is to "define their being." The process of defining, which often leads to the "manufacturing of other," creates a series of narratives regarding who and what (in this case, people of color) are and are not. Since such definitions are usually based on limited and skewed data and devote scant attention (at best) to social context, they are often negative, stereotypical, and psychologically damaging. Unfortunately, these narratives become not only "internalized noise" for many people of color, but very potent life-shaping organizing principles as well. Many people of color live with a consciousness of these narratives while simultaneously remaining unconscious to the ways in which they become internalized. The everyday life experiences of most people of color are profoundly organized (controlled) by the internalized noise. If the external narratives are that people of color are angry, dangerous, and violent, this becomes an organizing principle that is hard to ignore, especially when the external world often responds as if it were factual. Consequently, it becomes the burden of people of color to prove that they are exceptions to the narrative. Like silencing, being defined often leaves people of color feeling powerless, helpless, and trapped between spurious choices: they choose either to ignore the internalized noise and risk reinforcing broader narratives or to make a concerted effort to disprove them and ultimately be controlled by them.

People of color must engage in a process of exhaling as a prerequisite to having effective conversations about race. The process will enable them to identify all of the racially debilitating toxic messages that they have internalized and that ultimately interfere with their full participation in meaningful conversations about race. Through the process of exhaling, people of color can expunge from their psyches and soul many of the internalized messages that constrain them, such as those about whether they are smart enough, articulate enough, or good enough. The process is self-liberating and allows for a much freer and more uninhibited participation in challenging conversations about race.

**Tactic #3:** Focus on *being* congruent and communicating accordingly. Say what you mean and mean what you say.

## 4. Cease and Desist Caretaking of the Privileged

Many people of color have been historically and systematically "socialized" to provide caretaking for the privileged (Diller, 2007). This phenomenon has been reinforced by the systematic assignment of disproportionate numbers of people of color to positions as maids, butlers, janitors, nannies, cooks, and other servants. Along with these positions of servitude was an informal code of conduct that required the subjugated—-people of color—to be deferential, self-sacrificing, nonconfrontational, and hypercompliant in order to be considered good citizens. Since the code of conduct also allowed many whites to enjoy their lives free of a sense of injustice, guilt, or compassion for the suffering of others, the failure of people of color to uphold and adhere to it often resulted in some form of a punitive consequence that had to be endured.

Although people of color occupy a broader and more diverse range of occupations in the workforce today, vestiges of the code of conduct largely remain with regard to the interpersonal interactions between many whites and people of color. The contemporary expressions of caretaking have shifted from physical tasks such as tilling the soil, preparing food, and caring for children to more subtle emotional-psychological manifestations. For example, in cross-racial conversations, especially those involving race, many people of color will self-censor, use coded language, and resort to silence (voicelessness) to protect whites from experiencing discomfort. The motivation for the emotional caretaking is neither solely altruistic nor one-dimensional, as it serves the safety needs of both groups. It can be precipitated by the desire to pacify whites as a mechanism to avoid punishment or disapproval, or it can be a function of powerful internalized messages and voicelessness. Regardless of the motivation, it becomes virtually impossible to have effective and meaningful conversations when one party is not fully present, honest, or authentic in the relationship.

The prohibition against caretaking is not tantamount to being rude, disrespectful, or uncaring; instead, it means being authentic with oneself and others. It requires people of color to manage their anxiety and to remain emotionally centered and narrowly focused on the conversation even if whites are noticeably uncomfortable. There is a fundamental difference between being caring and caretaking; it is the latter that is under scrutiny in this section.

**Tactic #4:** Stay intimately engaged, but grant uninterrupted emotional space to whites to explore, understand, and experience the myriad of complex thoughts and feelings that race conversations are likely to provoke. Be caring without caretaking.

### 5. Maintain Investment in the Conversation

For many people of color, conversations about race are often fraught with frustration, emotional escalation, a sinking sense of futility, and withdrawal disguised as closure. For those in both the privileged and subjugated positions, the temptation to withdraw from the conversation is enormous. The importance of whites developing "thick skin" as a mechanism for staying in the conversation was discussed earlier. For people of color, maintaining investment in the conversation is an important key to effectively navigating it. Because racial conversations are often nonprogressive and symmetrical, many people of color often conclude that "white people just don't get it and don't want to get it." This sentiment often breeds contempt as well as a sense of futility, the consequence of which is usually a resignation from the conversation once it fails to progress beyond a certain point. While withdrawal from the conversation is understandable, the cut-off, unexpressed, suppressed feelings associated with it neither dissipate nor diminish over time. Instead they become the seeds for rage and an accumulated sense of angst that make future conversations more difficult and truly futile.

It is important for people of color to *stay in the conversation* even when convinced that "whites will never get it." After all, the purpose of the conversation should never be to convince whites or lecture or educate them. The purpose of the conversation and staying in it is to afford people of color the opportunity to define, not defend, themselves; to overcome voicelessness; and to increase the possibilities of having a transformative cross-racial interaction. The demonstrated understanding by whites should not be a precondition for remaining invested in the conversation. There is tremendous healing and transformative potential in dialog and conversation, and maintaining investment in the process is essential.

**Tactic #5:** Refrain from analyzing "the other" while simultaneously speaking from the core of one's thoughts, feelings, and experiences.

As noted earlier, these tasks are most effective and hold the greatest potential for promoting progressive conversations when they are executed simultaneously by the privileged and subjugated. They are not a panacea for racial injustice or transforming those who use them. Instead, the tasks are designed to provide a foundation for constructive engagement by outlining a set of rudimentary ground rules and principles for how we can begin to forge a different type of conversation across a vast racial divide and can actually dignify each other in the process (Smith, 1992). If we can do this, it certainly will place us on a promising path toward healing and transforming racial strife.

## CONCLUSION

Although race is, has been, and will be for the foreseeable future a major organizing principle in our society both inside and outside the workplace, conducting meaningful conversations remains a daunting feat. Attempts to discuss race often culminate in quickly aborted failed attempts, rapid escalation, and/or polarization. Our failure to engage in progressive conversations about race makes it difficult to address or transform antiracist practices in a thoughtful and productive manner. The PAST Model has been introduced as a semistructured framework for guiding conversations about race. Adherence to the model requires all participants to think critically about their racial positioning in a given conversation and then to execute the tasks associated with either their "privileged" or "subjugated" positions. Effective conversation is a precursor to transforming health and human services systems. Being a good steward of effective racial conversations requires one to "know thyself," particularly in terms of the relative power and privilege that one holds in a relationship.

## DISCUSSION QUESTIONS

1. In the vignette involving Mulani, the African American therapist, and her white supervisor, Helen, how could the PAST Model be used to help them effectively restart their conversation?

2. In the vignette involving Jaipaul, Richard, and Monique, if you were in a position to coach them through their contentious and failed conversation, using the PAST Model as your guide, where would you start? Whom would you start with and why?

3. Why do you think it is common during heated racial encounters for each of us to resort to our subjugated positions?

## REFERENCES

Berman Cushing, B., Cabbil, L., Freeman, M., Hitchcock, J., & Richards, K. (Eds.) (2010). *Accountability and white anti-racist organizing: Stories from our work.* Roselle, NJ: Crandall, Dostie and Douglass Books.

Cose, E. (2011). *The end of anger.* New York: HarperCollins.

Diller, J. V. (2007). *Cultural diversity: A primer for human services* (3rd ed.). Belmont, CA: Thomson Brooks/Cole.

Hardy, K. V. (2008). Race, reality, and relationships: Implications for the re-visioning of family therapy. In M. McGoldrick & K. V. Hardy (Eds.), *Re-visioning family therapy: Race, culture, and gender in clinical practice* (2nd ed., pp. 76–84). New York: Guilford Publications.

Hardy, K. V. (2013). Healing the hidden wounds of racial trauma. *Reclaiming Children and Youth, 21*(4).

Hardy, K. V., & Laszloffy, T. A. (1995). Therapy with African Americans and the phenomenon of rage. *In Sessions: Psychotherapy in Practice, 1*(4), 57–70.

Hardy, K. V., & Laszloffy, T. A. (2008). The dynamics of a pro-racist ideology: Implications for family therapists. In M. McGoldrick & K. V. Hardy (Eds.), *Re-visioning family therapy: Race, culture, and gender in clinical practice* (2nd ed., pp. 225–237). New York: Guilford Publications.

Patterson, K., Grenny, J., McMillan, R., & Switzler, A. (2005). *Crucial conversations: Tools for resolving broken promises, violated expectations, and bad behaviors.* New York: McGraw-Hill.

Singleton, G., & Linton, C. W. (2006). *Courageous conversations about race.* Thousand Oaks, CA: Corwin Press.

Smith, A. D. (1992). *Talk to me: Travels in media and politics.* New York: Anchor Books.

# PART THREE

# Systemic Impacts
# and Special Populations

# CHAPTER 9

# Children, Youth, and Family Serving Systems

## GERALD P. MALLON AND RUTH G. MCROY

The issue of race and culture in child welfare is often noted, but only recently has the issue begun to receive attention at the national level by professionals and practitioners. In the past decade, there has been progress, most notably by the Children's Bureau, State of Texas Department of Children and Family Services, Casey Family Programs, and the Child Welfare League of America, with significant efforts to openly and honestly address issues of race and culture. Disproportionate representation in foster care, one of the primary reflections of race and culture in the child welfare system, refers to the current situation in which particular racial and ethnic groups of children are represented in foster care at a higher or lower percentage than their representation in the general population. Children of color, belonging to various cultural, ethnic, and racial communities (primarily African American, Hispanic, and Native American), are disproportionately represented in the child welfare system and overwhelmingly experience disparate treatment, which is reflected in their having worse outcomes. The disproportionate representation of children of color in the child welfare and other social service systems (e.g., juvenile justice) is linked to social class, economic, and other factors that must be addressed to ensure that all children are fairly and appropriately served.

In this chapter, within the context of antiracist strategies for transforming the health and human services, we review the key facts and existing scholarship and discuss the broad range of issues concerning culture and race in child welfare systems. Special attention is given to providing a historical look at disproportionality as well as an examination of foster care inequities. The chapter ends with conclusions and a discussion highlighting implications for practice and policy improvement that will be helpful for those seeking to work toward greater equality within the child welfare system.

## STATISTICAL OVERVIEW: THE COLOR
## OF CHILD WELFARE

A close look at the latest statistics available from the Adoption and Foster Care Analysis and Reporting System (AFCARS) (U.S. Department of Health & Human Services [USDHHS], 2015) reveals that as of September 30, 2014, , 58% of the 415,219 children in the U.S. foster care system were children of color, yet only 48% of all U.S. children are children of color. The inverse is true for white children, who represent 52% of the U.S. child population under the age of 18 (Childstats.gov, 2015), yet only 42% (174,477) of white children were in out-of-home care in 2014 (USDHHS, 2015).

Further examination of ethnic differences among the populations of children of color reveals that African Americans (see http://www.hunter.cuny.edu/soc-work/nrcfcpp/info_services/disproportionate.html) and Native Americans (see http://www.nrcpfc.org/is/indian-child-welfare.html) have the highest overrepresentation of all ethnic groups in foster care. African American children made up 24% (97,540) of those in out-of-home care in 2014 yet constitute only 13.8 of the U.S. population of children and youth. Native American children are also overrepresented in foster care, as they made up 2% (9,517) of the foster care population and only .9% of the U.S. child population (USDHHS, 2015; Federal Interagency forum on Child and Family Statistics, 2015). Cross (2014) has noted that "over-reporting" of American Indians and African Americans, often stemming from unintended racial or cultural bias, can be a factor that leads to disproportionate representation of these population groups in care. Asian American children tend to be underrepresented in foster care, representing only 1% (2,107) of the total foster care population. Native Hawaiian/Pacific Islanders were even less represented, with 0% (693) of the foster care population (USDHHS, 2015). Much more information is needed to fully understand these disproportionately low foster care rates. Cheung and LaChapelle (2011) have called for empirical research to explore the actual occurrence of abuse in Asian American communities and the possibility of underreporting, as well as whether factors such as biases or perceptions of Asian American communities may lead to underreporting.

Recent data on Latino children and youth in the child welfare system reveal several interesting trends (see for additional information http://www.nrcpfc.org/is/latino-child-welfare.html). Nationally, Latino children represent 24% of the U.S. child population, and a slightly lower percentage, 22%, of the foster care population (USDHHS, 2015; ). However, , a closer look reveals that Latino children were "overrepresented in 19 states and underrepresented in 30 states in

2006" (Dettlaff, 2011, p. 122). Also, in some locations, Latino children may be underrepresented at the state level but overrepresented in a particular county. Dettlaff (2011) identifies several possible explanations for these trends. He suggests that this underrepresentation may be due to lower levels of maltreatment, family strengths, or protective factors that mitigate risk, or to "underreporting, especially of Latino children in undocumented immigrant families, and they are therefore less likely to come to the attention of child welfare systems" (Dettlaff, 2011, p. 123). It is important to point out that at one time Latino children were placed as "white" children in white homes and their cultural heritage was ignored and/or erased (Rivera, 2014).

### Native American Children

The issue of child welfare services for American Indian children has a long and complicated history fraught with trauma for Indian people and their communities (Cross, 2014). Before the passage of the Indian Child Welfare Act of 1978, Indian children were removed from their homes by the hundreds of thousands by child welfare professionals and agencies that believed Indian homes were generally unfit. Widespread poverty and social problems on reservations were not addressed but were cited as reasons for the wholesale removal of children to non-Indian homes. Cross (2014) notes that cultural differences also accounted for inappropriate removals. Foremost among these differences is the concept of "family" itself. Whereas in mainstream America the individual's primary source of identity is the nuclear family, in many Indian communities the individual is defined by his or her membership in the extended family, clan, and tribe. Extended-kin families share responsibility for the welfare of all family members. This practice is reflected in the names applied to relatives. Terms such as "mother," "father," "aunt," and "uncle" are interchangeable for all relatives of a child of a certain age, and "brother" or "sister" apply to cousins as well as to siblings in some traditional Indian cultures (Swinomish Tribal Mental Health Project, 1991). Often children in Indian families are raised, temporarily or permanently, by relatives (placed informally or customarily). Mainstream child welfare workers sometimes mistook these arrangements for abandonment.

Thousands more Indian children were placed away from their families in Indian boarding schools. In the late eighteenth century, the U.S. government desired to acculturate and assimilate American Indians (as opposed to instituting reservations), and promoted the practice of educating Indian children in the ways of white people. To aid this, the Civilization Fund Act of 1819 provided funding to societies (mostly religious) who worked on educating Indians, often at schools. Schools were founded by missionaries next to Indian settlements and reservations. As time went on schools were built with boarding facilities to accommodate students who lived too far to attend on a daily basis. Given English names, short haircuts, and uniforms, these children were not allowed to speak their own languages, often facing punishment for doing so, and were forced to take on Christianity. Overcrowding, poor sanitary conditions, and infectious disease were common in many schools. Students often ran away in an effort to get home to their families.

### African American Children

Since the majority of the research literature on racial disproportionality in foster care has focused on the African American population (Belanger, Green, & Bullard, 2008; Billingsley, 1992; Billingsley & Giovannoni, 1972; Carten & Dumpson, 1995; Chestang, 1972; Derezotes, Poertner, & Testa, 2005; Hill, 1997, 2006, 2011; McRoy, 1994, 2004, 2011a, 2011b, 2014; McRoy, Oglesby, & Grape, 1997; Roberts, 2002) due to their very significant overrepresentation, in this chapter we review the recent literature on the causes and correlates of African American disproportionality, and will present risk and protective factors as well as current policies and programs for addressing this problem. We will conclude with a discussion of the implications for child welfare practice with children, youth, and families of color.

## CONTRIBUTING FACTORS TO SYSTEMIC INEQUALITIES

To gain a more complete understanding of the causes of disproportionality of children of color in foster care, readers should consider the following (see Dougherty, 2003; http://www.nrcpfc.org/is/cultural-competence):

1. Exploring whether factors such as bias and service obstacles could lead to both overrepresentation and underrepresentation of specific groups of children in the child welfare system
2. Examining not just overrepresentation or underrepresentation of children in care, but assessing this disproportional representation at each decision point over time (Shaw et al., 2011).

As Anyon (2011, p. 242) observes, "at the national level, African American youth are overrepresented at every stage of the child welfare intervention process, and these disproportionalities grow as children move deeper into the system." That is, not only do African American children experience disproportionately higher rates of maltreatment investigation and abuse and neglect substantiation

(Fluke et al., 1999), they are also more likely to be removed from their parents and placed in foster care, more likely to stay in foster care for longer periods of time, less likely to be either returned home or adopted, and more likely to be emancipated from the child welfare system. In addition, the instability in foster children's lives makes it difficult for them to become productive citizens as they mature. Educational delays and emotional stress are associated with both maltreatment and multiple placements. Finally, youth of color aging out of care are at high risk for depression, homelessness, and economic dependency.

## REVIEW OF THE LITERATURE

A number of factors potentially contribute to the disproportionate representation of African American children in the foster care system, including disproportionate poverty among African Americans; vulnerable single-parent households; greater visibility to authorities responsible for child maltreatment reporting; and racism and bias in reporting, in addition to welfare policies, lack of resources, community of residence, increasing substance abuse, and lack of community-based treatment (Bass, Shields, & Behrman, 2004; Chipungu & Bent-Goodley, 2004; Green, 2002; Hill, 1997).

According to the 2007–2011 U.S. Census (2013), 14.3% (42.7 million) of the total U.S. population live below the poverty level. By race, the highest national poverty rates were found among Indians and Native Alaskans (27%) and African Americans (25.8%). Native Hawaiian and other Pacific Islanders had a national poverty rate of 17.6%. Among Latinos, the range was a low of 16.2% for Cubans to a high of 26.3% for Dominicans. The Asian population poverty rate was highest for Vietnamese at 14.7% and Koreans at 15.0% and lowest for Filipinos at 5.8%. According to Pelton (1989), there is a strong relationship among child abuse, neglect, and poverty. It is a well-established fact that most of the children in foster care come from single-parent households (Lindsey, 1991; McRoy, 2011). Moreover, poverty rates are highest for families headed by single women. For example, in 2010, 49.7% of black children lived with their mothers only (compared to 18.3% of white children) (Children's Defense Fund, 2011). Therefore, it is no surprise that these families would be more vulnerable. Single mothers rarely receive child support, and low wages make it very difficult to afford good child care.

Further, Courtney (1998, p. 95) has reported that "the incidence of abuse and neglect is approximately 22 times higher among families with incomes less than $15,000 per year than among families with incomes of more than $30,000 per year." Note also that physicians and other service providers may be more likely to attribute an injury to abuse in cases of children from low-income homes; in families of higher income, they might attribute the same injury to an accident (Newberger, Reed, Daniel, Hyde, & Kotelchuck, 1977; O'Toole, Turbett, &

Nalpeka, 1983). These differential attributions and labeling biases against low-income families may account for some of the relationships that have been found between poverty and abuse.

McRoy (2014) and others (Hill, 1997), acknowledging that African American children are much more likely to be poor than white children, suggest that growing depression and substance abuse of impoverished parents can also lead to neglect. In fact, according to the Child Welfare League of America (1997), in 1995 about one million children were found to be substantiated victims of child abuse and neglect and at least 50% had chemically involved caregivers. Parental substance abuse is one of the leading contributors to children being removed from their home and placed in care.

Parental incarceration is another factor leading more children into the child welfare system. Drug abuse and alcohol abuse are clear factors contributing to the incarceration of 80% of the 1.7 million men and women in prison today. In 2008, 1.7 million children had at least one parent in prison and 45% of these children were African American (U.S. Department of Justice, 2008).

## CUMULATIVE EFFECT: THE PATH TO OVERREPRESENTATION IN THE CHILD WELFARE SYSTEM

Poverty, child abuse and neglect, parental substance abuse, and parental incarceration all combine to increase the potential vulnerability of African American children. However, these factors alone do not fully explain their overrepresentation in the child welfare system. Barth (2001), Kapp, McDonald, and Diamond (2001), and others have suggested that it is important to understand disproportionality by examining a child's path into the system, beginning with research findings of the likelihood of maltreatment of African American and white children. For example, although Fluke, Yuan, Hedderson, and Curtis (2002) found that African American, Hispanic, and Asian/Pacific Islander children have a disproportionately higher rate of maltreatment investigations than white children, several researchers (Ards, Chung, & Myers, 1999; Sedlak & Schultz, 2001) reported that African American children are not at greater risk for abuse and neglect. Knott and Donovan (2010, p. 679) note "after controlling for child, caregiver, household and abuse characteristics, African American children had 44% higher odds of foster care placement when compared with Caucasian children" in their secondary analyses of the 2005 National Child Abuse and Neglect Data System (NCANDS) findings on child abuse investigations in 48 states and the District of Columbia. Also, the National Incidence Study (NIS)-3 data (Sedlak & Broadhurst, 1996; USDHHS, 1996) found no statistically significant race differences in the incidence of maltreatment. These findings indicated that children of color are not at greater risk for abuse and neglect compared with white children and that there are no differences in the incidences of maltreatment (Ards, Chung, & Myers, 1999; Sedlak & Schultz, 2001). However, much controversy was raised by the analysis of the NIS-4 data, which suggested that there is a black/white maltreatment gap (Bartholet, Wulczyn, Barth, & Lederman 2011) and that maltreatment rates are higher among African American families. Others have questioned whether this finding in the NIS-4 analysis reflects an actual change in maltreatment rates or an issue of survey methodology (Wells, 2011). A close look at differences between type of maltreatment and race has revealed that black children in low-income families may have higher rates of harm from physical abuse and white children in low-income households may be more likely to experience neglect (Wells, 2011).

Despite the varying findings related to incidence between groups, differences have been found in substantiation rates of abuse/neglect for African American children. Eckenrode, Powers, Doris, Munsch, and Bolger (1988) reported study findings that suggested child maltreatment reports are much more likely to be substantiated for African American and Hispanic children than are those for Anglo children. Using hypothetical vignettes of cases of sexual abuse, Zellman (1992) found that survey participants were more likely to believe that the law required a report to be made when children of color were described in the vignettes than when white children were described.

Although some studies have found no racial differences in allegations of sexual abuse by race or ethnicity (National Center on Child Abuse and Neglect, 1988, 1996), some have found differences in type of abuse by race. For example, Cappelleri, Eckenrode, and Powers (1993) and Jones and McCurdy (1992) found that white children were more likely to experience sexual abuse (as compared to neglect) than African American children.

## OUTCOME DISPARITIES: CONTEMPORARY AND HISTORICAL ANALYSIS

Not only are African American children and youth overrepresented in the child welfare system, but researchers have found numerous racial inequities in service delivery. Courtney and colleagues (1996) reviewed much of the literature on disparities in service provision and found research accounts of inequities in child maltreatment reporting, child welfare service provision, kinship care, family preservation services, exit rates and length of care, placement stability, and adoption. Although a few studies they reported did not find an association with race, the majority did. They also found that most of the racial differences reported were found between African Americans and whites rather than among other racial groups.

## AN HISTORICAL LOOK AT DISPROPORTIONALITY

Disproportionality, overrepresentation, and differential service delivery are not new issues in foster care. According to Lawrence-Webb (1997), under the Aid to Dependent Children program established in 1935, states could determine eligibility for receiving public assistance. Therefore, to rule out "immoral families" from receiving public welfare benefits, many states established "home suitability" and "illegitimate child" clauses. During this period, Florida removed 14,000 children (more than 90% of them African American) from public assistance, and in 1960, 23,000 children were removed from the welfare rolls in Louisiana (McRoy, 2004). Once children and their families were declared ineligible for public assistance, the children in these families were often labeled as "neglected" due to lack of financial resources and were subsequently brought before the court for child protection issues.

In response, the Flemming rule, named after U.S. Department of Health, Education and Welfare Secretary Arthur Flemming, was passed in 1961; it required the provision of service interventions to families identified as being "unsuitable" (Murray & Gesreich, 2004, p. 2). Although services were to be provided, many caseworkers began to emphasize removal of the child from the home as opposed to working with the family to correct the conditions. At the time, most eligibility workers were not trained social workers and lacked the skills needed for understanding family dynamics and clinical intervention techniques (Lawrence-Webb, 1997, p. 13). Moreover, according to Lawrence-Webb (1997, p. 14), the workers serving African American families were untrained in cultural sensitivity and held racial stereotypes about African American clients. Therefore, they were more likely to push for child removal. Once removed from their families and placed in foster care, these children were not given equal access to services. For example, in 1959, Maas and Engler reported that many African American children in foster care were in need of adoption but were less likely to be adopted than white children.

Beginning with the 1962 amendments to the Social Security Act, which made open-ended funds available for out-of-home placements, children began to be removed from "undesirable family situations." Jeter (1963, p. 32) reported that 81% of children entered care because their parents were either unmarried or the children came from "broken homes. In public agencies, the largest groups of children placed in foster care consisted of both Negro and American Indian children, 49% of the Negro children, and 53% of the American Indian children. In voluntary agencies the proportions were even higher, 57% and 59% [respectively] in foster care." Jeter (1963) also found ongoing discrimination in service provision, noting that African American children were primarily being served by public agencies; private voluntary agencies were primarily serving white children. Black children were remaining in foster care for longer periods of time than were white children, and adoption was not being offered on an equitable basis.

Over the years, additional studies have documented differential service provision. In 1982, Olsen reported that white and Asian American families had the greatest chance of being referred for services and Native American families had the least chance. African American and Hispanic children were least likely to have plans for contact with their families. Barth and colleagues (1986) reported that in their study of 101 physically abused children in California, African American children were more likely than children in other racial groups to experience permanent out-of-home placement. Close (1983) and Stehno (1990) found that African American children in care were more likely to remain in care longer, were less likely to have visits with their families, and had fewer contacts with caseworkers. Similarly, Fein, Maluccio, and Kluger (1990) found that in their study of 779 children who had been in out-of-home care in Connecticut for at least two years in 1985, white children and white foster families received more services and support than did children and foster families of color.

Goerge (1990) found that over an eight-year period, African American children in Cook County, Illinois, remained in care for a median of 54 months, whereas the median length of stay for all other children was 18 months. Goerge, Wulczyn, and Harden (1994) reported significant differences in many states regarding the median duration in care between African American and white children. In California, the median time in care was 30.8 months for African American children compared to 13.6 months for white children. In Illinois, African American children had a median duration of 36.5 months compared to 6.6 months for white children. In Michigan, African American children remained in care a median of 17.5 months, whereas white children had a median duration of 11.2 months. In Texas, although the duration of care was not as great, there was a difference of 7.3 months for whites and 9 months for African Americans.

McMurtry and Gwat-Yong (1992) reported in their study of 775 foster children in Arizona that African American children were half as likely to be returned home as white children. These authors also found that African American children were three times as likely to be in the foster care system and that they had been in care for longer periods than the other three ethnic groups studied. Black children spent an average of three or more years in out-of-home care, whereas white and Hispanic children spent an average of 2.5 years, and other children of color, 2 years. The third group consisted of children from mixed racial backgrounds.

Berrick, Barth, and Needell (1994), studying 600 kinship foster parents and nonrelative foster parents in California, noted that white foster parents were receiving more services than were other foster parents and that kinship foster parents (mostly African American) were less likely to have been offered such services as training, respite care, and support groups than were nonrelative foster parents. Courtney (1994) found that in California, African American children placed in kinship care went home at about half the rate of similarly placed white children. According to Courtney (1995), African American children had significantly higher reentry rates into foster care than all other children, even after controlling for the child's age, health problems, placement history, and Aid for Families with Dependent Children program eligibility. Finally, Courtney and colleagues (1996) reported that African American children were also less likely to be adopted than white or Hispanic children.

Barth reported some of the most compelling findings of service disparities in 1997. In his longitudinal study of 3,873 children in California who were younger than six years old upon entry into care, it was reported that age and race had substantial independent effects on outcomes. Barth (1997, p. 296) stated that when "controlling for age, African American children were considerably less likely to be adopted than Anglo or Latino children. The estimated adopted/remained in care odds ratio was more than five times as great for Caucasian children as for African American children." An African American infant had nearly the same likelihood of being adopted as a white child aged three to five years old. Also, in this California study, the odds of African American children being reunified from nonkinship foster care were one-fourth those of white children in care.

Other states have reported disparities as well. For example, a study by the Minnesota Department of Human Services (2002) to the state legislature on outcomes for African American children in Minnesota's child protection system noted significant disparities. The Minnesota Department of Human Services (2002) found:

> Black children are more likely to be reported as suspected victims of maltreatment by teachers, police, nurses, family members or neighbors. Additionally, after an initial screening, Black children are six times as likely as white children to be referred for a more formal investigation. Black children are nearly eight times as likely as white children to be determined victims of maltreatment. Only two in five African American families receive counseling, compared to three in five white families. If a child becomes legally free for adoption, Black children stay in care two years and three months, which is about six months longer than white children. One of the largest areas of disproportionality in Minnesota occurs in Hennepin County in which African American children represent 10% of the child population, yet 60% of the placement population.

Disparate outcomes are reported for African American children not only in the foster care system: similar patterns are found in the juvenile justice system. African American youth in 1997 accounted for 26% of those arrested, 31% of referrals to juvenile court, 44% of youth detained, 56% of those waived to criminal court, 40% of those sent to residential placement, and 58% of those admitted to state prison. Although white youth were reported as committing higher levels of weapons-possession crimes, African American youth were arrested at 2.5 times the rate of white youth for weapons offenses (Building Blocks for Youth, 2000; Green, 2002).

Moreover, according to the Child Welfare League of America, there is a link between child abuse and later juvenile delinquency arrests. A study in Sacramento, California, indicated that children who were reported abused and neglected were 67 times more likely to be arrested between the ages of nine and 12 than were other children (Johnson, 1997). This link suggests even more dire long-term consequences for minority children, because they are disproportionately represented in abused and neglected populations.

## ADDRESSING FOSTER CARE INEQUITIES
### Court-Mandated Systems Improvement

Over the years, there has been growing concern about state child welfare systems' failures to correct the problematic outcomes for children in out-of-home care. Children's Rights of New York, a legal advocacy organization whose mission is to promote and protect the rights of abused and neglected children in foster care systems, has filed class-action suits against at least 18 states and other jurisdictions (Children's Rights, 2011). Six states have met all the settlement requirements and have been released from federal court oversight; cases in four states are active, prejudgment cases; and eight states have yet to meet the requirements of a settlement and remain under federal court oversight: Wisconsin, Washington, DC, Tennessee, New Jersey, Mississippi, Michigan, Georgia, and Connecticut (Children's Rights, 2011). For example, in 1989, Children's Rights brought a class-action complaint against the state of Connecticut stipulating:

> For children who are African American and Latino, there is no system to ensure that sufficient numbers of appropriately trained, culturally sensitive, and bilingual persons exist to perform necessary evaluations and render appropriate treatment.... Defendants have failed to provide sufficient services statewide (and particularly to non-English-speaking and African-American families) to ensure timely access to services, which are necessary to ensure that reasonable efforts are and can be, made by DCYS to avert out-of home placements for all children. (*Juan F. v. Rell* 1989: 42, 47)

However, in September 2010, more than 20 years after the case was filed, a U.S. District Judge stated: "children in the state's care face unneeded delay and disruption, and continue to go without important services" (Bachetti, 2011); therefore, the judge ruled that Connecticut's Department of Children and Families would remain under federal oversight (Kovner, 2010). As of June 2011, the department had failed to fully comply with the court-ordered exit plan and remained under federal oversight (Bachetti, 2011).

Children's Rights also filed a class-action lawsuit against Governor Donald Sundquist and George Hattaway, then Commissioner of the Tennessee

Department of Children's Services (DCS), for failure to protect the approximately 10,000 children dependent on the department for care and protection. The complaint was filed specifically on behalf of Brian A. and eight other named plaintiffs who were in the Tennessee foster care system. According to the complaint:

> The Plaintiff Class includes approximately 9,000 children reported by the state to be in DCS custody who are dependent and neglected, "unruly" or were placed into custody voluntarily by their parent(s) or guardian(s). There are approximately 4,400 African-American children in DCS custody. The questions of law and fact raised by the claims of the named Plaintiffs are common to and typical of those raised by the claims of the putative Class members. Each named Plaintiff and each putative Class and Subclass member is in need of child welfare services, must rely on Defendants for those services, and is harmed by DCS's systemic deficiencies. (Children's Rights, 2004)

The following charges were subsequently brought against DCS (Children's Rights, 2004, p. 12):

> Lack of appropriate foster care placements, lack of adequate assessments, investigations and services to insure safety of children returned to home of parents or relatives. Also DCS routinely fails to provide appropriate caseworker, monitoring and supervision. Children often face abuse and neglect while in care, do not receive necessary services and treatment, and frequently spend many years moving from one inappropriate placement to another. The comptroller's report stated, "upon entering custody, African American children are not as likely to receive adequate services crucial to achieving permanency and improving family participation." Defendants' criteria or methods of administering adoption and permanency services also have a discriminatory effect on African-American foster children. Children spend years of time in care, lose much of their childhoods, move from one inadequate placement to another, lack appropriate services, are discharged at 18 without life skills, and the turnover rates for caseworkers are unmanageably high.

On July 30, 2001, a federal district judge approved the settlement reached by these parties in Tennessee. The settlement called for a technical assistance committee of five national experts in the child welfare field to assist in the implementation of the agreement; an independent monitor to determine whether the state was making reforms; a quality assurance program for statewide implementation; a system for receiving screening and investigating reports of child abuse and neglect; regional services to support and preserve foster children in the state's custody; maximum limits on caseloads and number of caseworkers overseen by a single supervisor; and time periods within which children must be moved through the adoption process. The agreement also called for the state to hire an independent consultant to conduct a statewide evaluation of the Tennessee foster care program to determine whether African American children in the plaintiff class were receiving disparate treatment or suffering disparate impact, to assess the causes for such disparities, and to recommend solutions.

The Tennessee settlement is perhaps one of the most comprehensive agreements rendered in this type of case. Through court monitoring of the state's delivery system and mandating caseload size and service outcomes, the state has been held accountable for its actions on behalf of children, youth, and families of color.

## ADDRESSING ORGANIZATIONAL ISSUES RELATED TO RACE AND CULTURE IN CHILD WELFARE SYSTEMS

Similar to recommendations made by others (Annie E. Casey Foundation, 2006; Johnson, Antle, & Barbee, 2009), we propose that organizations begin to address these issues of racial disparities by first making systemic changes using a seven-pronged approach:

1. **Ending Racial and Ethnic Disparities in Systems**: Reforming institutional structures that limit access to opportunities for racial/ethnic groups and disadvantaged families, and developing data-based strategies and resources around these issues
2. **Promoting Diversity**: Ensuring that practice reflects the diversity of the community and is grounded in respect for local cultures, experiences, and aspirations
3. **Developing Cultural Competence and Community Assets**: Building on the considerable culturally grounded strengths of diverse families and communities
4. **Examining Disinvestment and Gentrification**: Revealing longstanding patterns and practices of discrimination, neglect, and missed opportunities that result in communities losing power, strength, and vitality
5. **Providing Training and Technical Assistance**: Connecting communities, staff, and others to culturally relevant information, tools, and skill-building opportunities to make change happen
6. **Seeking to Create and Maintain a Diverse Staff at all Levels**: We realize that a rich diversity of racial backgrounds, ethnicity, gender, age, and points of view and to its effectiveness with the communities, clients, and leaders with whom we work.
7. **Recognizing the Unique and Inherent Strengths of Communities of People of Color**: People who have been pushed into the margins of the dominant society have developed a set of unique skills for negotiating what is often a hostile environment. Such skills can be reframed to promote growth and resilience.

## EFFECTIVE STRATEGIES

One of the most effective strategies for addressing race and culture in child welfare was taken on by the leaders of the Texas child welfare system, who took specific statewide steps to identify systemic racist practices and policies that harm African American families and have developed action plans to improve outcomes and decrease disparities. Texas child welfare leaders have become ambassadors for change by making disproportionality visible in their region and in the communities. They have improved their delivery of services, and the change has been visible both to clients and to the community at large. They demonstrate both accountability and passion through the belief that disproportionality was done and therefore can be undone. The core of addressing disparities within the child welfare system is developing a cultural change that embraces the principles of antiracism in everyday practices (James, Green, Rodriguez, & Fong, 2008).

Robert Hill (2004) advocates for the following systemic changes:

- Need to place higher priority on family preservation and reunification
- Need to provide more equitable financial and social support to kin caregivers
- Need for a federal subsidized guardianship law
- Need to mandate states to reduce minority overrepresentation in child welfare

As a response to the 2007 U.S. Government Accountability Office (GAO) report, the Casey-CSSP Alliance for Racial Equity in Child Welfare emphasized that federal and state policies and solutions must support the efforts of the state and county systems to effect positive change in addressing disproportionality in state and county child welfare systems. The alliance proposed several specific recommendations:

- Improve child welfare financing to promote permanency
- Provide family-strengthening and prevention services
- Implement strength-based decision-making approaches in all systems that serve children and families
- Enhance the capacity of federally funded data collection and reporting systems
- Report on racial and ethnic disparities in assessing state child welfare systems
- Increase involvement of families in the development and implementation of child welfare policies and practices
- Expand cultural competence training to adequately address disproportionality and disparate outcomes

Similarly, the alliance identified six dimensions that are needed in order to address and reduce racial and ethnic disproportionality in child welfare systems:

1. Create a policy and finance environment that supports achieving racial equity as an outcome through legislation, policy change, and finance reform
2. Identify promising practices and evidence-based solutions through research and evaluation
3. Create and enhancing youth, parent, and community partnerships
4. Create public will through well-designed messages and distribution
5. Develop a culturally competent child welfare workforce
6. Practice change by improving policies and practices (site-based implementation)

Child welfare agencies and the Casey Family Programs' Breakthrough Series Collaborative on reducing disproportionality and disparate outcomes for children and families of color suggested the following key components of the framework to address disproportionality in child welfare agencies:

- Agency mission and policies that support antiracist practice
- Cross-system leadership that addresses disproportionality and disparity in outcomes
- Collaboration with community and tribal stakeholders to support families
- Community partnerships to address child maltreatment, disproportionality, and racism and to help communities build the protective capacity of neighborhoods, tribes, and families
- Staff and stakeholder training about institutional and structural racism and its impact on decision making, policy, and practice
- Use of cultural values, beliefs, and practices of families, communities, and tribes to shape family assessment, case planning, case service design, and decision-making process
- Development and use of data in partnership with families and communities to assess agency success at key decision points in addressing disproportionality and disparate outcomes

## IMPLICATIONS FOR IMPROVED POLICY AND PRACTICE

Child welfare systems have a history of cultural preference and most have not been designed to serve culturally and racially diverse populations. For example, until the 1960s, public child welfare services—specifically, adoption services—systematically excluded African American children. Over the past four decades, the population served by the public child welfare system has become increasingly diverse, and for some populations it has become overly inclusive. Currently, child welfare systems attempt to protect children by relying on placement, with less attention to the family and community issues that make families and children of color more vulnerable.

Overrepresentation and racial disparities in child welfare service provision must be recognized and addressed in state systems (Green, Belanger, McRoy, & Bullard, 2011). If not, it is likely that there will be more class-action suits on behalf of African American and other children of color in care. More effective service provision can be achieved by addressing the problems of high caseloads; a shortage of experienced professional social workers, especially minority professionals (Briar-Lawson, McCarthy, & Dickinson, 2013); inadequate and minimally funded family preservation services; limited data and reporting capabilities; and insufficient alternatives to out-of-home placements.

Biased assessments may occur due to the lack of culturally competent child protective service workers who are aware of cultural differences and variations in childrearing (Leashore, Chipungu, & Everett, 1991; Stehno, 1982); because of this shortage, African American children may be more likely to be removed from their birth families. McMurtry and Gwat-Yong (1992, p. 47) have suggested that the nonminority staff lacking familiarity with black family norms might be more likely to find these families dysfunctional and to view reunification as not feasible. More than 25 years ago, Vinokur-Kaplan and Hartman (1986) reported that 78% of workers and 87% of supervisors were white and that the majority had not received cultural competency training.

Exacerbating this issue of cultural competency among staff is the insufficient number of experienced staff in the child welfare system. According to the GAO (2003), the average tenure of a child welfare worker is less than two years. Thus, inexperienced workers are responsible for large caseloads, including complex cases that have issues pertaining to child maltreatment, parental substance abuse and mental illness, domestic violence, HIV/AIDS, and numerous poverty-related problems. Acknowledging the problem of disproportionality and the above-mentioned issues within child welfare services, the Child Welfare League of America (2003b) has committed to a number of activities to address the issue, including the following: "engage member agencies to establish an action agenda to address this issue; present data and research; engage task forces to develop culturally competent policies, services, and practices; address workforce recruitment and retention issues to enhance diversity and cultural competence of staff; and address these issues at the national conference."

As another example of state responses to the need for enhanced cultural competency, in 2005, the Texas legislature mandated that the Texas Department of Family and Protective Services do the following:

"Provide cultural competency training to all service delivery staff; increase targeted recruitment for foster and adoptive parents to meet the needs of children waiting for homes; target recruitment efforts to ensure diversity among child welfare staff, and develop collaborative community partnerships to provide culturally competent services to children and families of every race and ethnicity" (James, Green, & Rodriguez, 2006, p. 9; Green, Bellanger, McRoy & Bullard, 2011).

Most importantly, ways must be found to help families so they are not at risk for having their children removed. Pelton (1989, pp. 52–53) has suggested that the reason for placement is that the family, frequently due to poverty, "does not have the resources to offset the impact of situational or personal problems which themselves are often caused by poverty, and the agencies have failed to provide the needed supports, such as babysitting, homemaking, day care, financial assistance, and housing assistance." Responses to cases in which a family is at risk should include support and preservation services. Promising practices include family group conferencing, family group decision making, and other strategies that involve families and/or youth in case planning and deciding what is right for the family. Community-based organizations that provide comprehensive wrap-around services, including employment assistance, substance abuse prevention and treatment, and family-centered prevention programs, particularly those with a built-in differential response (in which more than one response to a report is possible), are essential to help keep families intact and need to be explored by child welfare systems.

Another option for family preservation is legal guardianship, which represents an alternative to termination of parental rights and permits families to stay connected. Legal guardianship as a permanency goal is in many ways more concordant with many cultural and racial traditions that support the maintenance of strong ties with extended family. With ongoing support from states and local districts, kinship care is a placement option that has increased the likelihood that children of color will be placed with a family member (Testa & Miller, 2014).

The National Association of Black Social Workers (2003, p. 2) calls for state and local community boards to examine the impact of class on removal rates and challenges the "over-reliance on removing children from the home, as opposed to addressing structural issues, such as poor housing, income inequity and employment discrimination against people of African ancestry, in particular, and poor people, in general." The association also recommends:

> That each local child welfare agency convene a group of community members, selected by community and faith-based groups, to examine disproportionality in the child welfare system. Communities *should* be consulted and assisted with solving issues that impact their families. The problem of disproportionality must be addressed at the *local* level, with supporting federal mandates.

In a similar vein, Roberts (2011) found in her study of predominantly African American Chicago neighborhoods that in addition to concerns about differential placement rates of African American children, residents indicated that child welfare agency involvement in their neighborhood had significant negative effects on their communities. Specifically, Roberts called for agencies to partner with these vulnerable neighborhoods and target these areas for community-building initiatives and for the provision of supports and resources for families.

A leader in research for child welfare issues, Casey Family Programs, took on the issue of disproportionality in 2005. With a focus on improving community capacity, educating stakeholders, and designing culturally responsive services, Casey Family Programs partnered with nine state and four county-level jurisdictions in a collaborative effort entitled *Reducing Disproportionality and Disparate Outcomes for Children and Families of Color in the Child Welfare System* (Miller & Ward, 2011). Casey Family Programs designed this method-ology to help engage states and counties in change efforts that involved look-ing specifically at the influence of structural and institutional racism on the "dynamics of responding to families and decision making" (Miller & Ward, 2011, p. 273).

On a federal level, in 2007 the GAO was asked to analyze the factors leading to disproportionality and to report to the Chairman of the Committee on Ways and Means of the U.S. House of Representatives. The GAO (2007, p. 2) identified the following factors that have contributed to disproportionality:

> Families living in poverty had greater difficulty accessing housing, mental health, and other services needed to keep families stable and children safely at home. Bias or cultural misunderstandings and distrust between child welfare decision makers and the families they serve are also viewed as contributing to children's removal from their homes into foster care.

These findings reinforce previous research regarding disproportionality and dis-parate outcomes. They also found African American children were remaining in foster care longer due to difficulties in recruiting adoptive parents and greater reliance on relatives to provide foster care who were reluctant to terminate pa-rental rights of the child's parent or who needed federal adoption subsidies in order to adopt (GAO, 2007). The study found that many states have been trying to reduce bias by "recruiting and training staff with skills who can work with people of all ethnicities, and to reduce the number of children in care by doing diligent search for relatives who might adopt, recruiting African American adop-tive families, and offering subsidies for relatives seeking to adopt" (GAO, 2007, p. 2). The report also called for USDHHS to provide better technical assistance to states to analyze their data on disproportionality and to develop strategies to address this issue.

The federal government and individual states and advocacy organizations have launched a number of initiatives to respond to some of these findings. In 2008, the Fostering Connections to Success and Increasing Adoptions Act

(P.L. 110-351) was passed by the U.S. Congress in order to connect and support relative caregivers and to provide adoption incentives for families. It is hoped that subsidized guardianships will lead to an increase in the availability of homes for African American children and other children or color and reduce disproportionality (Center for the Study of Social Policy, 2009).

In 2009, the Alliance for Racial Equity in Child Welfare examined strategies in 11 states in order to identify practices to improve child outcomes for children in care and specifically to address disproportionality. They reported that many states are beginning to involve families and communities in developing action plans, in analyzing the impact of institutional practices and policies on families of color, and in collecting data and establishing benchmarks for achieving equity. For example, the Texas Legislature established a Center for the Elimination of Disproportionality and Disparities as part of the Texas Health and Human Services Commission. This center established an Interagency Council for Addressing Disproportionality to examine best practices, training, availability of funding, and outcomes of vulnerable populations in several systems, including juvenile justice, child welfare, education, mental health, and health and human services systems.

In 2011, the Black Administrators in Child Welfare, Inc. called for the use of a "racial equity lens in the development of policies, practices and procedures that are being used in agencies serving African American children" (Jackson & Jones, 2011, p. 4). They have identified specific "Racial Equity Strategy Areas" (e.g., innovative data, creative finance, parent and community engagement, youth-informed practice, culturally competent leadership, effective kinship services) that can be used to facilitate data-informed decision making by state and local policymakers and reduce overrepresentation (see www.blackadministrators.org).

It is clear that the issue of disproportionality is increasingly being brought to the attention of state legislators and advocacy groups. However, each year disproportionately high numbers of African American children and other children of color continue to be removed from their families and communities and placed in the child welfare system, only to experience disparate outcomes. Much more research is urgently needed to identify community-based, culturally appropriate, and effective family support, preservation, prevention, and intervention programs and policies to improve outcomes for all children, youth, and families in this country.

A recent report by the Annie E. Casey Foundation (2014) detailed nationwide racial disparities that put Asian and White children in a far more advantageous position than black, Latino, and American Indian children. The Casey Report is a newly devised index based on 12 indicators measuring a child's success from birth to adulthood, such as reading and math proficiency, high school graduation data, teen birthrates, employment prospects, family income and education levels, and neighborhood poverty levels. Nationally, composite scores were 776 for

Asian children, 704 for white children, 404 for Latino children, 387 for American Indian children, and 345 for black children. Wisconsin had the lowest score for its black youth at 285, followed by Mississippi and then Michigan.

Racial disparities occur due to barriers to the kinds of opportunities that children need in order to thrive and reach their full potential, much in the same way that poverty holds children back. Until systems face that fact with a comprehensive plan to mitigate these barriers, children and families of color will continue to suffer.

In the Casey index for American Indian children, South Dakota's score of 185 was the lowest of any racial group in any state—a result of the deep poverty that prevails on many of South Dakota's Indian reservations. Improvements should be pursued with a sense of urgency, but also with the understanding that progress in many cases will take years.

## CONCLUSION

This chapter examined critical areas for improving policy and practice in the field of public child welfare and suggested ways to achieve more favorable outcomes for the children, youth, and families served by the system. The discussion emphasized that addressing disparities and cultural and racial disproportionality in the public child welfare agency belongs to all members of the agency, from caseworkers on the front line to agency directors at the senior level—and indeed to administrators and board members. Each individual will have a unique role to play. Having a champion of the issue helps but is not enough. A firm and true commitment by top administrators is essential. Companion guides have been developed to illustrate the various roles that public child welfare agencies can play in eliminating disparities and reducing disproportionality, but without leadership, these efforts will be temporary as the "issue du jour" and will not have the sustainability to build capacity in the area of institutional racial and cultural competency. All children, youth, and families should receive fair and equitable treatment based on their identified needs: families should receive the kind of resources and services they need to be safe, well, and in permanent homes. Framing the relationship between institutional and structural racism and disparate treatment based on ethnicity and race raises awareness about how and why disproportionality occurs in public child welfare and the role the system can play to eliminate such disparate practices within the agency. The issues of disparity and disproportionality hold particular significance for the field of public child welfare because of their historical and enduring pervasiveness throughout society and evidence of disparate child outcomes. By committing to systematically examining this issue that is so deeply embedded within our society, systems, and individuals, public child welfare agencies can help the field to target interventions that will eliminate service disparities over time. This approach will, in turn, help to reduce the disproportionality observed in public child welfare.

## DISCUSSION QUESTIONS

1. In considering the issue of race and culture in child welfare, what is the one issue that you still have questions about?
2. In reflecting on the issue of race and culture in child welfare, what is the issue with which you continue to struggle professionally and personally?

## REFERENCES

Alliance for Racial Equity in Child Welfare. (October 2009). *Policy actions to reduce racial disproportionality and disparities in child welfare: A scan of eleven states.* Washington, DC: Center for the Study of Social Policy. Accessed at www.cssp.org.

Annie E. Casey Foundation. (2006). *Race matters: Organizational self-assessment.* Baltimore: Author.

Annie E. Casey Foundation. (2014). *Race for results: Building a path to opportunity for all children.* Baltimore: Author.

Anyon, Y. (2011). Reducing racial disparities and disproportionalities in the child welfare system: Policy perspectives about how to serve the best interests of African American youth. *Children and Youth Services Review, 33,* 242–253.

Ards, S., Chung, C., & Myers, S. (1999). Letter to the editor. *Child Abuse and Neglect, 23,* 244.

Bachetti, T. (June 23, 2011). Timeline: Connecticut Department of Children & Families under federal oversight. *Hartford Courant.* Retrieved on September 20, 2011, from http://articles.courant.com/2011-06-23/news/hc-dcf-timeline-0413_1_dcf-officials-consent-decree-caseloads

Black Administrators in Child Welfare. (May 2011). Kellogg, the Council on Accreditation, and BACW. *BACW News, 3.*

Barth, R. (1997). Effects of age and race on the odds of adoption versus remaining in long-term out-of-home care. *Child Welfare, 76,* 285–308.

Barth, R. (2001). *Child welfare and race: Reviewing previous research on disproportionality in child welfare.* Paper presented at the Race Matters Forum, Chevy Chase, MD, January 8–9, 2001.

Barth, R., Berry, M. Carson, M., Goodfield, R., & Feinberg, B. (1986). Contributors to disruption and dissolution of older child adoption. *Child Welfare, 65,* 359–371.

Bartholet, E., Wulczyn, F., Barth, R., & Lederman, C. (June 2011). *Race and child welfare.* Chicago: Chapin Hall at the University of Chicago.

Bass, S., Shields, M., & Behrman, R. (2004). Children, families, and foster care: Analysis and recommendations. *Future of Children, 14,* 5–29.

Berrick, J., Barth, R., & Needell, B. (1994). A comparison of kinship foster homes and foster family homes: Implications for kinship foster care as family preservation. *Children and Youth Services Review, 16,* 33–63.

Billingsley, A. (1992). *Climbing Jacob's ladder: The enduring legacy of African American families.* New York: Simon and Schuster.

Billingsley, A., & Giovannoni, J. (1972). *Children of the storm*. New York: Harcourt Brace Jovanovich.

Bozanich, D., Molinar, L., Lefler, J., Cole, C., & Crumpton, J. (2004). *Developing cultural competence through training, assessment, analysis, and implementation.* Paper presented at Second Annual Symposium on Fairness & Equity Issues in Child Welfare Training, University of California, Berkeley, April 27–28, 2004.

Briar-Lawson, K., McCarthy, M., & Dickinson, N. (2013). *The Children's Bureau: Shaping a century of child welfare practices, programs, and policies.* Washington, DC: NASW Press.

Building Blocks for Youth. (2000). *And justice for some: Differential treatment of minority youth in the justice system,* Retrieved April 18, 2004, from www.buildingblocksforyouth.org.

Cappelleri, J., Eckenrode, J., & Powers, J. (1993). The epidemiology of child abuse: Findings from the Second National Incidence and Prevalence Study of Child Abuse and Neglect. *American Journal of Public Health, 83,* 1622–1624.

Carten, A., & Dumpson, J. R. (1995). *Removing risk from children: Strengthening community-based services for African-American families.* Silver Spring, MD.: Beckham Publications Group.

Chestang, L. (1972). *Character development in a hostile environment.* Occasional paper no. 3. Chicago: University of Chicago.

Chibnall, S., Dutch, N., Jones-Harden, B., Brown, B., Gourdine, R., et al. (2003). *Children of color in the child welfare system: Perspectives from the child welfare community.* Washington, DC: Children's Bureau.

Childstats.gov. (2012). *America's children 2012.* Table POP 3 Race and Hispanic Origin composition: percentage of US children ages 0-17 by race and Hispanic origin in 2011. Retrieved November 24, 2013, from www.childstats.gov/americaschildren/tables.asp

Child Welfare League of America. (1997). *Child abuse and neglect: A look at the states.* Washington, DC: CWLA Press.

Child Welfare League of America. (2003a). *Special data tabulation of 2000 AFCARS, 2000 NCANDS and 2000 U.S. Census Data.* Washington, DC: Child Welfare League of America.

Child Welfare League of America. (2003b). *Children of color in the child welfare system statement.* Washington, DC: Child Welfare League of America.

Belanger, K., Green, D. K., & Bullard, L. B. (Eds.). (2008). *Racial disproportionality in child welfare: A special issue of Child Welfare Journal.* Washington, DC: CWLA.

Children's Defense Fund. (2011a). *Portrait of inequality 2011: Black children in America.* Retrieved August 20, 2011, from www.childrensdefense.org.

Children's Defense Fund. (2011b). *State of America's children.* Retrieved August 20, 2011, from www.childrensdefense.org.

Children's Rights. (2004). *Annual DCS case file review report for the State of Tennessee.* Retrieved from http://www.childrensrights.org/PDF/TAC_Report_Oct.pdf.

Children's Rights. (2011). *Class actions.* Retrieved on September 20, 2011, from http://www.childrensrights.org/reform-campaigns/legal-cases/.

Chipungu, S., & Bent-Goodley, T. (2004). Meeting the challenges of contemporary foster care. *Future of Children, 14,* 75–93.

Close, M. (1983). Child welfare and people of color: Denial of equal access. *Social Work, 28,* 13–20.

Courtney, M. (1994). Factors associated with the reunification of foster children with their families. *Social Service Review, 68,* 82–108.

Courtney, M. (1995). Reentry to foster care of children returned to their families. *Social Service Review, 69,* 226–241.

Courtney, M. (1998). The costs of child protection in the context of welfare reform. *Future of Children, 8,* 88–103.

Courtney, M., Barth, R., Berrick, J., Brooks, D., Needell, B., & Park, L. (1996). Race and child welfare services: Past research and future directions. *Child Welfare, 75,* 99–137.

Cross, T. L. (2014). Customary adoption for Indian and Alaska Native children. In G. P. Mallon & P. Hess (Eds.), *Child welfare for the twenty-first century: A handbook of practices, policies, and programs* (2nd ed., pp. 342–362). New York: Columbia University Press.

Cross, T., Bazron, B., Dennis, K., & Isaacs, M. (1989). *Toward a culturally competent system of care.* Washington, DC: Child and Adolescent Service System Program—CASSP Technical Assistance Center.

Derezotes, D., Poertner, J. & Testa, M. (Eds.). (2005). *Race matters in child welfare: The overrepresentation of African American children in the system.* Washington, DC: CWLA Press.

Dettlaff, A. (2011). Disproportionality of Latino children in child welfare. In D. Greene, K. Belanger, R. McRoy, & L. Bullard (Eds.), *Racial disproportionality in child welfare: Research, policy, and practice* (pp. 119–127). Washington, DC: Child Welfare League of America.

Dougherty, S. (2003). *Practices that mitigate the effects of racial/ethnic disproportionality.* Washington, DC: Casey Family Programs.

Eckenrode, J., Powers, J., Doris, J., Munsch, J., & Bolger, N. (1988). Substantiation of child abuse and neglect reports. *Journal of Consulting and Clinical Psychology, 56,* 9–16.

Federal Interagency Forum on Child and Family Statistics. America's Children: *Key National Indicators of Well-Being, 2015.* Washington, DC: U.S. Government Printing Office.

Fein, E., Maluccio, A., & Kluger, M. (1990*). No more partings. An examination of long-term foster care.* Washington, DC: Child Welfare League of America.

Fluke, J., Yuan, Y., & Edwards, M. (1999). Recurrence of maltreatment: An application of the National Child Abuse and Neglect Data System (NCANDS). *Child Abuse & Neglect, 23,* 633–650.

Fluke, J., Yuan, Y., Hedderson, J., & Curtis, P. (2002). Disproportionate representation in child maltreatment. *Children and Youth Services Review, 25,* 359–373.

Government Accountability Office. (July 2007). *African American children in foster care: Additional HHS assistance needed to help states reduce the proportion in care (GAO 07-816).* Report to the Chairman, Committee on Ways and Means, House of Representatives. Retrieved from www.gao.gov/cgi-bin/getrpt?GAO-07-816.

Goerge, R. (1990). The reunification process in substitute care. *Social Service Review, 64,* 422–457.

Goerge, R., Wulczyn, F., & Harden, A. (1994). *Foster care dynamics 1983–1992, California, Illinois, Michigan, New York and Texas: A report from the Multistate Foster Care Data Archive.* Chicago: Chapin Hall Center for Children, University of Chicago.

Green, M. (2002) Minorities as majority: Disproportionality in child welfare & juvenile justice. *Children's Voice, 6,* 9–13.

Green, D., Belanger, K., McRoy, R., & Bullard, L (Eds.) (2011). *Challenging Racial Disproportionality in Child Welfare: Research, Policy, and Practice.* Washington, DC: Child Welfare League of America.

Hill, R. (1997). *The strengths of African American families: Twenty-five years later.* Washington, DC: R & B Publishers.

Hill, R. (2004). *Disproportionality of minorities in child welfare: Synthesis of research findings.* Race Matters Consortium.

Hill, R. (2006). *Synthesis of research on disproportionality in child welfare: An update.* Casey-CSSP Alliance for Racial Equity in Child Welfare.

Hill, R. (2007). *An analysis of racial and ethnic disproportionality and disparity at the national, state and county levels.* Casey-CSSP Alliance for Racial Equity in Child Welfare.

Hill, R. (2011). Gaps in research and social policy. In D. Greene, K. Belanger, R. McRoy, & L. Bullard (Eds.), *Racial disproportionality in child welfare: Research, policy, and practice.* (pp. 101–108). Washington, DC: Child Welfare League of America.

James, J., Green, D., & Rodriguez, C. (2006, Nov. 2) *Reducing disproportionality in child welfare through collaboration and community engagement.* Paper presented at the Race, Ethnicity, and Place Conference, Texas State University, San Antonio, Texas.

Jackson, S., & Jones, E. (2011). *Reducing disparities: 10 racial equity strategy areas for improving outcomes for African American children in child welfare.* Washington, DC: Black Administrators in Child Welfare, Inc.

James, J. Green, D., Rodriguez, C., & Fong, R. (2008). Addressing disproportionality through undoing racism, leadership development, and community engagement. *Child Welfare, 87*(2), 279–296.

Jeter, H. (1963). *Children, problems and services in child welfare programs.* Children's Bureau publication no. 403-1963. Washington, DC: U.S. Department of Health, Education, and Welfare.

Johnson, J. (1997). *Study shows children reported abused and neglected are 67 times more likely to be arrested as pre-teens.* Washington, DC: Child Welfare League of America.

Johnson, L. M., Antle, B. F., & Barbee, A. (2009). Addressing disproportionality and disparity in child welfare: Evaluation of an anti-racism training for community service providers. *Children and Youth Services Review, 31*, 688–696.

Jones, E., & McCurdy, K. (1992). The links between types of maltreatment and demographic characteristic of children. *Child Abuse and Neglect, 16*, 201–214.

*Juan F. v. Rell,* Civil Action No. H-89-859 (D.C. Conn., Dec. 19, 1989) Retrieved September 1, 2011, from http://www.childrensrights.org/site/PageServer?pagename=cases.

Kapp, S., McDonald, T., & Diamond, K. (2001). The path to adoption for children of color. *Child Abuse and Neglect, 25*, 215–229.

Knott, T., & Donovan, K. (2010) Disproportionate representation of African-American children in foster care: Secondary analysis of the National Child Abuse and Neglect Data System, 2005. *Children and Youth Services Review, 32*, 679–684.

Lawrence-Webb, C. (1997). African American children in the modern child welfare system: A legacy of the Flemming Rule. *Child Welfare, 76*, 9–30.

Leashore, B., Chipungu, S., & Everett, J. (1991). *Child welfare: An Afrocentric perspective.* New Brunswick, NJ: Rutgers University Press.

Maas, H., & Engler, R., Jr. (1959). *Children in need of parents.* New York: Columbia University Press.

McMurtry, S., & Gwat-Yong, L. (1992). Differential exit rates of minority children in foster care. *Social Work Research & Abstracts, 28*, 41–48.

McRoy, R. (1994). Attachment and racial identity issues: Implications for child placement decision making. *Journal of Multicultural Social Work, 3*, 59–74.

McRoy, R. (2004). The color of child welfare. In K. Davis & T. Bent-Goodley (Eds.), *The color of social policy* (pp. 112–123). Washington, DC: Council on Social Work Education.

McRoy, R. (2011a). Contextualizing disproportionality. In D. Greene, K. Belanger, R. McRoy, & L. Bullard (Eds.), *Racial disproportionality in child welfare: Research, policy, and practice* (pp. 67–72). Washington, DC: Child Welfare League of America.

McRoy, R. (2011b). Selected resources for addressing African American adoption disproportionality. In D. Greene, K. Belanger, R. McRoy, & L. Bullard (Eds.), *Racial disproportionality in child welfare: Research, policy, and practice* (pp. 331–340). Washington, DC: Child Welfare League of America.

McRoy, R. (2014). Disproportional representation of children and youth. In G. P. Mallon & P. Hess (Eds.), *Child welfare for the twenty-first century: A handbook of practices, policies, and programs* (2nd ed., pp. 566–582). New York: Columbia University Press.

McRoy, R., Oglesby, Z., & Grape, H. (1997). Achieving same-race adoptive placements for African American children: Culturally sensitive practice approaches. *Child Welfare*, 76, 85–104.

Miller, O., & Ward, K. (2011). Emerging strategies for reducing disproportionality. In D. Greene, K. Belanger, R. McRoy, & L. Bullard (Eds.), *Racial disproportionality in child welfare: Research, policy, and practice* (pp. 271–295). Washington, DC: Child Welfare League of America.

Minnesota Department of Human Services. (2002). *Children's services study of outcomes for African American children in Minnesota's child protection system.* St. Paul: Minnesota Department of Human Services.

Murray, K., & Gesiriech, S. (2004). A brief legislative history of the child welfare system. In Pew Charitable Trust (Ed.), *The Pew Commission on children in foster care* (pp. 1–6). Washington, DC: Pew Charitable Trust.

National Association of Black Social Workers. (2003). *Preserving families of African ancestry.* Washington, DC: NABSW. Accessed at http://www.nabsw.org/mserver/ Preserving Families.aspx.

National Center on Child Abuse and Neglect. (1988). *Study findings: Study of national incidence and prevalence of child abuse and neglect.* Washington, DC: U.S. Government Printing Office.

National Center on Child Abuse and Neglect. (1996). *Child abuse and neglect state statute series.* Vol. 1: *Reporting laws.* Washington, DC: U.S. Department of Health and Human Services.

Newberger, E., Reed, R., Daniel, J., Hyde, J., & Kotelchuck, M. (1977). Pediatric social illness: Toward an etiologic classification. *Pediatrics, 60,* 178–185.

Olsen, L. (1982). Predicting the permanency status of children in family foster care. *Social Work Research and Abstracts, 18,* 9–19.

O'Toole, R., Turbett, P., & Nalpeka, C. (1983). Theories, professional knowledge, and diagnosis of child abuse. In D. Finkelhor, R. Gelles, G. Hotaling, & M. Straus (Eds.), *The dark side of families: Current family violence research* (pp. 349–362). Beverly Hills, CA: Sage.

Pelton, L. (1989). *For reasons of poverty.* New York: Praeger.

Rivera, H. (2014). Working with Latino families. In G. P. Mallon & P. Hess (Eds.), *Child welfare for the twenty-first century: A handbook of practices, policies, and programs* (2nd ed., pp. 662–675). New York: Columbia University Press.

Roberts, D. (2002). *Shattered bonds: The color of child welfare.* New York: Basic Books.

Roberts, D. (2011). *The racial geography of child welfare: Toward a new research paradigm.* In D. Greene, K. Belanger, R. McRoy, & L. Bullard (Eds.), *Racial disproportionality in child welfare: Research, policy, and practice* (pp. 13–22). Washington, DC: Child Welfare League of America.

Sedlak, A., & Broadhurst, D. (1996). *Executive summary of the Third National Incidence Study of Child Abuse and Neglect.* Washington, DC: U.S. Department of Health and Human Services.

Sedlak, A., & Schultz, D. (2001). *Race differences in risk of maltreatment in the general population*. Paper presented at the Race Matters Forum, Chevy Chase, MD, January 8–9, 2001.

Shaw, T., Putnam-Hornstein, E., Magruder, J., & Needell, B. (2011), Measuring racial disparity in child welfare. In D. Green, K. Belanger, R. McRoy, & L. Bullard (Eds.), *Challenging racial disproportionality in child welfare: Research, policy, and practice* (pp. 35–44). Washington, DC: Child Welfare League of America.

Stehno, S.M. (1986). Family-centered child welfare services: New life for a historic idea. *Child Welfare, 65*(3), 231–240.

Testa, M., & Miller, J. (2014). Guardianship. In G. P. Mallon & P. Hess (Eds.), *Child welfare for the twenty-first century: A handbook of practices, policies, and programs* (2nd ed., pp. 422–442). New York: Columbia University Press.

U.S. Census Bureau. (February 2013). *Poverty rates for selected detailed race and Hispanic groups by state and place: 2007–2011*. Washington, DC: Author. Downloaded April 3, 2013, from http://www.census.gov/prod/2013pubs/acsbr11-17.pdf.

U.S. Department of Health and Human Services. (2015). *Preliminary FY 2014 estimates as of July 2015 (The AFCARS Report)*. Retrieved March 2016, , from www.acf.hhs.gov/programs/cb/publications/afcars/report22.

U.S. Department of Health and Human Services, National Center on Child Abuse and Neglect. (1996). *The Third National Incidence Study of Child Abuse and Neglect*. Washington, DC: U.S. Government Printing Office.

U.S. Department of Justice. (2008). *Bureau of Justice statistics: Parents in prison and their minor children*. Washington, DC: U.S. Department of Justice, Bureau of Justice Statistics.

U.S. General Accounting Office. (2005). *Child welfare: Complex needs strain capacity to provide services. GAO/HEHS-95-208*. Washington, DC: U.S. General Accounting Office.

Vinokur-Kaplan, D., & Hartman, D. (1986). A national profile of child welfare workers and supervisors. *Child Welfare, 65*, 323–325.

Wells, S. (2011). Disproportionality and disparity in child welfare. An overview of definitions and methods of measurement. In D. Green, K. Belanger, R. McRoy, & L. Bullard (Eds.), *Challenging racial disproportionality in child welfare: Research, policy, and practice* (pp. 3–12). Washington, DC: Child Welfare League of America.

Zellman, G. (1992). The impact of case characteristics on child abuse reporting decisions. *Child Abuse and Neglect, 16*, 57–74.

# CHAPTER 10

# Systems Serving Ethnically Diverse Older Adults

CAMILLE HUGGINS

## INTRODUCTION

When asked why he was retiring as associate justice of the U.S. Supreme Court, Thurgood Marshall, the first African American appointed to the Court, responded, in a manner indicating that to him it seemed obvious, that he was "old and tired." At the age of 85, he would have been considered what is currently defined as "old-old," and having spent virtually his entire career fighting for the legal rights of blacks, there was just cause for him to be weary from spearheading what was for him and the country a long and still-ongoing battle.

Justice Marshall's years on the Court provided him with the opportunity to apply the knowledge and experience he acquired over a lifetime of making judicial decisions that were instrumental in securing the promises of democracy for more and more Americans. As a result of these notable achievements he experienced the gratification that came with the knowledge that his was a life well lived and his legacy would be preserved in American culture for future generations. His achievements in advancing the rights of blacks to full citizenship have made it possible for a large and growing number of American-born blacks to move into mainstream society. Consequently, the situation of black Americans may be viewed either as a cup that is half empty or one that is half full. Today, many blacks approach and move into late life looking forward to what the World Health Organization (2002) refers to as "active aging" with a view toward optimizing opportunities for health, participation, and security as they continue to age. Others approach this stage carrying the burden of the cumulative effects of lifelong racism and discrimination that account in part for the health and welfare disparities that occur among elderly persons of color (Manton, 2008). Further, in a society fascinated by youth, physical acuity, and attractiveness, older adults of color not only experience the effects of ageism but also face the added burden of discrimination and racism based on skin color.

## PURPOSE AND ORGANIZATION

With a focus on the experiences of immigrants, Latinos, and blacks, the discussion in this chapter is based on my experience working in health care facilities operating under the auspices of the Health and Hospitals Corporation, New York City's municipal hospital system. I have worked in nursing homes located in three of the city's five boroughs where poverty is concentrated among ethnic and racial groups as an administrator and direct service social worker. In my view, the city has one of the more progressive health and human service systems in the United States. The municipal hospital system provides health care services to all New Yorkers, as well as the foreign-born, irrespective of their immigrant status or ability to pay, and facilities are located in areas with high poverty rates and poor health outcomes that are densely populated by people of color. These neighborhoods are also popular resettlement sites for the city's newest immigrants from Mexico and African, Latin American, and Central American countries.

The city's older residents profit from having easily accessible community-based health care; they also receive other benefits, such as Meals on Wheels, reduced transit fares, and accessibility transportation for seniors. However, similar to the elderly of color who are aging in place in cities across the nation, they are also at increased risk for poverty, social isolation, loneliness, and the effects of stressors associated with urban life. My practice experiences are similar to findings from the literature as to the causes of the well-documented disparate health and well-being outcomes of older adults of color, which are driven by a complexity of factors. The discussion in this chapter examines some of these factors that are in play as these members of the elderly population, with support from government programs and health and human service providers, age in place in their families and communities, as well as their experiences in out-of-home care.

## DEMOGRAPHIC AND POPULATION TRENDS

Current census data indicate that the United States is an aging society, and the number of elderly persons of color (which includes African Americans, Hispanics, Asians, American Indians, and Pacific Islanders) is increasing in larger numbers than the white aged population. Currently, approximately 13% of the population is over the age of 65 years, and that number is projected to grow. It will also be the most ethnically diverse older population America has ever experienced, with the Latino and African American older adult population growing to over 19.8 million and 11.2 million respectively (U.S. Census, 2010). Immigration trends also contribute to the increasing diversity of the nation's elderly. As reported by the U.S. Census, in 2010 the foreign-born made up slightly less than 13% of the total population of America. The native homelands of the largest share of the country's foreign-born residents are Asia, Latin America, and Central America, according to the U.S. Census Bureau and the American Community Survey (2010).

New York State is third in the nation in terms of the number of older adults. According to data reported in the New York State Plan on Aging 2011–2015 (New York State Office for the Aging, 2011), of the 19 million people living in the state, 3.7 million are over the age of 60. The data further indicates that in the past decade the older ethnic and racial population has increased by 43%, which is projected to expand to 51% by 2020. Similar to national statistics, the New York plan reported a large and expanding ethnically diverse population, with approximately 29% of the population who are foreign-born. At the national level, the poverty rate for older adults is 13%, while in New York State it hovers at 18%. This is due in part to the high numbers of foreign-born residents and immigrants, who despite their high labor force participation are employed in low-wage jobs or those that pay less than the minimum wage.

## POLICY AND PROGRAM DEVELOPMENTS

The policy framework shaping practice with the country's elderly population was established by the Older Americans Act. The act, passed by Congress in 1965, has the legislative authority to make grants to states for community planning and social services, research and development projects, and personnel training in the field of aging. The law also authorized the creation of the Administration on Aging, which is administratively located in the U.S. Department of Health and Human Services (USDHHS) and serves as the focal point at the federal level for matters related to older Americans. The Administration on Aging (2010) authorizes a wide array of service programs through a national network of 56 state area agencies on aging. The National Caucus and Center on Black Aging and the National Hispanic Council on Aging are among the national organizations that advocate for an improved quality of life for special populations of elderly residents.

With the increase in the aged population, which will continue to grow as the baby boomer generation ages, gerontology has become one of the fastest-growing fields in the health and human services. Gerontology is concerned with the study of the physical, mental, and sociological aspects of the complex process of aging and the changes in individuals as they age, the effects on society, and the ways data can be used to monitor the effects on society and improve the quality of life of the aging population.

There is a corresponding increase in the need for helping professionals with degrees in the field of gerontology. In addition to practitioners to help older people age with dignity and provide supportive services to family members during this process, there is also a need for empirical research to inform evidence-based cultural and race-conscious practice with this population.

Social workers are especially well suited to play a central role in the field of gerontology because of their person-in-the-environment perspective that considers the well-being of the individual within his or her larger societal context, and their emphasis on valuing and respecting the self-determination rights of the individual. This perspective supports practice approaches that allow for a comprehensive assessment of the needs of the older person within the context of his or her family, community, and society; a commitment to removing barriers to needed services; and dedication to assisting the elderly to maintain a sense of dignity and independence. Further, social workers' ecological perspective promotes a concern for the social (Meyers, 2006) determinants of health and well-being that take into account the conditions in which people are born, grow, live, work, and age, including their experiences in health and human service systems. This orientation is especially useful for understanding the higher prevalence rates of chronic conditions of aging and poor health and well-being outcomes among older people of color. Social workers' concern for marginalized and stigmatized populations also supports the profession's interest in promoting health equity for special populations of the elderly. Included among these are LBGT older adults of color, those living with HIV/AIDS, and those who are homeless, who are virtually invisible. Many older adults of color in these special populations enter their retirement years without the social supports that are essential for successful aging and are not always welcome in long-term care facilities (Goldsen & Petry, 2011; Knochel et al., 2011).

## DEFINITIONS AND THEMES
## OF LATE ADULTHOOD

Because there is wide variation among the aged, there is no conclusive definition of an *older* adult. Gerontologists generally view aging through four processes: chronological age, which is measured in years; biological age, which is related to physical changes and decline in organs that are a part of the aging process; psychological age, which reflects changes in cognitive, sensory, and perceptual processes; and social aging, which is the capacity for adaptation to changing roles and relationships with family, friends, and other social networks (Hooyman & Kiyak, 2005). Seldom are all of these aging processes congruent with the person's chronological age.

The definition of the older adult may also be based on the time of transition from working to receiving a pension, using the standard established by a specific nation. In the United States this has been informally established as roughly between the ages of 55 and 65 (Kowal et al., 2012). With the enactment of the 1967 Age Discrimination in Employment Act, in the United States, as in other Western industrialized countries, establishing a mandatory age for retirement is unlawful, with the exception of certain organizations and occupations. Whereas in the past when people reached age 65, they were "put out to pasture," today, with Americans remaining healthy longer and living longer, they are more likely to work past the age of 65 years (WHO, 2002). This extended period of employment is in part due to financial need, advances in technology, structural changes in the labor force that have increased the number of jobs in the service sector that are less physically strenuous, and increased availability and use of preventive health care (WHO, 2002). Older Americans are also working longer because Americans love to work, and with the new emphasis on successful aging many take this as an opportunity to pursue occupational and career interests for which they have held a long-time passion but were unable to pursue for practical reasons.

While there is a tendency to group this entire older population into one category, there is a good deal of heterogeneity among the elderly. Because of this diversity, social scientists suggest that one stage is not sufficient to capture the many biological, psychological, and social changes occurring over the long period from the beginning of late adulthood to death. They propose establishing the following developmental stages. The young old, who are between the ages of 65 and 74, remain active in the community and maintain strong ties with families and friends. Many in this age cohort are still employed full time, may even serve in a caretaker role for grandchildren or their own parents, and continue to function well, with little loss in cognitive and physical capability. The middle old, who are between the ages of 75 and 84, may begin to experience chronic illness such as arthritis or cardiovascular or respiratory disease. This cohort may also experience additional stresses related to their cumulative losses, such as the loss of a life partner. Many persons at this stage begin to develop physical problems in terms of balance and have some loss of independent functioning but continue to remain in relatively good health. The old-old, those who are 85 and older, are sometimes referred to as the frail elderly. They become increasingly dependent and experience more disability and loss of physical and cognitive functioning. They experience a greater prevalence of dementia and Alzheimer's disease. With more and more elderly living beyond what used to be considered the normal lifespan, suggestions have been made to add another stage to capture the growing number of individuals who are living beyond the age of 100 years.

Late adulthood involves what are considered normative changes and losses of living. Included among these are changes in physical appearance, loss of physical acuity, and loss of independence. Roles in the family shift, and the older person is no longer the caretaker but the family member who needs to be cared for. With retirement comes the loss of influence and income associated with work and occupational status. Depending on the outlook and perspective of the older person, these predictable losses that come with aging may be seen as either opportunities or barriers for leading a purposeful and meaningful life.

A number of theoretical frameworks are available for understanding what are viewed as predictable personality and behavioral changes occurring at each developmental stage of the human life cycle. Erik Erikson's model of psychosocial development is frequently used by health and human service educators for teaching a developmental perspective for understanding human behavior and personality development because it gives consideration to the social environmental context within which people grow and develop over the full life cycle (Erikson, E.,1993). Erikson's psychosocial framework for understanding the developmental tasks of late adulthood is developed around themes of integrity versus despair. According to Erikson's theoretical framework, as older people characteristically look back to review the purpose and meaning of their lives, those doing so with feelings of acceptance, satisfaction, and accomplishment approach the end of their lives with integrity and see their approaching death as a natural part of the human life cycle. In contrast, the older person who reviews his or her life with feelings of disappointment, bitterness, and anger will approach the end of life with feelings of despair and a fear of death.

More and more social scientists are drawing on theories of successful aging as a normative part of the human life cycle. This approach endeavors to dispel stereotypes and myths associated with the aging process. These negative stereotypes are not true and contribute to ageism, which rationalizes the inequitable treatment of the aged in the general society, and their treatment in residential settings for the aged. Older people of color may be especially vulnerable to these stereotypes, which are closely associated with racial stereotypes about the behaviors and intellectual capacities of blacks and other people of color. Theories of successful ageing are based in the assumption that older people should not be abandoned or "put out to pasture" but encouraged and provided opportunities to remain actively engaged with life. For example, George Dawson, the grandson of a slave, was illiterate until the age of 98 but went on to write the book *Life Is So Good* at age 103. His reflections in the book provide insights for understanding the resiliency of older African Americans who are able to maintain healthy lifestyles and perspectives on life and living despite considerable hardship. Many blacks are able to achieve this level of acceptance even though they have faced considerable adversity over their lives because of their strong religious beliefs and the expectation that they will find their just rewards in the afterlife.

Based in similar assumptions as successful aging, activity theory applies social role theory to the aging process with the central assumption that older people maintain subjective well-being to the extent they remain active in many roles. This including modifying old roles as their environment changes and the ability to adapt and integrate new roles into their lives. Successful aging depends on adaptation and substitution for roles that are no longer available. This theoretical framework assumes a correlation between being active and engaged with successful aging, which is consistent with Americans' fondness for productivity and industry. Disengagement theory, which may be interpreted as a natural occurrence as death becomes imminent for the older person, is associated with the increasing loss of social roles and social contacts and a process of the mutual withdrawal of the individual and society.

Reminiscing is accepted as a universal characteristic of the elderly as they review their lives, with many planning trips to the ancestral home, musing over old photographs, and talking about life events. This process is important to their searching for the meaning and purpose of their lives.

## ETHNIC AND RACIAL DIVERSITY AMONG OLDER ADULTS

The following discussion focuses on the immigrant, Latino, and black elderly. "Black" and "African American" and "Latino" and "Hispanic" are used interchangeably in the discussion. There is, of course, considerable diversity both among and within these ethnic groupings that comprise of many ethnicities, races, cultures, histories, languages, and countries of national origin. This diversity must be taken into consideration when developing individualized culturally and race-conscious service plans for older adults of color who are members of these widely diverse and culturally rich ethnic groups. This is also the case with the immigrant population, since a large share of the newest immigrants to the United States are black and brown people arriving from Mexico, African, Latin American, and Central American countries; they experience discrimination based on both American attitudes about nativism and their skin color.

## THE IMMIGRANT ELDERLY

Older immigrants face complex structural obstacles that may contribute to their increased vulnerability to illness and limit the range of choices related to their health. The challenges associated with the migratory process itself are often compounded by having to acclimate to a new environment. Lack of documentation may create a reluctance and even fear to seek assistance from the formal health and human service systems. They also face considerable challenges related to language and communication. The experience for elderly immigrants is diverse, but some factors may be universal to this cohort.

Elderly immigrants coming to a new country in middle to late middle age are more likely to experience social isolation, are more likely to have limited

English skills, and are more closely identified with the traditions of their native countries. Consequently, they are likely to feel a greater degree of estrangement and alienation in the new country, and they tend to be more dependent upon their adult children. Immigration status can also serve as a barrier to obtaining needed health care. New immigrants are usually not able to access health care benefits provided under Medicare and Medicaid because of their immigration status and the punitive policy reforms under the 1997 Personal Responsibility and Work Reconciliation Act that made it possible for states to bar immigrants from participating in some federally funded programs. Nor can they qualify for Social Security retirement benefits if they or their spouse have not met the years-of-work requirements; some immigrants may have been employed in menial jobs such as domestics or seasonal farm and migrant workers that are not covered by social security (Ku, 2006; Okoro et al., 2005).

Elderly immigrants have unique psychosocial needs as they face end-of-life issues in a new country: they must come to terms with the loss of their home-land and all that entails, including the likelihood they will never return. In addition, most non-Western cultures place a high value on the elderly, honoring their wisdom and generational continuity, and this may be lost in a new country of which they have limited understanding and knowledge.

Immigration can be particularly problematic for poor immigrants, because they are often reuniting with families with limited resources. Many immigrants live in multigenerational households with extended family members (Vespa, Lewis, & Kreider, 2013). The tradition of incorporating new immigrants into an established household is considered a strength of the immigrant community. Such merging of families can provide a social support to ease the transition to the new culture and a financial safety net as newer members are able to establish an economic foothold by sharing household expenses. However, such arrangements may also lead to intergenerational conflicts and place older members at a increased risk for elder abuse.

Elder abuse takes many forms, including financial exploitation, passive or active neglect, and physical and emotional abuse. Elder abuse is not unique to this cohort of the aged population. It may result from physical and emotional stress on the part of the family member who is a caregiver, or unresolved inter-personal conflicts that surface with shifting roles as the older person becomes progressively dependent. In-home care aides who are poorly trained and moni-tored may also perpetrate elder abuse. Unfortunately, there are also some un-scrupulous individuals with questionable motivations seeking employment as an in-home aide for the elderly. Elder abuse may also occur in out-of-home set-tings operating in the health and human service sector as proprietary for-profit agencies serving the elderly. These agencies may receive funds from government contracts under purchase-of-care agreements, Medicare, Medicaid, and private pay. Due to low reimbursement rates, these facilities may not be able to afford to operate programs at an appropriate level of safety and care; the result may be poorly paid and insufficiently trained staff, high staff turnover, low morale, and an organizational culture that reduces the safety and quality of resident care.

While the prevalence of elder abuse in the immigrant community is not extensively reported in the literature, immigrant families are found to be at higher risk because of the social and environmental context of the immigration experience (Potocky-Tripodi, 2002). Immigrants arriving to the new country at an advanced age are challenged in their efforts to adjust to the cultural norms of the receiving country. This is exacerbated when the elderly immigrant is reuniting with a family that is well integrated into the cultural norms of the new country; the family members are likely more egalitarian in the behavioral expectations for gender and child and parent roles than those in their native homelands. Tensions emanating from differences in role expectation, the loss of filial piety and status that comes with age, and intergenerational conflicts can create situations ripe for conflict with grandchildren and adult children.

## THE LATINO ELDERLY

Similar to the immigrant elderly, Latino older adults are also especially vulnerable to the stresses of immigration and acculturation (National Council of La Raza, 2005). Latino elders face significant barriers to accessing appropriate care that are related to language and communication and low socioeconomic status. Even in families in which an adult is employed full or part time, Latinos have remained one of the poorest ethnic groups in the United States, and this is a central factor in the lives of Latino elders. Nationally, prior to the enactment of the Affordable Care Act, 33% of Latinos were medically uninsured, compared to 16% of all Americans (U.S. Census, 2008). Limited English proficiency among the Latino elderly is a significant barrier to health care; it includes such issues as the need for interpreters and the nuances of words in various languages. Of the some 18 million adults in the United States who speak a language other than English, 48% report they speak English less than very well. This can impact the amount and quality of health care received. For example, Spanish-speaking Latinos are less likely than whites to visit a physician or mental health provider or receive preventive health care, which may reflect the limited availability of interpreters. Even when interpreters are available, however, the quality of care may be perceived to be different by the patient. This may lead to feelings of dissatisfaction with the service, which of course has implication for retention and compliance with treatment plans. Latinos who are Spanish-speaking are found to be less satisfied with their quality of care (Alzheimer's Association, 2004).

Dementia and related illnesses of Alzheimer's and vascular dementia are the fifth leading cause of death among older adults (Alzheimer's Association,

2004). Alzheimer's disease is the most common form of dementia in old age, affecting more than 5% of the population older than age 65 years. It is estimated that by 2050 the number of Latino older adults suffering from Alzheimer's and related dementia illnesses could increase to more than 1.3 million (Alzheimer's Association, 2012; McEwen & Slack, 2005). In an effort to identify risk factors associated with Alzheimer's, recent years have seen an increase in epidemiological studies examining the link between years of schooling and risk for the disease. These studies are based in the assumption that enriched and stimulating environments increase the cortical thickness and number of brain synapses, thus creating a brain reserve that makes the more highly educated individual better able to ward off or manage the effects of the disease (Letenneur et al., 2000). Reports reflect these assumptions in the assertion that Latinos' susceptibility to dementia is due to low levels of education, as one in 10 Latino elders have no formal education (Alzhiemer's Association, 2004), combined with the high incidence in the Latino community of vascular disease, diabetes, and strokes (Alzheimer's Association, 2012). These studies are highly controversial and the findings are mixed and inconclusive, so the findings should be applied with caution.

One of the more striking disparities for Latinos is the high incidence of mental illness along with low utilization rates of mental health services. There are various subgroups within the Latino population with differing prevalence of mental illness, however, Latino elders overall have been identified as a high-risk group for depression, anxiety, and substance abuse (National Alliance on Mental Illness, 2006, 2010). One study found that Puerto Ricans have the highest overall prevalence rate of mental illness among all Latino ethnic groups (Alegria et al., 2007), and although there have been advances of evidence-based mental health services (Hilton et al., 2012) to overcome some barriers experienced by Latino older adults, many are found to terminate services prematurely or are reluctant to contact a mental health specialist (Jimenez et al., 2012).

These low utilization rates are supported in part by evidence that Latino communities are more likely to rely on family, religious and social communities for emotional support rather than professional mental health providers (National Alliance on Mental Illness, 2006, 2010). Utilization rates are also influenced by the stigma associated with mental illness in the Latino community, and the limited number of mental health professionals who are bilingual and bicultural (National Alliance on Mental Illness, 2006). The low utilization rates among Hispanics and other ethnic and racial groups was initially brought to light with the publication of the Supplement to the Surgeon General's Report on Mental Health (USDHHS, 2001). The report identified barriers to service access and retention related to the mistrust of formal mental health systems that was reinforced by clinician stereotyping, bias in standardized psychological tests and the clinical interview, and other forms of institutional racism (USDHHS, 2001).

## THE BLACK ELDERLY

American-born blacks, whose experiences in the United States are shaped by a history of slavery and systemic discrimination, make up 13.6% of the U.S. population (U.S. Census Bureau, 2010) and are no longer the country's dominant ethnic group. Changes in immigration law, globalization, and shifting world populations have increased the ethnic, linguistic, cultural, and religious diversity of communities of African descent within the continental United States. The country's oldest black immigrants, who have historically came from the Anglophone Caribbean and identify as "West Indians," and those from continental Africa, where dominant countries have been Ghana, Nigeria, Liberia, and Ethiopia, are being joined by the newest arrivals, who are coming from more than 50 African nations, Haiti, Latin and South American countries (U.S. Census Bureau, 2010).

Blacks in the African diaspora have the shared experience of a history of colonization that is anchored in doctrines of white supremacy and racial discrimination based on skin color. American-born blacks have a long and complicated history in the United States as citizens of a country that was slow to award them full citizenship even though they have been in the United States for generations. Despite gains in civil right legislation enacted since the 1960s, the legacy of slavery and discrimination continues to influence the social and economic standing of African Americans or American-born blacks. The cumulative effects of social and economic inequalities experienced over the entire life cycle are intensely felt by African Americans in late adulthood. The concept of intersectionality is useful for understanding the interactional and cumulative effects of gender, race, socioeconomic status, and age that are intensified in late life.

Poverty and socioeconomic disparities continue to have a disproportionate impact on some segments of the older adult African American population that is reflected in disparities in health and well-being outcomes. According to data from the US Census Bureau (2011), nationwide the poverty rate is 10.0% for older adults overall but 17.9% for African Americans 65 and older. Older African Americans have a high prevalence of poorer health, cognitive impairment, coronary artery and related diseases, and other diseases such as diabetes and hypertension. Obesity is of increasing concern and has continued to grow within all populations of the United States, with two out of every three Americans being considered overweight or obese. Although obesity is reported among the elderly population, the numbers are lower than those for the non-elderly adult population. Socioeconomic factors may play a role in obesity, which accounts in part for the overrepresentation of African Americans among the population of obese Americans. Relative to the elderly, obesity increases health care costs, and nursing homes are not always equipped with the equipment needed to maintain a safe environment for obese residents, whose weight prohibits the routine lifting and turning that is needed to prevent the development of bedsores (Bradway, DiResta, Fleshner, & Polomano, 2008).

The prevalence of mental illness in the African American community is similar to that of the white community and other ethnic groups (National Alliance on Mental Illness, 2010). Yet, because blacks are overrepresented among the poor, they are vulnerable to environmental stressors that influence mental health, including those related to coping with the stress of racism, discrimination, and racial stereotypes. African Americans sometimes experience more severe forms of mental health conditions due to unmet needs and other barriers which deters them from seeking professional help. According to the Health and Human Services Office of Minority Health (2010), African Americans are 20% more likely to experience serious mental health problems than the general population. As with Latino older adults, they tend to rely on family and religious and social communities for emotional support rather than seeking professional care (National Alliance on Mental Illness, 2010).

The results of a study conducted by this author found that U.S.-born black older adults who have been in the United States for generations have similar mental health beliefs and service utilization rates as white older adults, in comparison to black older adults who were foreign-born or recent immigrants to the United States (Huggins, 2013).

The elderly also experience a greater impact from natural disasters. Older black adults represented an overwhelming share of the deaths resulting from Hurricane Katrina, with the highest rates of deaths occurring among hospital patients and nursing home residents. The high death rates among the aged resulting from Hurricane Katrina can be attributed to illness and limited mobility, and ageist triage rationales that the critically ill and the aged were at the end of their lives and therefore the young should be saved first. The behavior of some older adults reflected a psychological predisposition shaped by the black experience: they were reluctant to leave as instructed before the storm arrived due in part to a perceived sense of self-efficacy based on skills learned from past experiences of coping with adverse situations, and a greater attachment to their homes, communities, neighborhood, and possessions, than were the younger victims of the disaster (Bytheway, 2007).

## AGING IN PLACE IN FAMILIES AND COMMUNITY

### Informal In-Home Caregiving

A strength of the African American and Latino communities is the sense of strong family and kinship ties, which includes fictive kin or those with whom there are strong emotional but no blood ties, and traditions of caring for aged family members in the home as they grow older versus placement in out-of-home settings. For black and Latino families, one or more family members are likely to fulfill the caregiving role for an older or disabled adult (Bullock, Crawford, & Tennstedt, 2003; Delgado & Tennstedt, 1997). Family caregivers of older adults are usually spouses or adult children. Caretaker roles are generally determined by gender, with females assuming the greater responsibility for taking on the caretaker role (Wakabayashi & Donato, 2005). Motivated by love, concern, and feelings of responsibility for their elderly family member, relative caregivers usually assume this role without knowing a great deal about how care should be provided or how to navigate an often-complicated health care financing and delivery system (Wallace, Levy-Storms, & Ferguson, 1995). Nor are some who are embarking upon the caregiver role knowledgeable about the progressive deterioration that is a normative part of the aging process, or how to cope with their own emotional feelings associated with the shifting of roles and physical strains of caring for older people as they become increasingly frail and unable to care for their personal needs and increasingly lose skills for independent living (Toseland et al., 2001; McCabe, Yeh, Lau, Garland, & Hough, 2003).

Although there may be a strong commitment among Latino and black families to caring for their older family members, the social roles of black and Latino women are changing concurrent with changing societal definitions of gender roles and the status of women in general. These changes, along with the increased labor force participation of women of color by choice, financial need, or changes in welfare policy requiring women to work as a condition of receiving welfare benefits, may make them less available to carry out a caretaker role that has traditionally been the responsibility of women. The increase in female-headed households and the greater labor force participation of women strains the informal caregiving social networks available to older adults (Rubin & White- Means, 2009). Black and Latino women may be employed in jobs with limited flexibility, and the balancing act of carrying out their responsibilities while meeting job expectations is difficult. Often the threat of loss of employment looms heavily as an added stress for the families of women carrying the dual role of a caregiver and primary family breadwinner (Bullock et al., 2003).

Older Americans are increasingly taking on the role of primary caretaker of their grandchildren either voluntarily or because the child has been remanded to their care under family court order. Grandparent-headed households have increased over 60% in recent decades; currently 5.8 million children are living with grandparents as the primary caregiver (Ellis & Simmons 2014). The reasons vary: teenage pregnancy, adult children who are military parents serving in Iraq and Afghanistan, and parents who are incapacitated due to addiction, mental illness, or incarceration (Dannison & Smith, 2002). Child welfare policy development eased the financial burden on older adults caring for children by order of the family court with the establishment of the kinship program. The program makes it possible for grandparents to receive the same rate of payment and access to services, including individuals who have a "family-like" connection to the child, as nonrelatives for providing foster care services. Continued policy developments under the Fostering Connections to Success and Increasing Adoptions Act of

2008 have expanded these benefits to allow for subsidized guardianship arrangements, making it possible for the grandparent to choose to stay in the workforce or at home as a stay-at-home caretaker.

### Out-of-Home Care

Because aging is a progressive and deteriorating process, older people rely on long-term care at higher rates than younger populations. Out-of-home care for the elderly is generally conceptualized along a continuum that moves from the least to the most restrictive form of care. With safety as the variable of the highest priority, best practices endeavors to maintain the care of the elderly person in a homelike environment that is modified as he or she progressively loses the ability for self-care and skills to live independently in residential settings. An assisted living facility is often the first choice in the continuum of care for older adults who need more personal care than can be provided in their own homes or in a retirement community but do not yet need the around-the-clock medical care and supervision provided in nursing homes.

Out-of-home care is funded out of pocket or by third-party reimbursement, Medicare, or Medicaid. Long-term health care insurance may be beyond the financial means of many older adults of color, and even fewer have the financial reserves to pay out of pocket the cost of long-term care. Therefore, there is a high reliance on the Medicare and Medicaid programs. Both were enacted in 1965 in the XIX Amendment to the Social Security Act under the "Great Society" programs. They are voucher programs that provide health care coverage to the aged and the indigent poor. Medicare is a universal entitlement program for which all Americans age 65 or older are eligible. Medicaid is means tested, and eligibility is open to individuals with incomes at or below the federal poverty level and those with catastrophic medical conditions. Low-income older adults with a medical disability receiving Medicare or Medicaid may also apply for additional cash support under Supplementary Security Income (SSI). Funding for these programs is shared by federal, state, and local governments. However, since they are state operated and administered, there can be considerable variation from state to state. Some states provide benefits by enacting Medicaid waiver programs that make it possible for older adults receiving Medicare to qualify for partial Medicaid reimbursement to support care in their own homes or to prevent undue hardship on their families. Because Medicare reimburses only for short-term acute hospitalization and a limited number of care days in rehabilitative centers, some older adults are discharged when they reach the limit of reimbursable patient care days, leaving the relative caregiver in the home with the burden of providing long-term care (Hinojosa, Rittman, Hinojosa, & Rodriquez, 2009).

Most states have put in place under their Area Agencies on Aged a Long-Term Care Ombudsman Program to advocate for the rights of residents of long-term care facilities. These programs accept and endeavor to resolve complaints on behalf of the residents and advocate policies that promote the improvement and quality of long-term care. Facilities are required to post in a conspicuous place information as to how the umbudsman can be contacted.

### Nursing Homes

Nursing homes have been and will continue to be an integral part of the long-term care continuum for meeting the critical needs of older adults with chronic illnesses, disabilities (Feng et al., 2011), or other skilled nursing needs. Latino and black older adults who reside in nursing homes are small compared to whites (Feng, Fennell, Tyler, Clark & Mor, 2011; U.S. Census Bureau, 2012). In 2010, of overall nursing home admissions, 85% were white, 8% were black, and less than 3.5% were Latino (U.S. Census Bureau, 2012). The low utilization of nursing homes can be explained by cultural differences in family structure and the expectation that black and Latino families prefer to have older adults remain in the home (Feng et al., 2011). For black older adults, there is a long history of being segregated and barred from nursing home admissions. Prior to the Civil Rights Act of 1964, nursing homes in the South were totally segregated by Jim Crow laws, and in the North were predominantly segregated by patterns of use and admission practices (Smith, Feng, Fennell, Zinn, & More., 2007). Today the Civil Rights Act of 1964 prohibits segregation and other forms of discrimination in any organization receiving federal funds such as Medicare and Medicaid. However, according to findings reported by Smith and colleagues (2007), nursing homes are still racially segregated, and blacks and Latinos continue to be treated differently in nursing home facilities across the country. Similar findings are reported by Fennell, Feng, Clark, and Mor (2010) and Feng and colleagues (2011), asserting that black and Latino older adults are typically cared for in facilities that are of poor quality, with serious deficiencies in staffing ratios and nursing care performance. Moreover, these findings indicate that in the low-income communities where many Latino and black older adults reside, the nursing homes are usually financially vulnerable, since they can rarely remain financially viable if they rely only on federal funding; to survive, they also need private-pay clients and those with health insurance (Feng et al., 2011).

There is little documentation about the extent of nursing home disparities, as there are few administrative reviews regarding admission practices or information on minorities' access to high-quality nursing home care (Feng et al., 2011). However, there is a high correlation between nursing home and residential segregation, as most nursing home closures and few nursing home openings occur in poverty-stricken communities (Feng et al., 2011).

## CULTURALLY COMPETENT
## RACE-CONSCIOUS CARE

Best practices for health and human service professionals practicing in geriatric settings are anchored in culturally competent, race-conscious approaches as discussed in the introduction and in preceding chapters of this book. Culturally competent practice across all fields of practice in the health and human services is based on the assumption that the patient's values and beliefs about health and well-being are shaped by various factors such as race, ethnicity, nationality, language, gender, sexual orientation, and physical and mental ability. These are all factors that are related to client retention and treatment compliance. Cultural competence in health care requires health care facilities and practitioners to have the knowledge, values, and skills required to understand and integrate these factors into the delivery and structure of the various heath care systems serving older adults of color. The USDHHS Office of Minority Health has made available the *National Standards for Culturally and Linguistically Appropriate Services in Health and Health Care* (Kane et al., 2007) in an effort to advance health equity, improve quality, and help eliminate health care disparities (Johnson et al. 2004). "Healthy People 2020" has expanded the goals of "Healthy People 2010" to achieve health equity, eliminate disparities, and improve the health of all groups. The geriatric health care field has made enormous advances in recognizing and incorporating new knowledge about the ways in which culture shapes conceptualization of health and wellness, symptom presentation, and help-seeking and service-using behaviors.

These developments increase awareness that the U.S. health care system serving the elderly and had trained of geriatric physicians are largely based in an American and Western cultural model of illness and wellness. The Western model reflects a Eurocentric worldview and is anchored in the physical sciences and a rational and objective cause-and-effect paradigm for interpreting symptoms, understanding etiology, formulating diagnoses, and planning treatment. Many communities of color and non-Western cultures are not anchored in this rational model but have belief systems that include spirituality, the concept of health as harmony and balance with nature, and the integration of mind, body, and spirit. Culturally competent practice with older adults of color requires an expanded knowledge base that draws upon a wide range of theories (Stone, Bryant, & Barbarotta, 2009). Practitioners should integrate findings from the emerging literature on antiracist approaches that deconstruct remnants of white supremacy in organizational policies and procedures and in the personal bias of individual practitioners. An expanded theoretical perspective that combines knowledge from the physical and social sciences provides a foundation for supporting and understanding the varied perspectives on illness and wellness in culturally different groups.

Establishing trust is a central challenge in providing culturally and racially appropriate health services to older people receiving care from predominately white health and human service systems. At the practitioner level, transference and countertransference (as discussed by Klein in Chapter 13 of this volume) involves the distortion of communication in cross-racial and cultural helping relationships because of the projections of one's internalized feelings onto another have implications for providing services older adults of color. Having seen or been victims of atrocities at the hands of authorities in their homelands, many new immigrants may be as wary of caregivers as they are of the care. And almost every racial and ethnic minority in the United States has experienced some atrocity and grave social injustice that threatened the survival of the group, and those actions have been undertaken as official governmental policy. These experiences are not easily forgotten, and with reminiscing being a characteristic of this life stage, feelings associated with these events are likely to surface in the relationship with the older person's primary care physician as well as other helping professionals who are responsible for providing the hands-on care to the older person and to family members. The health-seeking and health-using behaviors for this age population are also influenced a good deal by religious beliefs, and they may favor healing approaches that are anchored in spirituality and natural approaches. Religious and spiritual healing practices include prayer, meditation, reading and repetition of sacred oaths or affirmations or utterances to ward off evil spirits, the laying on of hands, and the use of amulets and other protective devices. The latest edition of the *Diagnostic and Statistical Manual*, published by the American Psychiatric Association (DSM-5, 2013), includes an expanded segment on culture-bound syndromes, mental health problems where clusters of symptoms are more prevalent among certain cultural groups. There are also folk illnesses or symptomatic clusters that are not recognized as diseases or syndromes in Western medicine but are very real for members of the culture.

More is also known about the relationship of stress and trauma in contributing to illness and medical problems, and this encourages the use of a trauma-informed model for shaping treatment interventions. Elders of color are overrepresented among the poor and therefore are at greater risk for presenting with stress-related illness. Further, this segment of the elder population may be suffering from the cumulative effects of these problems that have gone unrecognized and untreated over most of their lives. The Vietnam War veterans who are at retirement age or entering into old age may have not benefitted from the developments in the treatment of war-related post-traumatic stress disorder. Many of these veterans are African American males who were poor users of mental health services and may carry the effects of untreated trauma as they enter late life. Primary care professionals who are knowledgeable about the influence of culture in symptom presentation will use differential diagnosis and comprehensive social histories to avoid misdiagnosing symptoms that are similar in their presentations but may be due to untreated trauma, clinical depression, or dementia or Alzheimer's disease, or may reflect the normative processes of aging.

In 1997, the nursing home culture change movement was formed in an attempt to create caring communities where the residents' experience is enhanced and quality of life improved (Rahman & Schnelle, 2008). The movement was sparked by sweeping changes under the Nursing Home Reform Act of 1987, which mandates that nursing home residents be provided with services sufficient to attain and maintain their physical, mental, and psychosocial well-being (Koren, 2010). The movement's focus is to move the nursing home from an institutional to a homelike atmosphere while providing care that is "person-centered," making residents' preferences primary (Koren, 2010). These reforms also presented new opportunities for ensuring that nursing home menus include foods that are both nutritious and appealing to the ethnic preferences of residents, that the physical plant and décor reflect the ethnic diversity of residents, and that bilingual and bicultural staff are recruited who represent the race and ethnicity of residents.

## CONCLUSION

The nation's commitment to improving the quality of life of older Americans is reflected in a number of developments over recent decades. Every ten years since 1960, a White House Conference on Aging has been held to consider the situation of older Americans. The 1971 conference gave special consideration to the needs of the minority aged and the implications of increasing urbanization on the aging process and on the quality of life of older Americans. The 2015 conference is seeking to encourage broad public engagement in the continuing process of advancing policies and practices for older Americans. The provisions of the Elder Justice Act, enacted as a part of the Affordable Care Act, will be especially helpful to the urban elderly of color who are too often left isolated and lonely in impersonal urban apartments; this makes them especially vulnerable to scam artists who see them as easy prey for financial exploitation and other forms of abuse and neglect.

Despite these policy developments and positive practice trends, combined with medical advancements that increase life expectancy with fewer chronic illnesses, older adults of color continue to have poorer health and well-being outcomes. This is in part due to the cumulative effects of extensive economic hardship, social determinants influencing well-being outcomes, and environmental stressors that older people of color have often experienced throughout their lives. As asserted in the National Association of Social Workers (2014) statement on the continuing effects of racism in the United States, Latino and black older adults face cultural, naturalization, and minimization forms of racism in terms of restricted access to services and benefits based on cultural biases and disparate resources in their community.

This chapter highlighted the influence of race, ethnicity, and immigration status on older adults' health, life expectancy, and quality of life and discussed culturally competent approaches to enhance their chances for successful aging. Health disparities and access to appropriate health care were emphasized because health care is critical for successful aging.

## DISCUSSION QUESTIONS

1. Visit the website of the 2015 White House Conference on Aging and download the StoryCorps app that provides a format to record an interview with an older adult. Conduct an interview with a family member or an older person in your community and reflect on what you learned. http://www.whitehouseconferenceonaging.gov/
2. How would you finish the sentence: "Getting older is getting better for the elderly population. However, older persons of color are progressing at a slower pace because . . ."?
3. The narratives of former slaves were collected in the 1930s as part of the Federal Writers' Project of the Works Progress Administration. Read some of these narratives and reflect on the ways in which they enhance your understanding of the aged black experience. www.memory.loc.gov/ammem/snhtml/snhome.htm

## REFERENCES

AARP. A portrait of older minorities. Retrieved from http://research.aarp.org/general/portmino.html.

Agree, E. (1986). The AARP minority affairs initiative: A portrait of older minorities. Center for Population Research, Georgetown University, Washington, DC.

Administration on Aging. (2010). A statistical profile of Hispanic older adults aged 65+. U.S. Department of Health and Human Services. Available at www.aoa.gov/Aging_Statistics/minority_aging/Facts-on-Hispanic.

Alegría, M., Mulvaney-Day, N., Torres, M., Polo, A., Cao, Z., & Canino, G. (2007). Prevalence of psychiatric disorders across Latino subgroups in the United States. *American Journal of Public Health, 97*(1), 68–75.

Alzheimer's Association. (2012). *Alzheimer's disease fact sheet.* NIH Publication NO11642.

American Psychiatric Association. (2013). *Diagnostic and statistical manual of mental disorders (DSM-5®).* American Psychiatric Pub.

Anderson, L. M., Scrimshaw, S. C., Fullilove, M. T., Fielding, J. E., Normand, J., & Task Force on Community Preventive Services. (2003). Culturally competent healthcare systems: a systematic review. *American journal of preventive medicine, 24*(3), 68–79.

Bradway, C., DiResta, J., Fleshner, I., & Polomano, R. (2008). Obesity in nursing homes: A critical review. *Journal of the American Geriatric Society, 56*, 1528–1535.

Bullock, K., Crawford, S., & Tennstedt, S. (2003). Employment and caregiving: exploration of African American caregivers. *Social Work, 48*, 150–162.

Bytheway, B. (2007). *The evacuation of older people: The case of Hurricane Katrina.* Available at http://understandingkatrina.ssrc.org/Bytheway/index2.html, retrieved June 14, 2015.

Dannison, L. L., & Smith, A. B. (2002). *Grandparent headed families and head start: Developing effective services.* 6th National Head Start Research Conference, Washington, DC.

Delgado, M., & Tennstedt, S. (1997). Making the case for culturally appropriate community services: Puerto Rican Elders and their caregivers. *Health and Social Work, 22,* 246–55.

Ellis, R., & Simmons, T. (2014). Co-resident Grandparents and their grandchildren: Population Characteristics. Washington D.C.: U.S. Census.

Erikson, E. H. (1993). *Childhood and society.* WW Norton & Company

Feng, Z., Fennell, M., Tyler, D., Clark, M., & Mor, V. (2011). Growth of racial and ethnic minorities in U.S. nursing homes driven by demographics and possible disparities in options. *Health Affairs, 30,* 1358–1365. doi: 10.1377/hithaff.201.0126.

Fennell, M., Feng, Z., Clark, M., & Mor, V. (2010). Elderly Hispanics more likely to reside in poor-quality nursing homes. *Health Affairs, 29,* 65–73.

Furman, R., Negi, N., Iwamoto, D., Rowan, D., Shukraft, A., & Graff, J., (2009). Social work practice with Latinos: Key issues for social workers. *Social Work, 54,* 167–173.

Goldsen, J., & Petry, H. (2011). *The Aging and Health Report: Disparities and resilience among lesbian, gay, bisexual, and transgender older adults.* Seattle: Institute for Multigenerational Health.

Hilton, J. M., Gonzalez, C. A., Saleh, M., Maitoza, R., & Anngela-Cole, L. (2012). Perceptions of successful aging among older Latinos, in cross-cultural context. *Journal of Cross-Cultural Gerontology, 27*(3), 183–199.

Hinojosa, M., Rittman, M., Hinojosa, R., & Rodriquez, W. (2009). Racial/ethnic variation in recovery of motor function in stroke survivors: Role of informal caregivers. *Journal of Rehabilitation Research and Development, 46,* 223–232. Hooyman, N. R., & Kiyak, H. A. (2008). *Social gerontology: A multidisciplinary perspective.* Pearson Education.

Huggins, C. (2013). *Predictors of mental health treatment utilization among African American and Caribbean black older adults* (Doctoral dissertation, New York University).

Hyer, K., Temple, A., & Johnson, C. E. (2009). Florida's efforts to improve quality of nursing home care through nurse staffing standards, regulation, and Medicaid reimbursement. *Journal of Aging & Social Policy, 21*(4), 318–337.

Jimenez, D. E., Bartels, S. J., Cardenas, V., Dhaliwal, S. S., & Alegría, M. (2012). Cultural beliefs and mental health treatment preferences of ethnically diverse older adult consumers in primary care. *The American Journal of Geriatric Psychiatry, 20*(6), 533–542.

Johnson, R. L., Saha, S., Arbelaez, J. J., Beach, M. C., & Cooper, L. A. (2004). Racial and ethnic differences in patient perceptions of bias and cultural competence in health care. *Journal of general internal medicine, 19*(2), 101–110.

Kane, R. A., Lum, T. Y., Cutler, L. J., Degenholtz, H. B., & Yu, T. C. (2007). Resident outcomes in small-house nursing homes: A longitudinal evaluation of the initial Green House Program. *Journal of the American Geriatrics Society, 55*(6), 832–839.

Knochel, K. A., Crogan, C. F, Moore, R. P., & Quam, J. (2011). *Ready to serve? The aging network and LGB and T older adults.* Washington, DC: National Association of Area Agencies on Aging.

Koren, M. (2010). Person-centered care for nursing home resident: The culture-change movement. *Health Affairs, 29,* 312–317.

Kowal, P., Chatterji, S., Naidoo, N., Biritwum, R., Fan, W., Ridaura, R. L., . . . & Boerma, J. T. (2012). Data resource profile: the World Health Organization Study on global AGEing and adult health (SAGE). *International Journal of Epidemiology, 41*(6), 1639–1649.

Ku, L. (2006). *The slowdown in Medicaid expenditure growth.* Center on Budget and Policy Priorities.

Letenneur, L., Launer, L. J., Andersen, K., Dewey, M. E., Ott, A., Copeland, J. R. M., Dartigues, J-F., Kragh-Sorensen, P, Baldereschi, M., Brayne, C., Lobo, A., Martinez-Lage, J. M., Stijnen, T., & Hofman, A. (2000). Education and the risk for Alzheimer's disease: Sex makes a difference. *American Journal of Epidemiology, 151*(11), 1064–1071.

Manton, K. G. (2008). Recent declines in chronic disability in the elderly population: Risk factors and future dynamics. *Annual Review of Public Health, 29,* 91–113.

McCabe, K., Yeh, M., Lau, A., Garland, A., & Hough, R. (2003). Racial/ethnic differences in caregiving strain and perceived social support among parents of youth with emotional and behavioural problems. *Mental Health Services Research, 5,* 137–146.

McEwen, M. M., & Slack, M. K. (2005). Factors associated with health-related behaviors in Latinos with or at risk of diabetes. *Hispanic Health Care International, 3*(3), 143–152.

Meyers, S. (2006). Role of the social worker in old versus new culture in nursing homes. *Social Work, 52,* 273–277.

National Alliance on Mental Illness. (2006). *Latino community mental health fact sheet.* National Alliance on Mental Illness Multiculturalism Action Center.

National Alliance on Mental Illness. (2010). *African American community mental health fact sheet.* National Alliance on Mental Illness. www.nami.org

National Association of Social Workers. (2014). *Achieving racial equity: Calling the social work profession to action.* Social Work Policy Institute.

National Council of La Raza. (2005). *Critical disparities in Latino mental health: Transforming research into action.* Available at www.napolitano.house.gov/mhcaucus/reports/ Critical_Dispar ities_in_Latino_Mental_Health.pdf.

New York State Office for the Aging. (2011). *New York State Plan on Aging 2011–2105.*

Okoro, C., Young, S., Strine, T., Balluz, L., & Mokdad, A. (2005). Uninsured adults aged 65 years and older: Is their health at risk. *Journal of Health Care for the Poor and Underserved, 16,* 453–463.

People, H. (2013). Conclusion and future directions: CDC health disparities and inequalities report—United States, 2013. *CDC Health Disparities and Inequalities Report—United States, 2013, 62*(3), 184.

Potocky-Tripodi, M. (2002). *Best practices for social work with refugees and immigrants.* Columbia University Press.

Rahman, A. N., & Schnelle, J. F. (2008). The nursing home culture-change movement: Recent past, present, and future directions for research. *The Gerontologist, 48*(2), 142–148.

Rubin, R., & White-Means, S. (2009). Informal caregiving: Dilemmas of sandwiched caregivers. *Journal of Family and Economic Issues, 30,* 252–267. doi: 1007/ s10834-009-9155-x.

Smith, D. B., Feng, Z., Fennell, M. L., Zinn, J. S., & Mor, V. (2007). Separate and unequal: Racial segregation and disparities in quality across U.S. nursing homes. *Health Affairs, 26*(5), 1448–1458.

Stone, R. I., Bryant, N., & Barbarotta, L. I. N. D. A. (2009). *Supporting culture change: Working toward smarter state nursing home regulation.* The Commonwealth Fund Issue Brief.

Toseland, R. W., McCallion, P., Smith, T., Huck, S., Bourgeois, P., & Garstka, T. A. (2001). Health education groups for caregivers in an HMO. *Journal of Clinical Psychology, 57*(4), 551–570.

U.S. Census Bureau, (2014). *Income and Poverty in the U.S.*

U.S. Census Briefs. (2010). *The black population 2010.*

U.S. Census Bureau. (2008). *Component of population changes by race & Hispanic origin.*

U.S. Census Bureau. (2012). *Nursing home beds, residents and occupancy by state, 2009.*

U.S. Department of Health and Human Services. (2000). *Healthy People 2010.* Rockville, MD: Author.

U.S. Department of Health and Human Services. (2001). Mental Health: culture, race and ethnicity, supplement to "Mental health: A report to the Surgeon General." Rockville, MD. Author.

U.S. Department of Health and Human Services. (2003). Office of Minority Mental Health.

Vespa, J., Lewis, J. M., & Kreider, R. M. (2013). *America's families & living arrangements: 2012 population characteristics.* U.S. Department of Commerce.

Wallace, S., Levy-Storms, & Ferguson, L. R. (1995). Access to paid in-home assistance among disabled elderly people: Do Latinos differ from non-Latino Whites. *American Journal of Public Health, 85,* 970–975.

Wakabayashi, C., & Donato, K. M. (2005). The consequences of caregiving: Effects on women's employment and earnings. *Population Research and Policy Review, 24*(5), 467–488.

World Health Organization. (2002). *The world health report 2002: reducing risks, promoting healthy life.* World Health Organization. Switzerland.

# CHAPTER 11

# Barriers to Mental Health and Treatment among Urban Adolescent and Emerging Adult Males of Color

MICHAEL A. LINDSEY AND AMARIS WATSON

Living in a high-risk, urban environment has a deleterious influence on mental health outcomes among adolescent and emerging adult males of color (Lindsey et al., 2006, 2010a, 2010b; Lindsey & Marcell, 2012), hereafter referred to as young males of color. While prevalence rates of mental illness have continued to increase for this population (Lincoln et al., 2010; Ortega et al., 2006; U.S. Department of Health and Human Service, 2001; Williams et al., 2007), young males of color experience lower rates of mental health treatment than any other group (Alegría et al., 2008; Angold et al., 2002; Barksdale et al., 2009; Cummings et al., 2011; Keyes et al., 2012; Merikangas et al., 2011; Williams et al., 2007). Reasons for their lower utilization rates of mental health service include perceptual, social, and logistical barriers (Breland-Noble et al., 2011; Copeland et al., 2006; Lindsey et al., 2006, 2010, 2013), in addition to systemic-level factors, including organizational and financial obstacles (Lindsey et al., 2013; Snowden & Thomas, 2000; Vitale & Bailey, 2012; Wells et al., 2013). If we are to improve mental health outcomes and access to needed services for young males of color, multisector and multilevel interventions are required. This chapter will examine individual-level factors that are associated with the underutilization of mental health services among young males of color. In addition, this chapter will examine the ways in which services sectors (i.e., child welfare, juvenile justice) have contributed to mental health treatment underutilization. Finally, viable interventions and strategies that can be employed by service sectors to facilitate greater access

to care for this group will be considered. This final point will highlight important future directions in research and practice. This chapter will assist health and
human service providers in rendering culturally competent services and demonstrating an understanding of the individual and systematic barriers that influence
mental health service utilization among young males of color.

## PREVALENCE OF MENTAL ILLNESS AMONG YOUNG MALES OF COLOR

A definitive statement on the prevalence (i.e., the amount of new cases of disorders combined with the existing cases) of mental disorders among young males
of color cannot be made due to the underreporting of mental health needs for
this group. This is true even with strong survey methods and enhanced measurement precision (e.g., valid and reliable assessment measures). Large-scale, nationally representative studies like the National Survey of American Life (adult
and adolescent versions) and the National Comorbidity Survey (adult and adolescent versions), however, point to some viable prevalence rates among young
males of color. For example, according to the National Comorbidity Survey-
Adolescent version (NCS-A), boys have significantly higher prevalence rates of
any 12-month disorder than girls, mainly due to males' higher prevalence rates
of attention-deficit/hyperactivity disorder (ADHD; Merikangas et al., 2010).
Race-specific findings indicate that relative to white adolescents, Latino adolescents are 1.4 times significantly more likely to have a lifetime mood disorder,
while non-Latino blacks are significantly less likely to have a lifetime substance
abuse disorder relative to whites. There are no specific data on the interaction of
race by gender among available NCS-A studies.

   Data from the National Survey of American Life (NSAL) provide another es-
timate of the prevalence of mental illness among young black males. The NSAL
is a nationally representative survey of African Americans, Caribbean blacks,
and whites in the United States. It has adult- and adolescent-specific surveys.
One advantage of the NSAL is that it does have interactions by ethnicity and
gender. Williams and colleagues (2007) used data from the NSAL to examine
the prevalence of major depressive disorder (MDD) among Caribbean blacks,
African Americans, and non-Latino whites. Two major findings emerge from
their study. First, while the lifetime MDD prevalence rate was highest among
whites (17.9%) relative to Caribbean blacks (12.9%) and African Americans
(10.4%), each group experienced similar rates of 12-month MDD (i.e., 5.9%
among African Americans, 7.2% among Caribbean blacks, and 6.9% for whites).
Second, it appears that while the prevalence rate is highest for whites, the chronicity and burden of MDD seems to be greatest among blacks. That is, the
persistence of MDD is higher for African Americans (56.5%) and Caribbean

blacks (56.0%) than for whites (38.6%). Across each racial group, women had higher rates of MDD than men, but the gender difference was significant only for African Americans (Williams et al., 2007). Looking exclusively at depression among African American men in the NSAL, Lincoln and colleagues (2010) found that African American men aged 18 to 34 experience feelings of depression in higher doses than their older counterparts. African American men in this same age group also had higher levels of serious psychological distress than their older counterparts (Lincoln et al., 2010). Lincoln and colleagues' findings may explain the reasons that underlie the greater burden and chronicity of depression among blacks, especially African Americans.

In summary, nationally representative samples suggest that mental health need is greatest for females, but few of these studies document differential prevalence rates based on ethnicity. When ethnicity is considered, it appears that prevalence rates of mental health need are highest for whites. Another phenomenon, however, appears to be in play. While whites have higher prevalence rates of mental illness, the chronicity and burden of mental illness appears to be highest for young people of color. A look at mental health treatment rates reflects another troubling pattern.

## PREVALENCE OF MENTAL HEALTH TREATMENT AMONG YOUNG MALES OF COLOR

Large-scale epidemiologic studies indicate that the majority of adolescent and emerging adults who need treatment do not receive it (Costello et al., 2014; Merikangas et al., 2011; Villatoro & Aneshensel, 2014). The NCS-A study, for example, found that only about one-third of adolescents with a lifetime mental health disorder received services for their illness (36.2%; Merikangas et al., 2011). Although disorder severity is known to be associated with an increased likelihood of receiving treatment, half of adolescents with severely impairing mental disorders have never received treatment for their symptoms (Merikangas et al., 2011). Service use rates for a lifetime mental health disorder appear to be highest among those with ADHD (59.8%) and behavior disorders (45.4%) (Merikangas et al., 2011), indicating that the majority of youths receive treatment for a lifetime mental health disorder due to behavioral problems (rather than mood-related problems). The majority of adolescents also enter treatment with comorbid mental health disorders, which also seems to increase their odds of receiving treatment. For example, about 20% of youths with one class of disorder received treatment, while approximately 51% of those with two classes and 72.2% of those with three or more classes of disorders received services (Merikangas et al., 2011). This finding is consistent with other large-scale studies (Barksdale et al., 2009).

Non-Latino black and Latino adolescents with lifetime mental health disorders use mental health services at a lower rate in comparison to white youth across *both* mood and behavioral disorders, but the findings are statistically significant relative to mood disorders (Merikangas et al., 2011). This may be, in part, due to how the behavioral presentation of ethnic minority youth, particularly males, is interpreted by adults in their lives (e.g., teachers, principals). As a general matter, non-Latino black and Latino adolescents with mood disorders may be particularly vulnerable to being underserved in mental health treatment settings (this will be discussed further in a later section). When gender is considered, adolescent females are more likely to receive treatment for a lifetime anxiety disorder, while the opposite is true for adolescent males with lifetime ADHD (Merikangas et al., 2011).

Findings from the NCS-A study are confirmed by other nationally representative studies, particularly in regard to other diagnostic categories. For example, a study based on data from the National Survey on Drug Use and Health (NSDUH) found that treatment for 12-month MDD is lower among ethnic minority adolescents (African Americans, Latinos, and Asian Americans) relative to whites. Ethnic minorities were also significantly less likely to receive medication for MDD and treatment from a mental health provider relative to whites. Studies based on both the NCS-A and the NSDUH data reflect a disturbing trend of lower mental health service use for ethnic minority youth, especially among African American youth. The NCS-A, in particular, reflects the fact that relative to white youth, African American youth experience statistically significant lower use of specialty mental health, complementary/alternative medicine, and any mental health service use (Costello et al., 2014). In fact, while not statistically significant, African American adolescents are more likely than white adolescents to receive mental health service via human service sectors such as school-based and specialty mental health settings. Barksdale and colleagues (2009), in their examination of systems of care data, also found a persistent pattern of lower mental health service use (i.e., outpatient, school-based, and residential/inpatient services) for African American youth relative to white youth.

Large-scale, nationally representative studies have increased in sheer numbers, but vital information about outcomes specific for young males of color is missing. In particular, these studies miss an opportunity to determine within-group differences among young males of color regarding the factors that lead to unmet mental health need. We need to know the factors that underlie mental health service use among young males of color for several reasons. First, this information will lead to the development of interventions and strategies to remove barriers that contribute to the underutilization of mental health services. Second, we need to determine the role other service systems play (i.e., juvenile justice, child welfare, schools) as it relates to the mental health need and service use divide for young males of color. For example, as it relates to school- or juvenile justice–based mental health service use, what are the challenges related to addressing the mental health needs of young males of color? The following discussion will begin to extrapolate empirical findings regarding these challenges and point to possible solutions.

## FACTORS RELATED TO UNDERUTILIZATION

The factors that influence mental health service use among young males of color are best observed in the context of their help-seeking behaviors. A primary feature of psychological help seeking for this group pertains to their conceptualizations of masculinity—that is, what it means to be a "man" (Addis & Mahalik, 2003; Lindsey & Marcell, 2012). "Toughing it out," a prevailing notion among males of color, means that acknowledging an emotional or psychological need or asking for help is a sign of weakness. This is particularly true among those who live in urban, highly stressed environments (Lindsey et al., 2006; Watkins et al., 2014). Taking care of their own problems and exhibiting emotional control as an expression of masculinity prohibit the use of both informal and formal sources of help (Lindsey et al., 2010; Scott, McMillen, & Snowden, in press). Even being more introspective about emotional or psychological matters (e.g., spirituality, meditation) has been found to impede help seeking and formal mental health service use among black adolescent and young adult males (Lindsey & Marcell, 2012).

Another feature of help seeking salient to males of color is the tendency to have closed networks consisting of peers, family, and other close associates (Lindsey et al., 2010). For example, prior research among black adolescent males with depression suggests that families represent the primary source for psychological help seeking (Lindsey et al., 2010). In other words, young males from this group typically indicate turning to family members as the primary source of help (Lindsey et al., 2006, 2010). Family members are given primacy over professionals as the "appropriate" source for help. These perceptions are further reinforced in normative ways among familial networks (e.g., "Don't air the family's dirty laundry in public," "Mental health professionals get paid to listen to you, while family members have the best answers"; Lindsey et al., 2006). Thus, family sanctions with respect to help seeking and other normative expectations regarding the experience of participating in mental health services represent important barriers to service use among young males of color. Many are hesitant to utilize services due to the fear of stigma that will be exhibited from their social networks (Breland-Noble et al., 2011; Lindsey et al., 2006). Lindsey and colleagues (2013) found that young African American males experience feelings of embarrassment and shame that result from the stigma associated with mental health services among their social networks, as friends may deem them to be "crazy."

Young, Latino males may face even greater challenges that go beyond masculinity notions and the primacy of help seeking within the social network. For example, a study examining socioeconomic, cultural, and logistical barriers to service use among Latinos in Georgia found that cultural factors, including language barriers (e.g., lack of interpreters) and a general lack of understanding of the U.S. health system, served as barriers to treatment for Latinos (Vitale & Bailey, 2012). This finding is consistent with extant research that confirms the pivotal role language and cultural factors (e.g., immigration challenges) play in mental health service use among Latinos (Alegría et al., 2007; Keyes et al., 2012).

Matters of race and ethnicity can also influence help-seeking behaviors that do not lead to formal mental health service use. Many young males of color do not trust their service providers and feel as though providers cannot relate to them due to cultural differences (Lindsey et al., 2006, 2010). As previously mentioned, even family members transmit negative messages and beliefs that prohibit males of color from relating to mental health therapies and providers (Breland-Noble et al., 2011; Lindsey et al., 2006). Formal mental health treatment has been perceived, traditionally, as a help-seeking behavior engaged in by the "well-to-do," or the white middle-class (Lindsey & Marcell, 2012). Indeed, even the majority of mental health professionals do not reflect the same race and ethnicity of males of color. This leads to skepticism on the part of young males of color and fears that mental health professionals will not make a connection to them or will not be "down to earth" and exhibit "respect" for them (Lindsey & Marcell 2012). Males of color also have higher susceptibility to the stigma associated with mental health service use (Lindsey et al. 2010; Rose et al., 2011) and are likely to have poor involvement in treatment due to negative perceptions surrounding mental health services and providers.

## CONTRIBUTIONS OF SERVICE SECTORS TO MENTAL HEALTH TREATMENT UNDERUTILIZATION

### Child Welfare

While many service sectors contribute, in one way or another, to the mental health treatment underutilization among young males of color, we focus on two sectors in this chapter, child welfare and juvenile justice. Males of color with mental health needs are often overrepresented in service sectors like child welfare and juvenile justice. It is often the case that mental health problems among young males of color go unrecognized in these systems or, as mentioned earlier, are misinterpreted as behavioral problems or problems that otherwise do not warrant treatment. For example, extant research examining mental health treatment among child welfare–involved youth suggests that youth with sexual abuse histories are more likely to reach mental health treatment than youth with other types of trauma histories (e.g., removal from the family due to neglect; Horwitz, Hulburt, & Zhang, 2010). Girls tend to report higher levels of sexual abuse histories. Otherwise, gender tends to predict mental health treatment use among child welfare–involved youth, with boys often experiencing higher levels of treatment use (Farmer, Mustillo, Wagner, et al., 2010; Lindsey, Gilreath, Thompson et al., 2012). Age plays an additional important role in mental health treatment underutilization, particularly for young males of color aging out of foster care. Studies by McMillen (2004) and McMillen and Raghavan (2010) found that youth of color have increased levels of mental health needs that go untreated as they age out of the child welfare system. These findings suggest that as child welfare–involved youth gain more volition over their own decision making, some of the individual-level factors related to mental health service use discussed earlier in this chapter (e.g., stigma related to service use, social network influences on service use, greater reliance on informal sources of psychological health) prevail. Indeed, in a study of black males aging out of foster care, Scott (in press) found that young males from this cohort tend to rely more on their family members for support regarding a mental health problem than on professional sources of help. This is the case even in light of federal policies (i.e., the Foster Care Independence Act of 1999) that expanded access to services for older youth (up to age 21) in foster care.

## Juvenile Justice

The juvenile justice sector represents another arena in which males of color with mental health needs experience overrepresentation (Cocozza, Skowyra, & Shufelt, 2010; Shufelt & Cocozza, 2006; Skowyra & Cocozza, 2007). While minority youth make up 75% of the total population of youth in the juvenile justice system (Armour & Hammond, 2009), another 70% of these youth suffer from mental illness. Moreover, one in five of this 70% suffer from a severe mental illness that impairs their daily functioning (Hammond, 2007). Extant research also suggests that youth of color in this sector are less likely to access mental health treatment than their white counterparts (Dalton et al., 2009).

Young males of color often enter the juvenile justice system when symptoms of their mental illness go unrecognized and attract the attention of law enforcement (Geller & Bieber, 2006; General Accounting Office, 2003). In fact, the mental health needs of this group of youth may be multifold. For example, Cocozza, Skowyra, and Shufelt (2010) note that 79% of youth in juvenile justice systems with one mental disorder met criteria for a second, with the most common second disorder being a substance use disorder. In fact, young males of color with mental illness are likely to be imprisoned for minor and status offenses such as disrupting the public order, truancy, running away, smoking cigarettes, drinking alcohol, violating curfew, and disobedience (Cocozza et al., 2005); untreated mental illness may underlie all of these. In a study examining differences in mental health service use between African American and white youth going into a community-based system-of-care program, youth referred into systems of care from the juvenile justice system were significantly less likely to have received any services in comparison to those who were not (Barksdale et al., 2009).

The problems with mental health treatment in the juvenile justice sector have much to do with perceptions that juvenile justice officials have of young males of color and their families of origin. In her riveting book *The New Jim Crow*, Michelle Alexander chronicles the evolution of the mass incarceration system in the United States, which seems to disproportionately target young males of color. Alexander notes that from the very beginning of the formalized system of incarceration, and in its present form, the behaviors of young males of color were seen through a different lens relative to their white counterparts. The juvenile justice system has been complicit in its willingness to be a feeder system for the adult correctional system. Mental health treatment challenges within this system have largely remained unaddressed. Treatment services are either not available or are characterized by poor coordination and lack of collaboration between providers. Treatment services within the juvenile justice sector also fail to adequately identify or train providers who have experience in treating mental health and substance use disorders. These factors contribute to the mental health treatment underutilization of young males of color, and perhaps to the proliferation of a life within the corrections system.

## VIABLE STRATEGIES TO REDRESS THE MENTAL HEALTH TREATMENT UNDERUTILIZATION OF YOUNG MALES OF COLOR

We propose that the mental health treatment challenges of young males of color, while daunting, can be addressed via the careful coordination of intervention strategies and services. We offer solutions that can occur within the context of families and also at the provider level—to include those who actually provide the one-to-one services, and the settings or sectors in which services are provided.

### A Race-Sensitive Focus on Treatment Engagement

Despite the advances of evidence-based treatments and renewed policy efforts to improve access to care, the fact remains that the majority of youth in the United States do not receive treatment for their mental health needs (Costello et al.,

2014; Merikangas et al., 2011). No group is more disproportionately impacted by the lower likelihood of mental health treatment receipt than young males of color. As mentioned earlier, young males of color face a number of challenges regarding their conceptualizations of emotional and psychological struggles, and with respect to their conceptualizations of mental illness. Notions of masculinity and the primacy of social network support can hinder psychological help seeking that leads to formal care. Young Latino males face an even greater challenge if there are language differences between themselves and service providers. These challenges in service utilization call for a renewed focus on the need for targeted treatment-engagement interventions and strategies designed to meet young males of color where they are (i.e., facing the stigmatization associated with mental illness and treatment, and the uncertainty as to whether mental health professionals will truly understand their unique needs).

What we know is that some treatment-engagement interventions have a proven efficacy. In a recent analysis of the treatment-engagement literature, Lindsey and colleagues (2014) identified 22 successful interventions that have been applied to youth and families to improve mental health treatment utilization. Lindsey and colleagues point out, however, that these "common elements of treatment engagement" have been mostly applied to the caregivers of children with mental health needs, not the children themselves. The systematic review by Lindsey and colleagues confirmed the findings of an earlier review by Kim, Munson, and McKay (2012) that adolescents have been left out in terms of engagement interventions designed specifically for them.

This brings us to the matter of how best to engage young males of color in mental health treatment. While there are very few engagement interventions specifically targeted to adolescents (cf. Lindsey et al., 2013), we do know from available evidence what specific strategies might be targeted to improve mental health treatment for young males of color. We highlight a few here.

*Assessment* entails measuring the strengths and needs of young males of color with the goal of building rapport and treatment alliance with them. Assessment is an engagement strategy identified by Lindsey and colleagues' (2014) review as a strategy appearing with the highest frequency in randomized controlled trials of engagement interventions, and the strategy with the highest percentage of appearing in a winning treatment arm. This is a particularly important engagement strategy for young males of color, who might present to treatment with great reticence about pursuing mental health services. Building rapport by demonstrating genuine concern and care has been identified by young males of color as an important strategy for mental health providers to use when working with them (Lindsey et al., 2010).

A second important engagement strategy pertains to providing *psychoeducation about services*. This strategy involves providing information about what to expect from services, including frequency of sessions, session length, and roles of the therapist and client (Lindsey et al., 2014). Young males of color often equate mental health services as being part of a "system" that is inherently designed to mistreat or fail them (Lindsey et al., 2010). Mental health service providers are seen in the same light as police officers or even social workers, professionals with whom young males of color have not always enjoyed positive interactions. Thus, presenting mental health services as a source of support, explaining the nature of services to be delivered so that expectations about services can be clarified, and examining the needs of young males of color (e.g., need for interpretive services or clinicians who are bilingual) all reflect ways in which psychoeducation as an engagement strategy might yield stronger connections to treatment.

Finally, *motivation enhancement* involves identifying and probing the advantages to change, optimism, and intention to change. It also can include exercises designed to increase the client's readiness to participate in services, including exercises designed to mitigate psychological barriers to change and treatment participation (Lindsey et al., 2014). This is a key engagement strategy for young males of color, who often present to treatment with stigma regarding mental illness and services. Stigma-reduction strategies such as motivation enhancement can build up their cognitive and psychological strength to thwart off threats to the perception that services can be helpful.

## Greater Coordination of Treatment, with Schools as the Centerpiece

It is now clear, via large-scale, nationally representative studies, that schools have become the largest provider of mental health services in the United States (Costello et al., 2014). This is clear even from recent federal initiatives. For example, the Affordable Care Act calls for the expansion of school health centers and a greater focus on behavioral health within these centers (Carr et al., 2012). It makes sense, then, that efforts to improve treatment connections for young males of color be situated in schools—the natural ecology in which many of the problems of young males of color emerge. We discuss a few school-based intervention strategies here.

Few teachers and educators receive training on the signs and symptoms of mental illness. This leads to myriad problems as far as recognizing symptoms among young males of color and the appropriate interpretation of their behaviors. On average, black and Latino young males are suspended from school at higher rates than any other ethnic group (Aud et al., 2010). Some argue the differential is largely based on differential interpretation of behaviors—that is, young males of color are suspended or sent to juvenile detention, while young white males receive mental health treatment and probation. Teachers and administrators can play a huge role in curbing this tide. For example, we know from clinical

practice that a mental health outcome like depression can often have externalizing manifestations expressed in the form of irritability (Lindsey et al., 2013).
Irritable youth often get into fights or other forms of physically assaultive behaviors. Most schools have a zero tolerance policy regarding fights and physically assaultive behaviors. Yet, the depression or its correlate, anxiety, that may underlie
the expression of irritable behaviors is often overlooked or not seen at all. It would
be important to document how teacher and administrator training on the signs
and symptoms of mental health problems like depression, anxiety, or trauma-
related disorders might improve greater recognition of these mental health disorders, and also decrease suspensions among young males of color.

As the largest provider of mental health services to youth, specialty mental
health service providers and providers of child welfare and juvenile justice services might also have better coordination with school providers. It is unfortunate that many providers and sectors that serve youth often work in silos.
Rarely is there coordination between these entities. For example, it might be
possible for a youth to be seen in mental health treatment through child welfare services without the school's knowledge. If schools, the place where youth
spend the majority of their time, were the central focus of all mental health
service provision, then they could provide the requisite care to young males
of color. For example, we now know how to deliver an array of mental health
services within schools, from universal or school-wide interventions serving
all youth to indicated interventions targeting youth with more serious needs
(e.g., mental health disorders; Lever, Lindsey, Graham, & Weist, 2014). School-
based mental health service provision might also catch and address mental
health problems early enough to avoid further involvement in a service sector
like the juvenile justice system. Indeed, social workers and juvenile justice advocates might serve young males of color better by exploring the provision of
mental health treatment in schools.

## Greater Use of Evidence-Based Practice

A final area essential to redressing the mental health treatment underutilization
by young males of color pertains to the provision and expansion of evidence-
based mental health interventions. The mental health needs of young males
of color, while not as prevalent as the needs of young white males, are greater
in terms of chronicity and burden. Thus, when young males of color do access
care, they do so with intense needs and symptoms requiring the most efficacious
mental health interventions. The problem is that many specialty mental health
and even school-based settings struggle to keep up with the revolving door of
mental health personnel who need to be continuously retrained on a particular
evidence-based intervention. Training, to begin with, is quite costly. Thus, the

provision of effective services to young males of color becomes costly. These challenges are not unique to addressing the mental health needs of young males of color. What we argue, however, is that young males of color face a disproportionate number of issues that impact their mental health service use relative to other populations and, when combined with the aforementioned challenges regarding the delivery of evidence-based interventions, further complicate efforts to meet the mental health needs of this group. Mental health service providers should not be daunted by these challenges regarding the delivery of evidence-based practice to young males of color. Some have argued that these interventions are not always culturally attuned to the psychosocial needs of young males of color and call for the need for these interventions to be culturally adapted for this group. Similar to Huey and Polo (2008), we believe the reality remains that many young males of color have not been participants in randomized controlled trials, which document the efficacy of interventions.

## SUMMARY AND CONCLUSIONS

This chapter examined the individual-level factors associated with the underutilization of mental health services among young males of color. We also examined the ways in which service sectors (i.e., child welfare, juvenile justice) contribute to the underutilization of mental health services for this group, and viable intervention strategies to address these challenges.

Much of the focus, as we have argued, needs to be on addressing the factors (e.g., stigma, influence of social networks, expectancies regarding treatment) that lead to lower levels of mental health treatment among males of color. We need to employ strategies such as those mentioned in this chapter to facilitate stronger connections to evidence-based interventions among young males of color. We also need to ensure that providers of color (e.g., Latino providers who are bilingual) are trained so that provider characteristics that tend to get in the way of treatment connections might also be eliminated. Perhaps there are more strategies to employ, but we believe that the strategies we discussed are definitely a strong step toward meeting the mental health treatment needs of young males of color.

## DISCUSSION QUESTIONS

1. How can health and human service providers consistently render culturally competent services despite individual and systemic barriers?
2. What role can the child welfare and juvenile justice sectors play in the lives of males of color to facilitate greater access and connections to mental health services?

## REFERENCES

Addis, M. E., & Mahalik, J. R. (2003). Men, masculinity, and the contexts of help seeking. *American Psychologist, 58*(1), 5.

Alegría, M., Chatterji, P., Wells, K., Cao, Z., Chen, C. N., Takeuchi, D.,. & Meng, X. L. (2008). Disparity in depression treatment among racial and ethnic minority populations in the United States. *Psychiatric Services (Washington, DC), 59*(11), 1264.

Alegría, M., Mulvaney-Day, N., Woo, M., Torres, M., Gao, S., & Oddo, V. (2007). Correlates of past-year mental health service use among Latinos: Results from the National Latino and Asian American Study. *American Journal of Public Health, 97*(1), 76–83.

Angold, A., Erkanli, A., Farmer, E. M., Fairbank, J. A., Burns, B. J., Keeler, G., & Costello, E. J. (2002). Psychiatric disorder, impairment, and service use in rural African American and white youth. *Archives of General Psychiatry, 59*(10), 893.

Armour, J., & Hammond, S. (2009). Minority youth in the juvenile justice system, disaproportionate minority contact. In *Washington, DC: National Conference of Sstate Legislatures.*

Aud, S., Fox, M., & Kewal Ramani, A. (2010). *Status and trends in the education of racial and ethnic groups* (NCES 2010-015). U.S. Department of Education, National Center for Education Statistics. Washington, DC: U.S. Government Printing Office.

Barksdale, C. L., Azur, M., & Leaf, P. J. (2009). Differences in mental health service sector utilization among African American and Caucasian youth entering systems of care programs. *Journal of Behavioral Health Services & Research, 37,* 363–373.

Breland-Noble, A. M., Bell, C. C., & Burriss, A. (2011). "Mama just won't accept this": Adult perspectives on engaging depressed African American teens in clinical research and treatment. *Journal of Clinical Psychology in Medical Settings, 18*(3), 225–234.

Carr, D., Schaible, A., & Thomas, K. (2012). Health in mind: Improving education through wellness. In R. Davis & J. Levi (Eds.), *Healthy Schools Campaign and Trust for America's Health.* Available at http://healthyschoolscampaign.org/content/uploads/Programs/Health%20in%20Mind/Documents/Health_in_Mind_Report.pdf.

Cocozza, J. J., Skowyra, K. R., & Shufelt, J. L. (2010). *Addressing the mental health needs of youth in contact with the juvenile justice system in system of care communities: An overview and summary of key issues.* Washington, DC: Technical Assistance Partnership for Child and Family Mental Health.

Cocozza, J.J., Veysey, B. M., Chapin, D.A., Dembo, R., Walters, W., & Farina, S. (2005). Diversion from the Juvenile Justice System: The Miami-Dade Juvenile Assessment Center Post-Arrest Diversion Program. *Substance Use & Misuse, 40*(7), 935–951.

Copeland, V. C. (2006). Disparities in mental health service utilization among low-income African American adolescents: closing the gap by enhancing practitioner's competence. *Child and Adolescent Social Work Journal, 23*(4), 407–431.

Costello, E. J., He, J. P., Sampson, N. A., Kessler, R. C., & Merikangas, K. R. (2014). Services for adolescents with psychiatric disorders: 12-month data from the National Comorbidity Survey–Adolescent. *Psychiatric Services, 65*(3), 359–366.

Cummings, J. R., & Druss, B. G. (2011). Racial/ethnic differences in mental health service use among adolescents with major depression. *Journal of the American Academy of Child & Adolescent Psychiatry, 50*(2), 160–170.

Dalton, R.F., Evans, L.J., Cruise, K.R., Feinstein, R.A., & Kendrick, R.F. (2009). Race differences in mental health service access in a secure male juvenile justice facility. *Journal of Offender Rehabilitation, 48*(3), 194–209.

Farmer, E. M. Z., Mustillo, S. A., Wagner, H. R., Burns, B. J., Kolko, D. J., Barth, R. P., et al. (2010). Service use and multi-sector use for mental health problems by youth in contact with child welfare. *Children and Youth Services Review, 32*(6), 815–821.

Geller, J. & Bieber, K. (2006). The premature demise of public child and adolescent impatient psychiatric beds part II: Challenges and implications. *Psychiatric Quarterly*, 77, 273–291.

Hammond, S. (2007). Mental health needs of juvenile offenders. National Conference of State Legislatures.

Horwitz, S. M., Hulburt, M. S., & Zhang, J. (2010). Patterns and predictors of mental health services use by children in contact with the child welfare system. In M. B. Webb, K. Dowd, B. J. Harden, J. Landsverk, & M. F. Testa (Eds.), *Child welfare and child well-being—New perspectives from the National Survey of Child and Adolescent Well-being* (pp. 279–329). New York: Oxford University Press.

Huey, S. J., & Polo, A. J. (2008). Evidence-based psychosocial treatments for ethnic minority youth. *Journal of Clinical Child & Adolescent Psychology*, 37(1), 262–301. doi: 10.1080/15374410701820174

Keyes, K. M., Martins, S. S., Hatzenbuehler, M. L., Blanco, C., Bates, L. M., & Hasin, D. S. (2012). Mental health service utilization for psychiatric disorders among Latinos living in the United States: the role of ethnic subgroup, ethnic identity, and language/social preferences. *Social Psychiatry and Psychiatric Epidemiology*, 47(3), 383–394.

Lever, N., Lindsey, M. A., Grimm, L., & Weist, M. D. (2014). Preservice training for school mental health clincians. In M. D. Weist et al. (Eds.), *Handbook of school mental health: Research, training, practice and policy*. New York: Springer Publishing Company.

Lincoln, K. D., Taylor, R. J., Watkins, D. C., & Chatters, L. M. (2010). Correlates of psychological distress and major depressive disorder among African American men. *Research on Social Work Practice*, 21(3), 278–288.

Lindsey, M. A., Chambers, K., Pohle, C., Beall, P., & Lucksted, A. (2013). Understanding the behavioral determinants of mental health service use by urban, under-resourced black youth: Adolescent and caregiver perspectives. *Journal of Child and Family Studies*, 22(1), 107–121.

Lindsey, M. A., Joe, S., & Nebbitt, V. (2010). Family matters: The role of mental health stigma and social support on depressive symptoms and subsequent help seeking among African American boys. *Journal of Black Psychology*, 36(4), 458–482.

Lindsey, M. A., Korr, W. S., Broitman, M., Bone, L., Green, A., & Leaf, P. J. (2006). Help-seeking behaviors and depression among African American adolescent boys. *Social Work*, 51(1), 49–58.

Lindsey, M. A., & Marcell, A. V. (2012). "We're going through a lot of struggles that people don't even know about": The need to understand African American males' help-seeking for mental health on multiple levels. *American Journal of Men's Health*, 6(5), 354–364.

Merikangas, K. R., He, J. P., Brody, D., Fisher, P. W., Bourdon, K., & Koretz, D. S. (2010). Prevalence and treatment of mental disorders among US children in the 2001–2004 NHANES. *Pediatrics*, 125(1), 75–81.

Merikangas, K. R., He, J. P., Burstein, M., Swendsen, J., Avenevoli, S., Case, B., . . . & Olfson, M. (2011). Service utilization for lifetime mental disorders in US adolescents: Results of the National Comorbidity Survey–Adolescent Supplement (NCS-A). *Journal of the American Academy of Child & Adolescent Psychiatry*, 50(1), 32–45.

Ortega, A. N., Feldman, J. M., Canino, G., Steinman, K., & Alegría, M. (2006). Co-occurrence of mental and physical illness in US Latinos. *Social Psychiatry & Psychiatric Epidemiology*, 41(12), 927–934.

Shufelt, J. L., & Cocozza, J. J. (2006). *Youth with mental health disorders in the juvenile justice system: Results from a multi-state prevalence study.* Delmar, NY: National Center for Mental Health and Juvenile Justice.

Skowyra, K. R., & Cocozza, J. J. (2007). *Blueprint for change: A comprehensive model for the identification and treatment of youth with mental health needs in contact with the juvenile justice system.* Delmar, NY: National Center for Mental Health and Juvenile Justice.

Snowden, L., & Thomas, K. (2000). Medicaid and African American outpatient mental health treatment. *Mental Health Services Research, 2,* 115–120.

U.S. Department of Health and Human Services. (2001). *Mental health: Culture, race, and ethnicity–A supplement to "Mental health: A report of the Surgeon General."* Rockville, MD: U.S. Department of Health and Human Services, Substance Abuse and Mental Health Services Administration, Center for Mental Health Services.

United States. General Accounting Office. (2003). *Child Welfare and Juvenile Justice: Federal Agencies Could Play a Stronger Role in Helping Statesss Reduce the Number of Children Placed Solely to Obtain Mental Health Services: Report to Congressional Requeters.* The Office.

Villatoro, A. P., & Aneshensel, C. S. (2014). Family influences on the use of mental health services among African Americans. *Journal of health and social behavior, 55*(2), 161–180.

Vitale, M., & Bailey, C. (2012). Assessing barriers to health care services for Hispanic residents in rural Georgia. *Journal of Rural Social Sciences, 27*(3), 17–45.

Watkins, D. C., Hawkins, J., & Mitchell, J. A. (2014). The discipline's escalating whisper: Social work and black men's mental health. *Research on Social Work Practice,* 1049731514526621.

Wells, A., Lagomasino, I. T., Palinkas, L. A., Green, J. M., & Gonzalez, D. (2013). Barriers to depression treatment among low-income, Latino emergency department patients. *Community Mental Health Journal, 49*(4), 412–418.

Williams, D. R., Gonzalez, H. M., Neighbors, H., Nesse, R., Abelson, J. M., Sweetman, J., & Jackson, J. S. (2007). Prevalence and distribution of major depressive disorder in African Americans, Caribbean blacks, and non-Hispanic whites: results from the National Survey of American Life. *Archives of General Psychiatry, 64*(3), 305–315.

PART FOUR

# The Helping Relationship

# CHAPTER 12

# The Influence of Race and Ethnicity on Consumer Behaviors

MANNY J. GONZÁLEZ

## INTRODUCTION

Hispanics, interchangeably identified as Latinos, are one of the fastest-growing ethnic groups in the United States. The Latino population in the United States increased by 43% between 2000 and 2010 to 50.5 million, representing 16.3% of the total population (Pew Hispanic Center, 2011). The overall youthfulness, birthrate, and levels of immigration have contributed to the growth of the Hispanic population. In addition, the diversity of national-origin groups among Latinos has increased. Hispanics can be of any race and from over 20 national origins, with emerging communities of Dominicans, Colombians, Salvadorans, Nicaraguans, and Peruvians, for example, adding to the larger and more established communities of Mexicans, Puerto Ricans, and Cubans. According to the Pew Hispanic Center (2011), Mexicans are by far the largest Latino immigrant group, accounting for more than half of the Hispanic immigrant population, and they are the largest foreign-born group in the nation.

Hispanic immigration to the United States has reached unprecedented levels and has dispersed across the nation, including states, regions, cities, and towns that previously had virtually no Latino residents. Hispanics are concentrated in a number of metropolitan areas. The largest Latino immigrant groups—Mexicans, Cubans, Dominicans, and Colombians, as well as island-born Puerto Ricans—are located in four metropolitan areas: New York City, Los Angeles, Miami-Dade, and Chicago. Each area has a significant Latino population with a diversity of Hispanic national-origin groups. These areas are traditional destinations for the largest and most longstanding Latino groups (Mexicans, Puerto Ricans, and Cubans) and are the chosen destination of emerging Latino groups such as

Dominicans, Colombians, Salvadorans, and Guatemalans (Suro & Singer, 2002). Mexicans live largely in Los Angeles and several cities in Texas. Caribbean-born Latinos tend to live in New York or Miami.

Hispanics are one of the poorest ethnic groups in the United States. Latinos have high rates of poverty among full-time workers and poverty among working husbands in intact families with children, and may suffer from the effects of economic downturns more than non-Latinos and benefit less from periods of economic growth (Suro, 1998). In their report *Wealth Gaps Rise to Record Highs Between Whites, Blacks and Hispanics,* Kochhar, Fry, and Taylor (2011) found that median household wealth among Hispanics fell from $18,359 in 2005 to $6,325 in 2009. The percentage drop—66%—was the largest among all racial and ethnic groups. Low levels of educational attainment among Hispanics compound this negative economic shift.

In light of these demographic shifts, and the differences between and within the various Hispanic national-origin groups, including linguistic diversity and immigration status, understanding how race and ethnicity affects consumer or client behaviors within the helping process takes on increased significance. The mental health and psychosocial issues associated with the emigration experience are reason enough to justify integrating race and ethnicity into the clinical care of Hispanics and all persons of color. Drawing from the fields of health and mental health, the general objectives of this chapter are (1) to examine the sociocultural factors that influence the health, mental health, and illness behavior of Hispanics, including their use of medical, mental health, and general social work services; (2) to demonstrate how knowledge of social and cultural influences—including race and ethnicity—on health, emotional well-being, illness, and disability affects the accuracy of assessment and psychosocial diagnosis and the appropriateness of treatment planning and intervention; and (3) to explore how the use of health, mental health, and social services is enhanced by assisting individuals and families of color to mitigate the impact of negative factors and to tap into the positive influences of protective social and cultural factors. The general objectives of this chapter are consistent with the overall aim of the book: to address difficult service-delivery issues that are informed and sustained by interpersonal bias and institutional and structural racism and that contribute to persistent ethnic and racial disparities among marginalized and vulnerable populations treated within health and human service systems of care.

## "HISPANIC" VERSUS "LATINO": DOES IT REALLY MAKE A DIFFERENCE?

From an ethnic-sensitive perspective, it is important for practitioners to be attuned to what members of ethnic groups prefer to be called. As an anthropological construct, ethnicity—which is the key variable that informs the ethnic-sensitive perspective in the helping professions—underscores the importance of cultural differences among groups of people. It focuses on culture as a shared meaning as well as being rooted in individual lives. It is as fluid or stable as the culture of which it is a part. It is both an individual and a collective phenomenon that is externalized in social interaction and personal at the level of self-identification (see Devore & Schesinger, 1999). In their classic monograph *Bridging Ethnocultural Diversity in Social Work and Health*, Kumabe, Nishida, and Hepworth (1985) observed that ethnicity deals with an individual's sense of identification and provides a sense of belonging to a reference group. As a sociocultural variable, ethnicity is often displayed in the values, attitudes, lifestyles, customs, rituals, and personality types of individuals who identify with particular ethnic groups. Ethnicity points to a common heritage shared by a specific cultural group, and it includes the cultural phenomena of music, religious beliefs, history, worldview, language, preference for food, and perceptions of health and emotional well-being (U.S. Department of Health and Human Services, 2001). As a fluid and dynamic construct, ethnicity intersects with other key sociocultural variable such as race, gender, ability status, social class, and acculturation and immigration status (see Marsiglia, Flavio, & Kulis, 2009).

Informed by an understanding of ethnicity and its impact on service delivery, it is important to note that the terms "Hispanic" and "Latino" are used to describe people of Spanish descent who come from different countries, cultures, and sociopolitical histories (González & González-Ramos, 2005). Individuals of Spanish descent primarily identify themselves in relation to their specific country of origin (e.g., Cuban, Puerto Rican, Dominican, Mexican). Identifying with a specific country of origin is very important for many individuals of Spanish descent because it provides a sense of pride and uniqueness that is often reflected in their music, poetry, and food. Therefore, an important point to keep in mind when providing psychosocial services to Spanish-speaking individuals is that Hispanics prefer to be asked questions that allow for the unfolding of their journey from their homeland to the United States. Mental health clinicians and health care providers may find the following questions helpful when treating or working with individuals of Spanish descent:

- What is your country of origin?
- What do you miss the most from your homeland?
- How different is the United States from your country of origin?
- Do you travel frequently to your homeland?
- By what means of transportation did you come to the United States (e.g., ship, plane)? For example, many Puerto Ricans who migrated to the United States before World War II did so by ship and not air travel.

- What specific reasons or factors influenced your decision to leave your country and come to the United States?
- Do you plan to return to your homeland at some point in the future?

These questions give practitioners the opportunity to learn about the homeland that the client, consumer, or patient has left behind, the differences and similarities found within the Hispanic culture, and the reasons for moving to the United States (e.g., poverty, political persecution, limited access to health or educational opportunities). This type of questioning may also enhance the effectiveness of engagement in the helping process, assessment, and intervention planning.

Although the terms "Hispanic" and "Latino" are often used interchangeably in the United States to refer to individuals of Spanish descent, there appears to be an increasing debate among politicians, community activists, and Hispanic scholars as to which term is "politically correct" (see Engstrom & Piedra, 2006). The debate appears to be centered on the following points:

- "Hispanic" is a U.S. Census label developed to track the population growth of individuals of Spanish descent as well as trends in their level of education and socioeconomic status. For individuals of Spanish descent, the Hispanic label symbolizes a loss of identity by not recognizing the importance of a specific ethnic nationality, such as Cuban, Costa Rican, or Colombian.
- "Hispanic" is an English term that does not acknowledge gender, unlike the terms "Latino" and "Latina," which are gender specific.
- "Hispanic" is a politically conservative term, while "Latino/Latina" is viewed as a more progressive label.
- Many individuals of Spanish descent may oppose the use of "Latino" and "Latina," however, because the terms are historically linked to Spain and its conquering empire during the 15th and 16th century.

While recognizing this political debate, it is important to note that individuals of Spanish descent may prefer one term over the other, may use the terms interchangeably, or may choose to self-identify by ethnic nationality. Thus, in providing psychosocial services practitioners should simply ask individuals of Spanish descent their preference for self-identification: Hispanic, Latino/Latina, or a specific ethnic nationality. Offering a choice of preference for self-identification will not only assist in ensuring the effective implementation of specific interventions, but will also demonstrate respect for the diversity and difference often found within the Hispanic culture and communities of color.

## CULTURAL CHARACTERISTICS OF HISPANICS

Because Hispanics constitute a racially diverse group, any examination of their primary cultural characteristics must first be informed by an understanding of race and its impact on psychosocial functioning (see Borell & Rodriguez, 2010). Service delivery that is sensitive to the reality of race and ethnicity must be predicated on inclusiveness of the client's social reality, which includes the way specific cultural values or characteristics directly affect effective treatment. In fact, Proctor and Davis (1996), in discussing the challenge of racial difference in clinical practice, noted that racial differences in the helping encounter cannot be treated via a colorbind practice paradigm. They contend that colorblind practice is unrealistic because "race, reflected in skin color, is readily apparent and cannot be easily ignored" (p. 100). Race cannot be separated from an individual's self-definition, social reality, and sense of the world. Understanding the ethnocultural characteristics of people of color—and their impact on the helping encounter— requires a practice framework that places race and racial differences at the core of any therapeutic or service delivery initiative. As a socially constructed concept with profound implications for service delivery and the psychosocial treatment of people of color, it is important to underscore that race is not a biological category, and it ought to be viewed as a societal idea that has been used to divide groups of people into distinct racial categories (Borrell & Rodriguez, 2010; Marsiglia, Flavio, & Kulis, 2009; U.S. Department of Health and Human Services, 2001). Genetic studies (see Barbujani, Magani, Minch, & Cavalli-Sforza, 1997; Paabo, 2001) have confirmed that race, as a biological concept, has not survived the test of scientific investigation. Describing this scientific confirmation, Marsiglia and colleagues (2009, p. 9) write:

> Humans cannot be categorized reliably based on phenotypical characteristics, such as those aspects of physical appearance like skin color, hair texture, and bone structure that are often thought to be markers of one's racial background. This is a discredited idea that is a vestige of nineteenth-century phrenology, the study of the human skull based on the belief that mental faculties and personality could be determined from its shape.

In examining the cultural characteristics of any ethnic group through a racial lens, it important to recognize that racism and discrimination negatively affect health and mental health outcomes and place people of color at risk for specific mental health disorders such as depression and anxiety (see U.S. Department of Health and Human Services, 2001). Williams and Williams-Morris (2000) have identified the ways in which racism and discrimination may jeopardize and adversely affect the mental health of people of color. These include the following:

1. Racial stereotypes and negative images can be internalized, denigrating individuals' self-worth and adversely affecting their social and psychological functioning.
2. Racism and discrimination by societal institutions have resulted in lower socioeconomic status for minorities and poorer living conditions, in which poverty, crime, and violence are persistent stressors that can affect mental health.

3. Racism and discrimination are stressful events that can lead directly to psychological distress and physiological changes affecting mental health.

Many Hispanic scholars (see Sandoval and De La Roza, 1986; Gil & Vasquez, 1997; González & González-Ramos, 2005; Santiago-Rivera et al., 2002) have identified salient cultural characteristics that inform treatment strategies for the amelioration of distressed psychological social functioning among Hispanics. Key values or characteristics are *simpatia, personalismo, familismo, respeto,* and *confianza*. Two gender-specific roles (see Gil, 1980) also influence how attuned clinicians approach their Hispanic clients: *marianismo* (female self-sacrifice) and *machismo* (male selfrespect and responsibility). *Marianismo* and *machismo* have acquired such common pejorative usage that their actual centrality in the Hispanic maintenance of intrapersonal and interpersonal coherence is obscured. Religion or a sense of spirituality also informs the traditional Hispanic experience and may serve to enhance, or at times challenge, the curative process inherent within the helping process.

Hispanics' level of acculturation, socioeconomic class, family, and gender roles affect their adherence to traditional cultural values or characteristics and their utilization of psychosocial care. Examples include:

- *Simpatia* relates to *buena gente* (the plural form of a nice person). Hispanics are drawn to individuals who are easygoing, friendly, and fun to be with. Politeness and pleasantness, and avoidance of hostile confrontation, are valued, guiding social work clinicians to demonstrate these qualities in their demeanor and to anticipate the same in their client as the basis of engagement.
- *Personalismo* describes the tendency of Hispanic patients to relate to their service providers personally rather formally or as part of an institution. This serves the relational theory goals of authenticity and mutuality. It may not be reflected in the busy agency culture, requiring an outreach attitude by clinicians as they meet their Hispanic clients.
- *Familismo* is a collective loyalty to the nuclear and extended family that outranks the individual. Clinicians who are trained in individual techniques need to extend the relational perspective, in particular not-knowing and co-construction of meanings, to validate the significance of family. This includes *compadres* (godparents) as vital resources, particularly during times of crisis when instrumental and emotional support may be needed. *Familismo* remains strong even among highly acculturated families (Santiago-Rivera et al., 2002).
- *Respeto* (respect) dictates appropriately deferential behavior toward others based on their age, gender, social position, economic status, and authority. Clinicians must keep in mind that *respeto* implies mutual and reciprocal deference. The clinician receiving respect as a professional is equally obligated to

observe deferential courtesies to the patient based on age, gender, and other sociocultural characteristics.

- *Confianza* (trust) refers to the intimacy and interpersonal comfort in a relationship. The empathic attunement and mutuality of the relational approach are particularly central with Hispanic clients. *Confianza* generates interpersonal resilience overall, based on willingness to engage with the clinician and apply experiential learning.

Clinical practitioners ought to be mindful that these Hispanic-specific concepts offer practical guidance in racially and ethnic-sensitive practice with *all* populations. Their conscious centrality in work with Hispanic clients or patients may call for more overt demonstration of cultural protocols, particularly where there is diversity between clinician and client in cultural orientation. However, the essential features of sympathy/empathy, respect, individuality, and trust apply across most—if not all—helping encounters.

## GENDER-SPECIFIC ROLES

From a clinical point of view in both health and mental health care, gender role expectations and values constitute an area where transference and countertransference may create the strongest potential for cultural misalignment. These rational dynamics may be exacerbated by racial and ethnic factors (see Lum, 2004). Traditional gender roles within the Hispanic family structure are intrinsically linked to the concepts of *marianismo* and *machismo*. *Marianismo*, the term associated with Hispanic female socialization, implies that girls must grow up to be women and mothers who are pure, long-suffering, nurturing, pious, virtuous, and humble, yet spiritually stronger than men (Gil & Vasquez, 1997). *Marianismo* is associated with the Virgin Mary and therefore directly tied to the Roman Catholic faith. Although *marianismo* has contributed to a view of Hispanic women as docile, self-sacrificing, and submissive, it is clear from a family systems viewpoint that women (particularly mothers) are the silent power in the family structure.

Clinicians need to be alert to the temptation to view Hispanic female clients' deference to the clinician or submission in gender roles as a deficiency in self-esteem or self-assertiveness. Deconstructing and co-constructing the ways the client's posture toward others are the relational approach to seeing what is or is not inherent to the problem for clinical attention. In his seminal paper *Masochism, Submission, and Surrender*, Ghent (1990) clearly distinguishes deference from powerlessness or self-devaluation. The ethnic-sensitive and racially minded practitioner, seeking empathic attunement to the client's meanings and methods rather than superficial evaluation of manifest behavior, is well advised to regard surrender of dominance as a legitimate relational-interpersonal paradigm when matched by reciprocal protection and provision for the *machismo* role.

This observation underscores the importance of diversity practice in clarifying the value of an approach that recognizes that client behaviors are informed by ethnocultural processes that include racial and ethnic dynamics as well as individual psychological factors. Surrendering to the cultural and individual attributions of meaning and worth of the client does not represent submission as a professional but rather serves as a cornerstone of constructivist, nonpositivist, and clinical practice (Tosone, 2004). Similarly, clinical authority does not require dominance.

Hispanic *machismo*, contrary to being a cult of the gender role socialization of Hispanic males, has centered on the construct of manhood. *Machismo* has been defined in the social science literature as the cult of virility, arrogance, and sexual aggressiveness (Santiago-Rivera, 2002), and it refers to a man's responsibility of loyalty to friends, family, and community. He must provide for, protect, and defend his family (Sandoval & De La Roza, 1986), and in turn he commands respect from others. If clinicians are to succeed with Hispanic males, they must be skilled at proffering respect as a means of engagement, addressing any resistance in themselves as a countertransference phenomenon. Acculturation may conceal the degree to which Hispanic males and females adhere to *machismo* and *marianismo*, but the clinician's attunement to and acceptance of such important dimensions of self are needed to offset disruptions and impasses in clinical services with Hispanics (Sandoval & De La Roza, 1986).

## RELIGION AND SPIRITUALITY

Religion and spirituality are sociocultural domains that are informed by the variables of race and ethnicity. They may greatly influence how people of color seek psychosocial services, adhere to prescribed treatment plans, and engage with service providers in health, mental health, and other systems of care (see Congress & González, 2013; González & González-Ramos, 2005). Research studies (see Department of Health and Human Services, 2001) have shown a possible positive association between religion and spirituality and mental health promotion and mental illness prevention. Subjective well-being and life satisfaction are two important variables that appear to have a strong link with reported and/or observed levels of spirituality. For specific people of color, such as African Americans, religion and spirituality have been identified as predictors of improved self-perception, self-esteem, and adherence to health-related behaviors (Taylor, Mattis, & Chatters, 1999).

Clinical practitioners or providers of care might anticipate culturally normative ambivalence and confusion about how to use the clinical process without violating religious tenets. Ethnic-sensitive practice principles that are guided by an appreciation for racial differences and an understanding of marginalized and oppressed groups prescribe open and co-constructed exploration at all times to determine how a problem can be approached in ways congruent with the client's outlook (Ecklund & Johnson, 2007). When working with an Hispanic client, if the practitioner isn't open about the different outlooks between practitioner and client—the client may forgo treatment to keep his/her religious beliefs intact. (Flores & Carey, 2000; González & González-Ramos, 2005; Santiago-Rivera et al., 2002).

Religion and spirituality often are separated by the theoretical-treatment models that inform the helping process and psychosocial treatment. Fortunately, emerging psychosocial intervention approaches with culturally diverse populations—such as relational therapy—are stressing the integration of faith with physical and emotional well-being (see Rosenberger, 2014). Relational theory's nonjudgmental embrace of all contents, seeking only to identify its utility in the maintenance of self-fulfillment and functioning, poses no barrier to religious or spiritual beliefs in the helping process. From an interpersonal and relational perspective, Urrabazo (2000), for instance, has noted the curative potential of faith and religion in therapeutically assisting Hispanic clients, and more specifically undocumented Hispanic immigrants who have been robbed, raped, and beaten while crossing the border into the United States. Religion appears to emotionally sustain Hispanics who are continuously subjected to racism, discrimination, and social injustice. During times of psychological crisis or environmental distress, the religious belief systems of Hispanics may be used as an adjunct to conventional clinical practice, providing a healing community where self-validation, connection to others, guidance, and social support may be found.


## LANGUAGE

For many people of color, including Hispanics, language represents the primary means for retaining a sense of heritage, safeguarding cultural identity, and expressing emotionality. Language is an important element in the clinical treatment of Hispanics and other ethnic groups. It informs how this specific cultural group accesses, navigates, and utilizes services across systems of care. Similar to the variables of race and ethnicity, it serves to elucidate client behaviors within the helping process. Language, for example, has always assumed a central role in the provision of mental health care. Clinical theoreticians (see Woods & Hollis, 2000) have stressed the importance of understanding and assessing the client's language, as well as communication style, both at the manifest and latent level. In fact, the psychodynamic literature (see Fox, 2001) has even underscored the importance of comprehending and working with clients' preverbal and unconscious language.

Language, to a great extent, structures the creation of reality (Anderson, 1997). It is through the use of language that both mental health practitioners and clients are able to build and sustain a therapeutic relationship. The therapeutic relationship, in turn, becomes the medium through which change in the client's life can occur (Woods & Hollis, 2000). Because language has such a central place in the treatment of Hispanics, Castex (1994) has stressed that practitioners who wish to communicate effectively with Spanish-speaking and bilingual clients must first find out what language the client communicates best in, and then must demonstrate sensitivity to the fact that people who are in a state of crisis or who are experiencing significant psychological symptoms may struggle to communicate in a second language—namely, English.

Research studies (see Malgady & Zayas, 2001) have suggested a relation between linguistic inaccessibility and underutilization of mental health services by Hispanics. Treatment agencies, therefore, must ensure that Hispanics have access to competent bilingual mental health practitioners. In the absence of bilingual practitioners, agencies should employ or have access to well-trained translators who are proficient in English and Spanish. From an ethnic-sensitive practice perspective, it is not sufficient for human service organizations to employ bilingual/bicultural practitioners. Systems of care must ensure that the development and implementation of mental health policies and the delivery of clinical services reflect the Hispanic cultural values of *personalismo* (preference for personal contact/interaction), *bondad* (kindness), *respeto* (respect), and *dignidad* (dignity) (González & González-Ramos, 2005).

## OPERATIONALIZING RACE AND ETHNICITY IN THE HELPING PROCESS
### "Outline for Cultural Formulation"

In its 1994 edition of the *Diagnostic and Statistical Manual of Mental Disorder* (DSM-IV), the American Psychiatric Association (APA) acknowledged the significant role of culture in shaping the symptom presentation, expression, and course of mental disorders. This acknowledgment—which was evident by the development of the DSM-IV "Outline for Cultural Formation" and a glossary of specific idioms of distress and culture-bound syndromes—was an important milestone in systematically incorporating and operationalizing the sociocultural variables of race and ethnicity in the helping process, and in assisting clinicians to formulate a culturally informed assessment, diagnosis, and treatment plan (APA, 1994). Ecklund and Johnson (2007, p. 357) note that "the cultural formulation provides a systematic overview of a client's cultural background, the role of cultural context in the client's expression of distress or disturbance, and the effect that cultural differences may have on the relationship between client and professional." The major categories or components of the "Outline for Cultural Formulation" are (a) the cultural identity of the individual, (b) cultural explanations of the individual's illness, (c) cultural factors related to the psychosocial environment and levels of functioning, and (d) cultural elements of the relationship between the individual and the clinician.

In operationalizing the variables of culture, race, and ethnicity—via the use of the "Outline for Cultural Formulation"—the clinician is encouraged to do the following:

1. Inquire about the patient's cultural identity to determine their ethnic or cultural reference group, language abilities, language use and language preference.
2. Explore possible cultural explanations of the illness, including patients' idioms of distress, the meaning and perceived severity of their symptoms in relation to the norms of the patients' cultural reference group, and their current preferences for, as well as past experiences with, professional and popular sources of care.
3. Consider cultural factors related to the psychosocial environment and levels of function. This assessment includes culturally relevant interpretations of social stressors, available support, and levels of functioning, as well as patients' disability.
4. Critically examine cultural elements in the patient–clinician relationship to determine differences in culture and social status between them and how those differences affect the clinical encounter, ranging from communication to rapport and disclosure.
5. Render an overall cultural assessment for diagnosis and care, meaning that the clinician synthesizes all of the information to determine a course of care." (U.S. Department of Health and Human Services, 2001, p. 11)

It is important to the underscore that using the "Outline for Cultural Formulation" in health, mental health, and other systems of care enables practitioners to examine the impact of sociopolitical oppression, internalized racism, immigration and migration trauma, race-related stress, and acculturation on the adaptive or maladaptive functioning of Hispanics and other people of color. It also provides a means for practitioners to explore their own internalized bias and overt prejudices while developing a level of self-awareness that will facilitate competent cultural care of diverse client populations (see Ecklund & Johnson, 2007). Predicated on the DSM-IV "Outline for Cultural Formulation," the fifth edition of the *Diagnostic and Statistical Manual of Mental Disorders* (DSM-5) incorporates a greater degree of cultural sensitivity throughout (see APA, 2013). DSM-5 provides more detailed and structured information about cultural concepts of distress and culture-specific clinical syndromes. Included in the updated manual is a cultural formulation interview guide that is aimed at assisting clinicians to assess cultural factors influencing patients' perspectives of their symptoms and treatment options. It includes questions about patients' background in terms of their culture, race, ethnicity, religion, and geographic origin. The interview provides an opportunity for patients to define their distress in their own words and then relate this to how others, who may not share their culture, see their problems. This gives the clinician a more comprehensive foundation on which to base both diagnosis and care.

## Clinical Skills for Racially and Ethnic-Sensitive Practice

Proctor and Davis (1996) have identified a set of core practice skills that facilitate the helping encounter between clients of color and racially and ethnically dissimilar practitioners. The skillset is aimed at addressing the three overarching questions that many clients of color have when seeking health, mental health, or social service intervention:

> "Is the helper a person of goodwill?"
> "Is the help offered valid and meaningful to me?"
> "Is the helper trained and skilled?"

Answering these questions will facilitate the development of a cross-racial and cross-ethnic helping relationship that is qualitatively different from any racially dissimilar relationship that has been experienced by the client and service provider.

Drawn from person-centered and ecological approaches to clinical care (see Gitterman & Germain, 2008), the skills of respect, professional courtesy, tuning-in, and empathic attunement are critical in answering the first question. In addition to these skills, Proctor and Davis (1996, p. 99) note that "maintaining topic consistency, paraphrasing accurately, assuring confidentiality, and providing follow-up to the client's comments affirm the worker's sincere interest in the client." These skills are vital for engaging marginalized and oppressed clients who have had to adopt a sense of "healthy paranoia" to protect themselves from the reverberating affects of social injustice, inequality, powerlessness, and discrimination (see Grier & Cobbs, 1968).

Exploring and understanding the contextual factors that impinge upon the lives of people of color will assist clinicians or service providers to respond to the second question: "Is the help offered valid and meaningful to me? Does the practitioner have sufficient knowledge of my world to be of real assistance to me?" For instance, in their study of the impact of race on the health of Hispanic man, Borrell and Rodriguez (2010) found that Hispanic black men exhibit worse health outcomes than white Hispanic men along specific medical dimensions that measured diabetes, hypertension, feelings of sadness or hopelessness, and serious mental illness. Competent care of people of color requires mastery of both a broad and in-depth knowledge base that is predicated on a comprehensive understanding of the dynamics of race, racism, and discrimination. In fact, Borrell and Rodriguez (2010, p. 41) contend that "Ignoring racial heterogeneity among Hispanics may result in missing a great deal of information with regard to the role that race or color play in the health status of these individuals." From a clinical perspective, a culturally sensitive examination of the person-in-situation gestalt will assist practitioners to offer valid and meaningful care to individuals and families who have been marginalized by the dominant society because of racial and ethnic differences, and it will increase the practitioner's ability to engage and sustain these individuals in a meaningful helping relationship (see Woods & Hollis, 2000).

Giving something that works to clients during the initial phase of the helping process (e.g., the partialization of the presenting problem, information about a specific entitlement program, or concrete suggestions about financial or housing assistance) demonstrates that the practitioner possesses specialized knowledge and skill and gives the client a positive answer to the question: "Is the helper trained and skilled?" Proctor and Davis (1996) note that this question leads many racially diverse clients to wonder "Does the worker have professional expertise or mastery of skills that can resolve my problems?" The belief in the practitioner's ability is a cornerstone in the formation of the working alliance, an important dimension of the helping relationship (see Gitterman & Germain, 2008; Woods & Hollis, 2000). Without a working alliance with the practitioner, change in the client's life and situation may not be possible. The sociopolitical history of diverse populations and the unfair and inequitable treatment of people of color have created feelings of mistrust in the credibility of helping professionals. It is only through skill and competence in the context of an empathic helping relationship that feelings of mistrust can be carefully examined and managed.

In describing the importance of professional competence in the care of racially diverse populations, Proctor and Davis (1996, p. 102) state the following:

> The client's perception that the worker is competent has consequences far beyond the worker's own comfort level . . . Clients who view their helpers as competent are more likely to trust the worker, are more likely to be influenced by the worker, are more likely to continue in treatment, and are more likely to expect treatment to have a positive effect on the presenting problem. In short, a perception of worker competence appears to be critical to the success of the helping endeavor. [Practitioners] may wish that clients came to the helping situation already accepting their competence. Yet

workers may have to deliberately work toward a perception of their competence, particularly when perceptions are affected by societally based racial biases.

Professional competence may be conveyed in a number of ways, such as office arrangement, display of degrees and certificates, professional dress and comportment of the practitioner, and the display of journals and books on the office shelves.

## CONCLUSION

Providing psychosocial care to racially and ethnically diverse client populations is a challenging and rewarding professional endeavor. It requires skill, empathy, and an awareness of the socioeconomic and political factors that affect the lives of people of color in the United States. Health and human service practitioners must have an awareness of the impact of race and ethnicity on the behaviors of consumers or clients who seek services from health, mental health, or other systems of care. The primary objectives of this chapter were (1) to examine the sociocultural factors (e.g., cultural characteristics, language, gender roles, religion and spirituality) that influence health, mental health, and illness behaviors of Hispanics, including their use of medical, mental health, and general social services; (2) to demonstrate how knowledge of social and cultural influences—including race and ethnicity—upon health, emotional well-being, and illness affects the accuracy of assessment, psychosocial diagnosis, and the appropriateness of treatment planning and intervention; and (3) to explore how the use of health, mental health, and social services is enhanced by assisting individuals and families of color to mitigate the impact of negative factors and to tap the positive influences of protective social and cultural factors. The use of the "Outline for Cultural Formulation" and specific clinical skills in the care of diverse clients were identified as useful tools for assisting Hispanics and other racially and ethnically diverse individuals in acquiring adaptive behaviors that are consistent with protective cultural factors.

## DISCUSSION QUESTIONS

1. Identify and describe how race, language, and religion and/or spirituality influence the health, mental health, and illness status of Hispanics, including their use of medical, mental health, and general human services.
2. How might clinical practitioners in health and mental health settings incorporate or integrate the noted cultural characteristics of Hispanics (e.g., *familismo, personalismo, respeto, confianza*) in the helping process?

## REFERENCES

American Psychiatric Association. (1994). *The diagnostic and statistical manual of mental disorders* (4th ed.). Washington, DC: Author.

American Psychiatric Association. (2013). *The diagnostic and statistical manual of mental disorders* (5th ed.). Arlington, VA: American Psychiatric Publishing.

Barbujani, G., Magagni, A., Minch, E., & Cavalli-Sforza, L. L. (1997). An apportionment of human DNA diversity. *Proceedings of the National Academy of Sciences, USA, 94,* 4516–4519.

Borrell, L., & Rodriguez, C. (2010). The implications and impact of race on the health of Hispanic/Latino males. In M. Aguirre-Molina, L. Borrell, & W. Vega (Eds.), *Health issues in Latino males: A social and structural approach* (pp. 32–52). New Brunswick, NJ: Rutgers University Press.

Castex, G. M. (1994). Providing services to Hispanic/Latino populations: Profiles in diversity. *Social Work, 39,* 288–296.

Congress, E. P., & González, M. J. (Eds.). (2013). *Multicultural perspectives in social work practice with families* (3rd ed.). New York: Springer

Devore, W., & Schlesinger, E. (1999). *Ethnic-sensitive social work practice* (5th ed.). Needham Heights, MA: Allyn & Bacon.

Ecklund, K., & Johnson, W.B. (2007). Toward cultural competence in child intake assessment. *Professional Psychology: Research and Practice, 38*(4), 356–362.

Fabrega, H. (1990). Hispanic mental health research: A case for cultural psychiatry. *Hispanic Journal of Behavioral Sciences, 12,* 339–365.

Flores, M. T., & Carey, G. (Eds.). (2000). *Family therapy with Hispanics: Toward appreciating diversity.* Boston: Allyn and Bacon.

Fox, R. (2001). *Elements of the helping process: A guide for clinicians.* New York: Haworth.

Ghent, E. (1990). Masochism, submission, surrender: Masochism as a perversion of surrender. *Contemporary Psychoanalysis, 26,* 108–136.

Gil, R. M. (1980). *Cultural attitudes toward mental illness among Puerto Rican migrant women and their relationship to the utilization of outpatient mental health services.* Unpublished doctoral dissertation, Adelphi University, New York.

Gil, R. M., & Vasquez, C. I. (1997). *The Maria paradox.* New York: Perigee Trade.

Gitterman, A., & Germain, C. (2008). *Life model of social work practice: Advances in theory and practice* (3rd ed.). New York: Columbia University Press.

González, M. J., & González-Ramos, G. (Eds.). (2005). *Mental health care for new Hispanic immigrams: Innovations in contemporary clinical practice.* New York: Haworth.

Grier, W., & Cobbs, P. (1968). *Black rage.* New York: Bantam Books.

Kocharr, R., Fry, R., & Taylor, P. (2011). *Wealth gaps rise to record high between whites, blacks, Hispanics.* Washington, DC: Pew Research Center.

Kumabe, K. T., Nishida, C., & Hepworth, D. H. (1985). *Bridging ethnocultural diversity in social work and health.* Honolulu: University of Hawaii School of Social Work.

Lum, D. (2004). *Social work practice and people of color: A process-stage approach* (5th ed.). Belmont, CA: Brooks/Cole.

Malgady, R., & Zayas, L. (2001). Cultural and linguistic considerations in psychodiagnosis with Hispanics: The need for an empirically informed process model. *Social Work, 46*(1), 39–49.

Marsiglia, F. F., & Kulis, S. (2009). *Culturally grounded social work: Diversity, oppression and change.* Chicago: Lyceum.

Paabo, S. (2001). Genomics and society. The human genome and our view of ourselves. *Science, 291,* 1219–1220.

Pew Hispanic Center. (2011). *Census 2010: 50 million Latinos.* Washington, DC: Author.

Proctor, E. K., & Davis, L. E. (1996). The challenge of racial difference: Skills for clinical practice. In P. L. Ewalt, E. M. Freeman, S. A. Kirk, & D. L. Poole (Eds.), *Multicultural issues in social work* (pp. 97–114).Washington, DC: NASW.

Rosenberger, J. (Ed.). (2014). *Relational social work practice with diverse populations.* New York: Springer.

Sandoval, M. C., & De La Roza, M. (1986). A cultural perspective for serving the Hispanic client. In H. P. Lefley & P. B. Pedersen (Eds.), *Cross-cultural training for mental health professionals* (pp. 151–181). Springfield, IL: Charles C. Thomas.

Santiago-Rivera, A. L., Arredondo, P., & Cooper-Gallardo, M. (2002). *Counseling Latinos and la familia: A practical guide.* Thousand Oaks, CA: Sage.

Suro, R. (1998). *Strangers among us: Latino lives in a changing America.* New York: Vintage.

Suro, R., & Singer, A. (2002). *Latino growth in metropolitan America: Changing patterns, new locations.* Washington, DC: Brookings Institute.

Taylor, R. J., Mattis, J. S., & Chatters, L. M. (1999). Subjective religiosity among African Americans: A synthesis of findings from five national samples. *Journal of Black Psychology, 25,* 524–543.

Tosone, C. (2004). Relational social work: Honoring the tradition. *Smith College Studies in Social Work, 74*(3), 475–487.

Urrabazo, R. (2000). Therapeutic sensitivity to the Latino spiritual soul. In M. T. Flores & G. Carey (Eds.), *Family therapy with Hispanics: Toward appreciating diversity* (pp. 205–227). Boston: Allyn and Bacon.

U.S. Department of Health and Human Services (2001). *Mental Health: Culture, race and ethnicity—A supplement to "Mental health: A report of the Surgeon General."* Washington, DC: Author.

Williams, D. R., & Williams-Morris, R. (2000). Racism and mental health: The African American experience. *Ethnicity and Health, 5,* 243–268.

Woods, M., & Hollis, F. (2000). *Casework: A psychosocial therapy* (5th ed.). New York: McMillan.

CHAPTER 13

# Establishing Effective Cross-Cultural Alliances with Diverse Consumer Populations

EILEEN KLEIN

## INTRODUCTION

Health and human services organizations across the country are serving a population of increasing racial, ethnic and linguistic diversity. While American-born historically underserved populations have traditionally held high visibility on the caseloads of these organizations, current immigration and population trends indicate that in the coming years these agencies will serve populations of increasing diversity and complexity.

According to the National Migration Policy Institute, 41.3 million immigrants lived in the United States in 2013 (Zong & Batalova, 2015). This represents 13% of the total U.S. population of 316 million. The U.S. population that is foreign-born has increased by 1.3% between 2012 and 2013, or 524,000 people. According to the Pew Research Center, the black immigrant population from African countries grew from 570,000 to 1.4 million, an increase of 137% from 2000 to 2013. Africans make up 36% of the overall foreign-born black population, up from 24% in 2000. Half of the black immigrants in the United States were born in the Anglophone (English-speaking) Caribbean countries (www. pewresearch.org). The Latino population has increased sixfold in the United States, growing from 9.1 million to 53 million in 2012. Latinos currently represent 17% of the U.S. population; this figure is expected to reach 31% by 2060 (U.S. Census Bureau, 2012). As was discussed by González in Chapter 12, the Hispanic population has much within-group diversity that must be given consideration in the design and delivery of services.

These numbers emphasize that human services organizations must incorporate these demographic shifts in planning policy, programs and practice interventions, and professional workers must be prepared with the knowledge, skillsets, and competencies to serve clients who will likely have worldviews that are significantly different from their own. Relative to the immigrant and refugee populations, as suggested by Potocky-Tripodi (2002), a "pancultural" perspective that is broad enough to include the common experiences and practice approaches for a range of immigrant and refugee groups will be important. These agencies will also be required to incorporate corrective policies and practices that address the persistence of ethnic and racial disparities among segments of the population that identify as people of color that are of concern to this book.

This chapter focuses on challenges that health and human services organizations and professional workers confront in establishing inclusive organizational environments and practice responses that are conducive to making their services accessible and more widely available to racially and ethnically diverse consumer groups. The discussion endeavors to enhance understanding of the significance of culture, race, and racism in the provision of health and human services and the need for self-awareness on the part of the professional helper in recognizing the internalization of sociopolitical and ethnocentric orientations found to come to the fore when serving clients who are ethnically different from them.

## THE INCREASING DIVERSITY
## OF AMERICAN CULTURE

Culture encompasses a person's observable behavior, as well as the values and rules that govern that behavior. Culture helps people connect to others, share knowledge, and share a language in order to communicate and interpret their experiences (Murden, 2008). Lederach (1995, p. 9) stated that "Culture is the shared knowledge and schemes created by a set of people for perceiving, interpreting, expressing, and responding to the social realities around them." This sharing of knowledge and commonalities allows people to feel grounded within their community.

Since its beginning, the United States has been distinguished as a nation of immigrants, with the demographic composition of the immigrant population shifting over time. The newest arrivals to the United States in recent decades are increasingly black and brown people. In addition to confronting linguistic, cultural, socioeconomic, and political barriers that are characteristic of the immigrant and refugee experience, they confront the additional barrier of discrimination based on skin color that has been the most predominant form of discrimination in the United States.

During the Progressive Era in the United State of the mid- to late 20th century, the early social reformers were largely concerned with the plight of

European ethnic immigrant groups, thus leaving a service gap that prompted the development of specialized social welfare organizations to advocate for African Americans who were migrating to northern cities to escape Jim Crowism that was prevalent in the South during these years (Carlton-LaNey, 2001; Carten, 2015). With the increasing demographic diversity of the immigrant population arriving in the United States in the latter decades of 20th century, there was continuing growth in specialized ethnic associations. Chicanos created *mutualistas* to provide culturally sensitive services and mutual aid groups and to promote cultural activities to maintain their identity. Similar social welfare organizations were developed by Chinese immigrants (*Huiguan* associations) and Japanese immigrants (*kenjunkai*), and African Americans continued to expand their own mutual aid societies and self-help groups (Reisch, 2008).

The primary purpose of these specialized ethnic organizations was to help immigrants accomplish the basic task of integrating the cultural norms, traditions, and belief systems of the receiving culture into those of their countries of origin. The influx of white ethnic Europeans to America in the 18th and 19th centuries led to a favoring of the merging of cultures or assimilation, creating the notion of America as a "melting pot" (Bell, 2007). Within the context of increasing immigration, health and human service providers might ask what should be expected of new immigrants to the United States today. Should they assimilate into mainstream or dominant American culture and give up the traditions associated with their ethnic and national origins? Or should the task be one of acculturation, where new immigrants adopt and integrate the cultural norms of American society while holding on to those that are unique to their countries of origin?

Further, in considering the implications of the increasing ethnic diversity of the country for policy development and practice for the health and human services, we might ask whether it is better to view America as a "melting pot" or as a "salad bowl." The concept of a "salad bowl" is similar to that of pluralism or multiculturalism; it does not endeavor to reconstruct or change individuals but allows them to coexist in harmony and peace and with a respect for cultural differences. This model may allow for many different groups to mix together, even blend, while still maintaining distinct values and behaviors.

Pernell-Arnold (1998) writes about multiculturalism as helping her to interpret the diverse experiences she has had with different types of people around the country and how it is effective in paving the way for a connection. She views this as important for respecting and being inclusive of difference. Is being bicultural or multicultural helpful in allowing us to choose how to manage our actions and beliefs while encouraging freedom to choose? She refers to the need for us to embrace pluralism in order to recognize and accept differences. Modifying our approaches to accommodate individual or group difference will allow us to choose what traditions and values we wish to keep from each culture to which we are exposed and accept the right of others to do the same. The principle is that no cultural group is superior to or has the right to impose its values and belief systems on others.

These observations are pertinent for the design of inclusive services for the health and human services. Immigration status is found to be an important consideration for the organization, design, and provision of services. According to Leong, Park, and Kalibatseva (2013), immigrant status can be protective, serving as a buffer against the stressors associated with the immigration experience, or it can increase the risk of adverse life experiences. For instance, when immigrants to the United States engage in their ethnic culture and traditions, they are helped to feel a sense of identification and belonging that eases the transition into the new culture. Establishing bonds with other members of their ethnic group of identification supports social networking in their new environment, serving as another buffer against the stresses associated with the immigration experience. Moreover, some cultures place a high value on family cohesion that extends over generations to include extended family members, providing another support system for the successful engagement in the new cultural environment. However, linguistic differences, discrimination, and the transitional stressors associated with navigating between cultures may have an adverse effect on the health and mental health of individuals and families, and this may lead them to seek assistance from formal care systems.

## CROSS-CULTURAL HELPING ALLIANCES AND THERAPEUTIC RELATIONSHIPS

Qureshi and Collazos (2011) note that the therapeutic relationship is the key to providing effective services, and this can become compromised in cross-cultural treatment situations if the importance of the dynamics of these encounters is not acknowledged. Further, these authors examined the challenges in connecting stemming from communication styles, cultural values, and norms about healing that may play out at an unconscious level and compromise the worker–client relationship. For example, a client who is uncomfortable with self-disclosure as a cultural norm may be viewed as resistant or defensive to the therapist. These authors further state that transference reactions are often related to "the emotional and cognitive reactions toward another person that are predicated on past experiences" and are "independent of the person in question" (Qureshi & Collazos, 2011, p. 14).

The professional worker may have prejudicial feelings that lead to an avoidance of a discussion of race-related issues. This reaction may be self-protective and could result in viewing the client as "other" or as denying the importance of the client's race or culture when operating from a well-intentioned colorblind perspective. The client may have strong transference reactions to the professional worker perceived to be different that, if not acknowledged, can undermine and hinder the helping relationship or therapeutic alliance and the achievement of goals in the service plan. In light of these possible pitfalls, these authors suggest that clinicians be self-reflective, flexible, and adaptive and explore ways of effectively communicating and exploring with the client unexpressed feelings that may be related to worker–client cultural or ethnic differences. They refer to "ethnotherapeutic empathy," which "requires an awareness of one's own cultural values and the capacity to understand the other taking into consideration the play of cultural values" (Qureshi & Collazos, 2011, p. 16). Clients from non-Western cultures with very different cultures and traditions may identify these differences as problematic and as a barrier to their being accepted or fitting into the culture and norms of the host country.

Professional workers must adopt this perspective of ethnotherapeutic empathy as they endeavor to establish helping alliances and therapeutic relationships with clients of diverse ethnicities. In the development of a meaningful connection in which to exchange information, professional helpers must evidence an appropriate level of self-awareness and a willingness to continually explore their subjective biases and cultural and value systems to become aware of any unconscious prejudice that may interfere with the work they will undertake with culturally and ethnically diverse client populations. It is important to "explore the complex process of apprehending qualities of 'sameness' and 'otherness' in analytic pairs in which patient and analyst come from different cultural or class backgrounds" (Davies, 2011, p. 550). Connection to the "other" is transformative for both patient and therapist. This dimension contributes essential elements to the work and serves to strengthen a connection by recognizing similarities and differences in the therapeutic relationship that can translate into life experience.

As American society has become more multicultural, health and human services practitioners interact with clients from diverse cultures on a regular basis, and this increases the need for them to understand and integrate complex cultural issues about the health-seeking and services-using behaviors of these client populations into assessment protocols and practice interventions. In moving along the continuum of becoming culturally competent and race conscious, individuals must evidence an acceptance of the values of many cultures while still feeling comfortable with their own personal cultural identity. Usborne and Taylor (2012, p. 184) state that "if an individual has a clear and confident knowledge that the group with which he or she identifies has a particular set of characteristics, norms, and value inducing scripts, this knowledge will facilitate the individual's analyses and conclusions about what he or she should value, and how he or she should behave." Therefore, both therapist and client must acknowledge the significance of culture in any relationship to have an affirming outcome.

## MANIFESTATIONS OF TRANSFERENCE
## AND COUNTERTRANSFERENCE

As discussed above, transference and countertransference are important concepts to consider in the establishment of race-conscious helping alliances to
ensure authentic dialogs between the professional worker and client when engaged in cross-cultural helping relationships. The dynamics of transference and
countertransference, which involve the projections of one's internalized feelings onto another, can produce strong and sometimes irrational feelings and defensive reactions in both the client and the professional helper. These feelings
may intrude into the helping relationship and distort the interpretive meaning
given to the interaction and communication in cross-cultural encounters. The
complexities inherent in these relationships require workers to understand their
own culture and that of their clients so they can effectively manage the dynamics
that emerge at every stage of the helping process: beginning and engagement,
assessment and planning, service plan implementation, and evaluation and
termination.

During this process, the responses of professional helpers in cross-cultural alliance are driven in large measure by their own level of cultural identity. They
are not exempt from harboring racial and ethnic stereotypes or internalized feelings related to race operating at an unconscious level. Lum (2005, p. 7) offers
a five-stage continuum for supporting cultural competency and racial awareness for professional helpers: (1) understanding one's own cultural background;
(2) acknowledging the client's different culture, value, and belief systems and
behaviors; (3) recognizing that difference is not synonymous with inferiority;
(4) learning about the client's culture; and (5) adapting service delivery to an acceptable cultural framework.

In American culture, unconscious and socialization experiences that assign
unearned privilege to whites in American society and stereotypical beliefs about
African Americans and other people of color often surface in the helping relationship. These must be astutely managed by the professional worker. In a discussion of the dynamics of ethnocultural transference and countertransference between the professional worker and the client, Comas-Diaz and Frederick (1991)
identify the following as among the possible projections of internalized beliefs
based on socialization experiences and socially constructed stereotypes about
the behaviors of people who are perceived as different. These manifestations may
occur at any stage of the helping process. They may include on the part of the
client overcompliance and friendliness when there is a societal power differential
between the professional worker and the client, such as in the United States in
relationships when whites engage with African American and other black and
brown peoples. Mistrust, suspicion, and hostility based on past experiences of
discrimination and unethical treatment in the system may also be reflected in the

transference feelings on the part of the client. This dynamic may also engender in clients feelings and doubts about the ability of the professional worker to truly understand them since they are living virtually in two worlds. This may evoke feelings of guilt, defensiveness, or pity in the worker. These feelings may be especially intense for involuntary clients mandated to seek services by the courts. When operating from a colorblind perspective, the tendency on the part of both clients and helpers is to deny the ethnicity and culture and avoid discussing its impact on the client's life or on the presenting problems for which they are seeking help. The "clinical anthropologist" syndrome is one in which the professional helper becomes excessively curious about and preoccupied with the client's cultural background and spends the largest share of time in the relationship pursing these interests, which have little to do with the client's presenting problem.

## THE HELPING RELATIONSHIP

A helping relationship begins with the process of engagement and establishment of rapport. This involves respecting the client's needs, conveying empathy, clarifying roles and the therapeutic process, and removing any ethnic or racial barriers to building a working alliance. After clarifying the therapeutic process, there is a period of assessment of the presenting issues, mutual goal setting, and the development of a plan for intervention. The relationship continues to develop into one of trust, where the worker supports the client in an effort to reach mutually agreed-upon desired outcomes and build on this to move forward. When there is an agreement that goals have been reached and the client is prepared to effectively engage with the community, a plan for termination of services or referral is established. The ultimate plan is for the client to develop the skills to use to manage his or her environment and future challenges competently. This process works best when there is a helping relationship based on trust and openness so that there can be a comfortable exploration of present and underlying problems. The failure to achieve this level of authenticity may result in a premature termination of services because of the worker's feelings of lack of preparedness or discomfort with the client; this can account for high client dropout rates.

Lee (2011) reports the findings of several empirical studies indicating that professional workers reflecting multicultural competence in treatment have positive outcomes relative to client satisfaction and retention in services. The findings also indicated that therapeutic alliances with clients were improved when clinicians used racial or cultural references in their sessions that reflected a sensitivity to the client's perceived feelings of oppression, disrespect, and exclusion because of his or her race or ethnicity (Lee, 2011).

In Chapter 4 of this volume, Lee and colleagues examined in detail the importance of cultural competency on the part of the helping professionals at all levels of practice. Similarly, Murden and colleagues (2008, p. 192) summarized cultural competence as an awareness of culture, "respect for differences, ongoing self-assessment of perspective, alertness towards differences, continuing growth of cultural knowledge and resources, and adaptations to services." While this is critical to the relationship, professionals have to be mindful of the considerable within-group diversity among ethnic and racial populations. They should remember that knowledge of any culture does not make one an expert on that culture and that each person's perception of his or her cultural experiences is unique to that individual. Professionals must ask questions, consider the client the expert on his or her own lived experiences, and have the client reveal his or her own narrative in the helping process. Making assumptions about the client's experience based on the professional's interpretation or perceived meaning of the prior cultural information could lead to misdiagnoses and assessments that do not represent the client's own perspective. Professional helpers must also adopt a strengths-based perspective and a holistic view of the client and avoid an overemphasis on what are perceived to be symptoms of pathology; these may actually be culturally normative behaviors for the client. Helpers should keep a check on their curiosity about the client's culture if it prevents a full exploration of the complexity of the client's presenting problem.

Practitioners must acknowledge that whatever their ethnicity, their clients have both individual and group identities, According to Bell (2007), identity is constructed in relation to interaction with others as a part of the societal culture in which it is embedded. For example, individuals view themselves as interdependent with their place within society, their community, family, and history. In the United States, doctrines of white supremacy have shaped American culture for most of its history, and the group identity and socialization experiences of Americans have been formed within this historical context. Historical events can be presented from the perspective of the dominant group, which in America has led to the assignment of privilege and disadvantage on the basis of skin color. Unfortunately, the basis of the reality of service consumers and helpers alike is shaped by socially and politically constructed views of what is considered "normal," "real," or "correct" by the dominant group, leading to feelings of marginalization, low self-esteem, and damaging self-perspectives on the part of members of the nondominant culture (Hardiman, Jackson, & Griffin, 2007). These aspects of group identity formation are important to consider when professional workers, who may be identified or perceived as members of the "oppressor" group, are endeavoring to develop alliances with individuals who self-identify as persons of color or those who have experienced the real or perceived effects of marginalization in American culture.

Often diversity training is offered in traditional white-controlled health and human services agencies with a predominantly white staff in an effort to deconstruct the residual influence of societal racism and discrimination present in organizational structures, and to increase staff members' knowledge and level of cultural competence in providing effective services to the diverse consumer populations that make up their service caseload. However, this may not be enough to educate the staff or eradicate systemic and personal bias so that affirming services can be provided to meet the diversity of needs of clients from a range of racial and cultural backgrounds. Some argue that service provision by individuals of similar backgrounds can reduce systemic and personal bias. However, not only is the literature mixed as to the efficacy of worker and client matching, but it is highly unlikely that professional education programs can produce enough graduates who are people of color to match the volume of consumers of color seeking help from health and human service organizations.

Consideration must also be given to the service provider's own personal history, as well as issues that may arise in the helping process related to transference and countertransference. Daniel, Roysircar, Abeles, and Boyd (2004) found that psychologists who had training in self-awareness of their views on racism, homophobia, and ageism developed critical skills in cultural competence. This reinforces the need for helping professionals to develop insight, review what may be deeply engrained stereotypical thinking, and develop an increased level of self-awareness about working with clients who are culturally, racially, or ethnically dissimilar to themselves (as stressed by Davies, 2011) and the need for workers to know themselves.

## PRACTICE IMPLICATIONS

Goffman (1959) examined how individuals engage with others and establish a dialog that will guide their interpersonal interactions. He defined this as a complex process that may help to define the relationship, as well as provide advance information on expectations of each member of the interaction. We may relate information as a way to inform others of what is happening, while giving a positive impression. However, knowing what to expect of another prior to an interaction has not always been found to be helpful and may actually bias the individuals, thereby negatively impacting the outcome of their meeting. We must allow individuals to share their perceptions and reactions without a preconceived notion of what "should" be their experience. Being open and using active listening skills are essential to work effectively with others.

While not making assumptions and offering an outlet for clients to tell their story, we must be mindful when asking questions to be open and inclusive. Subtle cues indicating bias may cause a gap in forming a relationship. For example, when meeting with a female client, if you want to know if she has an intimate relationship or life partner, don't ask, "Do you have a boyfriend or husband?" While this may seem a benign question, it closes off the possibility of the client sharing that

she has a same-sex relationship since she may not want to shatter your expectations. Pleasing their providers is important for many clients since they feel this is
the only way to get the help they need for their presenting problems.

While cultural competency and respect for diversity are essential elements
in service provision, it is difficult to provide human services that are politically
or culturally neutral (Hugman, 2013). There is a difference between social diversity education and social justice education, according to Hardiman, Jackson,
and Griffin (2007). They define diversity education as helping one to appreciate
"social differences without an emphasis on power dynamics, or differential access
to resources" necessary for a meaningful, productive life. Social justice education, in their view, is focused "on understanding the social power dynamics and
social inequality that results in some social groups having privilege" and access
(p. 58). This power helps us to access resources and enhances our ability to gain
what is needed for a productive and meaningful life. Appreciating these definitions can help us understand the importance of the impact of our social group
affiliation. This is a basic and important element in educating helping professionals: it is vital not to make assumptions based on our own perceptions.

Individuals have to be viewed as a person-in-environment for us to promote
their well-being within that social context. According to Hugman (2013, p. 19),
"the definition of well-being itself is inevitably constructed for the notions of
'good' and 'right' that are very much a part of every culture." Therefore, if we acknowledge that an individual must be viewed within a cultural and social context,
we must let go of one of the basic assumptions of Western culture: that things
should be looked at on an individual level rather than within a cultural context.

Culture and race are played out in the therapeutic relationship and can compromise the therapeutic relationship. Differences in communication styles, cultural constructs of healing, and values and norms have a direct impact on the
transference process and, if not acknowledged, can hurt the outcome. A positive
consequence of understanding other cultures and ethnicities is that we may learn
alternative solutions to problems and expand our options. If we view multiple
perspectives, discover commonalities, identify differences, and work on reducing any conflicts that this may cause, we will be able to modify our interventions
based on the client's belief system (Pernell-Arnold, 1998).

## VIEWING OTHERS WITHIN THEIR
## CULTURAL CONTEXT
### Practitioner Role

Being "where the client is at" is a basic premise of any helping profession and
imperative for a successful outcome. For example, a client views the cause of his
illness as involving spiritual or outside influences and comes for help. To ignore

his interpretation of the presenting problem and causation and deny that his viewpoint has validity will alienate him and impede the helping process. Zane and colleagues (2005) found in their literature review that some ethnic-minority clients had better outcomes when paired with similar therapists, while other studies found this similarity to play only a minor role. They also found several studies reporting that client retention may not be impacted by similar therapist–client ethnicity. They did find, however, that when therapists and clients agree on treatment tasks and goals, there is a positive impact on the therapeutic alliance. Therefore, considering the client's perception of the problem will help to find a solution that is mutually agreeable and has a better chance of being implemented by the client.

Drozdek, Wilson, and Turkovic (2012) assert that context is essential in order to understand the individual. This is contrary to the traditional Western bio-medical model that places problems at the level of the individual. They opt for a holistic view of individual psychosocial processes. The Western focus on finding oneself through individual therapy sessions may not work well when personal autonomy is not a valued asset in some cultural groups. James, Noel, Favorite, and Jean (2012) found that when an entire community is impacted by social or economic stress, healing may involve collective rather than individual actions. They also noted that Western culture's reliance on scientific methods may lead to challenges in people's spiritual, cultural, or religious beliefs and impede the helping process.

The biomedical approach favored in Western cultures involves gathering in-formation as a first step. This may incorporate the latest scientific research and analysis of a client's presenting problem through a series of questions and pre-sented facts. This narrow way of evaluating a problem does not allow for consider-ation of the complete picture of a person's difficulties. Life events and perceptions of experiences do not occur in a vacuum but rather within an environmental and social context. Most mental health professionals, including social workers, are trained to view issues presented within the context of the person revealing them. This ensures that the situational and relational factors that play a part in causing or continuing the identified problem can be addressed in the helping process.

Therefore, we must be aware of our own bias or value judgments when work-ing with a client who comes from a cultural context different from our own. There may be inequities for a person who is a member of an ethnic minority, living in poverty, or associated with any group that is not considered mainstream or fa-vored in society. Adams and colleagues (2011, p. 12) referred to service delivery systems as being constructed in the context of "white Western norms and values." They indicated that it is important to understand clients using our knowledge of their history, beliefs, and value systems and to see them in a holistic way. Power differentials have existed for many individuals throughout their lives, and this impacts their problem definition. It is important to get the client's point of view and include his or her experience of social identity in the planning process. One's social identity can be categorized by race, gender, religion, class, ability, or age, for example, which encompasses the biopsychosocial approach to interventions and cannot be overlooked.

## Agency Role

In addition to staff members' awareness of the need to incorporate various aspects of a person's life to understand and provide intervention, the agency itself should be welcoming and inclusive. A way for organizations to show that they are accepting of diversity is to have physical indications of multiculturalism— for instance, having posters or artwork in the waiting room of different cultures, promoting cultural events, or having gatherings where traditions are shared with a group. Organizational culture plays a large role in promoting acceptance of difference, especially when this is viewed as a way to increase one's knowledge and broaden perspectives. This will enhance us as human beings and help everyone get along better in our multicultural and diverse society. Understanding and acceptance promote personal growth. This is the message that needs to be conveyed for affirmation and acceptance and ultimately will be critical for formulating a relationship. Perception of the climate of the agency and its personnel impacts the beginning process of establishing a relationship; it may make the difference between starting the process on a positive note or in a climate of distrust.

Human service agencies have a distinct organizational culture that affects the work they do with diverse client populations. An agency that works toward reducing patterns of racism and sexism will be more effective at serving diverse populations than one that simply acknowledges or celebrates difference (Hyde, 2004). Acknowledging that diversity is multidimensional is important in order to embrace it. There are dimensions of diversity that are inborn, cannot be changed, and have a major impact on one's early and future interactions in society, such as age, gender, disability, and ethnicity. There are also aspects of diversity that can be modified throughout life, such as education, socioeconomic status, and marital status (Lee, 2011). Understanding what is and isn't amenable to change is essential when developing skills in cross-cultural alliances. Cultures and traditions do not go away, but they may transform in another setting.

In addition, valuing diversity as an organizational approach will have a positive effect on employees. The agency's environment influences those who work there. The organization needs a mission that is consistent with embracing diversity. Employees must develop strategies that enable differences to be seen as educational rather than adversarial. Diversity, when promoted as a valued organizational culture, will increase the exchange of knowledge, ideas, and skills across employees. Ewoh (2013) describes the difference in organizations between affirmative action, Equal Employment Opportunity, and diversity: the first two are legal statutes and compliance issues, but diversity is related to being inclusive, respecting difference, and providing opportunities.

## MUTUAL RELATIONSHIP BUILDING

A working relationship can be established only if we engage individuals on an equal plane and incorporate their views into problem identification. In recent years, we have shifted to viewing the client as a partner in the helping process. We should be careful not to consider the professional as the expert on the issues presented, because people understand what is happening in a distinctive way. Kivlighan, Marmarosh, and Hilsenroth (2014) found that there was agreement among researchers that the therapeutic alliance should contain collaboration and reciprocity. Peeble-Wilkins (2003) refers to understanding clients with mutuality and within their own context as being at the core of effective collaboration.

Establishing and maintaining a working relationship, or therapeutic alliance, is essential for a positive collaboration between client and therapist. Bordin (1979, p. 253) defined three features of this alliance: "an agreement on goals, an assignment of a task or series of tasks, and the development of bonds." Beck, Friedlander, and Escudero (2006, p. 360) found that clients have to feel safe within the therapeutic process and have "good emotional connections with the therapist" to have a strong alliance with the therapist. Dybicz (2012) describes the need for a social worker to have expertise and authority to assist clients with their needs. He notes the importance of the ability to form a genuine connection in the helping process.

Hilsenroth, Peters, and Ackerman (2004) determined that establishing a therapeutic alliance begins during the assessment process. They found that this influences the entire treatment process thereafter. Therefore, from the very beginning of any client interaction, the establishment of a genuine and collaborative relationship with a client cannot be overlooked. This often begins with showing respect, interest, and warmth during the intake procedure and should be maintained and ongoing. Tailoring treatment for each individual is essential in forming an alliance. It is important to accept another person's identity as he or she defines it and go forward from there. Once this is established, there can be a collaboration to work toward mutually defined goals. Developing relationships, establishing therapeutic alliances, and showing empathy are topics that are covered in most training for the helping professions.

Training professionals to be culturally competent begins with helping them to understand and have an awareness of their own cultural identity and views about difference. This will help them to develop the ability to learn and build on the varying cultural and community norms they will encounter as individuals and for their clients while students. It is the ability to understand the within-group differences that makes each student unique, and students should be encouraged to celebrate the between-group variations that make our country a tapestry. This understanding informs and expands teaching practices in the culturally competent educator's classroom. This is a key for educators of clinical and helping professionals in making them effective in their careers in human services. While some information can be taught and encouraged in the educational process, students' personalities must be taken into account in the learning process.

Hersoug and colleagues (2009) found that clients are sensitive to therapists' attitudes. They found that a therapist who is seen as distant, indifferent, or disconnected will have a negative impact on the ability to form a positive working relationship. Their study indicated that attitude is not necessarily influenced by professional training; the therapist's comfort with closeness may be a more important factor. Another barrier to developing a mutual relationship is when the helping professional is using the time with the client to gather information without using exploratory questions that allow for a more thorough verbal exchange. This may happen when there is a focus on gaining the information that you need for an intervention based on preconceived notions or assumptions of prior knowledge. Facilitating another person's expression of his or her situation will lead to an understanding between the parties and the gathering of knowledge that may not have been anticipated. This will also help the relationship to develop based on mutuality and trust.

In addition, personal styles and characteristics of helping professionals have been found to affect their ability to work with diverse cultures. Weatherford and Spokane (2013) reported on studies that found a positive association between extraversion, openness to experience, empathy, and feminism to acceptance of diverse cultural groups. Homophobia, dogmatism, and neuroticism were reported to negatively impact attitudes toward cross-cultural groups. They also found various studies indicating that having a worldview associated with a feeling of superiority of one's cultural group, conventional ideas, and aggressiveness toward nonconforming groups may be a predictor of cultural prejudice. This is important since it may not be possible, based on their evidence, to educate or train all helping professionals to work effectively with diverse cultural groups.

The social group a person belongs to or identifies with often has an inherent status that gives the person an advantage. Advantaged groups can allow individual members to have greater access to opportunities and power, as well as feelings of dominance and privilege. Having an understanding of white privilege may enable a more positive intervention with racially diverse clients. White privilege, according to Peggy MacIntosh (1988), is an invisible knapsack filled with the proper codes, passports, and tools for a successful life. Historically, members of this group enjoy unearned social and political advantages for access to resources, whereas nonmembers may be viewed as disadvantaged, subordinate, targeted, or oppressed, which denies or limits their access to opportunities. Perceptions of those in the disadvantaged group may define and limit goals of its members. These feelings may also influence the person providing the help. Conscious and unconscious thoughts may interfere with one's ability to embrace training in the treatment of diverse clients (Bhui & Ascoli, 2012).

By monitoring their own emotional responses to a client in the helping process, professionals are more likely to be able to develop mutuality in the relationship and collaborate on solutions. Such awareness allows the social context for the client and worker to be validated as a framework to engage in a humanistic way. Clinician self-awareness will help to reduce operating as a professional information gatherer and move to operating with mutual recognition and empathic caring. Personal growth or behavioral change can occur when there is a reciprocal understanding and articulation of the process as a working model. When information is received, it is interpreted through our own beliefs and narratives, and this dictates our behavior or response. Ultimately, this will control our reaction and our experience to any treatment, either positively or negatively. Change will be possible if the internal validation allows for new frameworks and ideas to be accepted.

Knowing yourself is important for the well-being of both the client and the clinician. Tarver-Behring (1994) studied white women's identity formation. She found that as they became cognizant that they were not all the same, had within-group diversity, and were often devalued compared to men, they started to appreciate issues affecting women of color and reduce their feelings of ethnocentricity. This awareness helped them appreciate many of the complexities that go into forming identity. People who are not aware of the privilege within their own group may be resistant to accepting the need to work on cultural competence. Not only is consciousness raised, but defensiveness in response to denying inequality and oppression is reduced so that there can be positive self-development and increased cultural sensitivity.

Goh (2012) studied the integration of mindfulness and reflection exercises into undergraduate social work curricula. She found that the students had to learn active listening skills in order to form a bond with their clients. Active listening was inhibited by students' thinking ahead or multitasking while engaging with the client. Students may think ahead in an interaction so they can formulate an action plan for the client, or they may be uncomfortable with silence and begin to prepare to give advice. Raising awareness for students that this would be counterproductive for the relationship helped students become more aware of their own listening styles and make positive changes. Active listening, or empathic listening, is "being with and understanding clients and their world" according to Carl Rogers (cited in Goh, p. 588). Distorted listening can result when students use stereotypes or evaluate statements while engaging in a dialog. This may result in clients' being put into categories where they may not actually belong.

## OTHER CONSIDERATIONS

Other factors than culture and ethnicity also impact clients. Socioeconomic status has an important influence on our lives and ability to effect change. Generally, those with lower socioeconomic status are less likely to participate in the political process and advocate for equality in educational, employment, and community environments. This self-defeating process results in poorer physical and mental health and fewer chances to advance in society. Clients have to gain strength from our interventions to strive for what they are entitled to receive and have a voice that is heard. Clients who enter a helping relationship feeling traumatized and vulnerable need to connect to their treatment provider and develop trust and attachment to feel empowered to make changes in their situation. Some of the basic elements for developing trust are for the clinician to provide emotional availability, to be attuned and responsive to the client's emotional state, and to provide the client with predictability and consistency. Interventions, suggestions, and options provided need to be reliable and shared in an accepting environment for the client to benefit.

Novello (2004) reported on health disparities and inequality in health care for minorities, citing, among numerous other statistics, the following: (1) the cancer mortality rate was 35% higher for African Americans than whites; (2) African American men had a 60% higher incidence of prostate cancer than white men; and (3) Hispanic women had a 2½ times higher rate of cervical cancer than white women. She reported on a strong correlation between poverty and health status because of the lack of education on healthy foods, lifestyle choices, and access to health care. Iribarren and colleagues (2005) reported on great differences in death rates by sex and race because of AIDS, homicide, intentional injury, suicide, cancer, and coronary disease. These reports lend themselves to consideration of changes in social policy and preventive medicine, as well as health care access. Healthy lifestyles and education can be promoted to reduce health inequities, but when there is miscommunication between medical personnel, it may result in delays in treatment or insufficient information on how to take medication, leading to poor health outcomes (Snell, Allen, & Marsh, 2006). Health care is another area that requires understanding of cross-cultural alliances and cultural sensitivity for improved outcomes. The creation of a genuine bond between the helper and the client can be established through improving linguistic understanding, forming mutual expectations, and challenging assumptions while engaging in a helping relationship.

## CONCLUSION

In focusing attention on the client's perception of need and/or problem formulation, we can close the gaps presented by cultural, ethnic, and experiential diversity. Some suggestions on how to accomplish this have been developed in this chapter. They are certainly not exhaustive, but may help to start a dialog in agencies and training programs for human service staff.

One important topic not covered is the use of more than one staff member to evaluate and intervene with a client. Using a multidisciplinary approach to treatment, or working interprofessionally, has been helpful in engaging clients effectively. Professionals from different disciplines are taught to take a variety of approaches to a similar problem. Nurses, for example, may focus on the physical needs or health of a client as the priority, while social workers may include a plan to improve health as a part of an overall plan to improve the client's ability to function within the community. This does not make one philosophy better or more accurate, but when these professions engage a client together and respect each other's skills and training, it will lead to a fuller development of an intervention. In addition, working with other professionals to resolve a client's problems will lend itself to a more developed, comprehensive plan of action since there is an understanding of the problem from multiple points of view.

## DISCUSSION QUESTIONS

1. Convene or facilitate the convening of a workgroup in your agency that is representative of all levels of staff and the board of directors to take a comprehensive look at the agency—its mission, size, location, and the demographics of the staff and clients—and consider ways in which it might become more inclusive. Another way of doing this is to use an anonymous survey.
2. Consider the difference and similarities between immigrants and refugees and the implications for designing culturally relevant individualized service and treatment plans. Review your own family history of immigration or migration and the ways in which your personal experience is similar to that of recent immigrants to the United States.
3. The U.S. Department of Health and Human Services offers several cultural competence self-assessment tools (http://www.hrsa.gov/culturalcompetence/index.html). Retrieve and complete one of these to assess your level of cultural competency and race consciousness. Since there is no right or wrong answer, and since becoming culturally competent and race conscious is an evolving process, return and complete the tools at certain intervals and consider what accounts for any changes in your self-assessment.

## REFERENCES

Adams, J., Cushing, B., Bernabei, S., Golden, G., Hitchcock, J., Kremer, N, McLean, J., & Margolis, J. (2011). Clinical reflections on the impact of race and racism in the counselor/client relationship. *Mental Health News*, 13(1).

Beck, M., Friedlander, M., & Escudero, V. (2006). Three perspectives on clients' experiences of the therapeutic alliance: A discovery oriented investigation. *Journal of Marital and Family Therapy, 32*(3), 355–368.

Bell, L. A. (2007). Theoretical foundations for social justice education. In M. Adams, L. E. Bell, & P. Griffin (Eds.), *Teaching for diversity and social justice* (2nd ed.). New York: Routledge, Taylor & Francis Group.

Bordin, E. S. (1979). The generalizability of the psychoanalytic concept of the working alliance. *Psychotherapy: Theory, Research, and Practice, 16*, 252–260.

Bhui, K., & Ascoli, M. (2012). The place of race and racism in cultural competence: What can we learn from the English experience about the narratives of evidence and argument? *Transcultural Psychiatry, 49*(2),185–205.

Carlton-LaNey, I. B. (Ed.). (2001). *African American leadership: An empowerment tradition in social welfare history.* Washington, DC: NASW Press.

Carten, A. J. (2015). *Reflections on the American social welfare state, the collected papers of James R. Dumpson, Ph.D., 1930–1990.* Washington, DC: NASW Press.

Comas-Díaz, L., & Frederick J. M. (1991). Ethnocultural transference and countertransference in the therapeutic dyad. *American Journal of Orthopsychiatry, 63*(3), 392–402.

Daniel, J. H., Roysircar, G., Abeles, N., & Boyd, C. (2004). Individual and cultural-diversity competency: Focus on the therapist. *Journal of Clinical Psychology, 60*(7), 755–770.

Davies, J. E. (2011). Cultural dimensions of intersubjectivity: Negotiating "sameness" and "otherness" in the analytic relationship. *Psychoanalytic Psychology, 28*(4), 549–559.

Drozdek, B., Wilson, J. P., & Turkovic, S. (2012). Assessment of PTSD in non-Western culture: The need for new contextual and complex perspectives. In J. G. Beck & D. M. Sloan (Eds.), *The Oxford handbook of traumatic stress disorders.* (pp. 302–314). New York: Oxford University Press.

Dybicz, P. (2012). The ethic of care: Recapturing social work's first voice. *Social Work, 57*(3), 271–279.

Ewoh, A. I. E. (2013). Managing and valuing diversity: Challenges to public managers in the 21st century. *Public Personnel Management, 42*(2), 107–122.

Goffman, E. (1959). *The presentation of self in everyday life.* Bantam Doubleday Dell Publishing Group.

Goh, E. C. L. (2012). Integrating mindfulness and reflection in the teaching and learning of listening skills for undergraduate social work students in Singapore. *Social Work Education, 31*(5), 587–604.

Hardiman, R., Jackson, B., & Griffin, P. (2007). Conceptual foundations for social justice education: Conceptual overview. In M. Adams, L. E. Bell, & P. Griffin (Eds.), *Teaching for diversity and social justice* (2nd ed.). New York: Routledge, Taylor & Francis Group.

Hersoug, A. G., Hoglend, P., Havik, O., von der Lippe, A., & Monsen, J. (2009). Therapist characteristics influencing the quality of alliance in long-term psychotherapy. Clinical Psychology & Psychotherapy, 16(2), 100–110.

Hilsenroth, M. J., Peters, E. J., & Ackerman, S. J. (2004). The development of therapeutic alliance during psychological assessment: Patient and therapist perspectives across treatment. *Journal of Personality Assessment, 83*(3), 332–344.

Hugman, R. (2013). *Culture, values and ethics in social work.* New York: Routledge.

Hyde, C. A. (2004). Multicultural development in human services agencies: Challenges and solutions. *Social Work, 49*(1), 7–16.

Iribarren, C., Jacobs, D. R., Kiefe, C. I., Lewis, C. E., Matthews, K. A., Roseman, J. M., & Hulley, S. B. (2005). Causes and demographic, medical, lifestyle and psychosocial predictors of premature mortality: the CARDIA study. *Social Science & Medicine,* *60*(3), 471–482.

James, L. E., Noel, J. R., Favorite, T. K., & Jean, J. S. (2012). Development of a lay mental health worker project in post-earthquake Haiti: Challenges of post-disaster intervention in cultural context. *International Perspectives in Psychology: Research, Practice, Consultation, 1,* 110–126.

Kivlighan, D. M.Jr., Marmarosh, C. L., & Hilsenroth, Mark J. (2014). Client and therapist therapeutic alliance, session evaluation, and client reliable change: A moderated actor–partner interdependence model. *Journal of Counseling Psychology, 61*(1), 15–23.

Lederach, J. P. (1995). *Preparing for peace: Conflict transformation across cultures.* Syracuse, NY: Syracuse University Press.

Lee, E. (2011). Clinical significance of cross-cultural competencies (CCC) in social work practice. *Journal of Social Work Practice, 25*(2), 185–203.

Leong, F., Park, Y. S., & Kalibatseva, Z. (2013). Disentangling immigrant status in mental health: Psychological protective and risk factors among Latino and Asian American immigrants. *American Journal of Orthopsychiatry, 83*(2,3), 361–371.

Lum, D. O. (2005). *Culturally competent practice: A framework for understanding diverse groups and justice issues.* Third Edition. Belmont, CA: Thomson Brooks/Cole.

MacIntosh, P. (1988). *White privilege and male privilege: A personal account of coming to see correspondences through work in women's studies.* Wellesley, MA: Wellesley College Center for Research on Women.

Murden, R., Norman, A., Ross, J., Sturdivant, E., Kedia, M., & Shah, S. (2008). Occupational therapy students' perceptions of their cultural awareness and competency. *Occupational Therapy International, 15*(3), 191–203.

Novello, A. C. (2004). Cancer, minorities, and the medically underserved: A call to action. *Journal of Cancer Education, 21*(Suppl.), S5–S8.

Peeble-Wilkins, W. (2003). Collaborative interventions. *Children & Schools, 25*(4), 195–196.

Pernell-Arnold, A. (1998). Multiculturalism: Myths and miracles. *Psychiatric Rehabilitation Journal, 21*(3), 224–229.

Plutzer, E., & Wiefek, N. (2006). Family transitions, economic status, and voter turnout among African-American inner-city women. *Social Science Quarterly, 87*(3), 658–678.

Potocky-Tripodi, M. (2002). *Best Practices for Social Work with Refugees and Immigrants.* Columbia University Press.

Qureshi, A., & Collazos, F. (2011). The intercultural and interracial therapeutic relationship: Challenges and recommendations. *International Review of Psychiatry, 23*(1), 10–19.

Reisch, M. (2008) From melting pot to multiculturalism: The impact of racial and ethnic diversity on social work and social justice. *British Journal of Social Work, 38,* 788–804.

Snell, J., Allen, L., & Marsh, M. (2006). Patient inequities: An observation. *Psychology and Education: An Interdisciplinary Journal, 43*(2), 39–40.

Tarver-Behring, S. (1994).White women's identity and diversity: Awareness from the inside out. *Feminism & Psychology, 4*(1), 206–208.

Usborne, E., & Taylor, D. M. (2012). Using computer-mediated communication as a tool for exploring the impact of cultural identity clarity on psychological well-being. *Basic and Applied Social Psychology, 34,* 183–191.

United States Census Bureau. (2012). *Population Projections,* https://www.census.gov/population/projections/data/national/2012.html

Weatherford, R. D., & Spokane, A. R. (2013). The relationship between personality dispositions, multicultural exposure, and multicultural case conceptualization ability. *Training and Education in Professional Psychology, 7*(3), 215–224.

Zane, N., Sue, S., Chang, J, Huang, L., Huang, J., Lowe, S., Srinivasan, S., Chun, K., Kurasaki, K., & Lee, E. (2005). Beyond ethnic match: Effects of client–therapist cognitive match in problem perception, coping orientation, and therapy goals on treatment outcomes. *Journal of Community Psychiatry, 33*(5), 569–585.

Zong, J., & Batalova, J. (2015). Spotlight: Frequently requested statistics on immigrants and immigration in the United States. Available at www.migrationpolicy.org/article/frequently-requested-statistics-immigrants-and-immigration-united-states.

# CHAPTER 14

# Unpacking Racism, Poverty, and Trauma's Impact on the School-to-Prison Pipeline

ROBERT ABRAMOVITZ AND JESSICA MINGUS

I realized that I did have psychological problems and that I was a product of my environment. I understood that my problems frustrated me, confused me, made me . . . [r]espond aggressively. Impulsively. I kept digging a deeper hole, then getting depressed.

A 25-year-old man's reflections on his 10 years in the juvenile justice system

Cooper et al., 2007, p. 4

## INTRODUCTION

Since post-traumatic stress disorder (PTSD) was added to the third edition of the *Diagnostic and Statistical Manual of Disorders* (DSM-III) in 1980, an extensive body of research has documented the damaging effects of violence and trauma on the human psyche. As Corbin and colleagues (2010, p. 407) powerfully assert, the lessons learned about the harmful impacts of trauma are "seldom applied" to the adverse life experiences of black males. Similarly, our chapter argues that the lessons about the persistent and pervasive effects of trauma on development and functioning are too seldom applied to the experiences of boys and girls of color who have been exposed to overwhelming adversity in America's schools. To their profound detriment, the school environment all too often acts as a "traumatizing system" (Corbin et al., 2010, p. 408) that compounds harm and adversity because the interwoven forces of structural racism, "zero tolerance" school discipline practices, and clinical misdiagnosis drive inappropriate responses to the neurobiological and psychosocial symptoms of trauma exposure. This complex interplay between trauma exposure and the "traumatizing system" illustrates Carten's salient point in the preface that the "untested assumptions of helping professionals persistently distort their understanding of the life experiences of people of color, resulting in interventions that propagate racial oppression."

The overrepresentation of children of color in the juvenile justice system makes the urgency of this analysis evident. Children of color between the ages of 10 and 17 constitute 16% of the overall child population but 34% of those arrested, 38% of those adjudicated, and 68% of children in residential placements (Children's Defense Fund, 2014). Black males represent the largest population in confinement and black females are the fastest-growing subgroup in confinement (Morris, 2012). Moreover, the incidence of trauma exposure among juvenile justice–involved young people is drastically higher than the general population. A study of the extent of trauma exposure among juvenile justice–involved adolescents found that they experienced 4.9 trauma types, such as caregiver loss, domestic violence, and emotional or physical abuse, and more than half (62%) had their first exposure before the age of five. Of particular relevance to this chapter's thesis, 66% of this population reported externalizing problems in the clinical range—with rule breaking (37%) and aggressive behavior (34%) being most common—and 72% reported academic problems (Dierkhising et al., 2013). Upstream from the high incidence of "acting out" trauma symptoms among boys and girls in contact with the juvenile justice system, we encounter a steady current of young people of color subjected to school-based arrests and juvenile justice referrals in response to minor and arbitrary misbehavior, a phenomenon that contributes to the school-to-prison pipeline (Fabelo et al, 2011; New York City School-Justice Partnership Task Force, 2013). The collateral consequences of juvenile justice system contact—disrupted education, school dropout, barriers to employment, and increased recidivism (Nellis, 2011)—perpetuate the damaging effects of structural racism, poverty, and trauma on poor communities of color.

This chapter explores how structural racism, poverty, and misguided responses to symptoms of trauma in the educational and mental health systems act together to funnel an alarming number of young people of color with histories of trauma exposure into the juvenile justice system via the school-to-prison pipeline. Helping professionals who serve this population to recognize the vital gatekeeping function they play in these young people's lives serves as this chapter's purpose. Our discussion examines (1) the developmental delays in learning and behavioral difficulties caused by early childhood poverty and trauma exposure; (2) the influence of teachers' subjectivity and unchecked racial biases on their responses to students' learning and behavior problems; (3) the racial disproportionality of school discipline practices; and (4) how misattributions fuel clinical misdiagnosis and obscure youth of color's treatment needs and hinder receipt of effective care. We conclude by discussing approaches to prevention and intervention that aim to reduce poverty, build resilience in children and families, and promote positive relational approaches in schools to stem the tide of school push-out. We show that it is within our reach to foster powerful helping relationships by striving for a holistic understanding of the people we serve and unpacking the biases that can obscure the power of helping relationships.

## THE ORIGINS OF DEVELOPMENTAL DISPARITIES

Structural racism's social framework assigns unearned power and privilege to white people on the basis of their racial group affiliation, to the detriment and systematic disempowerment of communities of color. Although less blatant than in past generations, racism remains a pernicious and deeply entrenched social force in American daily life. Pervasive racial and ethnic disparities in opportunity and life outcomes yield similar patterns of inequality among black and Latino children (Acevedo-García et al., 2010).

The intimately intertwined effects of racism, poverty, and trauma on the body and mind chronically activate the neurobiological fight-or-flight stress system (the hypothalamic, pituitary, adrenocortical system (Loo et al., 2001; van der Kolk, 1996), resulting in a variety of long-lasting physical and mental health impairments (Teicher et al., 2001). Growing up or living under the stressful and frightening impact of poverty places infants and young children at increased risk for elevated cortisol levels, a neuroendocrine marker of chronic stress, compared to nonpoor children. (Kim et al., 2013). The developing brain's sensitivity to excess cortisol during the first five years of life makes children particularly susceptible to the effects of chronic or severe traumatic experiences, such as physical or sexual abuse or domestic or community violence exposure. These traumatic events negatively affect brain structures that are essential to memory function, the capacity to integrate cognitive and emotional information, and the development of linguistic and social-emotional skills (Teicher et al., 2001).

The Children's Defense Fund (2014) found that 16 million U.S. children lived in poverty in 2012. The 11.2 million poor children of color under age five were the most at risk. Further, approximately 1 in 5 black and 1 in 7 Latino children lived in extreme poverty compared to 1 in 18 white children (Children's Defense Fund, 2014). These poor children's families experience a higher exposure to a variety of risk factors (e.g., food insecurity, substandard housing, unemployment and underemployment, limited access to health care, underfunded and inferior schools, environmental pollution; (Lieberman et al, 2011). These poor communities also lack high-quality, stimulating day care and adequate parks and playgrounds. The higher likelihood that poor families of color will face such conditions contributes to either greater resource loss or low resource availability. This imbalance between risk factors and protective factors embeds these children in a toxic ecological system (Harris et al., 2007).

A low-income family's precarious supply of tangible resources makes them especially vulnerable to losses that can profoundly affect their children. Such instability increases feelings of helplessness and lack of control, which rank at the high end of the stress continuum (Abramovitz & Albrecht, 2013). The persistent lack of adequate resources triggers the individual members' "fight-flight-freeze" response (Carrión, 2006), leading to chronic cortisol production. Extended exposure to poverty in childhood also causes striking developmental differences in cognitive functioning and academic achievement. Negative effects on language development can be seen as early as 18 months (Eigsti & Cicchetti, 2004). Dearing (2008, p. 325) states that children persistently exposed to poverty from birth through age four years, the critical years for brain development, "may score on average score as much as 40%–60% of a standard deviation lower on intelligence tests" than children living in nonpoor families. The transmission of multiple stress exposures via the caregiver–child relationship directly affects the child's emotional development and cognitive stimulation, as it diminishes the caregiver's adaptive coping capacity and leads to emotional and physical problems that, in turn, interfere with healthy family, school, job, and community functioning. Harsh living conditions also indirectly compromise caregivers' ability to buffer children's exposure to these stressful and traumatic events, which affects their development (Chu & Lieberman, 2010).

## Community Violence's Disparate Impact

Data on youth of color's exposure to violence also reveal race and poverty's intertwined effects. An estimated 70% to 100% of children living in underresourced communities experience high rates of exposure to frightening, dangerous events. Youth ages 12 to 24 suffer more violent crime than any other age group in the United States (Rand, 2009). Very poor African Americans are nearly twice as likely to be victims of violence as whites at the same income level (80.2 per 1,000 people vs. 44.6, respectively). However, victimization rates progressively fall as income increases (National Crime Victimization Survey, 2007). During the 1990s, multiple studies documented extensive adolescent violence exposure (Schwab-Stone et al., 1999) and indicated that poor youth of color consistently experienced higher incidence rates than other adolescents (Garbarino et al., 2004). Black and Latino youth remain exposed to significantly higher rates of violence than white youth at every income level despite the steep drop in crime rates during the past 15 years (National Crime Victimization Survey, 2007; Stein et al., 2003).

## Interpersonal Violence's Disparate Impact

In 2013, approximately 679,000 U.S. children suffered maltreatment, resulting in a victimization rate of 9.1 per 1,000 children (U.S. Department of Health and Human Services [USDHHS], 2015). The highest victimization rates occurred among black children (14.6/1,000), Native American or Alaska Native children (12.5/1000), and children of multiple races (10.6/1,000). Latino children and white children had rates of 8.5 and 8.1 per 1,000, respectively. Asian children had the lowest rate of victimization, 1.7 per 1,000 (USDHHS, 2015). The highest rates of initial maltreatment occurred during the first five years of life (47%), and children under age one had the highest exposure rate: 23.1 per 1,000 (USDHHS, 2015). Turner, Finkelhor, and Ormrod (2006) found that children living in poor families had the greatest lifetime exposure to interpersonal violence. Comparisons between older and younger children have found that the youngest face the highest probability of residing in a home with domestic violence (Fantuzzo & Fusco, 2007).

The effect of maltreatment on children's development yields differing racial and ethnic group outcomes. Black and Latino young children face a greater likelihood of out-of-home placements, longer stays in foster care, more frequent placement changes, and a lower likelihood of parental reunification (Hill, 2007). Such stark outcome differences may reflect an unconscious bias against poor people of color that interacts with a family's lack of neighborhood and community resources to perpetuate differential reunification and permanency outcomes (Lieberman et al, 2011).

## Impact of Community and Interpersonal Violence

Children and adolescents who have experienced trauma do not have the option to leave it at the door when they enter school. Students with histories of trauma carry not only the memories of what happened to them, which can be re-experienced at any moment in the form of intrusive flashbacks, but also an internal alarm system that may be stuck in the "on" position that can cause significant emotional and behavioral dysregulation. Trauma exposure can yield two broad categories of symptoms: internalizing ("acting in") behaviors, such as dissociation, emotional numbing, or avoidance, and externalizing ("acting out") behaviors, such as hypervigilance, impulsiveness, outbursts, and aggression (Dierkhising et al., 2013).

Feelings of persistent distress, fear, and threat alter attention, concentration, and memory and impair learning, skill development, and the regulation of emotions and behavior necessary for academic and social success (National Scientific Council on the Developing Child, 2010). Classroom observation of the behavior of children exposed to high levels of community and interpersonal violence reveals some who feel safe and can sit comfortably in the same environment that triggers other children. Children who are exposed to intense fear due to chronic abuse and/or family violence exposure often experience an impaired capacity to differentiate between threat and safety because of their physiologically hyperaroused state. This impaired ability to accurately interpret facial expressions, tone of voice, and emotions leads to frequent misperception of threat in familiar situations (Masten et al., 2008). Students whose symptoms fall predominantly on the internalizing end of the spectrum may fade into the background, while those on the externalizing end will more likely draw heightened attention because their emotional and behavioral dysregulation is more likely to disrupt the learning environment and teacher–student and peer–student relationships. If traumatic adversity is not properly evaluated and considered, common emotional and behavioral symptoms that interfere with healthy school and peer relationships can be labeled as run-of-the-mill misbehavior rather than as signs of psychological distress that signal exposure to serious harm. It also bears note that countless American children are charged with the task of learning in what are intrinsically unsafe schools; these environments compound the fear and distress experienced by students with trauma histories, exacerbate their fear responses, and can cause subsequent traumatization.

## THE ROLE OF TEACHERS' SUBJECTIVITY

Schools are not dangerous but what looks not dangerous can be dangerous. We have to take a long, careful look at students. Who are the good kids, who are the bad kids, who are the ones who are dangerous?

Health teacher (Casella, 2003, p. 60)

Students who struggle to meet behavioral and academic expectations due to developmental difficulties are a common challenge across school settings. Since teachers function as gatekeepers, their response to student challenges plays a powerful role in whether students are referred for disciplinary action. The personal attitudes, assumptions, and expectations that shape their perceptions of *why* students behave in challenging ways must be carefully unpacked. Depending on their subjective lens, teachers may assign attributions to student behavior that carry with them very different connotations. For example, a seemingly restless, inattentive student could be characterized as "fidgety," "academically under-challenged," "rambunctious," or "deliberately disruptive," which would, in turn, evoke personal judgments about the student's character that can range from tolerant (e.g., "that's how s/he is") to intolerant (e.g., "s/he doesn't want to learn" or "s/he's unteachable"). Teachers' perceptions can have particularly serious consequences if challenging behavior is interpreted as a student's deliberate choice or an intrinsic trait. Such assumptions can cause teachers to view certain students more as problems rather than people with problems, which could spark conflict or punishment.

Teacher subjectivity plays a significant role in special education referrals. The learning disability and severe emotional disturbance classifications are "social model disabilities" typically diagnosed on the basis of "less readily measured and more context-dependent criteria such as behavior, intelligence, social skills and communication abilities" that rely on classroom teachers' observations rather than formal assessment tools (Vallas, 2009, p. 183). The emotional disturbance classification is frequently initiated by school discipline interventions such as repeated classroom removal, detention, and suspension (Vallas, 2009). Many symptoms of trauma exposure produce manifestations comparable to other psychiatric disorders such as learning problems, inattention, and behavioral outbursts. Thus, the emphasis on using behavioral designations to label youth's problematic behavior as markers of disability makes it more likely that the trauma histories can go unrecognized and mishandled by many educators (Griffin et al., 2011).

Teachers are in a unique position to promote more productive student interventions by shifting the discourse from "what is wrong" with students with behavioral challenges to "what has happened" to them. This change allows for recognition that school performance issues are a common outcome for students with histories of undetected trauma (Finkelhor et al., 2009).

## THE ROLE OF TEACHERS' RACIAL BIAS AND ETHNOCENTRISM

This paradigm shift can be hindered by teachers' unchecked racial bias and ethnocentrism. White teachers represent approximately 84% of America's K–12 educators (Feistritzer, 2011) and approximately two-thirds of teachers in schools with a predominant enrollment of students of color (Saffold & Longwell-Grice, 2008). Unconscious bias and cultural incongruence must be acknowledged as salient factors in student performance and conduct appraisals given the demographic differences between America's predominantly white school teachers and their students.

Hamre and colleagues (2008, p. 133) suggest that the "nature" of teacher–student conflict must be carefully examined "particularly when it is reported only by teachers" since their perceptions are influenced not only by students' actions but also by teachers' intrinsic personal factors. Teacher-initiated referrals for misconduct require similar scrutiny because unchecked racial bias can cause them to unconsciously adopt a danger/deficit framework for their interpretation of black and Latino students' behavior and learning problems.

Negative perceptions of black youth as somehow "deviant" due to implicit cultural bias can foster a learning environment in which "'whiteness' and the behaviors, skills and communication style that are associated with it" (Vallas, 2009, p. 190) are privileged while other ways of being are deemed inferior or delinquent. Teachers' negative attributions of students based on race, ethnicity, culture, or socioeconomic status can adversely impact their expectations of student behavior or achievement (Neal et al., 2003). In their simulated study, Neal and colleagues (2003) found that teachers' perceptions of male students' academic competence, aggression, and need for special education services correlated with their display of a walking style associated with African American culture. Tenenbaum and Ruck's meta-analysis (2007) showed that teachers commonly have lower academic expectations of black and Latino students and offer them less positive feedback than their white peers.

Similarly, racial bias or ethnocentrism can inform teachers' appraisals of whether or not a student is considered dangerous. Trauma-related functional impairments like hyperarousal and altered threat perception result in diminished emotional self-regulation and impulsivity. When school personnel's racist, ethnocentric assumptions about student conduct go unchecked, students' trauma-induced behavior can be interpreted as willful defiance or hostility. Casella's (2003) ethnographic study of two high schools that employed "zero tolerance" and preventive detention policies found that the students who were subjected to school disciplinary action (i.e., detention, out-of-school placement, court referral, or arrest) were predominantly black and Latino males characterized as threats based on their disputes with students or staff, many of which did not involve actual acts of violence. In some cases, students were characterized as dangerous by staff because of diagnostic labels, but many were judged as such on the basis of subjective attributions about their "character (their self-restraint, sexuality, reputation), their friends, their way of dressing and walking, their 'baggage,' their attitudes, and their backgrounds" (Casella, 2003, p. 59). Casella's narrative data indicated that students who displayed anger or engaged in conflict were handled as if they were threatening by nature and that this perception served as the catalyst for their school punishment or push-out.

## THE DISPROPORTIONATE IMPACT OF "ZERO TOLERANCE" DISCIPLINARY PRACTICES ON YOUTH OF COLOR

We get the bad guys out and keep the good guys in. I guess, in a way, it's the opposite of prison.

School police officer (Casella, 2003, p. 60)

How children of color with trauma histories fare in classrooms or the frequency with which their traumatic symptoms result in school discipline, suspension, or expulsion remains poorly documented. However, extensive data exist on the use of "zero tolerance" discipline policies, special education referrals, and the frequency of attention-deficit/hyperactivity (ADHD) diagnoses and medication prescriptions, which are three highly subjective methods of "managing" students whose externalizing behaviors interfere with students' ability to meet academic and behavioral expectations.

The use of exclusionary discipline practices has nearly doubled since 1974 due to the nationwide advent of "zero tolerance" policies. In 2006, 3.3 million students had at least one out-of-school suspension and 102,000 were expelled (Dignity in Schools, n.d.). Minor infractions like disruptive behavior, tardiness, and violations of the dress code account for the majority of suspensions (Losen & Martinez, 2013). Students' commission of these "offenses" easily catches them in the "zero tolerance" disciplinary policy net, which mandates predetermined consequences for certain behavioral infractions regardless of circumstances or personal history.

These stringent school discipline practices disproportionately impact black students across the socioeconomic spectrum (Skiba et al., 2011). National K-12 data for 2009–2010 indicate that black male students were suspended at over three times the rate of white students (17% versus 5%); black female secondary school students were suspended at the highest rate (18.3%) of any demographic (Losen & Martinez, 2013). At the elementary level, Latino students' suspension rate was only slightly higher than that of white students (1.7% vs. 1.1.%), but the rate steeply increased in secondary school (12.4% vs. 6.4%) (Losen & Martinez, 2013). Analysis of these troubling disparities has not identified differences in the nature or frequency of misbehaviors among students of different races and ethnicities but rather an institutional pattern of harsher and more frequent punishment of black and Latino youth (Skiba et al., 2011; Vallas, 2009). Black students are more likely to be disciplined for subjectively defined infractions like excessive noise, disrespect of authority, or loitering, whereas white students are typically punished for more objectively measurable offenses like smoking and vandalism (Skiba et al., 2002).

Moreover, children of color are overrepresented in special education programs, the population most at risk for school disciplinary actions. Students with disabilities who are served by IDEA (Individuals with Disabilities Education Act) receive one or more out-of-school suspensions at more than double the rate of their peers. Although they constitute 12% of the school population, they represent 25% of the total number of students who experience school-related arrests or law enforcement referrals (U.S. Department of Education Office for Civil Rights, 2014). An analysis of suspension data from 2,600 American middle and high schools found that the 36% suspension rate among black middle-school males identified as disabled was over five times the 6.6% rate for all students without disability status (Losen & Martinez, 2013). The disproportionately high repeated suspension and expulsion rates for special education students with emotional and behavioral disturbances represent a sort of "double jeopardy" for children exposed to trauma and adversity.

Educational gatekeepers' subjective assessments of student conduct are a critical link between racial disparity and negative outcomes in schools that employ "zero tolerance" policies. Actions initiated by these gatekeepers' have the power to promote or prevent students' diversion into the juvenile justice system depending on the interpretation given to the student's behaviors.

## THE ROLE OF PSYCHIATRIC INTERVENTION AND MISDIAGNOSIS

I survived being misunderstood. Being mis-diagnosed. I survived a lot of providers who thought I needed to be medicated.

25-year-old who spent ten years in the juvenile justice system

Cooper et al., 2007, p. 5

### Implications of the Failure to Consider Trauma Histories First

Labeling a youth's behavior as "aggressive" and/or "dangerous" may lead to a school referral to a pediatrician, social worker, or psychiatrist for medication. These professionals often default to a "one size fits all" approach that considers any disruptive behavior indicative of "probable ADHD." Calling even minor inattention or restlessness ADHD and requesting medication, often prior to a full clinical diagnostic process, obscures trauma's recognition, perpetuates misdiagnosis, and leaves it untreated (Schwarz & Cohen, 2013).

This fundamental misunderstanding of the difference between trauma disorders and ADHD contributes to the lack of recognition that traumatic stress symptoms such as hyperactivity or inattention often overlap with symptoms of ADHD, oppositional defiant disorder, or conduct disorder (Griffin et al., 2011). These "descriptive" diagnoses imply purposeful disruptiveness, which elicits continual disciplinary actions, special education referral, and/or suspension for students with ongoing unrecognized trauma-related affective and behavioral dysregulation. Often this results in their being pushed out of school.

### Overdiagnosis of ADHD

ADHD affects 11% of school-age children overall, making it the most frequently diagnosed childhood neurobehavioral disorder (Conway, Oster, & Szymanski, 2011, p. 60). An estimated 6.4 million children ages 4 through 17 have received an ADHD diagnosis at some point in their lives. The rate was 15% for elementary school boys and 7% for girls; it was 19% for high school boys and 10% for girls.

The overall rate of ADHD diagnoses increased by 16% since 2007, representing a 41% rise in the past decade (Centers for Disease Control and Prevention, 2013). This rise correlates with extensive ADHD drug advertising that convinced many parents, teachers, and pediatricians that most inattentive, restless children who struggle with schoolwork, lack friends, and misbehave suffer from ADHD (Schwarz, 2013).

No definitive test for ADHD exists. Diagnosing it involves extensive interviews with patients, parents, and teachers. Clinicians' ADHD diagnostic approach needs to be a systematic process that considers all other possible causes combined with routine trauma-exposure screening (American Academy of Child & Adolescent Psychiatry, 2010) before making the diagnosis. Bruchmuller, Margraf, and Schneider (2011, p. 132) found a higher false-positive rate compared with false-negative diagnoses, as opposed to "an equal number of false positive and false negative diagnoses" when ADHD diagnostic criteria are reliably used (p. 135).

### The Need for Routine Systemic Trauma History Screening

Failure to elicit either a trauma history or post-traumatic stress symptoms from most pediatric and mental health patients is routine (Havens et al., 2012). Often such a history is learned only when a client voluntarily reveals it (Read & Fraser, 1998). However, this seldom happens because most clients do not make the connection between their current behavior and past trauma exposures. Children referred for behavior problems or even discrete traumatic events require a structured assessment questionnaire to elicit the full trauma history, because probing for this possibility often reveals previously unreported stressful and traumatic events (Lieberman et al., 2011). Ghosh Ippen and colleagues (2009) showed that even when children's referral information contained either a single traumatic event (53%) or exposure to four or more traumatic events (6%), use of a standardized screening instrument found that the majority of the children (70.3%) had experienced four or more traumatic events and only 3% had a single traumatic exposure. The careful consideration of a trauma history needed to distinguish between ADHD and PTSD also gets "short circuited" by time constraints due to severe fiscal cutbacks at the publicly funded health and mental health services used by most families of color (Harrison et al., 2012).

PTSD's ability to cause harder-to-detect "internalizing" symptoms due to traumatic dissociation-related attention difficulties and intrusive re-experiencing underlines the significant need for a systematic approach. Even with a child PTSD diagnosis, the complex interaction between chronic trauma exposure's disruptive impact on psychosocial and neurobiological development and many other functional domains may remain unrecognized.

Consequently, many clinicians misunderstand trauma's pervasive developmental impact and tend to underdiagnose and/or misdiagnose traumatic stress disorders, especially for underserved populations (D'Andrea et al., 2012). To account for this discrepancy, the National Child Traumatic Stress Network proposed a new diagnosis, "developmental trauma disorder" (D'Andrea et al., 2012), for children with early-onset multiple trauma exposure. If PTSD and developmental trauma disorder's lasting neurobiological effects remain undiagnosed or are recognized only later in life, their persistence harms children well into adulthood and increases the cost of care across the system.

## The Implications of Medication Overuse

Sole reliance on psychiatric medications to manage traumatized children's disruptive behavior perpetuates the misdiagnosis problem. Children with trauma-related disorders prescribed stimulant medication generally show no benefit from it. If their behavior problems escalate, practitioners shift to "pharmacological restraint" using expensive atypical antipsychotic medications to treat "aggression" and dangerous "impulsive" conduct "symptoms." Use of these medications sharply increased among poor children on Medicaid from 1997 to 2006: they receive these medications five times more often than privately insured children (Harrison et al., 2012). Low-income children of color, who are overrepresented in foster care, received more than 53% of the antipsychotic prescriptions (Zito et al., 2007). Prevalent antipsychotic medication use also occurs in juvenile justice programs (Moore, 2009).

Poor youth of color exposed to "zero tolerance" discipline practices, racially biased subjective misinterpretation of their behavior, and learning problems experience increased disciplinary actions, expulsion, or special education referrals, which in turn initiate their introduction into the school-to-prison pipeline. In addition, in many cases conduct and learning difficulties are automatically presumed to indicate ADHD, and the diagnostic process fails to consider a child's possible trauma history; misdiagnosis and overreliance on medication result. Taken together, these actions and inactions significantly expedite the school-to-prison pipeline for poor youth of color in the absence of changed approaches.

## ALTERNATIVE APPROACHES

Grassroots advocacy campaigns mobilized by students and families directly affected by the school-to-prison pipeline and a growing research base have catalyzed recognition of "zero tolerance" discipline's harmful effects, especially its role in funneling students of color into the school-to-prison pipeline.

Recent federal guidelines urge the promotion of a positive school climate, non-punitive discipline practices, and ongoing data evaluation for public elementary and secondary schools to "ensure fairness and equity for all students" (U.S. Department of Education, 2014). Notably, the report highlighted the importance of supports for students who have experienced or may be at risk for trauma.

Efforts to overcome the host of negative life consequences and cumulative disadvantage faced by trauma-exposed children need to be driven by a moral imperative that support opportunities for healthy development and takes a comprehensive system change approach.

## Build Institutional Racism Awareness and Trauma Competence in Educational Settings

Needed system change is predicated on universal recognition among school professionals that trauma and adversity disproportionately impact children of color and that they have a critical role to play in buffering affected children from further harm and fostering inroads to critical support services. Operationalizing trauma-informed care in school settings helps to (a) appraise whether a school's infrastructure and operations help or hinder students facing adversity; (b) assess how students learn, behave, and interact to better identify root causes of their difficulties; and (c) employ strategies that foster emotional and behavioral regulation that, in turn, build children's academic and social competence (Cole et al., 2013). Effective implementation requires administrative leadership commitment, dialog and reflection on the interactive impact of institutional racism and trauma on school policies and staff–student dynamics, and ongoing evaluation of student outcomes to support racial equity and inclusion.

## Cultivate Safe, Supportive School Climates Committed to Inclusion and Retention

Positive, supportive student–teacher relationships represent a particularly important external resource for children with behavioral and emotional problems (Wang, Brinkworth, & Eccles, 2013). Trauma-sensitive schools emphasize safety, caring, clear expectations, and consistent rules, which help promote connectedness, positive engagement, and learning (Cole et al., 2013). Brockton, Massachusetts, and San Francisco schools dramatically lowered their suspension rates by 40% to 89% after starting school-wide trauma-informed programs (Stevens, 2014).

Since children's brains are highly malleable (Perry et al., 1995), positive experiences with patient, nurturing, and supportive school professionals present profound opportunities to alter the functional capacity of children exposed to trauma and elicit healthier interpersonal functioning over time. Collaborative Problem Solving (CPS) (Greene & Ablon, 2006) and restorative practices (Costello, Wachtel, & Wachtel, 2010) are noteworthy nonpunitive, relationship-based approaches to address challenging student behavior that promote emotional regulation, empathy, and positive skills development. CPS, a neurobiology- and trauma-informed approach, views challenging behavior as a reflection of cognitive skills functioning in three key domains (flexibility/adaptability, frustration tolerance, and problem solving) and lays out a flexible framework in which to develop "lagging" skills through alliance with the student (Greene & Ablon, 2006). Important school pilot study data showed a reduction in students' challenging behavior, behavior-related referrals, and rates of teacher stress (Schaubman, Stetson, & Plog, 2011). School-based restorative practices pair high behavioral expectations and clear boundaries with a high level of support in a community-centered climate (Costello, Wachtel, & Wachtel, 2010). Restorative practices work to promote positive, mutually respectful relationships and offer informal and formal approaches (e.g., affective statements and questions, small conferences) to address harm to people or relationships, promote personal accountability for wrongdoing, and create safe spaces for dialog between affected parties to discuss difficulties, identify solutions, and help prevent future episodes (Costello, Wachtel, & Wachtel, 2010). Both approaches share the view that problematic behavior should signal the start of a conversation with a student rather than the end of one.

## Invest in Policies and Programs that Alleviate Poverty and Build Resilience

The intertwined impact of racism, poverty, and trauma perpetuates a seemingly relentless process that ensnares thousands of young people of color in the school-to-prison pipeline. Changing this requires a commitment to universal availability of programs that build resilience. Ironically, approaches already shown to produce significant results exist but are not universally used. *Within Our Reach* (Schorr, 1988) cataloged a wide array of effective programs for "breaking the cycle of disadvantage," but our policies remain uninformed by what we know already works.

The most successful programs build resilience by investing in early intervention for all children and from their interruption of cascades of developmental risk. Three examples of the ability to significantly change the life trajectory of poor children of color stand out: the Nurse-Family Partnership (Olds et al., 2002), the Abecedarian program (Campbell et al., 2002), and the Perry Preschool Program (Schweinhart et al., 2005). Each program shared four common features: an emphasis on serving poor preschool children of color, early intervention, promoting children's school adjustment and learning, and a long-term outcome evaluation. These enriched early intervention programs enhanced participants' noncognitive skills and consistently produced a lasting impact not attainable by the public school's focus on cognitive test scores as a measure of success (Heckman & Masterov, 2004). Early intervention (a) raised cognitive and socioemotional abilities; (b) promoted staying in school; (c) reduced crime; (d) fostered workforce productivity; (e) reduced teenage pregnancy; and (f) promoted adult health. The Perry Program's follow-up at age 40 showed higher rates of high school graduation, salaries, and home ownership and lower rates of adult welfare assistance, single-parent births, and arrests than for the controls (Heckman, 2006). Benefit–cost ratios estimated to "range from $3.02 of benefits for each dollar invested" (Washington State Institute for Public Policy, 2008, p. 8) to over an $8 return per dollar invested produced rates of return of 6% to 10% per annum "compared to the post-war return on equity of 5.8%" (Heckman, 2011, p. 35).

Without these pre-kindergarten programs, the children typically experienced a common pattern of early and persistent language and cognitive difficulties most often responded to by strict discipline, suspension, and expulsion once they began school. Waiting until first grade to start remedies for the stressful effects of early life poverty, racism, and trauma on brain development compromises their effectiveness, even though brain plasticity continues into early adulthood (Karatoreos & McEwen, 2013). However, federal and state funding prioritizes programs for children aged 6 to 18 by a factor of three ($3,000 vs. $9,500/child) (Robert Wood Johnson Foundation, 2014). Lastly, recently published studies of improved family economic stability (Costello, Erkanli, Copeland, & Angold, 2010) or moving out of impoverished neighborhoods (Chetty & Hendren, 2015) showed significant benefits and replicated the finding that direct service provision beginning earlier in a child's life achieved even greater benefit. However, significant public policy initiatives focused on universal early investment in disadvantaged children's lives remain rare despite their proven capacity to save society money over the long term, to achieve individuals' productive participation in society, and to promote fairness and social justice.

On an optimistic note, recognition of the need for universal early life resilience promotion initiatives and trauma-informed programming is gaining national attention. For these efforts to be "within our reach," advocates for change stress cross-systems collaboration within education, child welfare, juvenile justice, and children's mental health services combined with a social justice and human rights perspective.

## DISCUSSION QUESTIONS

1. Convene a working group to evaluate the disciplinary policies and practices employed in your school. Consider the following questions with your

colleagues: What is the role of educator subjectivity in the assessment of student behavioral issues and the determination of appropriate consequences? What practical changes can be instituted to assess and counteract possible bias and further promote supportive intervention? What changes could be made to mediate the possibility of disproportionate impact on students with unidentified histories of traumatic exposure?

2. Identify at least 4 core concepts or data points that you think all personnel in your school should know about: a) child and adolescent trauma exposure and its impact on school functioning and b) racial disparities in school discipline practices as they relate to student performance and school inclusion. Develop a professional development module for staff that can also inform new staff onboarding.

3. Gather interested staff to research restorative practices for school settings and other non-punitive approaches to student intervention. How can these practices be integrated into your school incrementally and how might you assess their effectiveness?

## REFERENCES

Abramovitz, M., & Albrecht, J. (2013). The community loss index: A new social indicator. *Social Service Review, 87*(4), 677–724.

Acevedo-García, D., Rosenfeld, L., McArdle, N., & Osypuk, T. (2010). The geography of opportunity: A framework for child development. In. C. EdleyJr & J. Ruiz de Velasco (Eds.), *Changing places: How communities will improve the health of boys of color* (pp. 358–406). Berkeley, CA: University of California Press.

American Academy of Child & Adolescent Psychiatry. (2010). Practice parameter for the assessment and treatment of children and adolescent with posttraumatic stress disorder. *Journal of the American Academy of Child & Adolescent Psychiatry, 49*, 414–430.

American Psychiatric Association. (1980). *Diagnostic and statistical manual of mental disorders* (3rd ed.). Washington, DC: Author.

Bruchmuller, K., Margraf, J., & Schneider, S. (2011). Is ADHD diagnosed in accord with diagnostic criteria? Overdiagnosis and influence of client gender on diagnosis. *Journal of Consulting and Clinical Psychology, 80*(1), 128–138.

Campbell, F. A., Ramey, C. T., Pungello, E., Sparling, J., & Miller-Johnson, S. (2002). Early childhood education: Young adult outcomes from the Abecedarian project. *Applied Developmental Science, 6*(1), 42–57.

Carrión, V. G. (2006). Understanding the effects of early life stress on brain development. In A. F. Lieberman & R. DeMartino (Eds.), *Interventions for children exposed to violence.* Johnson & Johnson Pediatric Round Table series; 6.

Casella, R. (2003). Punishing dangerousness through preventive detention: Illustrating the institutional link between school and prison. *New Directions for Youth Development, 99*, 55–70.

Centers for Disease Control and Prevention. (2013). *National survey of children's health: State and local area integrated telephone survey, 2011–2012.*

Chetty, R., & Hendren, N. (2015). *The impacts of neighborhoods on intergenerational mobility: Childhood exposure effects and county-level estimates.* Harvard University Working Paper.

Children's Defense Fund. (2014). *The state of America's children:* 2014. Retrieved from Children's Defense Fund website: http://www.childrensdefense.org/library/ state-of-americas-children/2014-soac.pdf?utm_source=2014-SOAC-PDF&utm_ medium=link&utm_campaign=2014-SOAC

Chu, A. T., & Lieberman, A. F. (2010). Clinical implications of traumatic stress from birth to age five. *Annual Review of Clinical Psychology, 6,* 469–494.

Cole, S., Eisner, A., Gregory, M., & Ristuccia, J. (2013). *Helping traumatized children learn 2: Creating and advocating for trauma-sensitive schools.* Retrieved from Trauma and Learning Policy Institute website: http://traumasensitiveschools.org/tlpi-publications/.

Conway, F., Oster, M., & Szymanski, K. (2011). ADHD and complex trauma: A descriptive study of hospitalized children in an urban psychiatric hospital. *Journal of Infant, Child, and Adolescent Psychotherapy, 10,* 60–72.

Cooper, J. L., Masi, R., Dababnah, S., Aratani, Y., & Knitzer, J. (2007, July). *Unclaimed children revisited.* Working Paper No. 2. Retrieved from National Center for Children in Poverty website: http://www.nccp.org/publications/pdf/text_737.pdf.

Corbin, T., Bloom, S. L., Wilson, A., Rich, L. & Rich, J.A. (2010). Approaching the health and well-being of African American boys through trauma-informed practice. In C. EdleyJr. & J. Ruiz de Velasco (Eds.), *Changing places: How communities will improve the health of boys of color* (pp. 407–428). Berkeley, CA: University of California Press.

Costello, B., Wachtel, J., & Wachtel, T. (2010). *Restorative circles in schools: Building community and enhancing learning.* Bethlehem, PA: International Institute for Restorative Practices.

Costello, E. J., Erkanli, A., Copeland, W., & Angold, A. (2010). Association of family income supplements in adolescence with development of psychiatric and substance abuse disorders in adulthood among an American Indian population. *Journal of the American Medical Association, 303,* 1954–1960.

D'Andrea, W., Stolbach, B., Ford, J., Spinazzola, J., & van der Kolk, B. A. (2012). Understanding interpersonal trauma in children: Why we need a developmentally appropriate trauma diagnosis. *American Journal of Orthopsychiatry, 82*(2), 187–200

Dearing, E. (2008). Psychological costs of growing up poor. *Annals of the New York Academy of Science, 1136,* 324–332. doi: 10.1196/annals.1425.006

Dierkhising, C. B., Ko, S. J., Woods-Jaeger, B., Briggs, E. C., Lee, R., & Pynoos, R. S. (2013). Trauma histories among justice-involved youth: Findings from the National Child Traumatic Stress Network. *European Journal of Psychotraumatology, 4,* 1–12.

Dignity in Schools. (n.d.). *Fact sheet on school discipline and the push out problem.* Retrieved from Dignity in Schools website: http://www.dignityinschools.org/files/Pushout_ Fact_Sheet.pdf.

Eigsti, I. M., & Cicchetti, D. (2004). The impact of child maltreatment of expressive syntax at 60 months. *Developmental Science, 7,* 88–102.

Fabelo, T., Thompson, M. D., Plotkin, M. P., Carmichael, D., Marchbanks, M. P., & Booth, E. A. (2011). *Breaking school's rules: A statewide study of how school discipline relates to students' success and juvenile justice system involvement.* New York: Council of State Governments Justice Center; Public Policy Research Institute at Texas A&M University.

Fantuzzo, J., & Fusco, R. (2007). Children's direct exposure to types of domestic violence crime: A population-based investigation. *Violence and Victims, 22,* 158–171.

Feistritzer, C. E. (2011). *Profiles of teachers in the U.S. 2011*. Retrieved from National Center for Education Information website: http://www.ncei.com/Profile_Teachers_US_2011.pdf.

Finkelhor, D., Turner, H., Ormond, R., & Hamby, S. (2009). Violence, abuse and crime exposure among a national sample of children and youth. *Pediatrics, 124*(5), 1411–1423.

Garbarino, J., Hammond, R., Mercy, J., & Yung, B. R. (2004). Community violence and children: Preventing exposure and reducing harm. In K. I. Maton, C. J. Schellenbach, B. J. Leadbeater, & A. L. Solarz (Eds.), *Investing in children, youth, families, and communities* (pp. 13–30). Washington, DC: American Psychological Association.

Ghosh Ippen, C., Harris, W., Van Horn, P., Guendelman, M., & Lieberman, A. F. (2009). *Traumatic and stressful life events and young children: What are we learning? What can we do?* Paper presented at the University of California, San Francisco, Department of Psychiatry Research Retreat, Marin Headland Institute, Sausalito, CA.

Greene, R. W., & Ablon, J. S. (2006). *Treating explosive kids: The collaborative problem solving approach*. New York: The Guilford Press.

Griffin, G., McClelland, G., Holzberg, M., Stolbach, B., Maj, N. & Kisiel, C. (2011). Addressing the impact of trauma before diagnosing mental illness in child welfare. *Child Welfare, 90*, 69–89.

Hamre, B. K., Pianta, R. C., Downer, J. T., & Mashburn, A. J. (2008). Teachers' perceptions of conflict with young students: Looking beyond problem behaviors. *Social Development, 17*(1), 115–136.

Harris, W. W., Lieberman, F. A., & Marans, S. (2007). In the best interests of society. *Journal of Child Psychology and Psychiatry, 48*(3–4), 392–411.

Harrison, J. N., Cluxton-Keller, F., & Gross, D. (2012). Antipsychotic medication prescribing trends in children and adolescents. *Journal of Pediatric Health Care, 26*(2), 139–145.

Havens, J. F., Gudino, O. G., Biggs, E. A., Diamond, U. N., Weis, J. R., & Cloitre, M. (2012). Identification of trauma exposure and PTSD in adolescent psychiatric inpatients: An exploratory study. *Journal of Traumatic Stress, 25*(2), 171–178.

Heckman, J. (2006). Skill formation and the economics of investing in disadvantaged children, *Science, 312*, 1900–1902.

Heckman, J. J. (2011). The economics of inequality: The value of early childhood education. *American Educator,* Spring, 31–47.

Heckman, J. J., & Masterov, D. V. (2004, October). *The productivity argument for investing in young children*. Working Paper No. 5. Invest in Kids Working Group Committee for Economic Development.

Hill, R. B. (2007). *An analysis of racial/ethnic disproportionality and disparity at the national, state, and county levels*. Seattle, WA: Casey Family Programs.

Karatoreos, I., & McEwen, B. S. (2013). Annual research review: The neurobiology and physiology of resilience and adaptation across the life course. *Journal of Child Psychology and Psychiatry, 54*(4), 337–347. doi: 10.1111/jcpp.12054

Kim, P., Evans, G. W., Angstadt, M., Ho, S. S., Sripada, C. S., Swain, J. E., Liberzon, I., & Phan, K. L. (2013). Effects of childhood poverty and chronic stress on emotion regulatory brain function in adulthood. *Proceedings of the National Academy of Sciences USA, 110*(46), 18442–18447.

Lieberman, A. F., Chu, A., van Horn, P., & Harris, W. W. (2011). Trauma in early childhood: Empirical evidence & clinical implications. *Development & Psychopathology, 23*, 397–410.

Loo, C. M., Fairbank, J. A., Scurfield, R. M., Ruch, L. O., King, D. W., Adams, L. J., & Chemtob, C. M. (2001). Measuring exposure to racism: development and validation of a Race-Related Stressor Scale (RRSS) for Asian American Vietnam veterans. *Psychological Assessment, 13*(4), 503–520.

Losen, D., & Martinez, T. E. (2013). *Out of school and off track: The overuse of suspensions in American middle and high schools.* Retrieved from the Civil Rights Project website: http://civilrightsproject.ucla.edu/resources/projects/center-for-civil-rights-remedies/school-to-prison-folder/federal-reports/out-of-school-and-off-track-the-overuse-of-suspensions-in-american-middle-and-high-schools/OutofSchool-OffTrack_UCLA_4-8.pdf.

Masten, C. L., Guyer, A. E., Hodgdon, H. B., McClure, E. B., Charney, D. S., Ernst, M., Kaufman, J., Pine, D. S., & Monk, C. S. (2008). Recognition of facial emotions among maltreated children with high rates of posttraumatic stress disorder. *Child Abuse & Neglect, 32,* 139–153.

Moore S. (2009, August 9). Mentally ill strain juvenile system. New York Times. Retrieved from http://www.nytimes.com/2009/08/10/us/10juvenile.html.

Morris, M. (2012). *Race, gender and the school-to-prison pipeline: Expanding our discussion to include Black girls.* Retrieved from the African American Policy Forum website: aapf.org/2012/09/report-race-gender-and-the-school-to-prison-pipeline.

National Crime Victimization Survey. (2007). *Criminal victimization in the United States.* Retrieved from http://www.bjs.gov/index.cfm?ty=dcdetail&iid=245.

National Scientific Council on the Developing Child. (2010, February). *Persistent fear and anxiety can affect young children's learning and development.* Working Paper No. 9. Retrieved from http://developingchild.harvard.edu/resources/reports_and_working_papers/working_papers/wp9/.

Neal, L. I., McCray, A., Webb-Johnson, G., & Bridgest, S. T. (2003). The effects of African American movement styles on teachers' perceptions and reactions. *Journal of Special Education, 37*(1), 49–57.

Nellis, A. (2011). *Addressing the collateral consequences of convictions for young offenders.* Retrieved from http://sentencingproject.org/doc/publications/Collateral%20Consequences%20NACDL%202011.pdf

New York City School-Justice Partnership Task Force. (2013, May). *Keeping kids in school and out of court: Report and recommendations.* Albany: New York State Permanent Judicial Commission on Justice for Children.

Olds, D. L., Robinson, J., O'Brien, R., Luckey, D. W. Pettitt, L. M., Henderson, C. R., Ng, R. K., Sheff, K. L., Korfmacher, J., Hiatt, S., & Talmi, A. (2002). Home visiting by paraprofessionals and by nurses: A randomized, controlled trial. *Pediatrics, 110*(3), 486–496.

Perry, B., Pollard, R., Blakely, T., Baker, W. L., & Vigilante, D. (1995). Childhood trauma, the neurobiology of adaptation, and "use-dependent" development of the brain: How states become traits. *Infant Mental Health Journal, 16*(4), 271–291.

Rand, M. (2009). Criminal Victimization, 2008. Washington, DC: Bureau of Justice Statistics, 4. Retrieved from http://www.bjs.gov/content/pub/pdf/cv08.pdf.

Read, J., & Fraser, A. (1998). Abuse histories of psychiatric inpatients: To ask or not to ask? *Psychiatric Services, 49*(3), 355–359.

Robert Wood Johnson Foundation. (2014) *Time to act: Investing in the health of our children and communities.* Commission to Build a Healthier America Report, Retrieved from http://www.rwjf.org/en/about-rwjf/newsroom/features-and-articles/Commission.html.

Saffold, F., & Longwell-Grice, H. (2008). White women preparing to teach in urban schools: Looking for similarity and finding difference. *Urban Review, 40,* 186–209.

Schaubman, A., Stetson, E., & Plog, A. (2011). Reducing teacher stress by implementing collaborative problem solving in a school setting. *School Social Work Journal, 35*(2), 72–93.

Schorr, L. B. (1988). *Within our reach: Breaking the cycle of disadvantage.* New York: Doubleday.

Schwab-Stone, M., Chen, C., Greenberger, E., Silver, D., Lichtman, J., & Voyce, C. (1999). No safe haven II: The effects of violence exposure on urban youth. *Journal of the American Academy of Child & Adolescent Psychiatry, 38*(4), 359–367.

Schwarz, A. (2013, December 29). A.D.H.D. experts re-evaluate study's zeal for drugs. *New York Times.* Retrieved from http://www.nytimes.

Schwarz, A., & Cohen, S. (2013, March 31). A.D.H.D. seen in 11% of U.S. children as diagnoses rise. *New York Times.* Retrieved from http://www.nytimes.

Schweinhart, L. J., Montie, J., Xiang, Z., Barnett, W.S., Belfield, C.R., & Nores, M.. (2005). *Lifetime effects: The High/Scope Perry Preschool Study through age 40* (pp. 194–215). Ypsilanti, MI: High/Scope Press.

Skiba, R. J., Horner, R. H., Chung, C., Rausch, M. K., May, S. L., & Tobin, T. (2011). Race is not neutral: A national investigation of African American and Latino disproportionality in school discipline. *School Psychology Review, 40*(1), 85–107.

Skiba, R. J., Michael, R. S., Nardo, A. C., & Peterson, R. C. (2002). The color of discipline: Racial and gender disproportionality in school punishment. *Urban Review, 34*(4), 317–342.

Stein, B. D., Jaycox, L. H., Kataoka, S., Rhodes, H. J., & Vestal, K. D. (2003). Prevalence of child and adolescent exposure to violence. *Clinical Child and Family Psychology Review, 6,* 247–263.

Stevens, J. E. (2014). San Francisco's El Dorado Elementary uses trauma-informed & restorative practices; suspensions drop 89%. *Social Justice Solutions.* Retrieved from http://www.socialjusticesolutions.org/2014/01/29/san-franciscos...

Teicher, M., Andersen, S., Polcari, A., Anderson, C., Navalta, C., & Kim, D. (2001). Neurobiological consequences of early stress and childhood maltreatment. *Neuroscience & Biobehavioral Reviews, 27,* 33–44.

Tenenbaum, H. R., & Ruck, M. D. (2007). Are teachers' expectations different for racial minority than for European American students? A meta-analysis. *Journal of Educational Psychology, 99*(2), 253–273.

Turner, H. A., Finkelhor, D., & Ormrod, R. (2006). The effect of lifetime victimization on the mental health of children and adolescents. *Social Science & Medicine, 62,* 13–27.

U.S. Department of Education. (2014, January). *Guiding principles: A resource guide for improving school climate and discipline.* Retrieved from http://www2.ed.gov/policy/gen/guid/school-discipline/guiding-principles.pdf.

U.S. Department of Education Office for Civil Rights. (2014, March). *Civil rights data collection.* Issue Brief #1. Retrieved from https://www2.ed.gov/about/offices/list/ocr/docs/crdc-discipline-snapshot.pdf.

U.S. Department of Health and Human Services, Administration on Children, Youth and Families, Children's Bureau. (2015). *Child maltreatment 2013.* Retrieved from http://www.acf.hhs.gov/programs/cb/resource/child-maltreatment-2013

Vallas, R. (2009). The disproportionality problem: Overrepresentation of black students in special education & recommendations for reform. *Virginia Journal of Social Policy & the Law, 17*(1), 181–208.

van der Kolk, B. A. (1996). The complexity of adaptation to trauma: Self-regulation, stimulus discrimination, and characterological development. In B. A. Van der Kolk, A. C. McFarlane, & L. Weisaeth (Eds.), *Traumatic stress: The effects of overwhelming experience on minds, body, and society* (pp. 182–213). New York: Guilford.

Wang, M., Brinkworth, M., & Eccles, J. (2013). Moderating effects of teacher–student relationship in adolescent trajectories of emotional and behavioral adjustment. *Developmental Psychology, 49*(4), 690–705.

Washington State Institute for Public Policy. (2008, July). *Evidence-based programs to prevent children from entering and remaining in the child welfare system: Benefits and costs for Washington.* Document No. 08-07-3901. Retrieved from the Washington State Institute for Public Policy website: http://www.wsipp.wa.gov/ReportFile/1020.

Zito, J. M., Safer, D. J., Valluri, S., Garner J. F., Korelitz, J. J., & Mattison, D. R. (2007). Psychotherapeutic medication prevalence in Medicaid-insured preschoolers. *Journal of Child and Adolescent Psychopharmacology, 7,* 195–203.

PART FIVE

# *Replicating Best Practices*

# CHAPTER 15

# Giving Equal Access to the American Dream to All Kids

## *The Harlem Children's Zone*

### ANNE WILLIAMS-ISOM

## INTRODUCTION

We have allowed a system to take shape in America that does not truly give low-income children of color an adequate opportunity to educate themselves, get a high-skills job, and enter into the middle class as self-sustaining adults. The American dream is, by and large, walled off from millions of America's children. While many people have been too quick to give up on these kids, my experience has shown that with the proper supports they can overcome the many challenges they face and succeed. A comprehensive, long-term system that addresses each of these obstacles can even the playing field for these children.

In this chapter, I explore the very tangible, residual effects of structural racism in the health and human services as well as education sectors, particularly from the perspective of a child advocate. I highlight examples of concrete relational strategies and organizational approaches used to serve communities of color that have proven to be effective in practice—based on my experiences at both the New York City Administration for Children's Services (ACS) and the nonprofit Harlem Children's Zone® (HCZ). These approaches are increasingly reported in the literature as effective for achieving more favorable outcomes for this population of children. Both approaches show how we can proactively create culturally adept systems that help large numbers of children of color get on track and stay on track for success. This is the surest way to break the intergenerational cycle of poverty for individual children and their families as well as for the surrounding community.

## THE MAKING OF A CHILDREN'S ADVOCATE

I have been a child advocate my entire life. And when I say my entire life, I am including the realization that I had when I was nine years old that things were not quite equal for everyone. At that time in my life, one of the neighborhood boys—we called him Duck—was killed in an elevator shaft. He stepped out into the hallway of his apartment building one morning, waving goodbye to his mom. Without looking where he was going, he fell to his death down a dark elevator shaft. He was only twelve years old. That elevator had been out of service for weeks and residents had complained about it. But it took the death of this boy to bring about enough outrage from the residents to demand that it get fixed. Two things stuck with me from that experience. The first was that I should always speak up when witnessing injustice and the second was a nagging suspicion that the lives of black children were not valued as much as those of other children in our society. I remember thinking about and feeling that sense of racial inequality from a very young age. Who knew that thought would come to me many times as I grew older and ultimately lead me to pursue a career as an advocate for vulnerable children and their families?

I grew up in a lower-middle-class neighborhood in Queens, New York, with three older brothers and my Caribbean mother, who was raised by nuns in Port of Spain in Trinidad and Tobago after her mother died giving birth to her. The youngest of 14 children, my mother benefitted from the valuable skills that she was exposed to by the church. She eventually became a nurse and emigrated to the United States at the age of 27 to pursue the American dream. Her profession allowed her to make a living for herself and her children so that when she and my dad divorced, she was able to pay the mortgage on our modest home and pay tuition for us to attend a great local Catholic school because her own experiences had taught her the value of a good education. Because of my mother's emphasis on education, all of my siblings and I went to college and have good careers and beautiful families. We are all now working so that my mother's 13 grandchildren have better lives than she did, and helping them to achieve the American dream.

Such a simple story. Yet it seems so unattainable for so many children through no fault of their own. That feeling is what led me to law school and then to the ACS and the HCZ.

## CHALLENGES IN TRANSFORMING THE ADMINISTRATION FOR CHILDREN'S SERVICES

When I arrived at ACS, New York City's public child welfare agency, in 1996, there were nearly 42,000 kids in foster care. Incredibly, an ACS report (2012) found that in 1992 and 2002, children of color represented 93% and 95%, respectively, of all children living in foster care. It was at this time that I learned the meaning of the term "disproportionality." And sadly my childhood suspicions about the inequitable treatment of black children were confirmed the more I learned about the experiences of children of color who were served by public systems. These children and their families were rarely given the supports they needed to keep them safely in their own homes and communities. Tragic stories of child fatalities—like Duck in the elevator shaft—or exposure to life-threatening circumstances in their daily lives became an all-too-common reminder of what disproportionality really looked like.

The ACS is the governmental agency that has the gargantuan responsibility of protecting all of the city's children. Within this population, much of the agency's work focuses on the highest-risk cases—children who are facing imminent danger. African American children are overrepresented in this cohort. In 1987, approximately 16,500 of New York's African American children—1 in every 32 black children—were residing in foster care. While 32% of the city's children were African American, about 63% of ACS incident reports, foster care entries, and foster care residents were African American (ACS, 2012). Even as the total number of children in foster care declined significantly over the following two decades, according to data reported by the ACS (2012) the disproportional representation of African Americans on the foster care caseload increased. Directionally, the racial disproportionality represented in New York City mirrors that of data trends and presenting problems reported in child public welfare systems across the nation.

The causes of the persistence of such widespread racial disparity remain open for debate. My viewpoint, however, on that question is informed by firsthand knowledge of the extensive data generated by the agency on a daily basis as a member of the ACS executive staff. Together, these data tell painful stories that help us understand how the cycle of generational poverty stubbornly persists. The stories told by these data reveal the depth of structural inequalities confronted by disadvantaged young people. Importantly, these data also instruct us about the potential levers and tools that are available to human service professionals that can reverse the cycle of intergenerational poverty and change their life outcomes.

During my 13 years at ACS, I saw that the city's public child welfare system was not equipped to proactively help troubled families. This is illustrated by the experience of a mom I had known for years whom I will call Rose. She was justifiably angered that the city's child welfare system, in its attempt to keep her children safe, actually made them more vulnerable by removing them from her home.

A victim herself of abuse and neglect as a child, she left her home and sought refuge in a marriage at too young of an age. Unsurprisingly, she found herself with an abusive husband and two young children. She was unable to go to college, hold a steady job, and secure stable housing. As a result of a call from a neighbor to child protective services, an ACS investigation determined that her children were living in unsafe conditions and placed them in foster care. Then, the unimaginable happened: Rose's 10-year-old daughter was sexually abused while in foster care.

On a call with me after her children were returned, Rose shared that her daughter was becoming extremely rebellious—skipping school, abusing drugs and alcohol, and engaging in other risky behaviors. We both knew that if her daughter did not get the necessary interventions, she would be on the same downward spiral that Rose experienced early in life. As Rose struggled with her daughter, her school called in a report against Rose for "educational neglect."

Shocked that she was going through this again, Rose invited me to accompany her to a school conference. I observed school administrators who were woefully ill equipped to deal with the serious issues that Rose's daughter was facing. I actually felt some sympathy for the school. The school administrators felt that the city's child welfare agency was the only resource they had. Rose again challenged me to walk in her shoes by sitting in on the agency's visit. The worker observed the apartment and interviewed Rose and the children, and eventually it was determined that the allegation against Rose for educational neglect was unfounded. In other words, the agency found that Rose had in fact done everything that she could to get her daughter connected to mental health services to help address the trauma she experienced as a result of the sexual abuse. However, Rose's predicament was complicated by a school that did not have the resources to help.

Rose's circumstances were representative of many of the parents who came in contact with the child welfare system. While Rose held herself and her husband accountable for the consequences of their actions, which led to her daughter's traumatic foster care experience, the system had failed Rose and her children because it did not offer any services to help keep her family together. The best and only intervention the system could offer was foster care. While the option may keep children safe for a short period of time, it exposes them to the trauma of separation and, in the case of Rose's daughter, substitute care that was far worse. My years in contact with Rose helped me see that what families really need are supports—access to a good education, a job, and good mental health and counseling services and not judging and finger-pointing. Through Rose, I also learned that most of the parties were victims of a system that was not meant to be the first source of support. We needed a better solution.

During my tenure, New York's child welfare agency began to adopt procedures that grew out of the lessons learned from stories like that of Rose. We began to recognize that if we were going to truly change the trajectory of a child's life, we had to address the root causes that put the child in unsafe living situations, and that doing so would require the involvement of the entire community surrounding the child. We also recognized that if we were to deepen our involvement in communities of color, this required a heightened competency around racial issues. While deputy commissioner, I helped to create a racial equity task force, as discussed by Hardy in Chapter 8 of this volume, that facilitated regular race dialogs on key topics at every level of our organization—from the lawyers and administrative staff to child protection workers to our leadership. My experience as an Annie E. Casey Leadership Fellow was critical as it trained me to lead effective conversations around racial disparity and disproportionality with groups of people from different backgrounds and racial experiences. As a result of this work, not only did individuals become more attuned to the racial undercurrents that influenced their decision making, but also, as an organization, we became more adept in working with children and families of color.

To deepen our community engagement, we closely examined up-and-coming national models, such as the neighborhood-based services system, and applied new elements to our approach to child welfare. Under my leadership, we created community partnerships, welcoming participation from a broader range of stakeholders who cared about our children—teachers, priests, even crossing guards and family friends. We formalized this and other strategies by creating parent and community advisory boards, which provided feedback on how our services could amplify local efforts to help our kids. We leveraged these new relationships to improve service coordination and tailor neighborhood strategies. We scaled these shifts through launching the Community Partnership to Strengthen Families Project, which applied these strategies to almost a dozen high-need areas with a disproportionate number of foster care placements. A key successful strategy included the implementation of family team case conferences, led by trained and experienced social workers, that regularly engaged parents, caregivers, service providers, and community partners in the service planning process (Chahine, van Straaten, & Williams-Isom, 2005).

This period of outreach and our renewed focus on prevention substantially reduced the agency's reliance on foster care. An ACS report (2012) stated that, at its peak in the early 1990s, nearly 50,000 children resided in foster care; by the middle of the last decade, this number had gone down to between 10,000 and 20,000. More children were able to stay among their families, friends, and communities as the agency's approach evolved.

## THE HCZ: A DIFFERENT MODEL

I was always an admirer of HCZ from afar. It just made sense to me that in order for children to be successful and safe they needed to be surrounded by caring adults and have access to the best institutions that provided basic services, such as schools, health care, and libraries, and safe places to play and participate in recreational activities. Further, they needed constant access to the full range of these services throughout their childhood years as a prerequisite for reaching successful adulthood. HCZ is a model that supports my perspective on the provision of services to children and their families that evolved in my thinking over working many years at ACS: the best way to keep children safe is to ensure that they are surrounded by prepared and caring adults, who are themselves anchored in strong, well-resourced communities.

The brilliance of the HCZ model is in its simplicity. It is based in the assumption that children should be given everything they need from the moment they are born until they graduate from college. It says surround them by the best people in their fields. It says teach the adults in their life to be the best and most well-prepared caretakers and parents. It says surround them with the best teachers and afterschool providers and give them access to the highest-quality arts, music, and recreation. And it says do that 24/7, 365 days of the year. It says that for the most vulnerable children, we need to provide the best: not whatever is available, not the mediocre, but the absolute best.

When you look at some of the statistics of Central Harlem, where HCZ operates, you see a community that had been neglected for many years. For example, as reported by the New York Department of Health and Hygiene (2006) and the Citizen's Committee for Children (2008, 2011), 65% of children are born into poverty, 33% of adults have not completed high school, 68% of the children are born to single mothers, and 40% of the children living in HCZ are obese or overweight.

We at HCZ know, based on recent research, that childhood poverty is now looked at as a disease and a public health issue, especially when that poverty is concentrated. As Dr. Perri Klass (2013) said in a recent *New York Times* article:

> Poverty damages children's dispositions and blunts their brains. We've seen articles about the language deficit in poor homes and in the gaps in school achievements. These remind us that more so than in my mother's generation, poverty in this country is now likely to define many children's life trajectories in the hardest terms: poor academic achievement, high dropout rates and health problems from obesity and diabetes to heart disease, substance abuse and mental illness.

When you overlay these outcomes with the effects of several decades of institutional racism, you get a community that has been neglected and children who have almost nothing compared to what children have who live 30 blocks away from them. You need a bold solution to reverse this—not just another program, but a bold new undertaking and paradigm shift.

The HCZ story is really one of very traditional community organizing and shows how, through a deep partnership with the community, a strategy has been built one program at a time until a seamless pipeline of services was developed for children aged 0 to 23.

## BUILDING A COMPREHENSIVE PIPELINE: FROM RHEEDLEN TO THE HCZ PROJECT

The organization we call HCZ began as Rheedlen, a program founded to prevent truancy among children. When elementary-age children miss school, it usually is a red flag of something going on at home. For that reason, Rheedlen addressed truancy as a symptom and worked with families.

The agency grew, responding to the many needs in the community as well as opportunities that arose. When Mayor David Dinkins proposed allowing community groups to open public school buildings to run programs after school, Rheedlen jumped at the chance to gain access and better serve children and families in Harlem. In 1990, the organization began operating the Countee Cullen Community Center, which became a prototype for the Beacon model, providing an array of services in a safe environment for children and adults.

The crack epidemic that swept through many American inner cities in the 1990s exacerbated the already tough challenges for children in Harlem. Geoffrey Canada, who was Rheedlen's president/CEO at the time, was keenly aware that Rheedlen's good work was happening against the backdrop of a neighborhood that was, for the most part, failing its children. He began to think that what was necessary was a solution that worked at a larger scale, appropriate to the size of the challenge. The goal was to create a culture in the neighborhood where success was the norm, not the exception, where kids looked around and saw other kids in or on their way to college, where hope replaced hopelessness.

After a one-block pilot project, the organization created a 10-year business plan for the HCZ Project, which would grow to cover almost 100 blocks in Central Harlem. The HCZ Project aimed to tackle all the challenges that families were facing—from education to safety to health. Today the agency serves more than 13,000 children, from birth through college. If we were a separate school district, we would be the 10th largest in New York State. While the geographic boundaries have been reached, we continue to deepen and improve the efficacy of our work so we get it right for every child every time.

While we have scaled immensely since our Rheedlen days, our approach has remained the same. We continue to root ourselves in community-based decision making and solutions. For example, as we constructed our 135,000-square-foot building to accommodate 1,300 students of our Promise Academy charter school, the St. Nicholas Community Advisory Board played a pivotal role in how we built the complex and continues to impact how we think about best using the newly built school and community center building in the middle of the St. Nicholas public housing development.

More broadly, we literally depend on the community to help us improve it—over half of our approximately 2,000 full-time and part-time staff live in Harlem or similarly situated communities. They are our eyes and ears on the ground, building the relationships needed to identify and match family members to our appropriate services. They also spend locally so our organization acts as an economic engine. In the process, they are transforming the community from within.

We have built a comprehensive system that continues through college because we know that piecemeal academic supports are often not enough. Environmental factors such as safety, housing, and parental behavior can impact the odds of high school and college completion. We needed to be able to address these factors early and effectively at each stage of a child's development. Our early childhood youth programming focuses on building a strong foundation for children by teaching new parents how to nurture the learning and developmental skills needed to be ready for kindergarten.

Our early childhood parenting program, the Baby College®, is a good example of how our relationship with the community helped us design our services. Initially proposed by HCZ's community advisory board, the program was created to expose caregivers with children aged zero to three to best-practice parenting techniques. Since 2000, we have served more than 5,500 new and expecting caregivers. Seeing the impact of the lack of black fathers in households, we wanted to send a message about the importance of having both parents involved in a child's development in the Baby College program. As a result, since its inception, the percentage of dads who participate continues to increase. Moreover, we are proud of the work of our recently appointed black male program director, whose team successfully recruits black males to participate alongside their female partners for the nine-week Saturday parenting workshops.

We are committed to making the dream of college a reality not only for the students at our Promise Academy charter schools, but also for the thousands of students we serve who attend New York City public schools. We keep track of and support their academic progress, assisting in tutoring and college prep, offering enrichment exposures, and advocating for them in their schools. We monitor and improve their physical health through our Healthy Harlem fitness and nutrition initiative. We support them with their social and emotional needs. And when they near the end of our pipeline and head off to college, as historically more than 93% of our high school seniors do each year, we stay connected to them. This year, we plan to help over 250 incoming college freshmen acclimate themselves to the new environment, and we continue to support more than 900 of our students currently in college—encouraging them through their sophomore slump, providing them with opportunities to build job skills through internships, and preparing them for life after college.

## THE URGENCY TO BRING THE HCZ MODEL TO OTHER COMMUNITIES

Although HCZ provides an array of services, our primary focus is on education. The U.S. Census Bureau (2012) found that the returns on investing in education are enormous: a college graduate may earn over twice as much as a high-school dropout on an annual basis. Sadly, the income of a household where a child is raised is highly predictive of the child's academic achievement—creating an intergenerational cycle of poverty. When measured by standardized reading test scores, Reardon (2011) found that the performance gap between high-income and low-income families has grown by as much as 40% since the 1970s. Improving the education of children is a sure path to life success, so it is the cornerstone of our work at HCZ.

Finding the right path, though, means reversing entrenched inequalities in the public education options available to low-income African American children. Quantitative evidence provided by the National Center for Education Evaluation (2011) highlights what many of us have observed anecdotally: the distribution of high-performing, experienced teachers is unequally weighted toward wealthier school districts and communities. And the situation is compounded for African American students. Research by the Civil Rights Data Collection Project (Diverse Education, 2011) has shown that nationally, schools with majority black student populations are twice as likely to have inexperienced teachers as are pre-dominantly white schools within the same districts.

We know that our young people in Harlem need even more than strong teach-ers and schools. In underserved communities, the exit from generational poverty is often blocked by the hurdles outside the classroom—from inadequate health care and housing to unsafe streets and a lack of recreational spaces. America's poorest students lack access to enriching experiences—trips to the zoo, exposure to the performing arts and athletics, summer programs—that expand middle-class children's understanding of the world around them. Analysis by the After-School Corporation (2013) has estimated that this gap is equivalent to 6,000 or more hours of enriching activities by the time a child reaches the sixth grade.

Offering the right set of exposures and opportunities for children and their families that ultimately change the beliefs of an entire community and provide evidence of a different path represents an enormous lift for any single intervention, program, or leader to tackle on its own. It requires a wide range of supports that are common in middle-class communities but are partially or even entirely missing in poor neighborhoods. Unfortunately, the creation and coordination of sufficient re-sources is far beyond the scope of most of our existing social service agencies, which are organized to deliver targeted interventions to crisis situations such as ACS.

At HCZ, we have built a different kind of agency—one that is rising to the chal-lenge of really changing the odds for children over time across Central Harlem.

## EXECUTIVE LEADERSHIP INSIGHT: HOW OUR LEARNING HAS SHAPED THE HCZ PIPELINE

Over the years, our team has seen hundreds of children defy the odds and prove the efficacy of HCZ's long-term comprehensive model. Children who had been woe-fully behind grade level in elementary school, in middle school, and even sometimes into high school were—with the right interventions—able to get themselves on track and stay there. Importantly, our programming has evolved over time, often through observation of what isn't working in outside systems, but also through taking a hard look at what's working and not working in our own programs.

Many of us have observed the harm that adults can do by jumping to conclusions and lowering their expectations for children. Armed with this insight, our collective belief has become the operating principle for the entire HCZ organization: if Plan A and Plan B don't work for a child, it simply means coming up with Plan C, D, and all the way to Plan Z, if necessary.

Having watched generations of children be undermined by public schools in low-income neighborhoods of color, HCZ jumped at the chance to create a high-quality charter school in Harlem when invited to do so by New York City Mayor Michael Bloomberg. Opening a school was not the typical expansion for an organization that worked as a partner with public schools, but our leadership felt that schools—the centerpiece of a child's academic life—were routinely dooming kids to failure and that no one was stepping forward with the appropriate level of action to stop the tragic cycle.

In every way, Geoffrey and the executive team made it clear to frontline staff, students, and parents that the school was going to be different: it was going to take on the tough cases, it was not going to give up on children, and it was going to tackle the students' challenges both inside and outside the classroom. Whether the child needed extra tutoring, a pair of glasses, or a social worker to address a chaotic home life, the Promise Academy was going to mitigate the problem. As chronicled in journalist Paul Tough's (2008) *Whatever It Takes*, the school opened with kindergarten and sixth-grade cohorts in September 2004 with a plan to add two new grades each year as each grade moved up.

The first few years of the Promise Academy were rocky, and the school's board of trustees began to give up hope for the middle school. As the board and staff began to think about starting a new high school for the middle-school children, board members said they thought the school should solely take in younger children and close the existing middle school, sending the children elsewhere.

Geoffrey and the school administration asked the board for a last chance to turn around the middle school. The board members agreed to a year-long probationary period but said they could not sanction opening a new high-school division. The painful compromise meant telling the eighth graders and their families that there would be no Promise Academy High School for them to matriculate into, and that they would need to find a different high school. It also meant that the middle-school staff needed to be revamped. As Geoffrey Canada told Tough (2008, pp. 254–255) in *Whatever it Takes*:

> It's not the kids. It's us. The kids are middle school kids from Harlem who come from troubled environments and have lots of problems. That's who they are. Yes, they're difficult. If they were not difficult, I'd be quite shocked. But we didn't do our job. . . .

Saying it was the behavior, that something was wrong with the eighth-graders, that is just a cop-out.

The HCZ and Promise Academy leaders restated to the families our commitment to continue to work with the students in conjunction with their new schools and to make sure they got through college, but parents and students understandably felt upset. While the school eventually righted itself over the next year and resumed taking in older students and starting a high school, Geoffrey has often said that letting go of that eighth-grade class was the worst experience of his professional career: it felt like a retreat of his personal commitment to stick with every child regardless of how well or poorly he or she was doing.

Today the school—along with its sister school, Promise Academy II—is stronger but still struggles with students who have enormous challenges in their lives. Nonetheless, there is no mistaking the mission: we are committed to doing "whatever it takes" to get every student through college, a lesson rooted in our observation of what doesn't work in much of the existing system and the hard-won lessons of our own work.

## QUICKLY ADVOCATING FOR THE BEST SOLUTION FOR THE CHILD AND HIS FAMILY: A PARENT'S STORY

I met Mrs. Milton after we received a report about a parent with a chronically absent son in the first grade at one of our Promise Academy charter schools. We scheduled a meeting for Mrs. Milton with me, the principal, and Geoffrey Canada, the CEO of HCZ at the time.

It was immediately apparent that Mrs. Milton was overwhelmed. Her oldest son was living with her, as well as her four-year-old daughter. Three months prior, she had given birth to another boy.

We discussed with her how important it was for her son to come to school. We also talked about the importance of getting the four-year-old connected with our Harlem Gems' preschool. We even had the opportunity to connect her to our Baby College program and told her that we would help her work on her résumé.

This story highlights the management structure at HCZ that is essential to the organization's success: highly qualified managers and leaders who are very hands-on; a system in our schools that detects early warning signs; and a process for providing immediate access to services when a family is in need.

What happened next was an unfortunate but illustrative part of the story. While the mother was at the Baby College, a family worker noticed that the baby did not look as if he were thriving. Based on the reports we got, her first grader and the new Gems student both were still frequently absent and tardy. We got together as a full team and decided that we had to call the case into the Statewide

Central Register of Child Abuse and Maltreatment because the baby was not being fed properly. ACS went to the house to investigate and placed the children in foster care. The mother was devastated and, while we knew it was the right thing to do, many of the HCZ staff experienced secondary trauma.

Because of the good relationship we had with ACS, we were able to make sure that the kids were able to come back to the Promise Academy and the Gems program after a couple of weeks. That way they were with people they trusted and knew for a good part of the day. We kept the dialog with the mother open, even though she felt betrayed. Both Geoffrey and I decided to talk to her directly. We explained to her that we had to make sure that the kids were safe and that, as mandated reporters, if we felt the children were not safe, we were obligated to call it in.

We also explained that her kids would be back home one day and that we would work with her closely to make sure she received all the services and supports she needed so that she could be a stronger mom to them. Through the months that the children were in foster care, HCZ worked with the foster care agency, legal aid attorney, and lawyers for the children to be sure that not only did the mom get the mental health, parenting, and job-finding support that she needed, but that the children were able to keep in contact with her. After almost a year in care, the children came home. One of the first places the mother stopped when the kids came home was to visit Geoffrey and me. The HCZ family did not miss a beat: we gave her diapers, a gift card, a Metrocard for public transportation, and household items.

Mrs. Milton's story is not over, so we continue to support her and her kids. Her story illustrates the importance of having an HCZ in someone's life: an agency that is concerned about safety and security for children first but that is also able to strengthen families; an agency that provides support as needs change. It is this type of relationship with the students and families we serve and the preventive, ongoing nature of our work that is keeping kids safe. Last year, of more than 600 families served in our preventive programs that work directly with New York's child welfare agency, only 2.5% experienced a placement into foster care.

## BEING AN ONGOING SUPPORT SYSTEM FOR YOUTH: A STUDENT'S STORY

Another story that illustrates why the HCZ model is so important is that of Paul Ortiz (a pseudonym). Paul entered the HCZ Promise Academy in the sixth grade. While Paul was a good student, he seemed to get into trouble during and after school. Geoffrey mentored him in a martial-arts class, paying special attention to Paul.

As Paul went through school, he maintained a B average, but he became more rebellious, skipping school and smoking marijuana. His principal suggested that

Paul and his family be referred to HCZ's preventive services. Preventive services attempted to stabilize the family by helping them to learn how to negotiate the conflicts between Paul's need for independence and his parents' need to protect him.

One evening, past his curfew, he was hanging out with friends on the street when a car drove by and a shooter sprayed bullets into the crowd. Paul was hit in his arm. This happened on a Saturday night, but our staff was notified, and both Geoffrey and I got calls immediately.

We hoped that this would be a life-changing experience for Paul. It gave us the opportunity to show him what it was going to be like for him if he decided to choose the path we had been trying to keep him from. We met with him regularly and told him that we refused to lose him. We stood by him and his parents and got him to graduation day.

By the end of his first semester in college, though, Paul was put on probation for damaging school property after a late-night party. Under the coaching of staff at our College Success Office, Paul was able to write a letter of apology to school administrators. The school decided that while he could no longer stay in the dorms, he was able to stay in school.

By the second semester, his bad grades and his involvement in another incident led to the school asking Paul to leave for a year. We again used this experience to help Paul understand how his choices were related to the consequences. We learned in more, giving him the support needed to transfer to a new school. We connected him to a part-time job. While we addressed his needs, we held him accountable and made sure he knew we loved him.

As of this writing, he is now back in his original school, working part time and making better decisions. He tells us that he wants to go to medical school, and we know that we will always be a part of his family.

## OUR EVOLVING MANAGEMENT APPROACH

The way in which we built the HCZ project is as illuminating as the results. Our approach is influenced by the experience of HCZ's leadership, and our method constantly drives how we respond to the changing needs of Mrs. Milton, Paul, and other residents in the neighborhoods we serve. First, we know from experience that bringing about large-scale change means starting small. For example, we provided academic and college readiness supports to nearly 1,200 high schoolers in the 2013–2014 school year. We created "student advocates" to work with each student and monitor his or her progress in several areas through individualized action plans. Our advocates are assigned to a specific group of students, and case teams are structured around each youth and his or her family and school and community stakeholders. This practice, which we call academic case management, has allowed us to reach our overall program goals while meeting the singular needs of each child. Moreover, it has created an ongoing, effective process for bringing together the right internal team to tackle the toughest student and family cases.

Second, we have learned how to complement our rigorous data collection with management practices that stress accountability and lead staff to continually think about the work and how it can be improved. Our "Efforts to Outcome" database is customized to track the levels of our efforts, but also our results.

To improve the quality and consistency of our work, I initiated a regular internal program performance review process with staff that we call HCZ Stat, which was inspired by the Child Stat process at ACS. The HCZ Stat process serves as a critical lens through which senior staff can observe what is working and not working across our program sites and quickly put our collective expertise together and brainstorm potential solutions. HCZ Stat brings together leaders from our education, programmatic, evaluation, and other departments to review individual student data. It offers a forum in which our leadership can look at program-level data on attendance, grades, graduation, retention, and other topics, sharing agency-wide and case-specific observations and insights. It also allows staff from across our agency to strategize together to improve our work.

## SCALING WHAT WE LEARNED: BECOMING A NATIONAL MODEL

We know that Harlem is not the only neighborhood in need. Too many communities around the country have been mired in generational poverty and could benefit from a place-based, comprehensive long-term strategy like the HCZ model. For that reason, HCZ has been proud to serve as a blueprint for community development efforts around the country. In 2003, we founded the Practitioners Institute at HCZ to provide formal sharing for leaders across the country and around the world. In total, we have hosted groups from 68 countries around the world and 227 cities across the United States.

Fulfilling a campaign promise, President Barack Obama identified HCZ as the inspiration for the federal Promise Neighborhoods program. Beginning in 2010, this federal discretionary grant program has awarded over $200 million to nonprofits, institutes of higher learning, and tribal organizations who want to build coordinated supports in areas of concentrated poverty, using the familiar framework based on HCZ's cradle-to-college pipeline. HCZ joined PolicyLink in founding the Promise Neighborhoods Institute to support these grantees and others by codifying and sharing best practices in what it takes to transition neighborhoods on the brink into communities of sustainable opportunity. The Center for the Study of Social Policy has since joined us as a partner in this work.

Yet HCZ isn't a panacea that can be simply "dragged and dropped" onto struggling neighborhoods. Our work has been successful precisely because it was built from the ground up—rooted in the unique assets and challenges of Central Harlem, woven into the fabric of life in our community.

## CONCLUSIONS

The comprehensive HCZ model is a new paradigm for disrupting the intergenerational cycle of poverty and providing a pathway for more children to achieve the American dream. Moreover, it presents a proven, community-based model for moving from a reactive approach to a preventive one, and from sporadic interventions to ongoing support of children and their families. HCZ is also a flexible, constantly evolving organization, pivoting and expanding to meet the needs of its children and families as they arise over the years.

Our model is built on several important principles. We work with children from birth and stay with them until they graduate from college, putting in place a series of best-practice programs for each stage of a child's development. We work to strengthen families and the communities to make sure children are surrounded by adults who are equipped to keep children on track. We have created a culture of high expectations for both our staff and our participants—one in which success is the norm, not the exception. To ensure everyone is accountable, we rely on data to both guide and evaluate our programs. Lastly, we feel it is critical to bring the system to scale so the effort begins to match the pervasive extent of the problem across America.

Fifty years and billions of dollars after President Lyndon Johnson's war on poverty, the problem is still with us, leading many to believe it is hopeless. Having given up on these young people, society has shown its frustration by relying on short-sighted solutions such as building prisons—which are expensive and, by and large, produce no valuable outcomes—rather than on making the cost-effective investment in comprehensively supporting children so they can succeed.

The large-scale success of HCZ in a neighborhood that has been synonymous with intractable poverty gives us hope—and, more importantly, proof—that we can fix this. The success of our children and families has shown that with the right supports, all black and brown children can succeed—even those who come from vulnerable families and communities. By wrapping our arms around children of color and supporting their families as our trusted partners, we can reverse long-standing inequities in academic performance, health, and life trajectory.

While our model has been heralded as an innovation, at its core it is not. The "secret" to its success is hiding in plain sight: we make sure children have the resources they have in middle-class communities, we don't take our orders from rigid government policies, and we avoid bureaucracy that puts obstacles in the way of kids getting what they need. We find our answer in the community lifting itself up, and our approach reflects the belief that *every* community can and should build systems that give all its children a real and fair chance at fulfilling the American dream. It is our dream that HCZ's work will prove by example that there is a solution to generational poverty—one that is ultimately good for our children, our communities, and our country.

## DISCUSSION QUESTIONS

1. What are the advantages of a more proactive, comprehensive, and family-oriented approach when working with historically underserved minority youth?
2. To what extent are the specific individual strategies and leadership practices mentioned in this chapter applicable to your line of work or at your organization?

## REFERENCES

After-School Corporation. (2013, October). *The 6,000-hour learning gap.* Retrieved from http://www.expandedschools.org/policy-documents/6000-hour-learning-gap.

Chahine, Z., van Straaten, J., & Williams-Isom, A. (2005, April). The New York City neighborhood-based services strategy. *Child Welfare Journal, 84*(2), 141–152.

Citizens' Committee for Children of New York. (2008). *Keeping track of New York City's children, Appendix A.*

Citizens' Committee for Children of New York. (2011). *Keeping track online: Children born into poverty.* Retrieved from http://data.cccnewyork.org/profile/location/3/community-district#12/central-harlem/3/89/a/a.

Diverse Education. (2011, August). *Study: Minority, low-income students lack adequate access to educational opportunities.* Retrieved from http://diverseeducation.com/article/16180/.

Klass, P. (2013, May 13). Poverty as a childhood disease. *New York Times.* Retrieved from http://well.blogs.nytimes.com/2013/05/13/poverty-as-a-childhood-disease/.

National Center for Education Evaluation. (2011, April). *Do low-income students have equal access to the highest-performing teachers?* Retrieved from http://ies.ed.gov/ncee/pubs/20114016/pdf/20114016.pdf.

New York City Administration for Children's Services. (2012). *Report from Management and Outcome Reporting, Office of Management Analysis, Research, and Planning; Division of Policy, Planning, and Measurement.*

New York City Department of Health and Mental Hygiene. (2006). *Take Care Central Harlem. NYC community health profiles* (2nd ed.). Retrieved from http://www.nyc.gov/html/doh/downloads/pdf/data/2006chp-302.pdf.

Reardon, S. F. (2011). *The widening academic achievement gap between the rich and the poor: New evidence and possible explanations* (p. 1). Retrieved from http://cepa.

stanford.edu/content/widening-academic-achievement-gap-between-rich-and-poor-new-evidence-and-possible.

Tough, P. (2008). Graduation. In *Whatever it takes: Geoffrey Canada's quest to change Harlem and America* (pp. 254–255). Boston: Houghton Mifflin Co.

U.S. Census Bureau. (2012). *Work-life earnings by field of degree and occupation for people with a bachelor's degree: 2011.* Retrieved from http://www.census.gov/prod/2012pubs/acsbr11-04.pdf.

# CHAPTER 16

# A Racial Equity Staff Development Strategy for Public Human Service Organizations

CHRISTIANA BEST-GIACOMINI,
ALEXIS HOWARD, AND HENRY ILIAN

This chapter focuses on a staff development strategy that was implemented in a public child welfare organization in the northeastern part of the United States to address worker bias because it was believed that worker bias contributed to the disproportionality and disparate outcomes of people of color in this municipality. As cited in the United States Government Accountability Office (2007) report, caseworker bias directed at families and children in the child welfare system is one of many factors that contribute to high rates of disproportionality and disparity for people of color, particularly black children in the nation's child welfare system. The issue of worker bias resonated deeply with the authors because of their experience working in the child welfare system as well as narratives obtained from a focus group of child protective workers who were on the staff of a public child welfare organization while they were graduate students enrolled in a master of social work (MSW) program. The authors are not suggesting that worker bias exists in isolation of institutional and systemic racism. However, the existence of negative attitudes toward African American parents within the child welfare system is prevalent, as was found in a study of Michigan's child welfare system (Center for the Study of Social Policy, 2009), and it bears directly on attempts to alter attitudes. A large-scale investigation using qualitative methods found that the belief was prevalent within the child welfare system that African American children were better off away from their biological families (Center for the Study of Social Policy, 2009). Hence, the shared belief in the inferior parenting abilities of African Americans resulted in practices that worked against a strengths-based approach that would incorporate efforts to keep children at home. This underlying assumption is not far from the value beliefs that Billingsley and Giovannoni (1972) found existing over 30 years ago, a dominant belief shared by the wider society.

This chapter provides the reader with an understanding of the authors' planning, implementation, and evaluation of the staff development strategy. It also includes detailed descriptions of each workshop and the analysis of the evaluations presented in tables and figures.

## THE CHILD WELFARE CHANGE MODEL

A taskforce on disproportionality and disparity was convened at the public child welfare organization: the Racial Equity and Cultural Competence Task Force. Its members included a racially diverse representation of its staff and external stakeholders and other professionals committed to addressing and resolving the disparate treatment of people of color in the child welfare, juvenile justice, early care and education, and other systems. One of the charges of this committee was to inform training, hiring practices, organizational policies, and frontline practice where needed to ensure continuity and sustainability in promoting equitable outcomes for children, families, and staff. The taskforce facilitated "Undoing Racism" training by the People's Institute for Survival and Beyond for its members and the executive leadership of the public child welfare organization. Following the training, the taskforce organized a series of seminars for the organization's leadership regarding race, racism, and the child welfare system, bringing in local and national speakers with expertise in racial disproportionality and disparity. The purpose of these seminars was to build knowledge and educate taskforce members and other organizational leaders about racial disproportionality and disparity. Among the notable accomplishments of the taskforce was the push for the public child welfare organization to share data on disproportionality and disparity. The data are made available to the organization's staff and the child welfare community.

As the work of the taskforce on racial disproportionality and disparity evolved, so too did the work of the schools of social work in the region. In 2008 a notable university in the area hosted a conference on disproportionality and disparity featuring the author and researcher of the 2007 United States Government Accountability Office report (Hill, 2007); (U.S. GAO, 2007). , l The conference and GAO report provided many in the child welfare community and the schools of social work with data that substantiated what they knew anecdotally about the conditions of children of color in the child welfare system, nationally. In a debriefing among members of the taskforce following the 2008 conference, one of the managers remarked, "This is the information we need to do effective work with families." Another manager said, "This is a first for public child welfare to engage in discussions around race, oppression, structural racism and oppression of the oppressed; we need more."

The conference sparked enthusiasm and passion among practitioners, researchers and leaders in the child welfare community. This momentum within created a sense of eagerness to "do something." It pushed some members of the taskforce who were also members of the university–agency partnership to action, which led to the development and implementation of this staff development strategy.

## UNIVERSITY–AGENCY PARTNERSHIP COMMITTEE

The university–agency partnership committee is a staff development collaborative comprising the leadership of the public child welfare organization and the deans of the schools of social work in the region. This committee is an established partnership that focuses on the professionalization of child welfare services staff. The group convened a subcommittee to address issues of racial disproportionality and disparity using a staff development intervention/strategy. The subcommittee was chaired by three people who represented different racial and ethnic groups as well as the agency and university partnership. The subcommittee developed and implemented a staff development strategy that was designed for 60 child protective workers who were also MSW students attending one of the schools of social work while working for the public child welfare organization.

The rationale for the target population of the staff development strategy to be MSW student who were also child protective workers was twofold. First, this was a group for whom one of the authors and co-chairs was administratively responsible. Second, this group was identified as emerging leaders, given their anticipated career pathway within the organization.

## THE STAFF DEVELOPMENT STRATEGY

The staff development strategy had four goals:

- Train child welfare workers so they will become conscious of their practice from a racial equity perspective;
- Raise awareness of MSW/child protective workers on disproportionality and disparity;
- Educate MSW/child protective workers on issues of disproportionality and disparity; and
- Develop an online bibliography on racial disproportionality and disparity to address issues of sustainability.

The aim was to expose upcoming leaders to new ideas and understandings. The underlying belief was that making a new group of leaders aware of disproportionality and disparity would help to shape their practice today and in the future. The strategy was built on the assumption that these frontline practitioners would one day become leaders and would be able to influence their staff, colleagues, and many others in the child welfare system.

Students volunteered to work with the facilitators and chairpersons to share in the content and process of the workshops. This process gave them an opportunity to help identify the challenges they experience in engaging families. While the approach to staff development was based on the research around individual worker bias in child welfare, the proposed training framework incorporated an ecological structural perspective with the notion that each worker's decision-making processes are influenced by larger societal factors (Chisom & Washington, (1996). The strategy also incorporated a cultural humility perspective (Ortega & Fuller, 2011) in which the child welfare worker takes on the role of a learner about cultural experiences, which equalizes the power in the worker–client relationship.

The strategy consisted of four workshops over nine months, facilitated by consultants with expertise in racial equity and child welfare. Facilitators were selected based on their understanding of racism and its impact on oppressed communities as well as the effects of internalized racial oppression. The selected workshops included the following topics: (1) self-care and internalized oppression; (2) the cultural genogram; (3) skills and strategies for facilitating challenging discussions on race, power, and privilege in our work relationship; and (4) unpacking race at the family team conference meeting.

Following the workshop presentation, the MSW students/child protective workers were given an evaluation to complete. After each workshop, the facilitator engaged the participants in discussions because it was thought that some of the workshop contents might elicit emotional responses that the staff/students should process before returning to the workplace.

## PLANNING FOR THE WORKSHOPS

Planning for the workshops involved the use of themes that emerged from a focus group with MSW students from the previous year who were also staff members of the public child welfare agency. These themes were used to guide the workshop content.

The racial and ethnic demographics (race, ethnicity, culture) of the staff and the clients are very similar. But while there were many similarities between the client population and the students/staff, there were also biases. In the earlier focus groups, an MSW student/staff member commented, "part of the reason we returned to get advanced degrees is so we could move out of the community." This translated into: we struggled to achieve our education so we can get out of the community, and now we have to return for work. While some staff/students provided narratives of pride in having come from the community, others did not want to relive the memories of poverty. The issue of class as it relates to educational level and socioeconomic status creates some discomfort for the staff when working in poverty-stricken communities.

Another theme, the use and misuse of power and authority in worker–client interactions, was also an area illuminated by focus group participants. There were numerous narratives in which the use of power was influenced by biases and prejudices. An example of the use or misuse of power is the following comment:

> I went into my investigations with a baseball bat, ready to charge my clients because this was the only way I knew how to interview and get the information I needed to complete the interview. If they don't comply they are resistant with services, and will deal with me in court. This was the old me. My social work education has really encouraged me to self-reflect. If I was a client I would not have wanted myself as a worker back then.

## WORKSHOP #1: SELF-CARE AND INTERNALIZED OPPRESSION

Self-care as an intervention for child welfare staff is discussed in the literature. Child welfare staff is exposed to secondary trauma on a daily basis (Collins, 2009; National Child Traumatic Stress Network [NCTSN], 2008). In a study of New York City's Children's Service staff, symptoms of post-traumatic stress disorder were noted by 60% of staff exposed within the past week to a traumatic work experience, and 60% of staff reported symptoms of psychological distress (NCTSN, 2008). In addition to recurring exposure to trauma frequently encountered in their capacity as first responders who investigate allegations of child maltreatment, other negative job characteristics exist to these workforce members. These negative characteristics include high caseloads, mandated clients, work in potentially dangerous communities, an inflexible or unpredictable work schedule, and public scrutiny when a child is injured or a child fatality occurs.

While many child welfare leaders understand the need to provide organizational support to staff regarding self-care issues, there does not seem to be a connection for these leaders between self-care for staff and internalized racial oppression. Our planning for this workshop focused on this relationship, which we thought was particularly relevant for workers who are demographically similar to the clients they serve.

> Internalized racial oppression is the incorporation and acceptance by individuals within an oppressed group of the prejudices against them within the dominant society. Internalized oppression for the marginalized group is likely to consist of self-hatred, self-concealment, fear of violence, feelings of inferiority, resignation, isolation, powerlessness, and gratefulness for being allowed to survive. Internalized racial oppression is the mechanism within an oppressive system for perpetuating domination not only by external control but also by building subservience into the minds of the oppressed or marginalized groups. (Pheterson, 1986, p. 146)

The aim was to create an organizational climate in which conversations about internalized racial oppression were safe to express. The facilitator set the stage for staff to understand that working with traumatized populations is painful work. Time was spent on responses to trauma, which included detachment and how it manifests itself for us with our clients. Further exploration focused on how detachment translates into distancing ourselves from the families and devaluing the clients and families we work with. Exploration for staff occurred on what it is like for families to work with a helper who is detached or distant. The workshop also provided an opportunity for students to engage in self-reflection, or what Suarez, Newman and Reed (2008) refer to as the critical consciousness, necessary in social work practice.

With the facilitator's coaching, students explored the concepts and terms of oppression and internalized oppression and how structural and individual biases are demonstrated in the work. The public child welfare system, like many of the systems our families interface with, reinforces organizational oppression (Alliance for Racial Equity in Child Welfare, 2011), the same oppression that marginalized, vulnerable families deal with on a daily basis.

Discussions also focused on how oppression can be counteracted by making space for clients to be their own experts in the work, by truly examining the concept of authentic engagement, and by using the theoretical framework of empowering clients to engage in mutually agreed-upon goals (Altman, 2005).

## WORKSHOP #2: THE USE OF THE CULTURAL GENOGRAM AS AN EXPERIENTIAL WORKSHOP

The workshop on the cultural genogram (Hardy & Laszloffy, 1995, p. 232) was adapted by the workshop facilitator. The content of the cultural genogram is based on family systems work and was modified for the needs of the child welfare professional (Warde, 2012). It reintroduced the staff to the concept of a cultural being and their own cultural identity. The facilitator gave examples of his own professional journey and evolution as a cultural being.

The main goal of the cultural genogram is to raise cultural awareness and sensitivity by assisting trainees to understand their cultural identities. The aim was to help the students/staff gain insight into and appreciation of the ways in which culture impacts their role as child protective workers and influences the lives of clients they serve. The tool consists of a series of questions to promote self-reflection and to illuminate the influence culture has on the family system. It encouraged frank discussions that revealed and challenged culturally based assumptions and stereotypes. The aim was to assist the child protective workers in discovering their culturally based emotional triggers and to aid them in exploring how their cultural identities may impact their work style.

## WORKSHOP #3: SKILLS AND STRATEGIES FOR FACILITATING CHALLENGING DISCUSSION ON RACE, POWER, AND PRIVILEGE IN OUR WORK RELATIONSHIP

This workshop was designed to raise awareness of power, privilege, oppression, and their implications in the child welfare system. Its aim was to help child protective workers gain an in-depth understanding of diverse races, classes, and cultures. The workshop navigated some of the "-isms" that prevent us from truly caring for other human beings, while contributing to a balance of power and responsibility between the child protective workers and their clients. The content is grounded in an awareness of the complexities of intersectionality and our many positions within the larger society (Suarez, Newman, and Reed, 2008).

The workshop was also designed to focus on the power differential inherent in the child welfare worker role. The formal authority given to child protective workers or social workers in child welfare practice is full of complexities (De Jong, & Berg, 2001; Bundy-Fazioli, Briar-Lawson, & Hardiman, 2009; Waldfogel, 1998). This phenomenon of power within the worker (professional role) and client (consumer of service) is not a new concept within child welfare practice (Cohen, 1998). The workshop was tailored to meet the needs of workers for whom the professional role may have been the only position in which they ever experienced power.

The power and privilege workshop was grounded in an empowerment framework intended to be particularly relevant for this cohort of women who were predominately of color. Empowerment practice is a process grounded in feminist theory and has proven successful in increasing feelings of well-being for oppressed women (Goodman et al., 2007; Jager & Carolan, 2009; Perez, Johnson, & Wright, 2012). There is an emphasis on the combination of internal and external factors and the impact on women's well-being (Chadiha, Adams, Phorano, Ong-Ling, Byers, 2003; Worell, 2001), which reinforced the notion of self-care. Staff/students were actively engaged in numerous activities in which they moved around the room based on their individualized status in society. Facilitators identified the status categories (race, gender, religion, color, sexual orientation, educational level, socioeconomic level, and body ability), and participants moved into collectives based on their status. In these groups they discussed their common experiences, especially concerning their power or lack of it.

The facilitators highlighted that despite the internalized racial oppression that many of the workers experienced, in some situations they had power based on the context of the relationship or their position within society. Their job function may afford them power, or perhaps their religion, or perhaps their experiences; it was how they exercised this power that was important.

## WORKSHOP #4: UNPACKING RACE AT THE FAMILY TEAM CONFERENCE MEETING

This was the only workshop that aimed to develop skills focusing on a specific practice intervention, the family team conference. The family team conference model, also known as team decision making, is grounded in a strengths-based framework of practice (Child Welfare Policy and Practice Group, 2001). This practice intervention is based on respect for family differences and engagement in mutually defined goals despite the family's mandated status. Cultural differences are honored within a well-being framework while the worker assesses for risk and protective factors.

In incorporating a developmental approach to learning (Bennett, 1986), this workshop's rationale was to support the workers' newly gained insight and awareness and begin to apply their knowledge and skills to a specific practice intervention. A role-play was designed to illustrate sensitivity to culture, norms, and engagement using a culturally competent lens.

A facilitator with knowledge of the issue of racial disproportionality and disparity played the role of the family team conference facilitator and volunteers played family members and community representatives. Special attention was given to (1) accepting and respecting the family's culture, (2) using culture and exploring for strengths that may be culturally based, and (3) using knowledge of the family's culture to engage family members. Finally, participants who were observers during the role-play were engaged in examining structural influences can create barriers for families in the child welfare system.

## PARTICIPANTS' REACTIONS TO THE WORKSHOPS

Over 200 participants rated four of the six workshops using a specially constructed rating instrument supplied by one of the workshop developers, who was a consultant to the project. Responses were analyzed using SPSS version 20. Bar charts were created with Microsoft Excel. Across all sessions of the four workshops, a total of 215 participants completed rating instruments. The breakdown is shown in Table 16.1.

*Table 16.1* NUMBER OF PARTICIPANTS ATTENDING EACH WORKSHOP

| Workshop | N |
| --- | --- |
| Cultural Genogram | 55 |
| Self Care | 48 |
| Race, Power, and Privilege | 50 |
| Unpacking Race | 62 |

## DEMOGRAPHICS

The rating instrument asked about the participant's gender, whether the participant identified as a member of the majority culture, and whether he or she identified as a person of color. There was no specific question regarding ethnicity. Not
all participants provided answers for all questions. Aggregating all sessions of the
four workshops, 173 participants (93%) were female and 13 (7%) were male; 157
(85%) identified themselves as persons of color and 28 (15%) did not. Fifty-nine
(36%) identified themselves as being part of the majority culture, although some
participants told those collecting the rating instruments that they had associated
majority culture with religion; in this case, they were answering affirmatively because they were Christian. One hundred five (64%) did not see themselves as
part of majority culture.

## THE RATING INSTRUMENTS

There were two versions of a rating instrument used. These differed in the inclusion of a set of questions on the impact of the workshops on participants' interest
in exploring the issues presented and on motivators for exploring these issues,
and on the inclusion of six rather than five statements for participants to rate in
evaluating the impact of the workshops. The "Unpacking" workshop, which otherwise used the shorter version, included four questions on participants' readiness to apply the workshop content in the family team meeting. The other workshops used the longer one.

Both versions asked participants to respond to a series of statements relating
to the impact the workshop had on their involvement with the issues addressed.
The rating scale was anchored at the end points, and rating was on a continuum
from 1, "Very inaccurate" to 4, "Very accurate."

## RATINGS
### Understanding of Myself as a Cultural Being

The first item was "The Workshop helped me to examine or deepen my understanding of myself as a cultural being and implications for the workplace whether
I think about it all the time or never think about it." Ratings clustered between 3
and nearly 4, although those for the "Unpacking" workshop were lower than the
rest, with an average rating of slightly less than 3.1. This workshop received lower
ratings, on average, on all of the other items as well.

Across the workshops, these ratings indicate considerable agreement with
the statement, and the ratings for the "Internalized Racism" workshop received
the highest average, which was the case for all of the other statements as well.
Those who identified themselves as not of the majority culture tended to rate this

statement higher than those who identified with the majority culture across all
the workshops: 3.47 (103 raters) versus 3.22 (59 raters). This difference was statistically significant at $p < .05$ [$t = 2.151$; $df = 160$; $p = .032$ (two-tailed)]. A one-
way between-subjects ANOVA was conducted to compare the effect of the different workshops on ratings for this item. There was a significant effect at the $p <$
.05 level for the four workshops: [$F(3, 212) = 11.461, p = .000$]. Post hoc comparisons using the SPSS Tukey B procedure found statistically significant differences
at the $p < .05$ level between, on the one hand, the "Race, Power, and Privilege
(RPP)" and "Internalized" workshops and, on the other hand, the "Unpacking"
and "Cultural" workshops. The average ratings are displayed in Figure 16.1.

## Own Power and Privilege

The next item stated "The Workshop helped me to identify and/or further reflect
upon my own power and privilege and implications for the workplace whether
I think about it all the time or never think about it." As the bar chart shows, the
"Internalized" and "RPP" workshops averaged considerably higher than the
"Cultural" and "Unpacking" ones. The differences between those identifying
themselves as majority (3.19, 59 raters) and nonmajority (3.35, 103 raters) were
not statistically significant at $p < .05$ [$t = 1.446$; $df = 160$; $p = .150$ (two-tailed)].
A one-way between-subjects ANOVA was conducted to compare the effect of the
different workshops on ratings for this item. There was a significant effect at the $p <$
.05 level for the four workshops [$F(3, 211) = 9.104, p = .000$]. As with the preceding
item, post hoc comparisons using the SPSS Tukey B procedure found statistically
significant differences at the $p < .05$ level between, between, on the one hand, the

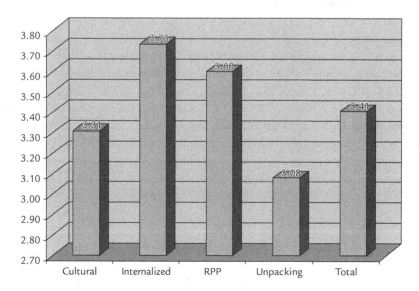

**Figure 16.1:** Understanding of Myself as a Cultural Being.

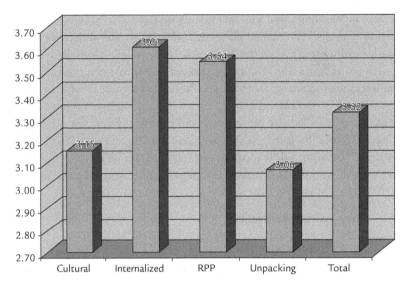

**Figure 16.2:** Own Power and Privilege.

"RPP" and "Internalized" workshops and, on the other hand, the "Unpacking" and "Cultural" ones. The average ratings are displayed in Figure 16.2.

## Own Values, Beliefs, and Attitudes

The third item was "The Workshop helped me to identify and/or further reflect upon my own values, beliefs and attitudes and implications for the workplace whether I think about it all the time or never think about it." Again, the ratings for the "Internalized" and "RPP" workshops were higher than for the other two, and the average for the "Unpacking" workshop was below the rest. With this item also, those who identified themselves as not of the majority culture tended to rate this statement higher across all four workshops than those who identified with the majority culture: 3.46 (103 raters) versus 3.22 (59 raters). This difference was statistically significant at $p < .05$ ($t = 2.106$; $df = 159$; $p = .037$). A one-way between-subjects ANOVA compared the effect of the individual workshops on ratings for this item. There was a significant effect at the $p < .05$ level for the four workshops [$F(3, 211) = 7.190$, $p = .000$]. Post hoc comparisons using the SPSS Tukey B procedure found statistically significant differences at the $p < .05$ level between the "Unpacking" workshop and the other three. The average ratings are displayed in Figure 16.3.

## Own Biases, Prejudices, and Assumptions

The fourth item was "The Workshop helped me to identify and/or further reflect upon my own biases, prejudices, and assumptions and implications for the

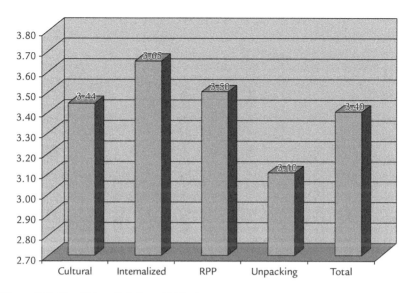

**Figure 16.3:** Own Values, Beliefs, and Attitudes.

workplace whether I think about it all the time or never think about it." As with the other questions, the ratings for the "Unpacking" workshop were lower than the others, with average ratings just above 3.0. With this item again, those who identified themselves as not of the majority culture tended to rate this statement higher than those who identified with the majority culture: 3.41 (103 raters) versus 3.14 (59 raters). This difference was statistically significant at $p < .05$ ($t = 2.328$; $df = 159$; $p = .021$). A one-way ANOVA compared ratings on this item across the workshops. There was a significant effect at the $p < .05$ level for the four workshops [$F(3, 211) = 9.258$, $p = .000$]. Post hoc comparisons using the SPSS Tukey B procedure found statistically significant differences at the $p < .05$ level between, on the one hand, the "Unpacking" workshop and, on the other hand, the "RPP" and "Internalized" workshops. The "Cultural" workshop showed no statistically significant differences with any of the others. Average ratings on this item are displayed in Figure 16.4.

## Multiple Identities

The fifth item was "The Workshop helped me to begin to explore or further explore the effects of my multiple identities and implications for the workplace whether I think about it all the time or never think about it." This item was not included in the rating instrument for the "Unpacking" workshop. The averages on this item were in line with the preceding ones. The average of 3.22 (36 raters) for those who identified with the majority culture was lower than the 3.37 (75 raters) for those who identified as nonmajority. This difference was not statistically significant at $p < 0.05$ ($t = 1.081$; $df = 109$; $p = .282$). A one-way between-subjects

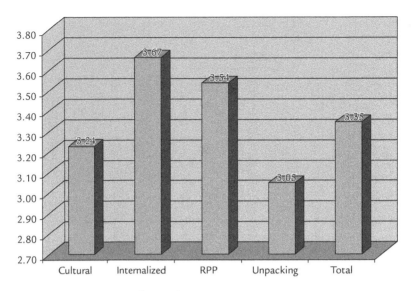

**Figure 16.4:** Own Biases, Prejudices, and Assumptions.

ANOVA was conducted to compare ratings on this item across the workshops workshops. There was a significant effect at the $p < .05$ level for the three workshops $[F(2, 151) = 7.488, p = .001]$. Post hoc comparisons using the SPSS Tukey B procedure found statistically significant differences at the $p < .05$ level between the "Unpacking" and "Cultural" and "RPP" and "Internalized" workshops. The average ratings are displayed in Figure 16.5.

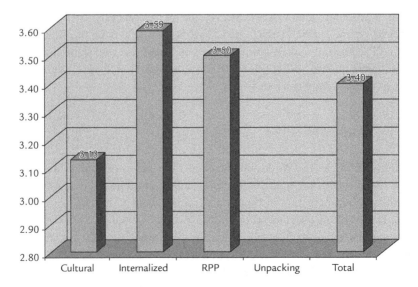

**Figure 16.5:** My Multiple Identities.

### Effectiveness in Working in an Increasingly Diverse and Global Society

The final common item on workshop content was "The Workshop helped me to further develop my effectiveness in working in an increasingly diverse and global society regardless of my prior experience." Women tended to rate this item higher than men (3.41 vs. 3.0), although there were only 13 men who responded as opposed to 170 women. This difference was statistically significant at $p < .05$ ($t = 2.058$; $df = 181$; $p = .041$).

As with the other workshops, those who identified themselves as nonmajority tended to give higher ratings, 3.40 versus 3.22. This difference was not statistically significant at $p < .05$ ($t = 1.540$; $df = 159$; $p = .126$). Again, a one-way between-subjects ANOVA was conducted to compare ratings on this item across the workshops. There was a significant effect at the $p < .05$ level for the four workshops [$F(3, 210) = 4.365$, $p = .005$]. Post hoc comparisons using the SPSS Tukey B procedure found statistically significant differences at the $p < .05$ level between the "Unpacking" workshop and the "RPP" and "Internalized" workshops. The differences between the "Cultural" workshop and the others were not statistically significant. The average ratings are displayed in Figure 16.6.

### Participants' Awareness of and Concern with the Issues Addressed

The rating instrument used with the "RPP," "Cultural," and "Internalized" workshops included an item made up of a series of statements reflecting participants'

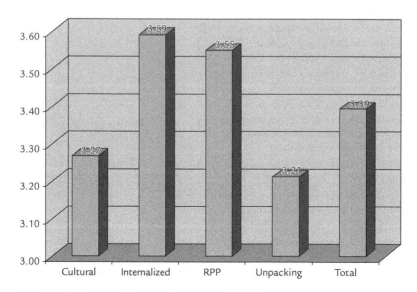

**Figure 16.6:** Working in an Increasingly Diverse and Global Society.

awareness of and concern with the issues addressed before and after the workshops. In all, there were 155 rating instruments from these three workshops. Participants were asked to select one of these statements, but 21 did not select any and 33 selected more than one.

The questions fell into two groups. The first looked at how often participants thought about the issues presented in the workshops (Table 16.2) and the second concerned reasons why the issues were important to them (Table 16.3). Of the 134 participants who provided answers to this section, 111 (83%) answered the items regarding how important the issues were to them and 102 (76%) answered the items that addressed why they were important. As Table 16.2 shows, nearly half of those answering the "How Often" items chose "Before today, I thought about these issues some of the time but this workshop helped me to identify new issues I don't usually think about," and only a few ($n = 8$) had not previously thought about the issues. It is possible that many of those not answering also had not given much thought to the issues.

The statements selected suggest that these issues were very much on the minds of participants both before and as a result of the workshops. Only 12 of the responses (representing only nine persons) were to statements indicating lack of interest in the issues addressed. The rest, as Table 16.2 shows, chose statements that indicated that these issues were on their minds either some or all of the time.

*Table 16.2* HOW OFTEN PARTICIPANTS THOUGHT ABOUT ISSUES

|  | Number of Responses | Percent of Responses | Percent of Participants |
|---|---|---|---|
| Before today, I never really thought about these issues. | 8 | 7.21% | 5.97% |
| Before today, I never really thought about these issues and I don't really see how they're relevant to workplace roles, tasks and relationships. After today, I don't really see myself continuing to explore them. | 4 | 3.60% | 2.99% |
| Before today, I never really thought about these issues but I now understand how important they are to workplace roles, tasks and relationships and I will continue to explore them. | 16 | 14.41% | 11.94% |
| Before today, I thought about these issues some of the time. | 16 | 14.41% | 11.94% |
| Before today, I thought about these issues some of the time but this workshop helped me to identify new issues I don't usually think about. | 53 | 47.75% | 39.55% |
| Before today, I thought about these issues all of the time. | 14 | 12.61% | 10.45% |
| **Total** | 111 | 100.00% | 82.84% |

*Table 16.3* WHY ISSUES IMPORTANT

| | Number of Responses | Percent of Responses | Percent of Participants |
|---|---|---|---|
| Before today, I thought about these issues all of the time because of who I am as a cultural being. | 27 | 26.47% | 20.15% |
| Before today, I thought about these issues all of the time because of the work that I do. | 30 | 29.41% | 22.39% |
| Before today, I thought about some of these issues all of the time but now I will think about others to pertain to who I am as a cultural being and issues of power and privilege. | 45 | 44.12% | 33.58% |
| **Total** | 102 | 100.00% | 76.12% |

Identifying or not identifying as a person of color had no statistically significant effect on whether items were chosen.

The most frequent response to why the issues presented were important to participants was the third option, (See Table 16.3) that some of the issues presented were previously on the participant's mind all of the time but now he or she will think about other issues pertaining to himself or herself as a cultural being and to issues of power and privilege.

## DISCUSSION

### Participants' Responses to the Workshops

Our ability to derive lessons from the evaluation instruments used for these workshops is somewhat undercut by the use of two instruments and also by lack of a question on ethnicity. The latter omission is somewhat compensated by the question on identification with the majority culture, which may actually be the more relevant question when it comes to people's experience of race. It would also have been helpful to know how long workshop participants had practiced in child welfare before entering their master's programs.

The average ratings for the four workshops were all in the same order. "Internalized" received the highest ratings, followed by "RPP," "Cultural," and "Unpacking." With most of the statements, the differences among the workshops held up statistically, although, since this was not a random sample, the statistical results should be taken as suggestive rather than in any way definitive. It is, nevertheless, noteworthy that those who identified themselves as not belonging to the majority culture tended to give higher ratings, although the differences were not in all cases statistically significant.

There appear to be two lessons in this. First, content that most directly addresses the experiences of frontline workers regarding issues of race and class (in this case, MSW students, predominantly female and predominantly persons of color, who have come from frontline practice) is highly valued by these workers. This is buttressed by comments that were offered that often displayed a high degree of discomfort in working with mandated clients who are poor and live in unpleasant surroundings in dangerous neighborhoods, with race as the unspoken subtext. Second, content aimed toward preparing frontline workers to apply insights around race in the child welfare system, even workers who have been exposed to social work content and skills in a master's program, may need a different kind of presentation than was offered in the "Unpacking" workshop.

## Lessons Learned

Over the course of the implementation of this model, several critical lessons were learned. Each contains implications for action-oriented interventions on multiple levels: the individual level, the collective workforce level, and the organizational level.

### Internalized Racial Oppression

Addressing the pain associated with internalized racial oppression for this cohort of public child welfare workforce members became a core element woven throughout all of the workshops. Themes generated from the cohort were clearly linked to their perceived feelings of oppression, particularly relevant for students with racial and ethnic origins within the African diaspora.

An abundance of literature speaks to the complexities of internalized racial oppression and the potential impact of this oppression on one's emotional well-being (Bailey, Chung, Williams, Singh, and Terrell, 2011; Brave Heart Chase, Elkins, and Altschul, 2011; Pyke, 2010; Rosenwasser, 2002; Utsey, Ponterotto, Reynolds, and Cancelli, 2000). What became evident during the workshops was how this oppression was unconsciously embedded in the day-to-day practice. It was essentially a part of the interpersonal domain of the worker–client relationship. Hence, while much attention has historically been given to training and educating child welfare staff on the skills of engagement, there was seemingly a gap in addressing the position of power, the emotionality of power, and the relevance of internalized racial oppression. These factors seem significant in effectively engaging families in the child welfare system from oppressed communities. While workers expressed knowing the skills, little attention was given to the underlying internalized racial oppression, which can create barriers to engagement.

As greater trust was developed, the students were able to engage in a reflective process about the manifestation of their own internalized racial oppression. They examined the ways in which their often negative perceptions of families resulted in blaming families, and how these perceptions may impede engagement. As students became increasingly aware of internalized racial oppression and its impact, they were able to hear their own use of oppressive language, specifically in how they articulated and reinforced the national narrative of "pull yourself up by your bootstraps." This narrative was reinforced when they blamed families for being poor, and when they used this narrative as a yardstick by which to measure members of the community who were unable to accumulate economic status. This increased awareness made them able to analyze their use of authorized power.

Experiential learning was a critical element in helping to unpack the emotionally laden material. The experiential process allowed them to gain power over their learning by engaging in a participatory approach to learning and processing new knowledge (Dickson, Jepsen, & Barbee, 2008). Being able to gently challenge individual biases was a developmental process, and the less-than-traditional approach to staff development was introduced at the time when the students were undergoing a transition into their professional formation. They were being exposed to a mindfulness practice in the schools of social work and became more familiar with engagement in a self-reflective practice.

### Group Identity

The group experience of being a part of a workforce with a collective attachment to historical and structural racism and trauma is a complex lesson learned on the group level. Brave Heart and colleagues (2011) describe the implications for group members impacted by historical trauma, which is notably experienced by many oppressed groups. This workforce cohort made us aware that they too identified as a stigmatized group by their group identification as members of an oppressed group.

The members of this cohort, while forming a professional identity as new MSWs, were always aware of their personal identity as members of an oppressed group with similar group identification to the communities they served. However, rather than align with the communities they served—who were in many respects demographically similar to themselves—they emotionally distanced themselves from these communities. They initially only spoke of those aspects of their group identity that they perceived as distinctively different from the communities they served (i.e., their educational level, their professional status, and other achieved statuses).

Much like internalized racial oppression, the emotional impact of dealing with people who belong to the same race and ethnicity as oneself but may be engaged in activities that are viewed by society in a negative way contributes to emotional distancing. According to Goffman (1963), individuals from the stigmatized group experience some ambivalence in their identity, particularly when they witness people from their own group behaving in a stereotypical way that can be considered acting out the negative attributes that were ascribed to them by the wider society. Further, as individuals from the stereotyped group observe their group members engaged in the perceived negative behaviors, they often reject them by distancing themselves from them (Goffman, 1963).

We observed this protective factor—distancing themselves from their clients—employed by the participants collectively. The students expressed their lack of humanity in the work frequently; indeed, it became a constant theme. Viewing the clients as "numbers" and depersonalizing them were analyzed as aspects of the emotional distancing. When the families are racially similar to the workers and are seen as engaging in negative or stereotypical behaviors (e.g., abusing or neglecting children, substance abuse, domestic violence), one can make a case for emotional distancing as presented by Goffman (1963). As the students evolved throughout the training, the discussions began to focus on the similarities of their stories and national narrative—the idea that they too had "pulled themselves up" by entering MSW programs. As we probed further, we examined what supports were in place and how they as agents of change could help families identify or gain similar supports toward achieving life goals.

### The Organizational "Space"

How does the internalized oppression and collective trauma of a workforce play out in organizational life? As the students gained awareness, they gradually identified how the dominant ideology was embedded in the fabric of the organizational life. Over time, the students as a collective cohort realized that an organizational "space" was needed where discussions of racially equitable practices could occur. This concept of space, both figuratively and literally, was essential to any proposed sustainability plan for the transfer of knowledge to occur. The students called attention to the different agency practices used when dealing with families of a certain race, status, and/or perceived power. Hence, families with child protective cases who are from the dominant race, particularly those who are professionals, who reside in middle-class and upper-middle-class neighborhoods, who are educated, or who have some social capital, are treated differently and have better outcomes than those who are from oppressed groups, are poor, are uneducated, or live in communities that have high rates of crime. The poor families were often not told what their rights are; in fact, so that child protective workers can to do their jobs expediently and without any barriers, their rights were sometimes overlooked or not respected. Child protective workers are given the message, both from agency practices and procedures and from their own internalized racial oppression, that they should precede with caution when dealing with privileged groups. The child protective investigations are sometimes disrupted by private attorneys who inform their clients of their rights—specifically, they do not have to speak to the child protective workers—or these attorneys contact the supervisor and upper management directly to attempt to intervene on behalf of their clients. Consequently, clients who exercise their rights interfere with the routine ways investigations are conducted. Therefore, for the most part, clients belonging to privileged groups have their rights recognized by the agency. This dual agency practice was a constant theme that was described and shared by the staff.

As MSW students, the staff were in the midst of learning about social work values such as social justice and racial equity. However, their education was occurring outside of the organizational context. Therefore, the university–agency partnership which facilitated the trainings, which the public child welfare organization sponsored, spoke volumes in terms of organizational priorities. The message heard by the cohort was that the organization was taking responsibility for their development of equitable practice. As hooks (2003) notes, the organization was going beyond engaging in a critical conversation and moving toward a liberating conversation.

Moving in this direction of liberation meant that the organization must create a space to sustain an equitable practice. Students, as emerging leaders, were engaging in critical liberating discussions about how the practices they deemed discriminatory were core practices of the larger societal structures. Hence, by training identified emerging talent within the organization, we were attempting to employ, as Freire (2010) described, a new cohort of emerging leaders with an awareness of internalized racial oppression who were prepared to intervene against oppression on both micro and macro levels.

## DISCUSSION QUESTIONS

1. Systemic discrimination/racism can be described as patterns of behavior, policies or practices that are part of the structures of an organization, and which perpetuate advantages to people of European decent and disadvantages for people of color, particularly Black and Native American families, How can organizations like the northeastern child welfare organization discussed in this chapter, address systemic racism in a comprehensive way?

   a. What can be done to change organizational culture in regards to achieving racial equity?

2. Implicit bias refers to the attitudes or stereotypes that affect our under-standing, actions, and decisions in an unconscious manner. What are some other strategies organizations can use to raise awareness of the existence of unconscious bias?

3. This chapter described a staff development model that focused on MSW grad-uate students in increasing their awareness of a racial equitable child welfare practice. What aspects of the model can be transferred and used in other prac-tice setting?

## REFERENCES

Alliance for Racial Equity in Child Welfare. (2011, December). *Disparities and dispro-portionality in child welfare: Analysis of the research.* Available at www.cssp.org/publications/child-welfare/alliance/Disparities-and.Disproportionality in child welfare.

Altman, J. (2005). Engagement in children, youth, and family services: Current re-search and promising approaches. In G. P. Mallon & P. M. Hess (Eds.), *Child wel-fare for the 21st century: A handbook of practices, policies and programs* (pp. 72–86). New York: Columbia University Press.

Bailey, T. M., Chung, Y. B., Williams, W. S., Singh, A. A., & Terrell, H. K. (2011). Development and validation of the internalized racial oppression scale for black in-dividuals. *Journal of Counseling Psychology, 58*(4), 481–493.

Bennett, M. J. (1986). A developmental approach to training for intercultural sensitivity. *International Journal of Intercultural Relations* (Special Issue: Theories and Methods in Cross-Cultural Orientation), *10*(2), 179–196.

Billingsley, A., & Giovannoni, J. (1972). *Children of the storm: Black children and American child welfare.* New York: Harcourt Brace Jovanovich.

Brave Heart, M. Y. H., Chase, J., Elkins, J., & Altschul, D. B. (2011). Historical trauma among indigenous peoples of the Americas: Concepts, research, and clinical consid-erations. *Journal of Psychoactive Drugs, 43*(4), 282–290.

Bundy-Fazioli, K., Briar-Lawson, K., & Hardiman, E. R. (2009). A qualitative examination of power between child welfare workers and parents. *British Journal of Social Work, 39*(8), 1447–1464.

Center for the Study of Social Policy. (2009). *Race equity review: Findings from a qualitative analysis of racial disproportionality and disparity in Michigan's child welfare system.*

Chadiha, L A. Adams, P., Phorano, O., Ong-Ling, S.L., Byers, L. (2003). Stories told and les-sons learned from African-American female caregivers' vignettes for empowerment practice. *Journal of Gerontological Social Work, 40*(1–2), 135–144.

Child Welfare Policy and Practice Group. (2001). *Family team conferencing.* Available at http://www.childwelfaregroup.org/documents/FTC_History.pdf; downloaded 11/14/14.

Chisom, R., & Washington, M. (1996). *Undoing racism: A philosophy of international social change.* Northern Kentucky University.

Cohen, M. (1998). Perceptions of power in client/worker relationships. *Families in Society: The Journal of Contemporary Social Services. 79,* (4), 433–442

Collins, J. (2009). *Addressing Secondary Traumatic Stress: Emerging Approaches in child wel-fare.* Child Welfare League of America.

De Jong, P., & Berg, I. K. (2001). Co-constructing cooperation with mandated clients. *Social Work*, 46(4), 361–374.

Dickson, G. L., Jepsen, D. A., & Barbee, P. W. (2008). Exploring the relationships among multicultural training experiences and attitudes toward diversity among counseling students. *Multicultural Counseling and Development*, 36, 113–126.

Freire, P. (2010). *Pedagogy of the oppressed*. New York: The Continuum International Publishing Group, Inc.

General Accounting Office. (2007). *African American children in foster care: Additional assistance needed to help states reduce the proportion in care*. Washington, DC: GAO.

Goffman, E. (1963). *Stigma: Notes on the management of spoiled identity*. Englewood Cliffs, NJ: Prentice-Hall Inc.

Goodman, L. A., Litwin, A., Bohlig, A., Weintraub, S. R., Green, A., Walker, J., & Ryan, N. (2007).Applying feminist theory to community practice: A multilevel empowerment intervention for low-income women with depression. In E. Aldarando (Ed.), *Promoting social justice through mental health practice* (pp. 265–290). Florence, KY: Lawrence Erlbaum.

Hardy, K. V. and Laszloffy, T. A. (1995). The cultural genogram: Key to training culturally competent family therapists. *Journal of Marital and Family Therapy*, 21 (3), 227–237.

Hill, R. B. (2007, Nov. 16). *Reducing disproportionality in child welfare*. Presentation to the Columbia University School of Social Work Forum.

hooks, b. (2003). *Teaching community: A pedagogy of hope*. New York: Routledge.

Jager, K. B., & Carolan, M. T. (2009). Locating community in women's experiences of trauma, recovery, and empowerment. *Qualitative Inquiry*, 15(2), 297–307.

National Child Traumatic Stress Network. (2008). Policy Brief: Workforce Strategies. Retrieved from http://www.nctsnet.org/about-us/national-center.

Okazaki, S. (2009). Impact of racism on ethnic minority mental health. *Perspectives on Psychological Science*, 4(1) 103–107.

Ortega, R. & Fuller, K.C. (2011). Training child welfare workers from an intersectional cultural humility perspective: A paradigm shift. *Child Welfare*, 90(5), 27–50.

Perez, S., Johnson, D. M., & Wright, C. V. (2012). The attenuating effect of empowerment on IPV-related PTSD symptoms in battered women living in domestic violence shelters. *Violence Against Women*, 18(1), 102–117.

Pheterson, G. (1986). Alliances between women: Overcoming internalized oppression and internalized domination. *Signs*, 12(1), 146–160.

Pyke, K. D. (2010). What is internalized racial oppression and why don't we study it? Acknowledging racism's hidden injuries. *Sociological Perspectives*, 53(4), 551–572.

Rosenwasser, P. (2002). Exploring internalized oppression and healing strategies. *New Directions for Adult and Continuing Education*, 94, 53–61.

Suárez, Z., Newman, P., & Reed, B. G. (2008). Critical consciousness and cross-cultural/intersectional social work practice: A case analysis. *Families in Society: The Journal of Contemporary Social Services*, 89(3), 407–417.

Supervision practices to impact disproportionality with African American clients in child welfare. *Protecting Children*, 25(1), 99–108. Available at http://www.ucdenver.edu/academics/colleges/medicalschool/departments/pediatrics/subs/can/disparities/From%20Old%20Site/assets/docs/bridging-the-cultural.pdf; downloaded 11/10/14.

United States Government Accountability Office (2007). African American children in foster care (GAO-07-816).

Utsey, S. O., Ponterotto, J. G., Reynolds, A. L., & Cancelli, A. A. (2000). Racial discrimination, coping, life satisfaction and self-esteem among African Americans. *Journal of Counseling and Development*, 78(1), 72–80.

Waldfogel, J. (1998). *The future of child protection*. Cambridge, MA: Harvard University Press.

Warde, B. (2012). The cultural genogram: Enhancing the cultural competency of social work students. *Social Work Education, 31*(5), 570–586.

Worell, J. (2001). Feminist interventions: Accountability beyond symptom reduction. *Psychology of Women Quarterly, 25*(4), 335–343.

# CLOSING THOUGHTS FROM
# THE EDITORS

## ALMA J. CARTEN, ALAN SISKIND,
## AND MARY PENDER GREENE·

The President of the United States, in commenting on the nation's continuing struggle with race, remarked that racism is deeply rooted in American history and DNA. The U.S. Supreme Court invalidated a component of the 1965 Voting Rights Act, ruling that it did not take into account the nation's progress on matters of race. Large numbers of whites recently marched with blacks in protest of the shooting of unarmed African American males by white police officers. But, as routinely asserted by master trainers of the "Undoing Racism" workshop, most white Americans are oblivious to the ways in which race shapes every aspect of their personal lives, including where they live, worship, work, and play.

The easy coexistence of these disparate views reflects the perplexing, paradoxical pieces of the puzzle that have shaped American culture on matters of race. When looking toward the future, the millennials, the generation of Americans born after 1981, have been reported as the most racially tolerant generation in U.S. history. Yet a video recently surfaced on social media of members of a white college fraternity chanting racial slurs, and the Pew Research Center has found that white millennials hold similar views on race as the older generation; while they see themselves as racially progressive, they are less willing to express these views publicly. Taken together, these contradictions on matters of race indicate that the work is far from done. America, and the field of health and human services, will continue to grapple with vexing matters of race in the coming years.

While preparing this book we have witnessed events that dramatically illustrate the indelible mark of racism on American culture. Perhaps one of the most tragic of these was the Charleston church massacre and murder of nine African Americans by a self-proclaimed white supremacist with the intention of igniting a race war. President Obama's eulogy for the victims is an example of what we have referred to in this book as "speaking truth to power." The eulogy will become a part of the historical record documenting the changing face and the tenacity with which doctrines of white supremacy have persisted in America for future generations to reflect upon.

Other recent events that have implications for the health and human services are the Supreme Court's rulings on the Patient Protection and Affordable Health Care Act (ACA) and same-sex marriage. The court's ruling not to end the subsidies ensures that this vital safety net will continue for Americans who need them. It underscored that health care is a right for all Americans, and health care coverage will continue to the special populations discussed by some of the authors in this book. The Court's ruling on same-sex marriage ends the tradition of "othering" the LGBT community, whose members now have the right to marry whomever they love—as do all other Americans. The National Association of Social Workers was among the organizations that signed on to the American Psychological Association's amicus brief sent to the Supreme Court documenting that there was no scientific evidence to support claims that same-sex marriages undermines the institution of family and is harmful to children.

We know from history that these progressive policy advances will evoke backlash. And the current national discourse on immigration reveals the country's feelings of nativism, now overlain with racism, and suggests that gaining consensus on immigration reform is far off.

Nonetheless, we hold to the optimism with which the book was undertaken. This optimism was based on the success of New York City's experience with bringing the People's Institute for Survival and Beyond's "Undoing Racism" workshop to health and human service providers and academic communities. We concede that the success of this undertaking was due in part to the city's history of interracial cooperation, progressive and liberal social policy development, combined with a similar strong historic collaborative partnership between the public and private health and human service sectors. The city is also distinguished for being at the forefront in the development of pioneering programs. These include the creation of racial and ethnic equity in the awarding of government provider contracts to not-for-profit agencies, and the spawning of minority-governed agencies and ethnic professional and advocacy associations. Currently, men and women of color are employed in the city's social welfare infrastructure in executive-level positions in the not-for-profit sector and as commissioners in city government, and New York City's mayor has embarked on a reform agenda to address the social and economic inequalities that are the root cause of the racial and ethnic disparities observed in all fields of practice in the health and human services in New York and across the nation.

We recognize that other social service jurisdictions located in states that favor a conservative social agenda in conducting health and human service programs may not enjoy these benefits that contributed to the success of New York's experience. We call attention to the success of the Texas experience, as outlined in the foreword to this book by Joyce James, who provided leadership to the statewide initiative. Texas, which is counted among the nation's conservative states, implemented a reform agenda anchored in antiracist principles that resulted in the virtual transformation of the state child welfare system. It became a national model for addressing the racial disproportionality that was pervasive in the nation's foster care system.

The primary purpose of the book was to disseminate information about lessons learned from the New York City experience to a national health and human service audience. Some of these lessons we believed might be replicated in other jurisdictions. Other goals were to encourage cross-racial dialogs and add to the literature on antiracist strategies as one way of closing the ethnic and racial disparities in the health and human services. In reviewing the book, we are confident that it makes a significant contribution to the literature on antiracist/culturally competent approaches for the health and human services. The book seems to raise more questions than it answers, which we interpret as a success. The individual chapters mirror the diverse points of view that in racial dialogs are axiomatic. For example, in Part One, which examines the organizational context, the authors for the most part consider the issues exclusively through the lens of race and eschew the colorblindness that is embedded in Dr. King's iconic *I Have a Dream* speech, in which he envisioned an America in which people are judged not by the color of their skin but by the content of their character. For these authors a colorblind approach denies the significance of race and results in a justification and entrenchment of race-based discrimination. In subsequent chapters, the authors suggest that with the increasing diversity of the country's cultural landscape, matters of race are no longer a binary black/white dialog. They argue that the potential for solving complex social problems for which consumers seek help is enhanced when helping professionals actively seek to build cross-cultural affinity teams and embrace diversity and multiculturalism to create new opportunities for innovation and positive change in organizational and program development. Acknowledging the salience of race, still others suggest that race alone is too narrow of a lens and fails to acknowledge other characteristics that intensify or mitigate the stigmatizing effects of race; they advance a rationale for a culturally competent research system.

It is a fair appraisal that all of the authors agree that the nation's health and human service system, like all other American institutions, reflects the traditions, values, and customs of the host society—and in Americann society, the inequitable treatment of individuals identified as "the other" cannot be ignored. The discussion in each chapter directly and indirectly speaks to the social control function of social welfare systems, which have as one of their main tasks controlling deviance and rehabilitating those individuals who are likely viewed as "the other" and whose behavior is subsequently determined to be inconsistent with socially constructed behavioral norms. The authors considering the situations of special populations argue that too often past efforts, sometimes well intentioned, have done more harm than good, and offer alternative empirically tested, corrective front-end preventive approaches. They assert that these race-conscious approaches have the potential to reverse the harmful effects of culturally incompetent interventions that were actually repressive forms of social control that aimed to maintain the status quo. Authors encourage practitioners to "know thyself" in an examination of the effects of transference and countertransference that can distort the interaction in the helping alliance at any stage of the helping process. They also offer clear guidelines for engaging in productive, nondefensive cross-racial dialogs.

The book ends with a description of what we believe are exemplary programs in the private and public sectors. These are data driven and illustrate that the "personal is political" and that it is possible to change organizations and practice where there is the political will and committed leaderss who are willing to step off the trodden path. With a motto of "success is the only option," the not-for-profit agency is promoted by the President of the United States as worthy for consideration as a national model for replication to break the cycle of poverty and transform the lives and communities of low-income children of color and their families. The change model used by the public sector agency was designed around antiracist principles and endeavors to redress what has been a strong resistance to examining the intersection of race and class in the nation's child welfare system and centuries of well-documented racist practices that accounts for the disproportionate representation of children of color in foster care at the same time they are found to receive the least desirable forms of care.

We hope that the book has increased sensitivity to matters of race and racism in the health and human services and encouraged a commitment to change systems and practices that contribute to the persistence of racial and ethnic disparities. We believe that the helping professionals in these organizations can and should lead the way in applying the values of their codes of ethics in all aspects of the work, including organizational operations and practice interventions. Knowledge building in this area continues to take shape and relies heavily on the research and practice wisdoms of a broad range of thoughtful, skilled, and experienced scholars and practitioners. We hope that this volume informs and stimulates further thinking and action in the field and promotes continuing collaboration between practitioners and researchers as together we endeavor to define coherent theories to inform evidence-based antiracist practices for the health and human services. Achieving this goal is a long-term effort and very much a work in progress.

Our major task as editors was to bring together into one product the diversity of voices on the controversial topic of race and racism. In the editorial process we endeavored to be ever-mindful of preserving the uniqueness of the work of a roster of outstanding scholars and practitioners, not all of whose contributions are anchored in the antiracist ideology. Two of the editors, Alan Siskind and Mary Pender Greene, while preparing the book have continued to provide leadership to the "Undoing Racism" initiative in New York City and at the national level. Their vision and commitment to the "Undoing Racism" philosophy has been a constant guiding force of our working together and bringing the book to a conclusion. They offer the following observations.

In recognition of our enduring commitment to the "Undoing Racism" philosophy and ideology, Pender Green and Siskind offer the following as some of our critical understandings, especially about white privilege, that are based in the "Undoing Racism" perspective, which, for the two of us, is the fundamental starting point for any work on transforming health and human service organizations using antiracist principles.

Failing to acknowledge race, even understanding that our approach need not be binary, results in denial, minimization, or rationalization of social injustice and the individual's experience of discrimination. A critical and fundamental step in the transformation of a human service organization using antiracist principles is to educate (or re-educate) leaders of those organizations about white privilege. People often do not know how to engage in organizational systems in ways that promote racial equity. Too often, racism is viewed only as overt, blatant prejudice involving individual acts of cruelty and intolerance, while systemic inequities are neither considered nor understood. Focusing on individual bias and individual achievement reinforces structural racism. Since hard work and sacrifice are almost always necessary for success, failure to acknowledge systemic supports and barriers places the onus back on the individual. The ability to live, work, learn, and play within this framework without thinking about the role of race is the essence of white privilege. Thus, white privilege places people of color at a disadvantage. People of color have less access to control of social systems and to resources that would ensure full and equitable participation in the society.

Because many in our field continue to view racism as individual acts of meanness, they view the discussion of racism in the profession as a personal affront and/or a challenge to the good work they are doing. Furthermore, nonprofit institutions often have histories of religious affiliations and missions that highlight the importance of "charity." Some of these values of caring for others encourage tackling racism, but others give us places to hide. Although we might feel that there is a given connection between religious values and confronting racism, this connection does not always exist. Experience teaches also that some of the resistance to looking at and dealing with racism in our human service systems comes from organizational cultures where professionals already perceive themselves as people who are antiracist (and perhaps in some important ways are) and who sacrifice the better salaries and benefits found in the corporate world to do good work.

These issues and others indicate that it might be particularly difficult for social workers and other human service and mental health workers to acknowledge and take the responsibility for doing something about organizational racism in human services. Agencies must learn to be accountable for evaluating how historical and current privilege is expressed in promotion opportunities (or the lack of them); establishing and maintaining mentoring systems for all staff; and developing race-sensitive recruitment systems, staff and program evaluation systems, and job descriptions.

As younger generations continue to evolve in their attitudes about human differences and similarities, we see more biracialism, more fluidity in gender and sexual identity, less religiosity, and less conformity with tradition. There is, at least in some areas of the country, more acceptance and even celebration of diversity. We hope these dynamics are leading to more openness in examining and changing how current societal norms and systems of white superiority are manifested in and perpetuated by social service and mental health organizations. While globalization, the increasing impact of technology, and the rapid dissemination of information pose challenges to developing consensus about issues of racism, we suggest that these changes also provide immense new opportunities. To make the most of these growing opportunities and open doors, we propose that the senior staff and board members of human service organizations have two major tasks in moving their institutions toward multicultural, antiracist practice: vision and accountability.

An antiracist vision includes the ability to imagine and communicate the essential nature of multicultural, antiracist practice as necessary for meeting and advancing the programmatic goals of the organization. Such vision calls for an honest analysis of power and privilege within the organization as well as an evaluation of how organizational culture and practices might impede the full inclusion of all staff and clients.

Earlier in this book, we suggested that in order for antiracist executives to be accountable, they must be willing to take action to identify and oppose oppressive or discriminatory practices and to commit the time, energy, and resources necessary to support antiracist practices. Given the increasingly intense competition for resources within and between organizations, it is easier to say that we cannot accomplish these objectives—but it is critical that we do. Our effectiveness and credibility as human service organizations depend on it. These issues are especially important in our field because of the significant impact they have on our work with clients and our relationships with each other.

When we stop assuming that we know what we don't know, we start to more effectively hear each other and our clients. By bringing all voices to the table, we can fill in the gaps in our knowledge and begin to rectify the distortions in our perceptions. Clarity of understanding about race, culture, and racism results in antiracist policies and program design, authentic relationships and evaluation tools, and organizational goal attainment. Real change can begin only when organizational leaders understand the ways in which white people have learned to understand race and racism and experience white-skin privilege, as well as the ways in which people of color understand race and racism and experience various forms of racism and microaggressions.

# AUTHOR INDEX

# SUBJECT INDEX